The Ultimate Dividend Playbook

The Ultimate Dividend Playbook

Income, Insight, and Independence for Today's Investor

Josh Peters

WILEY

John Wiley & Sons, Inc.

Published by John Wiley & Sons, Inc., Hoboken, New Jersey

Published simultaneously in Canada

For general information on our other products and services or for technical support, please contact our Customer Care Department within the United States at (800) 762-2974, outside the United States at (317) 572-3993 or fax (317) 572-4002.

Wiley also publishes its books in a variety of electronic formats. Some content that appears in print may not be available in electronic books. For more information about Wiley products, visit our Web site at www.wiley.com.

ISBN-13 978-0-470-12512-0

Library of Congress Cataloging-in-Publication Data:

Peters, Josh.
    The ultimate dividend playbook : income, insight, and independence for today's investor / Josh Peters.
    p. cm.
    Includes index.
    ISBN 978-0-470-12512-0 (cloth)
    1. Dividends. 2. Stocks 3. Investments. I. Title.
HG4028.D5P48 2008
332.63'22—dc22

2007038108

Printed in the United States of America
10 9 8 7 6 5 4 3 2

Contents

Acknowledgments   VII

Introduction   IX

Chapter 1   Income? From Stocks?   1

Chapter 2   Dividends, Values, and Returns   25

Chapter 3   Corporations: Dividend Machines   49

Chapter 4   Dividend Insight   69

Chapter 5   Dividends Past, Present, and Projected   87

Chapter 6   Is It Safe?   101

Chapter 7   Will It Grow?   125

Chapter 8   What's the Return?   149

Chapter 9   Independence   169

Chapter 10   Managing a Dividend Portfolio   183

Chapter 11   The Future of Dividends   205

Epilogue 221

Appendix 1 The Nuts and Bolts of Dividend Payments 225

Appendix 2 Dividends and Taxes 241

Appendix 3 Banks 257

Appendix 4 Utilities 277

Appendix 5 Real Estate Investment Trusts 295

Appendix 6 Energy Partnerships 313

Appendix 7 Other Dividend Opportunities 333

Index 337

Acknowledgments

THE TWO INDIVIDUALS most directly responsible for bringing my ideas to life, both in this book as well as in the monthly issues of *DividendInvestor*, are Morningstar designer Christopher Cantore and editor Sylvia Hauser. These fine professionals both worked long hours on short deadlines without sacrificing the humor, creativity, and keen eyes for detail I've come to rely on over the past three years. I can't thank either of them enough.

My content was improved mightily by the feedback of Pat Dorsey, Morningstar's director of equity analysis, and Haywood Kelly, chief of security analysis. Maureen Dahlen, Courtney Dobrow, and Paul Justice, along with many other folks I've worked with at Morningstar and John Wiley & Sons, helped speed the writing and editing process to its blessed conclusion. And since seeds without soil might just as well be stones, I have to add my thanks to Morningstar founder Joe Mansueto and individual investor segment president Catherine Odelbo. Along with Pat and Haywood, they've provided the patient, inquisitive environment in which I could develop the strategies I'm now able to pass along to you.

There's basically no chance I would even be interested in stocks if it wasn't for the early encouragement of my parents, Henry and Susan Peters. I'm sure they were puzzled by a 13-year-old's desire to hang out at brokerage offices rather than at hockey rinks, but they ensured I was able to learn everything I could. And my primary teacher, in so many things in addition to the stock market, was and still is Glen Bayless. He took that kid with a $200 account under his wing when there was nothing (except possibly a bit of amusement) in the deal for him. I can never repay the debt I owe my mother, father, and "big brother" Glen; I can only hope to serve others as generously as I have been helped in life.

The biggest thanks of all go to my wife, Jaime, for the marvelous grace, wisdom, and beauty with which she has immeasurably enriched my life. It is to her that I dedicate this book.

Introduction

You may have heard that the basic idea of the stock market is to buy low and sell high. Pardon me for saying so, but that sounds like a lot of work. An investment represents money that is supposed to work for me, right? Having earned my money once already, why should I have to work for it all over again?

When it comes to redundant and wasted effort, nothing tops the stock market. I came to the conclusion long ago that investors, professional and individual alike, work much harder than necessary. As J. P. Morgan once promised, stock prices will fluctuate—everyone knows that. Even blue-chip businesses can see their market values swing 50 percent or more over the course of a single year. These ups and downs seem to promise great wealth, if only the investor can time the buys at low points and the sales at high ones.

The trouble with this mentality—in addition to poor odds of consistent success, of course—is that it puts almost 100 percent of the responsibility for profits on the back of the stockholder rather than the stock. It's as though the stock market is not about business at all, but rather a grand game pitting wily investors against each other in attempts to beat the market.

Yet the fact remains that stocks are capable of providing attractive returns to their owners. Treated as partnership stakes in profit-seeking businesses, stocks are highly useful tools—tools for storing value, tools for generating income and accumulating wealth, tools effective enough to meet a lifetime's worth of financial goals. But if we are to shed the game mentality of our fellow investors, our stocks must provide an alternative source of reward. Rewards with no additional effort. Rewards not subject to the whims of Wall Street. Above all, rewards paid in cash.

Those rewards are cash dividends. This book is not only about how dividends work, but about how dividends can work for you.

I should state up front that *The Ultimate Dividend Playbook* is about as far from a get-rich-quick guide as you're likely to find. In *Morningstar DividendInvestor*, I once wrote that subscribers shouldn't expect the 1,000 percent returns other newsletters promise, at least unless they were willing and prepared to follow my advice for the next 25 years. But that's the point: A 10 percent annual return, well within the reach of a simple, low-maintenance dividend strategy, turns $100,000 into $1.1 million over a quarter of a century. As of this writing, it's also possible to generate income from a portfolio of dividend-paying stocks equal to 6 percent or 7 percent of its initial value without any need to trade. Best of all, this income can and should grow faster than the cost of living. In a world where we're lucky to find bonds and CDs paying even 5 percent, and these options providing no respite from the threat of inflation, I hope these observations will come as welcome news.

Rather than promise sky-high returns—which would probably sell a lot more copies of this book—only to deliver the mud beneath my boots, this book sticks to three core principles:

1. *Income.* At the bottom of it all, it is income, not capital gains, that most investors need to meet their financial goals. Fortunately, many conservative, well-managed, and economically attractive businesses are prepared to provide good income through dividends.
2. *Insight.* Dividends are worth much more than the sum of income they generate. No matter how routine on the surface, each dividend is a critical signal of the financial health, growth, and value of a business.

3. *Independence*. The taste for gambling and speculation is not equally distributed through the population—and thank heaven for that! I strongly suspect that most investors would just as soon not live their lives entangled with Wall Street's never-ending pageant of fear and greed. Dividends, by contrast, set the investor free from fickle market prices and unreliable capital gains.

What Are Dividends, Anyway?

Glad you asked! Strictly speaking, a dividend is a transfer of assets (almost always cash) from a corporation to its shareholders.

A share of stock—any stock—represents a bit of partial ownership in a business. A successful business typically has a good deal of assets (even after deducting its debts), and management employs these assets to turn profits.

Yet a corporation is an entity separate from its shareholders. You might look at a corporation as a lockbox containing all the assets and earnings of the business. As a shareholder, you own part of that lockbox, but you don't have direct access to its contents. The key to the lock is held by the corporation's management. Only when they decide to unlock the box and hand part or all of the cash inside to shareholders do those shareholders—the ultimate owners of the box—get to benefit directly from what is held inside.

Not all corporations, even those with enormous profits and sizable cash reserves, are willing to unlock the box for shareholders' benefit, preferring instead to keep control of the cash for themselves. But many corporations do. Some pay out only a little, while others—the kinds of stocks we're interested in—pay out a lot.

Furthermore, corporations that have paid dividends in the past have a very strong tendency to continue dishing out cash in the future. The box is opened and cash disbursed on a predictable basis, and over time, these payouts tend to grow larger and larger. From the investor's perspective, the value of a share of the box isn't about the box itself, but rather the growing stream of cash it will provide in the years and decades to come.

To consider just one example out of hundreds, let's look at the shareholder experience at Associated Banc-Corp (ASBC) over the past 20 years. At the end of 1986, shares of Associated sold for $4.08 apiece (adjusted for subsequent stock splits, as are all similar references in this book). Back then, Associated's *dividend rate*—the amount of cash paid on each share annually—was running

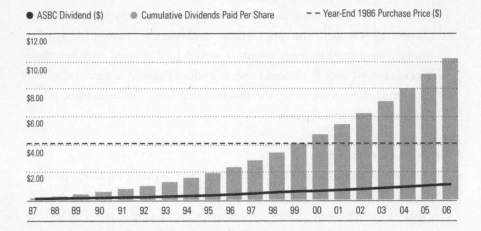

● ASBC Dividend ($)   ● Cumulative Dividends Paid Per Share   – – Year-End 1986 Purchase Price ($)

Figure I.1   Associated Banc-Corp (ASBC): Cumulative Dividend Income

at just 10.6 cents a share. Dividing the 10.6 cents in annual dividends by the stock price of $4.08, we can say the stock provided a dividend yield of just 2.6 percent. The investor looking for income probably could have walked into one of Associated's bank branches and received a much higher rate of interest.

Dividend yields may look like interest rates, although neither the dividend nor the stock that is paying it has a fixed, guaranteed value. But unlike the interest paid on a bond or a CD, Associated's dividend payments rose every single year thereafter. (See Figure I.1.) Despite the initial yield of just 2.6 percent, just look how those dividends accumulated!

By 1999, Associated had paid out cash dividends equal to the purchase price of the stock 13 years earlier. Seven years later, by the end of 2006, those cumulative dividends were 2.5 times the 1986 stock price. In 2006 alone, payments totaling $1.14 a share were equal to 28 percent of the 1986 purchase price. And even this was not the end: Associated raised its dividend yet again in early 2007. If history is any indication (and in this case, I believe it is), many more decades of steadily rising payments lie ahead.

But before you focus too closely on this ascending pile of accumulated dividends—attractive though it is—step back to visualize the peace of mind this kind of performance inspires. Between 1986 and 2006, a period containing some of the great bull runs of all time, I count three major bear markets, a number of smaller corrections, and four major stretches of rising stock prices.

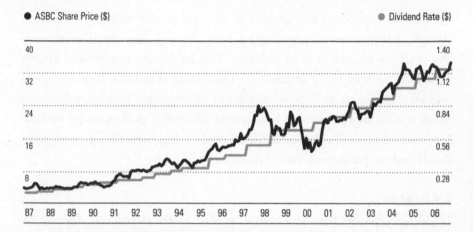

● ASBC Share Price ($)   ● Dividend Rate ($)

Figure I.2   Associated Banc-Corp (ASBC): Share Price and Dividend History

Yet for the truly patient holder of the stock through this whole period, these fluctuations mattered not one bit. I can't go so far as to say that a dividend strategy is maintenance-free—one needs to be aware of factors that could slow dividend growth or even lead to reduced or eliminated payments—but it's hard to imagine a better way to have your money working for you, rather than the other way around!

And not only did Associated's rising dividend provide more and more income as the years rolled by, but each dividend increase made the stock more desirable to own. Those dividends drove the market price of the stock higher in tandem, as shown in Figure I.2.

You may look at this chart and conclude that Associated's stock price alone might seem to have been a pretty nice investment; who needs dividends? But let's now invoke the concept of total return: capital gains and dividends working together to provide profits and build wealth. Associated's stock price rose an average of 11.3 percent annually over this 20-year stretch. Without dividends, that would have turned a $10,000 investment into roughly $85,000. But with dividends—specifically, dividends reinvested into additional shares along the way—that same $10,000 investment compounds into a stake worth $161,000, nearly twice as much as from capital gains alone. The total return on the stock over these two decades was not just the 11.3 percent average annual capital gain, and not just the 3.2 percent average yield, but an average total return of 14.9 percent annually.

I chose Associated not because it is a spectacular example of success, though in its own way it certainly has been. Instead, Associated is noteworthy precisely because it is so ordinary. This bank may not be well known across the country, but it certainly is to hundreds of thousands of depositors and loan customers in Wisconsin. Dozens of seemingly humdrum banks in other corners of the country have generated similar performances, as have hundreds of firms in other industries. The unifying factors are growing dividends and the patience to collect them.

A Role Model

Dividend investors have few heroes, at least as far as you can discover by browsing the bookshelves at Barnes & Noble or reviewing a year's worth of cover stories in *Fortune* or *BusinessWeek*. Indeed, dividends may be the most misunderstood aspect of investing in stocks, to the extent people bother to understand dividends at all. Most professionals are indifferent to dividends, and a surprisingly large minority are downright hostile. Even the fans of dividends you might see on TV or read about in a magazine are usually on their way somewhere else, collecting dividends just to kill time while waiting for other opportunities to crop up. True fans, those who understand the critical role of dividends over the long run, are very rare in the professional ranks.

As editor of a monthly newsletter devoted to the topic, *Morningstar DividendInvestor*, I am one of those rare professionals. And while I admire Warren Buffett, Peter Lynch, Marty Whitman, and many other famously successful and articulate investors as much as anyone, my true hero is—drum roll, please—Marjorie Bradt.

Don't spend too much time trying to place her name; she's never been featured on CNBC or mentioned in the *Wall Street Journal*. She's never written a book about investing or managed a mutual fund. Indeed, the stock market has never even been a hobby of hers. Yet I'm willing to bet that Marjorie's long-term investment record beats the vast majority of investors over the past half century.

I became familiar with Marjorie's remarkable record while working as an assistant to a stockbroker in 1999. Marjorie and her husband, Don, were getting their ample estate in order, and they needed cost basis information for their seven-figure portfolio. Given this task, I was handed a folder six inches thick with old statements, some dating back to the 1950s. The best information I had was their current portfolio, almost all of which consisted of the various corporate descendants of AT&T, the original Ma Bell.

Working backward from what they owned in 1999, I noticed that Marjorie's account was marked by a distinct lack of active management. All she did, it seemed, was reinvest her dividends—quarter after quarter, year after year, decade after decade. When AT&T broke up into a long distance-only carrier and the seven baby Bells, Marjorie held on to all eight stocks. When Southwestern Bell bought Pacific Telesis and Ameritech, she held on. When AT&T went on to spin out Lucent, and US West spun out MediaOne, she held on to those, too.

After more than a day's worth of work, I finally found the root of Marjorie's wealth: a handful of gifts of AT&T stock given to her by her father between 1955 and 1962. Their original value totaled $6,626. Very early on, she signed up for AT&T's dividend reinvestment plan. Instead of getting penny-ante dividend checks every three months, she turned those payments into additional shares, which led to more dividends, and so on. As AT&T prospered and raised its dividend rate, the value of each share rose as well—as did the Baby Bells' dividends and share prices. By 1999, this investment had blossomed into a portfolio of ten separate stocks worth more than $1 million—all of them descendents of the original Ma Bell.

I was astounded. Here was all this wealth, but Marjorie hadn't lifted a finger to earn it. She hadn't foreseen the raging inflation of the 1970s, the surge in gold, the run of small caps, then large caps, then small caps again. She didn't predict anything—and she didn't have to. She just held and held, reinvesting every dividend, letting these rising dividend payments do all of the work.

The beauty of Marjorie's experience is its simplicity: Anyone could have done the same, even if virtually no other investors did. No PhD, MBA, or CFA was required; math skills learned in junior high school could suffice. Marjorie didn't have to trouble herself with a market-timing strategy or the pursuit of the next Microsoft. And it isn't as though AT&T was a diamond in the rough in the 1950s; back then the company owned almost every telephone in America. Other companies were growing faster, but millions of investors held stock in Ma Bell, drawn in by the same thing that made AT&T attractive to Marjorie's parents: large, steady, and growing dividends.

Marjorie thus traded the usual investor attempts at prescience for a combination of dividends and patience—and rarely does one find an example of such a richly rewarding investment strategy.

The Ultimate Dividend Playbook

This book is devoted to putting the three dividend plays of income, insight, and independence into practice. These are the tactics I've used to make investment recommendations in *Morningstar DividendInvestor,* and in the aggregate, these stocks are providing exactly the kind of income and income growth I've set out to earn. Prices rise and prices fall; dividend growth may exceed my expectations or disappoint. But the well-rounded model portfolios I manage are delivering the cash to meet real-world investor needs.

As this book unfolds, I'll take you through the insides of a corporation and the factors that allow it to pay and raise dividends; I'll show you how to separate safe dividends from risky ones, and how to construct a portfolio of dividend-paying stocks to meet your financial needs. Along the way I hope to share a little business acumen and a lot about dividends, and to frame an approach—emotional as much as intellectual or financial—that will equip you for a rewarding investing career.

I

Income? From Stocks?

Congratulations are in order! If you've picked up this book, you probably have some money to invest. Perhaps you've just retired with a couple of hundred thousand dollars, maybe even a million or two. Funny thing about money, though: It doesn't come with instructions. Television commercials for the *Wall Street Journal* in the 1980s used this line to suggest that the *Journal* was the next best thing. I appreciate the *Journal*'s insightful missives as much as anyone. For the most part, though, you and your money are largely on your own.

Whether your accumulated savings are large or small, we can begin by asking what you want from the money. "To get rich" is a straightforward and honest answer, but it may not quite get to the heart of the matter. Fortunes have been and will be made by investors who can outguess the market, especially with large quantities of other people's money. It's also true that very few of us will reach the ranks of the superrich. Even on Wall Street, there's only so much dough to go around.

Then again, it's not necessary for one's investments to generate fantastic fortunes. Buying groceries, paying the gas bill, taking a vacation now and again—these are the bread-and-butter activities of Main Street, both before retirement and after. The goal of saving and investing, then, is to replace the paychecks earned by the sweat of your brow with paychecks from your investment portfolio. Income—steady, reliable, predictable, and rising income—is the objective.

Portfolios: Piles and Flows

There was a time, a generation ago or thereabouts, when the average working stiff didn't have to think too hard about retirement. We were thriftier back then, with a lot fewer financial choices. Savings went into passbook accounts that paid 5 percent interest. Paying off the mortgage was a well-earned cause for celebration. The boss took care of retirement income, through defined-benefit pension plans. And whatever the pension couldn't cover, Social Security and a modest accumulation of savings would.

Though held in derision and contempt today, defined-benefit pensions plan were reasonably well suited to the needs of the average worker and retiree of the time. Only a tiny proportion of the American public is trained in investment analysis and portfolio management. We all memorized the state capitals and learned how to dissect frogs, but they didn't teach much (if anything) about personal finance in school. Having employers and their investment managers take responsibility for investment decisions made a lot of sense. Leaving asset-allocation and security-selection decisions to the professionals allowed ordinary folks to concentrate on their jobs and personal lives.

Of course, defined-benefit pensions had significant drawbacks; this is why they've all but disappeared from the private sector. When an employee changed jobs—a phenomenon that became much more frequent in the 1980s and 1990s—accumulated pension benefits would stay with the original employer, usually at a sharply diminished value. The monthly pension benefit in retirement was typically fixed, meaning its purchasing power would shrink over time because of inflation. And if the employer went bankrupt, retirees could find their monthly pension checks slashed.

In the early 1980s, a new vehicle came along to replace defined-benefit pensions: the defined-contribution plan, most frequently in the form of a 401(k) account. *Defined contribution* describes these plans perfectly: The only known factor is how much money is put in; no one guarantees any particular amount of money the beneficiary will one day take out. Employees, not employers, are responsible for saving. Employees, not employers, determine how these savings are invested. And retirees, not the former employers, have to figure out how to turn accumulated assets into income. In fact, 401(k) plans are often lauded for providing employees with the freedom to choose their own investments. But no freedom exists without responsibility—a responsibility few people are adequately trained to shoulder.

In addition to shifting the responsibility for saving and investing from boss to worker, 401(k) plans changed the focal point of retirement planning. The defined-benefit plan was all about *flows* of cash—the pensioner's monthly check. The worker might receive a statement of benefits showing how much he was eligible to collect; translating this into a budget was easy. The value of the assets in the plan that would provide these payments was not terribly relevant and was rarely of interest to the beneficiary. The 401(k) plan, by contrast, shows you every three months how much you've accumulated—the emphasis is on the size of the *pile*. Someone close to retirement might have a statement balance of $500,000, but how much of the pile can be safely extracted each month is a matter of guesswork.

Living Off the Pile

Let's all say hello to Sally, who has just retired with $500,000 worth of savings in her 401(k) account. Her situation is not too different from millions of newly retired Americans, possibly even you. Sally's expenses are manageable, especially after taking Social Security income into account, but she still figures to draw $30,000 worth of cash from her portfolio every year.

Sally's account is invested in a handful of stock mutual funds. Over the past 20 years, these funds have done a wonderful job helping her accumulate this $500,000 balance. Assuming that her mix of funds mirrors the industry average, they provide very little dividend income: a yield of about 1 percent, or $5,000 annually. Not much more than a rounding error in the big scheme of things, these dividends have always been reinvested automatically. To generate income—or at least cash flows that look like income—Sally plans to sell off $30,000 worth of mutual fund shares every year.

This is a strategy we might call living off the pile. Sally is implicitly assuming that her portfolio will grow more valuable over time, enough that drawing $30,000 a year out of the account won't actually cause its value to fall. If her savings were simply dollar bills stuffed in a mattress (earning an investment return of zero), she'd run out of money in less than 17 years. But Sally knows, or thinks she knows, that the stock market returns 10 percent a year on average. A 10 percent gain for a $500,000 portfolio means an annual dollar increase of $50,000. Even after taking out $30,000, Sally figures she'll still be $20,000 ahead at year-end.

This rising balance is important to Sally because she's counting on being able to draw more money out of the account next year and still more the year after that. Like anyone, she's feeling the effects of inflation—at the grocery store, the gas pump, the car dealership, you name it. As the cost of living rises, her portfolio withdrawals will have to grow. If inflation runs at 3 percent annually, that $30,000 withdrawal in year one will have to rise to $30,900 in year two, $31,827 the year after that, and so on.

Fooling around with a spreadsheet, she makes five-year projections based on 10 percent portfolio returns and a $30,000 withdrawal that grows 3 percent annually, as shown in Figure 1.1.

	Year 1	Year 2	Year 3	Year 10	Year 25
Beginning Balance	500,000	520,000	541,100	727,615	1,574,767
Asset Return (10%)	50,000	52,000	54,110	72,762	157,477
Withdrawal	−30,000	−30,900	−31,827	−39,143	−60,982
Ending Balance	**520,000**	**541,100**	**563,383**	**761,234**	**1,671,262**

Figure 1.1   Living Off a $500,000 Pile: Projected Balances and Withdrawals

On the surface, this doesn't seem like a bad strategy. It does assume a 10 percent return from stocks—a bit higher than I think the market is capable of over the long run, as I show in Chapter 5. But even though Sally's withdrawals rise with each passing year, her account balance is rising faster. Maybe she can take even more than $30,000 annually out of the account and add exotic travel to her plans. At the very least, it provides a bit of room for the market to fall short of a 10 percent return without blowing up her portfolio.

Hearing of Sally's strategy, I should introduce her to this fellow I know. His name is Mr. Market.

Meet Mr. Market

Even though the market is made up of millions of individual buyers and sellers, it forms something of a collective consciousness of its own. Ben Graham, the father of value investing, understood this when he suggested the character of the mythical Mr. Market. He's the guy on the other end of your stock trades. When you buy, it's his shares you're buying. When you sell, you're selling to him. Every moment of every trading day, Mr. Market can be found quoting prices for publicly traded stocks.

To understand Mr. Market, we must begin with the premise that price and value are distinct concepts. On Wall Street—as with any economic transaction—price is simply what you pay, but value is what you get in return. The value of a stock is a function of its capacity and propensity to return cash to its owner. Were Mr. Market a steady, reasonable man, his price offers would reflect these future cash returns perfectly. A $1,000 investment today would provide $1,000 worth of value, no more and no less.

But Mr. Market is not what you'd call a steady business partner. An incurable manic-depressive whose actions define the words *fear* and *greed,* Mr. Market will offer ridiculously high prices for a given stock at one point and insanely low prices the next. Mr. Market is the guy who does most of the obsessing about quarterly earnings, economic reports, and so-called technical trends in stock prices. Does anyone really believe that the value of large, well-established, profitable businesses should change 50 percent or more over the course of a year? But Mr. Market's prices fluctuate that widely all the time.

So who's in charge of your money, you or Mr. Market? No one wants to admit to being in Mr. Market's thrall, but the observed collective behavior says otherwise. Rather than buying low and selling high, we see the market's individual participants doing the opposite: buying high and selling low. These are the ancient and ineradicable emotions of greed and fear in action. And if you're interested in seeing what this Mr. Market fellow looks like, you might want to check a mirror. There's at least a bit of him in all of us.

I'm not sure that most of us are prepared to engage Mr. Market, even if the odds can—through great effort—be tipped in the investor's favor. As with any active strategy, the onus of the buy-high-and-sell-low approach is on the stockholder, not the stock. The investor does the bulk of the work to earn his expected return; whatever the underlying business may be up to is of secondary importance. And at the end of the day, success or failure will be measured when the stock is sold: that is, success or failure depends on Mr. Market's attitude shifting from gloom to glee.

Sally and Mr. Market

This volatility is not necessarily a problem. This year's drop leads to next year's rebound; those who hang on to investments in good companies will be fine. Indeed, the investor who has the ability to add money consistently— whether stock prices are high or low—will wind up with more shares, lower purchase prices, and higher returns than a portfolio without inflows. This is a financial phenomenon known as *dollar-cost averaging*, and it's a terrific tool for growing and compounding wealth. (See accompanying box.)

But Sally's investment strategy is about to change dramatically. Every year, Sally will have to sell shares to generate cash. If prices are high, she'll have the luxury of selling fewer shares and leaving more money working for her financial future. If prices are low, she'll have to sell many more shares at lower prices to generate the same amount of cash. As a result, her selling prices will be lower than the average level of the market. She's still going to be dollar-cost averaging, all right—dollar-cost averaging in reverse.

Dollar-Cost Averaging

Stock prices fluctuate. Even watching a stock for a couple of minutes will tell you that much. However, for the investor who is steadily adding to a position in a stock (or portfolio), this volatility actually reduces average cost and increases subsequent profits.

How can this be? Let's check the math. You're hoping to build a nice-size position in a particular stock, but you don't have all the money right now. You can invest $12,000 now, another $12,000 in three months, and another $12,000 three months after that. Initially, your investment buys you 200 shares at $60 apiece. Later, the stock has dropped—but at a lower price of $50, your $12,000 buys you 240 shares instead of 200. By the time of your final purchase, the stock has shot up to $80, and you're only able to buy 150 shares. Figure 1.2 depicts this sequence.

	Dollars Invested ($)	Stock Price ($)	Shares Bought
First Purchase	12,000	60.00	200
Second Purchase	12,000	50.00	240
Final Purchase	12,000	80.00	150
Totals	**36,000**	—	**590**
Average Price of Stock	—	63.33	—
Average Cost per Share	—	**61.02**	—

Figure 1.2   Dollar-Cost Averaging in Practice

The average price of the stock over this period is $63.33, the simple average of the three purchase prices. But because you're able to buy disproportionately more shares at lower prices, your average cost per share (the $36,000 invested divided by the 590 shares your money purchased) is $61.02, about 3.7 percent lower than the simple average price. Simply by buying in equal dollar amounts, you'll wind up paying less per share and earning higher profits in the future. And if this discount of 3.7 percent doesn't look like that big of a deal, just try adding it up and compounding it over a long stretch of time.

This math works with equal force when selling shares in fixed dollar amounts. Had these three transactions been sales instead, the average selling price would have been at the 3.7 percent discount—and your returns would suffer as a result.

A little tinkering with her previous projections shows just how damaging this reliance on market prices can be. Just a couple of bad years in a row, especially early on, can turn what looks like a sustainable investment strategy into a problematic one. So let's throw some bad years at the spreadsheet: a 25 percent drop in the stock market in year one followed by a 20 percent drop in year two. Then let's bake in a rebound, enough to bring the stock market's cumulative return into positive territory by the end of year five. (If this sounds draconian, I can only say it's not quite as bad as the 2000–2005 bear market and subsequent rebound was.)

By the end of year two, Sally's account has lost more than half of its value (see Figure 1.3). The biggest risk here is probably that Sally panics and sells out at the bottom, locking in those losses forever. For the purposes of this example, though, we'll assume Sally hangs on for the recovery. But even if she

	Year 1	Year 2	Year 3	Year 4	Year 5
Beginning Balance	500,000	345,000	245,100	286,803	311,382
Asset Return	−125,000	−69,000	73,530	57,361	31,138
Withdrawal	−30,000	−30,900	−31,827	−32,782	−33,765
Ending Balance	**345,000**	**245,100**	**286,803**	**311,382**	**308,755**
Asset Return (%)	−25.0	−20.0	30.0	20.0	10.0
Cumulative Annual Return (%)	−25.0	−22.5	−7.9	−1.6	0.6

Figure 1.3   Living Off a $500,000 Pile: Projected Balances and Withdrawals after a Bear Market

does, her account has been permanently damaged. Over this five-year stretch, the stock market's cumulative return is slightly positive, yet her cumulative returns are a negative $31,971. By selling to fund her withdrawals, she wouldn't have those funds working for her in the rebound.

Worse yet, her year five withdrawal exceeds 10 percent of the account's balance. A 10 percent annual return won't be enough to maintain Sally's spending level. If she doesn't change her withdrawals, and the market returns a perfect 10 percent in all the years thereafter, her account will run out of money in less than 20 years. Alternately, she could slash her annual withdrawal rate by $10,000, but what's the consolation in that?

I'm not laying out this negative scenario to scare you away from stocks altogether—far from it. But the lesson here is simple: *Mr. Market cannot be relied upon to provide dependable income.* This clown will force you to sell shares of stock precisely when selling is the worst thing to do. Will Sally want to cancel her vacation plans just because the Dow Jones drops a thousand points? And can she really afford the 20 percent or 30 percent cut in income that a bear market might require? Some economies can be had, but let's be realistic: Income that is subject to market price risk is not the stuff of a sustainable retirement strategy.

Are Fixed-Income Investments the Solution?

After Sally sees my bear market scenario, she's ready to dump her stocks and buy bonds. A bond offers the investor a fairly straightforward relationship: You give a government, corporation, or some other institution your money for a predetermined period of time, during which you'll receive a fixed rate of interest. At the end of that stretch, you get your money back. Case closed, more or less.

The primary trouble with bonds, at least in recent years, is that the yields they offer are substantially lower than the long-term returns provided by stocks. The yields on bonds and their close cousins, bank certificates of deposit, change all the time, but these days you can't get a government-guaranteed yield greater than 5 percent, even if you're willing to part with your principal (the original investment) for 30 years.

Looking at rates available on long-term Treasuries, Sally figures she could pour her 401(k) into 30-year bonds and generate a 5 percent yield, or $25,000 worth of income a year. That would require her to trim her budget by $5,000 annually, but the extra security alone would make this trade-off worthwhile.

Unfortunately, there's another problem with fixed-income investments, and it's right there in the name: The income they provide is fixed; it doesn't grow. There are a variety of ways to tinker with a bond portfolio and increase its yield, but from a big-picture point of view, the only way to get a bond portfolio's income to grow is to reinvest a portion of its income in additional bonds. Of course, those reinvested dollars aren't available for living expenses.

So now Sally faces a very difficult choice. She can either spend all $25,000 of her interest income, knowing this figure will never rise, or she'll have to live on even less so that this income can grow.

Choice 1

Let's say Sally withdraws all of her interest income every year, and, as a consequence, her income doesn't grow. Figure 1.4 illustrates how the purchasing power of her income will change under several inflation scenarios.

At even a 2 percent rate of inflation, the purchasing power of this income stream will drop 9 percent in 5 years, 18 percent in a decade, and 33 percent in 20 years. At a steeper 5 percent rate of inflation, the purchasing power erosion is significantly faster—Sally's effective income would drop 22 percent after 5 years and a whopping 62 percent after 20. Spending all of one's earnings from a fixed income portfolio points the way to a steadily eroding standard of living.

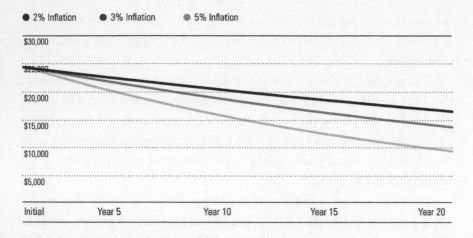

Figure 1.4   Fixed Income: Purchasing Power of $25,000 over Time

Choice 2

Sally could withdraw less than $25,000, leaving some of her interest income available to buy additional bonds. How much? That depends again on the rate of inflation.

Here we can call on a useful concept known as *real return*. Investment returns are usually expressed in nominal terms—percentages of dollars and cents—but nominal returns fail to take inflation into account. By subtracting the inflation rate from a nominal return, we can see what the real return is—that is, the net gain in purchasing power.

A good rule of thumb is that an investor should withdraw no more than the real return on a fixed-income portfolio. Withdrawals in excess of this figure will deplete the future purchasing power of the portfolio's income and value. Instead, the portion of the nominal return that represents inflation should be held back and reinvested, to keep the portfolio's real value stable.

For Sally's bond portfolio, Figure 1.5 demonstrates the (ugly) figures.

If inflation manages to hold to a 2 percent rate, Sally should withdraw no more than $15,000—just half of her original target. If inflation runs even higher, her allowable withdrawal drops further. At a 5 percent inflation rate, she technically shouldn't withdraw anything at all; at even higher rates of inflation, she'd have to add dollars to the account just to keep its real value stable.

Nominal Return	Less: Inflation	Real Return	Nominal Income	Real Income
5%	2%	3%	$25,000	$15.000
5%	3%	2%	$25,000	$10,000
5%	5%	0%	$25,000	$0

Figure 1.5   Fixed Income: Nominal Income versus Real Income

The Third Way: Income from Stocks

Maybe I'm being a bit harsh with these examples. Fixed-income investments like bonds and certificates of deposit, as well as what you might call general stocks (those chosen without respect to dividends), may well have a part to play in your portfolio. Immediate annuities, investments where you turn over your funds to an insurance company in exchange for fixed monthly payments for life, could have a role as well. (You can't get your money back—as soon as you buy the annuity, the funds belong to the insurance company—but the yields tend to be quite a bit higher to compensate.) At any rate, the broader topic of asset allocation isn't the main focus of this book.

But what if there was a class of investments that could offer good current income that would grow as fast as or faster than inflation without any need for the investor to hold back part of this income for reinvestment? There is: stocks with large dividends.

To illustrate this phenomenon, I'll begin by drawing on an unconventional example.

Foremost among those who have made tons of money off Mr. Market over the years is Warren Buffett, a billionaire whose eminent wisdom and down-home charm have made him a household word. You might wonder how Buffett merits mention in a book about dividends, since his Berkshire Hathaway holding company has declared only one dividend on his watch—in 1966. (He has since suggested, perhaps only half jokingly, that he must have been in the bathroom when Berkshire's board voted to pay out that 10 cents a share.) The fact that Berkshire Hathaway hasn't paid a dividend in 40 years hasn't hurt the price of a Class A share, which has risen from $15 to more than $100,000. Buffett figures he can do a better job investing Berkshire's cash than shareholders can on their own, and just about anyone—even someone devoted to dividends like me—would have to grant him that.

Early in his investment career, back when the assets at his disposal could be expressed in six or seven figures rather than eleven or twelve, Buffett focused his attention squarely on Mr. Market. Beginning in the 1970s, however, his emphasis started to change. He started buying entire companies—in essence, buying every single share of stock those companies had. The penny-ante investors under Mr. Market's spell might be willing to sell their little bits of ownership at wildly undervalued prices, but knowledgeable businesspeople who control entire corporations are not. And once a company is off the public markets, there is no more Mr. Market to play games with. You won't find the value of See's Candies, Nebraska Furniture Mart, or Dairy Queen quoted in the papers or on the Internet. Because Buffett has bought these companies wholesale, these businesses do not even exist as far as Mr. Market is concerned.

If Buffett has given up the ability to trade these businesses on the stock exchanges, he must be obtaining an attractive return in some other way. That way, I have no doubt, is through dividends—large and growing ones, at that. Outside shareholders don't see these payments since they are conducted entirely underneath the larger Berkshire umbrella. But the earnings of Dairy Queen are not simply piling up inside that subsidiary's checking account; much, if not most, of the cash Dairy Queen and its Berkshire siblings generate is being returned to Berkshire. These returns aren't being delivered by Mr. Market; they come from the operations of the businesses themselves with only the lightest touch from Buffett himself.

Very few of us are in a position to acquire entire corporations and set dividend policies that suit our personal needs. Yet that does not mean that investors of ordinary means must simply take whatever Mr. Market dishes out, for good or for ill. To the extent that a corporation chooses to pay out part of its earnings as dividends, its shareholders find themselves in a position similar to the controlling owner of a business. The larger the dividends relative to the size of the investment, the more shareholders can control their own fate. Dividends allow the investor to harvest cash returns that are fully and completely independent of market prices. It isn't Mr. Market who pays dividends; only the underlying corporations can do that, and they can do it very well indeed.

Where the Dividends Are

I figure that American corporations are dishing out some $250 to $300 billion worth of dividends annually, a gargantuan sum by any standard. This estimate only pales in comparison with the aggregate market value of the stock market: $15 trillion or thereabouts. As large as this dividend stream is, it's still less than 2 percent of the market's total value.

In fact, dividend yields have been so low (less than 3 percent) for so long (continuously since 1994) that it's little wonder that stock investors as a group have all but forgotten their contribution to overall returns. This was not always the case: Historically, dividends have been a much more significant contributor to total return—a comprehensive measure of investor profits that takes both dividend income and capital appreciation into account. Only in the 1990s did dividends fall from favor, and even a recent comeback hasn't come close to offering the yields of the past (see Figure 1.6).

The good news is that today's dividends are not equally distributed. Many stocks pay no dividends at all, and hundreds more make only token payments of cash (such as United Healthcare's 0.1 percent yield). This leaves a relative minority of firms paying the bulk of the market's cash dividends. Certain fields— which just happen to be less volatile and more profitable than American business in general—turn up as providing the best prospecting grounds for dividend income.

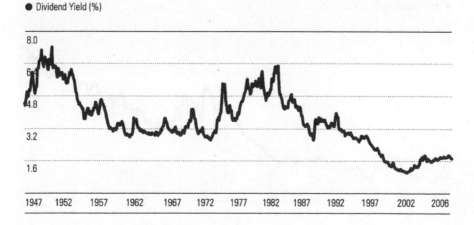

Figure 1.6 Dividend Yield of the S&P 500, 1947–2006

▶ *Banks.* While other segments of the U.S. market let their dividends lag, banks have continued to dish out cash, making them the market's leader in terms of total dividends paid. Bank stocks frequently offer yields between 3 and 5 percent with generally excellent dividend growth as a group—double the rate of inflation or higher. The record of Associated Banc-Corp, which I mentioned in the Introduction, is fairly typical, but much larger banks have superb records as well. (See Figure 1.7.)

▶ *Utilities.* Ever since electric and natural gas utilities ceased being growth stocks back in the 1950s, the basic appeal of these stocks has been high current income. The industry is not nearly as profitable as banking, which has made it tough for many utilities to increase their dividends as fast as inflation. Still, well-chosen utilities have historically been able to supply current yields of 4 percent or more while keeping pace with inflation. (See Figure 1.8.)

▶ *Consumer staples.* People still eat during recessions. They also continue to buy beer, soap, and razor blades. This group encompasses food, beverages, household products, and the like, and as a group these enterprises are enormously profitable. Sales growth is relatively slow—there's a limit to how much overall gains in household wealth will translate into higher consumption of detergent and toothpaste—but these firms also provide decent, above-average yields with growth prospects double or triple the rate of inflation. (See Figure 1.9.)

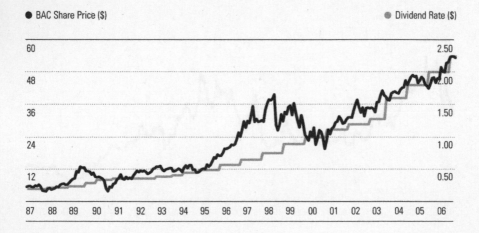

Figure 1.7   Bank of America (BAC): Share Price and Dividend History

● PNY Share Price ($)   ● Dividend Rate ($)

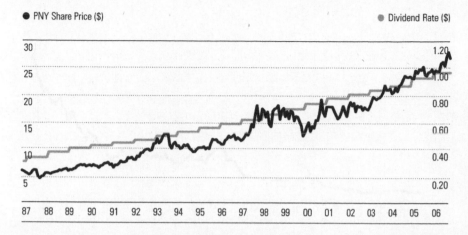

Figure 1.8   Piedmont Natural Gas (PNY): Share Price and Dividend History

● MKC Share Price ($)   ● Dividend Rate ($)

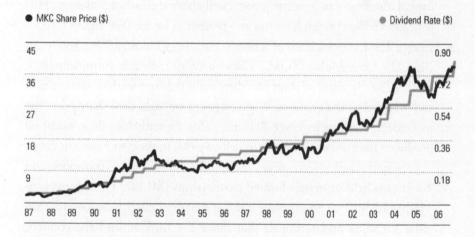

Figure 1.9   McCormick & Company (MKC): Share Price and Dividend History

▶ *Real estate investment trusts.* These firms make an interesting trade-off: In exchange for not paying federal income taxes at the corporate level, they agree to pay out at least 90 percent of their taxable income to shareholders as dividends so (as you might expect) the government can tax it. The bulk of this industry is simply in the landlord business: owning office buildings, malls, warehouses, and hospitals; collecting the rent; and mailing most of it out to investors. Like utilities, growth prospects in general are relatively modest; unlike utilities, no regulator places a ceiling on profitability, so effective

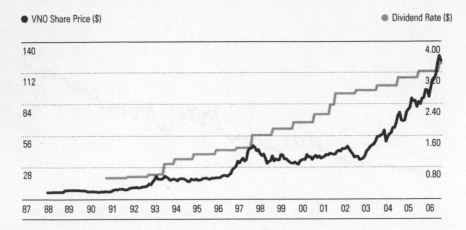

Figure 1.10   Vornado Realty Trust (VNO): Share Price and Dividend History

capital allocators can generate growth well above the industry average. Historically, dividend yields have run at 6 percent or better. (See Figure 1.10.)

▶ *Energy.* There are two kinds of action in the energy industry. First, you've got Big Oil—ExxonMobil (XOM), Chevron (CVX), British Petroleum (BP), and the like. By virtue of sheer size, these firms dole tremendous quantities of cash out to their shareholders. When oil prices are high, their share prices rise in tandem, resulting in lower dividend yields. Nevertheless, these major oil producers have usually been able to deliver yields in the 3 to 5 percent range.

Second, and even more interesting, are energy transportation businesses held in master limited partnerships (MLPs). These firms generally have little or no exposure to oil and natural gas prices; instead, they own the pipes and terminals that move the stuff around the country. These are as cash-rich businesses as you're likely to find, and like the REIT structure, MLPs typically hand almost all of their cash flow back to investors, creating yields of 6 percent and up. (See Figure 1.11.) Not only that, but the industry has demonstrated excellent income growth for investors. (The only hitch is that MLPs carry certain tax characteristics that make them more complicated to own than ordinary common stocks and REITs; more on this in Appendix 6.)

The industries I've mentioned are well known for rich dividend yields and at least decent dividend growth, but even these are not alone. For example, few industrial manufacturers provide decent current yields, but General Electric

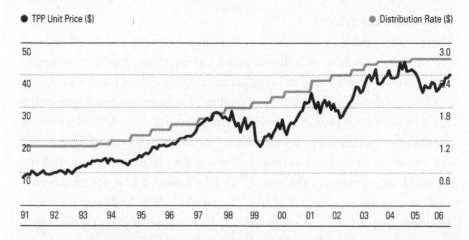

● TPP Unit Price ($)   ● Distribution Rate ($)

Figure 1.11   TEPPCO Partners (TPP): Unit Price and Cash Distribution History

(GE) has often been priced to yield 3 percent or more since the bottom of the 2000–2002 bear market—*and* has been increasing its dividend at a 12.3 percent annualized rate over the past 20 years (see Figure 1.12).

I don't cite these examples to make recommendations; whether a particular stock, regardless of yield or growth, is worth buying is a topic for later chapters. I merely mean to demonstrate that the equity investor is not limited to the dismal yield of the market averages or fixed-income investments with low real returns. Individual stocks, chosen for their dividend characteristics, can bridge the gap between fixed-income yields and equitylike growth prospects.

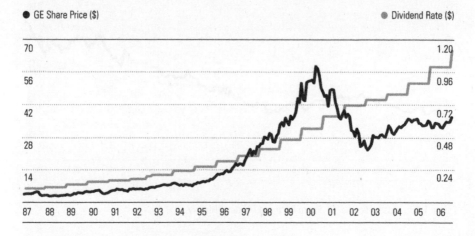

● GE Share Price ($)   ● Dividend Rate ($)

Figure 1.12   General Electric (GE): Share Price and Dividend History

The Ultimate Example

There are no perfect stocks out there, but some come closer than others, and one stock in particular—California-based real estate investment trust Realty Income (O)—comes closer to being perfect than any other I know of.

This landlord specializes in freestanding, single-tenant retail properties. But if its business is predominantly collecting rent, it treats shareholders—not just tenants—as customers. It bills itself as "the Monthly Dividend Company," and I have yet to find any company so devoted to large, consistent, and rising dividend payments as this one. CEO Tom Lewis and his lieutenants routinely invoke the expectations of "the 75-year-old lady in Dubuque for whom dividends aren't a luxury, but a necessity"—not only when pitching their stock to investors, but also when making business decisions. Far from being the lip service this line might otherwise represent, this deep sense of responsibility to shareholders is evident in the firm's long-term performance. (See Figure 1.13.)

Realty Income is not a buy at any price (no stock is; see General Electric's stock price chart if you doubt me), but its basic characteristics are exactly those meant to meet the real-world needs of income seekers. Between 1994 and 2006, its annual dividend payments to shareholders rose an average of 3.7 percent per year. That may not sound like a lot of growth, but the stock also provided an average dividend yield of 7.5 percent during this time.

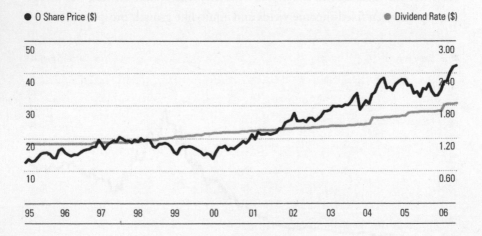

Figure 1.13　Realty Income (O): Share Price and Dividend History

Note that Realty Income's stock price does not always go up. Mr. Market is at work here, too: The market price of these shares fell 30 percent between August 1997 and March 2000. Without the dividend, it would have been tough to hang on to Realty Income shares during that stretch of almost three years of decline.

But even as Realty Income's yield rose and fell inversely to its market price, its monthly dividend rate never declined. Through thick and thin, bear and bull, those cash payments to shareholders kept right on rising. The investor holding Realty Income shares for the dividend didn't need to panic, nor was there any need to trade back and forth to generate a worthwhile return. Realty Income, not the shareholders, did all the work.

Realty Income is exactly the kind of stock that can meet Sally's needs. Bought at a reasonable price, it can provide a yield of 6 percent or more, filling Sally's need for cash. This dividend should also grow at least as fast as inflation, keeping the purchasing power of Sally's income stable. I wouldn't recommend investing Sally's entire portfolio in this one company—no stock's dividend is safe enough for that—but a mix of stocks with similarly attractive dividend characteristics seems to me to offer the best way to meet real-world financial goals.

Dividend Reinvestment

Maybe you don't need current income from stocks—you're far from retirement, and what you want is for your money to grow. I have wonderful news: Dividend reinvestment is just as good a way (or better) to build wealth and future earning power as the pursuit of capital gains.

Take Realty Income, for example. Between the end of 1994 and the end of 2006, its market price rose from $8.56 a share to $27.70. You could have paid $856 for 100 shares and earned a capital gain of $1,914, an increase of 10.3 percent per year on average.

That's not at all bad on its own, but a rising stock price was only half of the story:

▶ Realty Income also paid out $13.57 a share in dividends over those dozen years. That same $856 investment kicked out $1,357 in cash payments. The total return on those 100 shares was not $1,914, but $3,271.

(continued)

▶ Not only that, but the shareholder who used those monthly dividends to buy additional shares saw his ownership stake grow from an initial 100 shares to 249 shares over those dozen years. The final gain of that strategy—$6,039—was almost double the sum of the return with dividends taken in cash (see Figure 1.14).

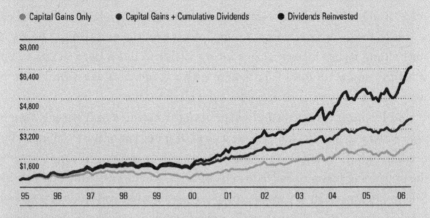

● Capital Gains Only   ● Capital Gains + Cumulative Dividends   ● Dividends Reinvested

Figure 1.14   Realty Income: Hypothetical Dividend Reinvestment

Having accumulated earning power with reinvested dividends, you're free to stop anytime and start taking your dividends in cash. In this case, the 100 shares that once provided $90 worth of dividend income per year has become 249 shares paying some $378 annually—the investment's earning power has multiplied more than fourfold. Given the right group of well-chosen dividend payers, with high yields, rising dividend rates, and reinvestment compounding to your benefit, you might never need to sell in search of higher-yielding investments—even at retirement.

Many brokerage firms and even individual dividend-paying companies make it easy to reinvest dividends through automatic dividend reinvestment plans—also known (regrettably) as DRIPs. I'll describe how DRIPs work in more detail in Appendix 1.

(My sole knock on Realty Income is the fact that it doesn't sponsor a DRIP. Doing so would cost the firm a meaningful amount of money, and it would rather pay those funds out as dividends. Fortunately, most brokerage firms also offer low-cost dividend reinvestment programs, even for stocks that don't offer DRIPs of their own.)

What Do You Want to Own?

While the current income provided by high-yield stocks is attractive, the single best side effect of the dividend harvest strategy is that it helps shift the investor's attention away from ever-fluctuating stock prices. Instead, the income stream—sound, large, and growing—becomes the ultimate source of reward and the benchmark of success.

Let's try a little experiment. Imagine that it's noon on a Wednesday, the markets are open, and you've got some cash to invest. Then you receive word that when the stock market closes today, it's going to stay closed indefinitely—at least five years, maybe a decade or two. There's nothing wrong with the economy: Corporate profits are strong, dividends are safe, and nobody has repealed capitalism. But whatever you own when that closing bell rings, you're stuck with for the foreseeable future. What do you want to hold?

Were this to happen in the real world, I have no doubt that Mr. Market would have a full-blown seizure. Investors who own stocks in anticipation of capital gains would flee and prices would crash.

As for me, I'd be loading up on Realty Income and other high-yield stocks like it. With enough dividend income and dividend growth to justify my investment, what do I need the market for? I'm not a seller on this day; I'm a buyer with both hands. Assuming Realty Income can keep up a 4.5 percent growth rate in annual dividends (it's been growing even faster than this recently), I stand to get all of my money back in less than 14 years, and even then I expect the firm will continue to pay ever-rising dividends to shareholders. (See Figure 1.15.)

Fortunately, I know of no plans on the part of the government, the stock exchanges, or anyone else to shut down the stock market. I wouldn't want this to happen; I like being able to buy stocks when I have money to invest, including the money that comes in through dividends I don't need for living expenses. And it is valuable to have a place to sell shares when good reasons arise; maybe I decide I need a new pickup truck, and selling a few shares of Realty Income makes more sense than borrowing from a bank. Maybe I discover that Realty Income is headed for trouble, or some other dividend-paying stock is positioned to provide even more income, faster income growth, or a combination of the two. But the underlying principle remains the same: Up, down, or closed, I'm not relying on the market to deliver my return.

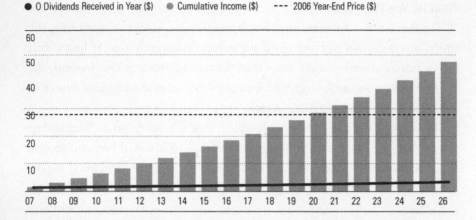

Figure 1.15   Realty Income: Cumulative Dividend Projections

This approach, which works well for any individual stock, stands to be even more effective when managing a portfolio. The focus is on the dividend stream: How large is it, how safe is it, and how fast is it growing? In *Morningstar DividendInvestor*, I look at myself not so much as a portfolio manager but as a manager of two streams of income—one as large as safely possible, the other smaller but rapidly growing. I suggest the same approach to Sally: Use your $500,000 to pick yourself a basket of stocks that collectively provide $30,000 worth of income, and then watch that income grow. Having arranged for your portfolio paychecks up front, you can let your statement value flop all over the place—as it surely will—without having to rely on Mr. Market.

The Case for Individual Stocks

Most of the stock held by American investors is held through intermediaries of one kind or another, primarily mutual funds. Some funds, as well as the new crop of dividend-oriented exchange-traded funds (ETFs), talk about dividends as being part of their strategy. Many are called equity-income funds; some even throw the word *dividend* into their names. With dividends becoming more popular in recent years, a lot of new money has flowed into these funds.

If you outsource your stock picking to others, however, you're obliged to make several trade-offs.

▶ *Fees.* If you own a stock like Realty Income directly, you'll collect 100 percent of the dividend income it provides. By contrast, if you own Realty Income through a mutual fund, the management fees and other expenses of the fund will be deducted from its dividend income before the fund itself distributes cash to investors. The average equity-income mutual fund covered by Morningstar offered a yield of 1.7 percent in mid-2007, even though the underlying portfolios provide yields of 2.3 percent on average. Not only are these equity-income funds failing to seek much income, but fees and expenses are claiming at least a quarter of what little there is.

▶ *Strategy.* While there's no shortage of dividend fund and ETF choices, their strategies seem to fall into one of two camps. One group will buy stocks with the highest yields possible to generate maximum income, though often without much regard to growth or sustainability. The dividend ETFs generally fall into this camp, while some actively managed funds go so far as to manufacture dividend income by buying stocks in advance of one-time special payouts or simply in advance of the ex-dividend date. The other, larger group of equity-income funds will buy stocks *with* dividends, but not necessarily *for* or *because* of those dividends. These funds are, like their dividend-indifferent peers, more interested in capital gains and beating the indexes. I have yet to find a fund with a true and consistent dividend strategy, where the emphasis is on a rising stream of income. (And unlike a stock, whose dividend rate is a predictable dollar amount, the actual quarterly or annual dividend distribution of a mutual fund can vary as the portfolio changes.)

▶ *Need matching.* With so many choices available, it's possible you may find a fund that throws off the kind of income you seek. But the bulk of these funds' yields are so modest that the investors looking to withdraw 3 to 4 percent or more of their portfolio values annually will wind up selling shares. They'll be right back to living off the pile.

There's nothing necessarily wrong with opting for a mutual fund or ETF that emphasizes dividends, as long as these trade-offs seem reasonable to you. However, I think the case for owning individual dividend-paying stocks directly is stronger: You can match your need for income with the stocks that can provide it, and then you'll get 100 percent of the income they generate.

Naturally you (or your adviser) will have to do some homework; the companies, not the market, provide the returns in a true dividend strategy, but not all dividend streams are worth owning. Fortunately, a research approach centered on dividends (the one in this book) is not at all complicated—and the kinds of stocks this process involves are more attractive to own than the market in general.

The Bottom Line

Establish, nurture, and harvest a stream of income: What a liberating concept! But perhaps I've gotten a bit ahead of myself. Later in this book I'll have much more to say on the task of managing a portfolio from the income stream perspective. Next on the docket, however, is a journey through the land of dividends—why they matter, where they come from, and what they have to tell us.

Chapter 1: Rules and Plays

▶ Even though portfolio withdrawals made up with capital gains may look like income, they are a very poor substitute for dividend and interest payments.

▶ Fixed-income returns are much more predictable than the total returns from stocks. Predictably low, that is, after inflation is taken into account.

▶ High-yield stocks combine the best of both worlds: the steady income of fixed-income securities and the growth only stocks can offer.

Dividends, Values, and Returns

WALL STREET HAS an army of professionals determined to make investing seem like rocket science. To be a sophisticated player in bonds, for example, you've got to understand concepts like duration, convexity, and option-adjusted spreads. If advanced bond analysis requires a doctorate in mathematics, the stock market throws in heavy doses of physics: Momentum, more than anything, seems to rule the day-to-day action. And on Wall Street, it's always other people's money that they're playing with. Possibly even yours.

The common denominator to all investments and strategies is *cash*. The buying and selling of securities generates most of the cash flow on Wall Street, but marketability is not the same as return. For an investment security to have value—be it stock, bond, or whatever—it has to return cash to its owner independently of any effort on the owner's part.

Dividends, as I show in this chapter, provide the essential basis for stock value, even for stocks that might not be paying dividends at present. Without dividends, or at least the prospect of dividends, stocks are little more than handsome pieces of paper. With dividends, shares of stock take on true investment merit.

This chapter begins with the premise that all investment value relies on future returns of cash, and it ends with the observation that for stocks, future returns are a function of dividend yield and future dividend growth. We have to contend with some math along the way—I hope you won't find it too boring—but these lessons are vital to understanding the principles found in the remainder of this book.

Begin with the Humble IOU

To illustrate the dividend dynamics that give stocks value, let's begin by backing up into the simpler world of bonds. Bonds and stocks have more in common than you might think: The value of both is derived from their future returns of cash. The principal differences are (1) bonds return the original bondholder's investment at some point in the future, whereas stocks do not; and (2) the income of a bond is generally fixed, while that of a stock can and usually does rise over time.

Let's start by creating a simple IOU, also known as a bond. In exchange for giving me $10,000 today, I promise to return your $10,000 one year from now. I even give you a piece of paper, complete with my legally binding signature, that gives you the power to enforce your right to timely repayment in court. From your point of view, this loan is an investment. From mine, it's a debt.

If you're a good friend of mine, and I happen to be a bit down on my luck, you might let me have the $10,000 without interest. You might even be willing to be flexible on the repayment terms if my fortunes haven't improved by then. But if this is a true arm's-length transaction, the time value of your money, as well as any risk that I might fail to repay, must enter into your decision to make this loan. So let's add a reward. Not only do I promise to repay your $10,000 loan, but I'll chip in another $800 when the IOU comes due. With our terms now mutually agreed upon, that piece of paper with "IOU" in bold print at the top is now a claim on my personal assets, including my future earnings.

The extra $800 I promise to repay in a year's time represents *interest*, which provides you with income in addition to the return of the original loan amount (known separately as *principal*). The ratio of interest income to the IOU's principal—its *yield*—is $800 divided by $10,000, or 8 percent. This rate is fixed in the terms of our contract, hence the term *fixed-income investment*. You figure this 8 percent will more than offset the likely rate of inflation and provide a decent reward for trusting in my ability to repay. As long as you hold on to this bond until I pay it off, the market price doesn't enter into the equation.

Total Return on an IOU

Just after I've cashed your check for $10,000, you open the newspaper to discover that someone at the other end of town is offering a cherry-red 1966 Mustang in prime condition. The asking price? As if to spite you, the asking price is exactly $10,000. Unfortunately (from your perspective, at least), you can't force me to return your cash early. I have no legal obligation to pay the IOU off for a full year. The only way to get something back for your investment is to find someone else to take the IOU off of your hands.

What you need now is a liquid market for IOUs—a group of buyers and sellers with capital to invest. A $10,000 loan is too small to take to the nation's financial exchanges, and I doubt many banks would take serious interest, either. You want to head someplace where people have heard of Josh Peters and know he's a respectable fellow who pays his bills on time. Where do you head? The bakery down the street, perhaps, or maybe the corner bar. Chances are that someone will have both capital to invest and sufficient knowledge of me to make such an investment.

Strolling into the bakery, the first friendly face you see is your brother-in-law Bernie. He should have some idle dough to invest, right? You describe the situation and show him the IOU note. He rubs his chin for a moment, smiles, and offers you $9,500.

Ouch! To sell right now, you'd have to take a $500 loss. But consider the situation from Bernie's point of view. The terms of the IOU haven't changed; whoever happens to hold it when the IOU comes due will receive $10,000 in principal and $800 in interest. If Bernie buys the IOU for $9,500, he'll score a $500 *capital gain* in addition to the income. Not only that, but his effective yield will be higher than the 8 percent interest rate specified in the IOU. With profit coming from two sources—interest and capital gains—we need a more comprehensive statistic known as *total return* to describe Bernie's prospects.

At a $9,500 purchase price, Bernie's prospect for total return breaks down as follows:

$$\$800 \text{ of income} \div \$9,500 \text{ investment} = \text{yield of } 8.4\%$$
$$+ \$500 \text{ capital gain} \div \$9,500 \text{ investment} = \text{capital gain of } 5.3\%$$
$$= \$1,300 \text{ total profit} \div \$9,500 \text{ investment} = \text{total return of } 13.7\%$$

Your pain—in the form of a low selling price—becomes Bernie's gain. This leads us to a critical observation that applies to IOUs and all other types of securities:

All else being equal, as price falls, yield and future total return prospects rise.

"Thanks, but no thanks," you tell Bernie, and you move on to the bar. Surely someone else is willing to pay a higher price! Passing through the door of the corner watering hole you see more folks from your neighborhood. If you apply a little salesmanship, perhaps you can extract a higher price. Setting aside all claims to personal dignity, you climb atop the bar and shout, "Who in this room wants to make an 8 percent return in the next year?"

Interest rates at the bank being pitifully low, you've got the room's attention. You describe the situation in a bit more detail: how reliable Josh is, how he just got a new six-figure job, how his great aunt Tillie plans to leave him half of her estate. A can't-miss prospect!

Your next-door neighbor Joe looks up and says, "Okay, I'll take that 8 percent." You heave a sigh of relief and turn toward him. Then Rick from across the street interrupts, shouting, "Hey, wait a second. I'll settle for 7.5 percent." Before you can face Rick, Cindy from the drugstore bellows, "Seven percent over here." You've got a bidding war on your hands. Finally Morty, the village clerk, stands up and says "Five percent and that's my final offer." Dumbfounded by your good luck, you shout "Sold!" The IOU market is now closed; all you have to do is complete the transaction. Morty reaches for his checkbook but you pause: Just how much did Morty agree to pay?

Here we draw on a financial concept called *present value*—the value of some future cash payment, less some discount to reflect a required return. Since we know exactly how much cash I will pay to the IOU's holder one year hence—$10,800 including interest—the formula for figuring price is not terribly complicated:

$$\text{Future Cash Payment} \div (1 + \text{Rate of Return}) = \text{Present Value}$$

Replacing 5 percent with its decimal equivalent (0.05), we can calculate what Morty has agreed to pay for the IOU.

$$\$10{,}800 \div (1 + 0.05) = \$10{,}286$$

Not only will you get your ten grand back, you'll earn a profit of $286 for your troubles. But by paying a premium to its original value, Morty is going to take an equal capital loss on the IOU's principal. This will be more than made up by the interest income, but he won't earn the 8 percent return that you would have by holding the IOU until repaid, much less the 13.7 percent return that Bernie demanded. Recalling our earlier formula for total return:

$$\$800 \text{ of income} \div \$10{,}286 \text{ investment} = \text{yield of } 7.8\%$$
$$+ \ \${-}286 \text{ capital loss} \div \$10{,}286 \text{ investment} = \text{capital loss of } {-}2.8\%$$
$$\overline{= \$514 \text{ total profit} \div \$10{,}286 \text{ investment} = \text{total return of } 5.0\%}$$

With three parties now involved, let's look at where we stand. It doesn't matter who holds the IOU when it comes due; I owe that person a total of $10,800 in one year's time; my obligations are unchanged. You've come out $286 ahead, a tribute to your fine selling skills and, possibly, the slightly inebriated state of the IOU marketplace. Morty will also come out ahead with a 5 percent total return, but not by as much as you would have over the full term of the IOU. This demonstrates that my earlier observation regarding price and return runs equally in reverse:

All else being equal, as price rises, yield and future total return prospects decline.

Every marketable investment holds the prospect of a change in price, presenting the opportunity for capital gains or losses. For those securities providing income, that income component comes into play as well.

From IOUs to Stocks

Imagine if we meddled with the terms of this IOU a bit. You'll still give me $10,000, but now I have no obligation to repay. Rather than fixing income at a specific rate of interest, I instead make a vague promise of sharing my future earnings with you every so often—though I won't make any guarantees. Sound attractive?

As an IOU, these terms stink. Bonds have maturity dates at which time the investor's principal is returned; stocks offer no such promise. Instead, a common stock is assumed to be a *perpetuity*, able and (we hope) willing to pay dividends as long as the corporation paying it exists. Moreover, dividends are not fixed. No common stock carries any exact promise to pay.

But to have value, a stock still has to offer the shareholder the prospect of a cash return. Stocks can provide their owners with cash in four ways.

1. First, there are dividends. By sharing earnings with shareholders, corporations provide investors with a direct reward for the use of their capital. However, unlike the interest on an IOU (or bond), there's no guarantee of income. Per-share dividends may go up in the future; then again, they may drop.

2. A corporation may sell the entire firm for cash to a private buyer, usually another corporation. The shareholders receive equal cash payments in exchange for giving up ownership.

3. A corporation may decide to liquidate itself. Ceasing operations, the firm sells its assets, pays off any debts, and divides whatever is left among shareholders. This represents a final cash payment (akin to the repayment of principal on a bond) that severs the relationship between the now nonexistent corporation and its owners.

4. Finally, there's the stock market, where a shareholder can convert his shares back into cash by selling to someone else.

These four sources of cash provide the entire basis for a stock's value. Yet some of these sources are more reliable than others. Looking at these in reverse order:

▶ Investors obviously benefit from being able to buy and sell shares, but the fact that shares can be converted into cash at any time by selling ignores a key question: On what basis does the market establish a price? The shares you might own of, say, General Mills (GIS) aren't worth more or less than anyone else's; those shares need to provide the prospect of future cash payments regardless of who owns them. Therefore value can only be a function of the other three factors.

▶ Profitable liquidations are very rare, at least for shareholders. Sure, the value of General Mills' assets exceeds its liabilities, but on paper this difference only amounted to about $16 a share at the end of 2006. A market price in the mid-$50 range tells us that the company is worth much more as a going concern. Why would General Mills liquidate—especially when doing so would terminate the employment (and compensation!) of senior executives?

  In practice, corporations only liquidate themselves when they run out of money after heavy operating losses. In the bankruptcy liquidation process, there is rarely any money or value left for common shareholders.

▶ The prospect of a buyout or takeover plays a critical role in keeping a corporation's stock price in the ballpark of underlying business value. When price dips well below the present value of future cash-generating ability, private-equity firms like Kohlberg Kravis Roberts or the Blackstone Group know they can earn good returns by taking control of the entire company. Competitors like Kellogg (K) or Kraft (KFT) might see the same kind of opportunity.

  But if a KKR or Blackstone were to buy General Mills, what would they really be doing? They're not going to take the capital General Mills has invested in the cereal business and convert it into gravel pits or computer chips; the manufacture of Cheerios will go on much as it has in the past. What private buyers really obtain is control over the cash flow that General Mills generates; they want the ability to extract payments that look very much like dividends on whatever terms they choose.

By process of elimination, then, we discover that a stock's value rests squarely on its dividend prospects. Even for profitable corporations like Dell (DELL) and Cisco Systems (CSCO) whose managers steadfastly refuse to pay dividends (that being so old economy!), their stocks have value only because their assets and earning power strongly suggest that they *could* pay dividends. Were these firms' share prices to diverge too widely from their business value, shareholders would band together to demand dividends, possibly firing the board of directors in the process. If that effort failed, some extremely well-heeled private-equity buyer would acquire control of these corporations to extract whatever cash payments it wanted. Without the ability and propensity of corporations to pay dividends to their owners, it would be much more difficult for individual investors—those without the ability to acquire control of the corporations they own—to unlock the true value of their investments.

The Honor System

Instead of offering contractual guarantees, stocks operate on an honor system of sorts. Dividends may be discretionary, but per-share dividend rates are also *sticky*. Having set a regular dividend rate for its shares, a corporation is reluctant to renege on something that, if technically not a promise, carries an implicit obligation to go on paying. This is not necessarily true in other countries, but American investors like to be able to count on a predictable dividend stream. Dividend cuts or eliminations (known to dividend types like me as *omissions*) are just short of a full-blown betrayal of trust, and may signal financial troubles to come.

Better yet, the fact that dividends aren't fixed (like the interest rates on bonds) allows those dividends to rise as the issuing corporation grows and prospers—and dividends rise much more frequently than they fall.

Present-value math still applies to stocks as perpetuities, albeit in a slightly different fashion. To illustrate, let's compare the cash flows of a $1,000, five-year bond with a fixed interest rate of 8 percent against a $10 stock paying annual dividends of $0.80 a share. (To make the math easier to grasp, we'll assume we spend the same $1,000 to buy 100 shares of that $10 stock.) Assuming for the moment that investors will be satisfied with an annual return of 8 percent from each, the cash flows of future years, discounted to today's value, are demonstrated in Figure 2.1.

	Year 1	Year 2	Year 3	Year 4	Year 5	Total
5-Year Bond, Par Value $1,000	80.00	80.00	80.00	80.00	1,080.00	1,400.00
Present Value of Cash Flows	74.07	68.59	63.51	58.80	735.03	1,000.00
100 Shares of a $10 Stock	80.00	80.00	80.00	80.00	80.00	400.00
Present Value of Cash Flows	74.07	68.59	63.51	58.80	54.45	319.42

Figure 2.1   Comparing Cash Flow, Bond versus Dividend-Paying Stock

The $1,000 bond will return $1,400 in cash to its holder over five years; after taking the time value of money into account, discounting each year's cash flow by 8 percent per year, the bond is indeed worth $1,000. Well over half of this cash flow comes from the return of the bond's principal at maturity.

The stock, by contrast, is not obliged to return its original purchase price. After five years, its cash flow totals only $400. Discounted by the same 8 percent required return of the bond, these future cash payments are worth just $319 in today's dollars. If the corporation were to drop dead five years hence and cease paying dividends, its stock is worth no more than $3.19 a share today. But if the firm remains financially fit, that $0.80 a share of yearly dividends can go on and on. There will still be a lot of value left in the stock even after five years.

We could add more years to our spreadsheet; after 10 years, the stock will have returned dividends worth $5.37 a share in today's dollars; after 25 years, $8.54 a share. But even then, we're missing the value of still more dividends in the decades thereafter. Such is the nature of a perpetuity: We presume that it, like the Energizer bunny, will keep going . . . and going . . . and going . . .

Fortunately, mathematicians have provided us with a handy shortcut. The present value of a perpetuity with a fixed level of income is simply this:

Income ÷ Required Return = Present Value

Applying this math to our common stock, annual dividends of $0.80 a share divided into 8 percent (or 0.08, expressed in decimal terms) is indeed $10. If we decide to require a 9 percent return, the value of this stock falls from $10 to $8.89 a share. If we settle for 7 percent, then the stock is worth $11.43.

Again, we see this inverse relationship between price and return: A higher price produces a lower return and vice versa. (If I seem to belabor this point, it's only because it is critical to understanding future total returns.)

A Rising Dividend Stream

If the world were filled with stocks offering 8 percent yields, the role of a rising dividend stream would not be so important. In the low-yielding markets we live with today, most stocks derive the bulk of their value not from the level of current dividends but from the potential for future dividend growth.

Consider machinery manufacturer Graco (GGG), which has recently been paying dividends at an annual rate of $0.66 a share. Assuming investors demand a 10 percent return from their Graco shares, the stock—with no dividend increases—should trade for no more than $6.60 a share. But check the price: In mid-2007, those shares were trading around $40. Graco's current yield was less than 2 percent. Clearly, these shareholders are looking for dividends much higher than $0.66 a share in the years to come.

Specials, Splits, and Spin-Offs

Not everything that is called a dividend represents the kind of reliable, predictable income we seek. Some cash dividends, known as special dividends, represent one-time payouts. Companies may also issue special dividends in the form of stock, either as additional shares in the same company (stock splits) or shares of a subsidiary (spin-offs). In Appendix 1, I tackle the subject of special dividends in much more detail. As I show there, these dividends are not so special after all. What we seek are regular cash dividends—those that we can assume will be paid at predictable intervals and amounts into the indefinite future.

A rising dividend stream is much more valuable than a flat one. Instead of assuming a flat $0.80 dividend from my earlier example, let's assume that it rises 5 percent annually, and we continue to require an 8 percent annual return from the stock. What does the math look like? See Figure 2.2, where I forecast 100 years' worth of dividends to approximate perpetuity value.

The number that leaps off the page is the total dividends paid—$2,088.02 over the course of a century. Converting those payments into present dollars

	Year 1	Year 2	Year 3	Year 4–100	Total
$0.80 Dividend Grows at 5%	0.80	0.84	0.88	2,085.50	2,088.02
Present Value of Cash Flows	0.74	0.72	0.70	22.91	25.07

Figure 2.2   A Rising Dividend Stream

shrinks their value dramatically, but even that sum of $25.07 a share is suitably impressive relative to the value of a flat dividend stream. And even after forecasting 100 years' worth of dividends, there's still value we have yet to capture (the assumption of perpetuity is, after all, the prospect of forever).

Yet again, the math department stands ready to lend us a hand. Rather than forecasting 100 (or 1,000 or 10,000) years individually, a formula known as the Gordon Growth Model (GGM) shortens the math to this:

$$\frac{\text{Current Income}^1}{(\text{Required Return} - \text{Growth Rate})} = \text{Present Value}$$

On this basis, a stock with (1) an $0.80 dividend in the first year, (2) a required return of 8 percent, and (3) a growth rate of 5 percent is worth $26.67 a share: $0.80 divided by (0.08 − 0.05) is $26.67.

Preferred Stocks

Not all dividends grow. In fact, some dividends are guaranteed not to. From their name, you might assume that preferred stocks offer significant advantages over the mere common stocks I discuss in this book. However, the term *preferred* conveys only two advantages:

1. Dividends on preferred stocks must be paid before any dividends are sent out to common shareholders.
2. In the event the company liquidates, preferred shareholders receive their principal (par, stated, or liquidation value) back before common shareholders do.

(continued)

---

[1] The standard presentation of the GGM uses current income × (1 + growth rate) in the numerator. I've dropped the adjustment for first-year dividend growth for the sake of simplicity.

However, in exchange for this superior claim on dividends and liquidation value—factors that only become important when a company has fallen on hard times—almost all preferred stocks give up the potential for dividend growth. In virtually every case, the dividend rate on a preferred stock is fixed when it is issued, and there it will stay.

These factors—and many others—make preferred stocks a type of fixed-income security, rather than a true equity investment. They trade on the basis of their dividend yields, credit ratings, and (where applicable) maturity dates, just like bonds. And, like bonds, preferred stocks may have a role to play for some investors. As for me, I'd much rather focus on stocks whose dividend rates can and will rise over time.

The Grand Conclusion

With the Gordon Growth Model, we can place a value on any dividend-paying stock with just three inputs: the dividend rate, the dividend growth rate, and a required return. The dividend rate is easily obtained; growth is harder to figure, but both historical growth rates as well as the research process I describe in Chapter 7 can help us build a reasonable forecast. The last figure—required return—is the most troublesome. Just how much reward should we require for committing our hard-earned capital to a particular stock?

To a large extent, the answer lies in the eye of the beholder. Ten percent may not be a bad rule of thumb, approximating as it does the historical total return average of broad market indexes over very long stretches of time. (Not that I'd necessarily count on 10 percent in the future; in Chapter 5, I make the case that future returns for the market are more likely to run in the neighborhood of 8 percent.)

What is not subjective, however, is the stock's current price. A 15-second surf on the Internet will reveal the price at which a stock can be bought. The current quotation may not represent what the stock is actually *worth* (chances are excellent, in fact, that it does not), but with an algebraic flip of the Gordon Growth Model we can turn the stock price into an input and the required return—now the *prospective* return—into the output. The resulting calculation is at once elementary and insightful:

$$\frac{\text{Dividend Rate}}{\text{Stock Price}} + \text{Dividend Growth} = \text{Prospective Return}$$

Because the first term (the dividend rate divided by the stock price) is simply the current dividend yield, another statistic easily obtained on the Internet and elsewhere, we can shorten a stock's total return prospect to:

$$\text{Dividend Yield} + \text{Dividend Growth} = \text{Prospective Return}$$

It is just that simple! I guess I could name this the Peters Total Return Model, but that seems a bit over the top. Instead, I refer to this phenomenon as *dividend total return*.

Dividend Yield and Dividend Growth

Let's put some meat on this math lesson with some examples, starting with Kimberly-Clark (KMB). If the name doesn't ring a bell, a trip down the right grocery store aisles will; think Kleenex, Huggies diapers, and Scott paper towels. Apparently we Americans are going through more of these products as time goes on, because their maker has been able to raise its dividend in each of the past 13 years. Looking at the past decade, we observe a pleasant upward trend. (See Figure 2.3.)

Even before probing Kimberly-Clark's fundamentals, we can see that the company's growth fluctuates from year to year. Between 1996 and 2001, dividend growth averaged only 4 percent annually. The succeeding five years show steeper annual progress, with average growth near 12 percent. It's too early to tell whether the overall growth rate of 7.9 percent is a good estimate of what to expect in the future, but with some variations already evident in the past, it's probably not a bad proxy.

What else do we know? In early 2007, Kimberly-Clark raised its dividend yet again, this time by 8.2 percent. The fact that the 2007 increase is almost equal to the growth rate of the past 10 years lends additional support to the notion that dividends should go on rising at about 8 percent annually. The past is no guarantee of future performance, of course—which is why Chapter 7 is devoted to forecasting future dividend growth potential.

Year	Div Rate	Growth %	Price	Yield	Year	Div Rate	Growth %	Price	Yield
1986	0.31	—	9.82	3.2	1999	1.04	4.0	65.44	1.6
1987	0.36	16.1	12.29	2.9	2000	1.08	3.8	70.69	1.5
1988	0.40	11.1	14.56	2.7	2001	1.12	3.7	59.80	1.9
1989	0.65	62.5	18.38	3.5	2002	1.20	7.1	47.47	2.5
1990	0.68	4.6	21.00	3.2	2003	1.36	13.3	59.09	2.3
1991	0.82	20.6	25.34	3.2	2004	1.60	17.6	65.81	2.4
1992	0.82	0.0	29.50	2.8	2005	1.80	12.5	59.65	3.0
1993	0.86	4.9	25.94	3.3	2006	1.96	8.9	67.95	2.9
1994	0.88	2.3	25.19	3.5					
1995	0.90	2.3	41.38	2.2	**Averages**		Div Growth %		Yield
1996	0.92	2.2	47.63	1.9	1986–2006 (20 yrs)			9.7	2.6
1997	0.96	4.3	49.31	1.9	1996–2006 (10 yrs)			7.9	2.2
1998	1.00	4.2	54.50	1.8	2001–2006 (5 yrs)			11.8	2.5

Figure 2.3   Kimberly-Clark: Dividend Record

For now, though, I'll simply assume 8 percent is a sustainable rate of growth for Kimberly-Clark.

With quarterly dividends now running at an annualized $2.12, and the stock changing hands at roughly $71 in mid-2007, Kimberly-Clark offered a current dividend yield of 3 percent. Adding to that yield the dividend growth of 8 percent suggests the shares are priced to offer a total return of 11 percent in the years to come.

Is an 11 percent annual return good enough? Consumer product firms such as Kimberly-Clark tend not to be terribly risky, but all else being equal, I would demand a higher prospective return from a stock yielding 3 percent than I would from a similar business providing current income of 5 or 7 percent. A return of 11 percent looks good but not great—and not one that leaves much margin for disappointment. (Look for much more on this topic in Chapter 8.)

Kimberly-Clark provides a good example because both its yield and growth point to a realistic-looking dividend total return prospect. But recall my mention of low-yielding Graco shares earlier: With a dividend rate of $0.66 a share on a $40 stock, its yield is just 1.7 percent. The record of dividend growth is a much different story: Graco has raised its dividend in 9 of the past 10 years for a compound growth rate of 18 percent. Were Graco to

Year	Div Rate	Growth %	Price	Yield	Year	Div Rate	Growth %	Price	Yield
1986	0.035	—	1.46	2.4	1999	0.130	0.0	10.63	1.2
1987	0.035	0.0	1.33	2.6	2000	0.166	27.3	12.26	1.4
1988	0.046	31.1	1.68	2.7	2001	0.178	7.2	17.36	1.0
1989	0.053	14.8	1.57	3.4	2002	0.196	9.9	19.10	1.0
1990	0.060	12.9	2.00	3.0	2003	0.220	12.5	26.73	0.8
1991	0.060	0.0	2.34	2.5	2004	0.373	69.6	37.35	1.0
1992	0.067	12.1	2.05	3.3	2005	0.520	39.3	36.48	1.4
1993	0.074	10.8	3.19	2.3	2006	0.580	11.5	39.62	1.5
1994	0.084	14.1	2.87	2.9					
1995	0.095	12.3	4.02	2.4	**Averages**			Div Growth %	Yield
1996	0.111	16.9	4.84	2.3	1986–2006 (20 yrs)			15.1	2.0
1997	0.111	0.0	7.37	1.5	1996–2006 (10 yrs)			18.0	1.3
1998	0.130	17.7	8.74	1.5	2001–2006 (5 yrs)			26.6	1.1

Figure 2.4   Graco: Dividend Record

maintain this rate of growth into the indefinite future, our total return formula points to a total return of 19.7 percent annually. Now there's some *real* dividend potential! (See Figure 2.4.)

The trouble is, 19.7 percent is not a realistic annual return to expect from *any* stock in perpetuity, nor is a growth rate of 18 percent sustainable for any business indefinitely. Look at it this way: For Graco's dividend to grow that fast over the next 50 years, the firm's total annual outlay for dividends would have to rise from $43 million in 2007 to $728 *billion* 50 years later. No matter how outstanding its prospects (and they are in fact very good), Graco is not capable of expanding that quickly into the indefinite future. In Graco's case, a 10 percent growth rate seems more likely than the past decade's 18 percent, but with a 1.7 percent yield, we could still expect a total return of around 11.7 percent going forward.

One more example is in order at the opposite end of the growth spectrum: Consolidated Edison (ED). This electric utility is notable for three things:

1. Con Ed does a superb job of keeping the lights on in New York City (notwithstanding the 2003 power failure that blacked out parts of eight states—I know, I was there).

2. It has raised the dividend on its common stock for 33 straight years—no mean feat.
3. Unfortunately, Con Ed has one of the *worst* dividend growth rates of any company with a lengthy streak of annual increases. Between 1996 and 2006, its per-share dividend rate rose at a paltry average of 1.0 percent per year. (See Figure 2.5.)

A low growth rate is not necessarily bad, so long as the yield is high enough to compensate. Stocks with low dividend growth prospects should offer high current yields, and vice versa—and these two numbers need to add up to something worthwhile. But in mid-2007, Con Ed's dividend rate of $2.32 and market price of $46 resulted in a yield of only 5 percent. The implications of the past (annual dividend growth of 1 percent) and present (5 percent yield) are dismal: a dividend total return prospect of just 6 percent annually. That's not much more than an investor could get with a risk-free bank CD. I may not know for sure how low of a return would still be adequate for a low-risk business like Con Ed—but I'm sure it's higher than 6 percent.

Year	Div Rate	Growth %	Price	Yield	Year	Div Rate	Growth %	Price	Yield
1986	1.34	—	23.56	5.7	1999	2.14	0.9	34.50	6.2
1987	1.48	10.4	20.88	7.1	2000	2.18	1.9	38.50	5.7
1988	1.60	8.1	23.25	6.9	2001	2.20	0.9	40.36	5.5
1989	1.72	7.5	29.13	5.9	2002	2.22	0.9	42.82	5.2
1990	1.82	5.8	23.63	7.7	2003	2.24	0.9	43.01	5.2
1991	1.86	2.2	28.63	6.5	2004	2.26	0.9	43.75	5.2
1992	1.90	2.2	32.63	5.8	2005	2.28	0.9	46.33	4.9
1993	1.94	2.1	32.13	6.0	2006	2.30	0.9	48.07	4.8
1994	2.00	3.1	25.75	7.8					
1995	2.04	2.0	31.75	6.4	**Averages**			Div Growth %	Yield
1996	2.08	2.0	29.13	7.1	1986–2006 (20 yrs)			2.7	5.9
1997	2.10	1.0	41.00	5.1	1996–2006 (10 yrs)			1.0	5.4
1998	2.12	1.0	52.88	4.0	2001–2006 (5 yrs)			0.9	5.1

Figure 2.5   Consolidated Edison: Dividend Record

Dividend growth isn't the only variable. Stock prices change all the time, and since dividend rates are presumed to be fixed in the short run, yields change every time prices do. This is an inverse relationship: A higher stock price means a lower yield, while lower prices mean a higher yield. Were Con Ed's stock to drop from $46 to $33, its yield would rise from 5 percent to 7 percent. Assuming growth stays at 1 percent, Con Ed's dividend return prospect would rise from a questionable 6 percent to an arguably adequate 8 percent.

Either way, Con Ed's dividend is sending clear signals: Either the company's growth rate will have to be significantly better in the future than it has been in the past (and there's some reason to believe it could be), or investors are paying too much for the stock and accepting insufficient yields and total returns as a result.

Dividend Returns and Realized Returns

Recall that the premise underlying the dividend total return formula (yield plus growth equals return) is the assumption that, to collect that return through dividends alone, the stock must be held forever. That's nice as theory goes, but it's not terribly practical. Being a long-term investor, I don't buy stocks with a specific sell date in mind; instead, I present myself willing and able to hold as long as the company and its dividend stream treat me well. But even if a handful of stocks—and we don't know which ones—subsequently prove worthy of ownership into the indefinite future, many if not most stocks an investor buys will eventually be returned to the marketplace.

While the market price need not matter much when you're holding a stock and collecting its dividends, it's of obvious importance when it comes time to sell. The final piece of this total return puzzle is the impact of dividends on the future market price of a stock.

Let's say you were the final buyer of 100 shares of General Mills in December 2005, paying $49.32 a share for a total investment of $4,932. Perhaps you like the cereal maker's history of rising sales and profits; perhaps you're just a fan of Honey Nut Cheerios. Either way, you're looking for General Mills to generate income and increase your wealth.

General Mills was paying dividends at an annual rate of $1.36 a share at the end of 2005. Based on your purchase price of $49.32, your initial yield was 2.8 percent. In 2006, you expect your 100 shares to provide $136 worth of dividend income. That yield alone won't make the stock worth owning, of course; you want growth. How much growth? By rearranging the Gordon Growth Model yet again, we can find the answer:

Required Return – Dividend Yield = Required Dividend Growth

If we require at least a 10 percent annual return from General Mills, this formula tells us that the firm's dividends need to grow by at least 7.2 percent annually. Fortunately, General Mills provided you with wonderful news during 2006: Management raised the dividend three separate times. By year-end, the indicated dividend rate had risen from $1.36 to $1.48 a share, an increase of 8.8 percent—ahead of the 7.2 percent you expected.

From one standpoint, an extra $0.12 a share of annual dividend income may not sound like much of a gain. Your dividend checks in 2007 stand to be only $12 higher than the ones you cashed in 2006; relative to your original investment of $4,932, this represents a improvement of just 0.2 percent. However, the real impact of this dividend increase on the stock's value is significantly larger. The fact that the dividend went up has made the stock more attractive to own—a fact that surely ought to be reflected in the stock's market price.

Before asking what this dividend *did* do to the stock price, let's first consider what it *should* do. The fact that this one dividend increase came in ahead of your 7.2 percent requirement for growth is certainly a plus, but this alone doesn't suggest that all future increases will run at a higher rate as well. For now, we'll assume that future dividend growth will continue to run at 7.2 percent. We'll also assume that 10 percent remains a fair total return on an investment in General Mills. These two factors tell us that General Mills should continue to offer a yield of 2.8 percent.

The only variable that has changed, for our purpose at this moment, is the dividend rate. Calling the Gordon Growth Model into action one more time, we can discover how much value this dividend increase added to General Mills' shares.

Before

$$\frac{\text{Dividend Rate of } \$1.36}{\text{Return of } 10\% - \text{Growth of } 7.2\%} = \$49.32$$

After

$$\frac{\text{Dividend Rate of } \$1.48}{\text{Return of } 10\% - \text{Growth of } 7.2\%} = \$53.67$$

Note: Figures may not align precisely due to the rounding of yield and growth terms.

We find that the value of General Mills' future dividend stream has increased by $4.35 per share—a gain identical to the 8.8 percent hike in the dividend rate. By adding this gain in value to the $1.38 in dividends General Mills paid during 2006 (higher than the $1.36 you initially expected, thanks to an increase at midyear), the stock's dividend total return was 11.6 percent. This is exactly what the basic math of dividend yield (2.8 percent) plus dividend growth (8.8 percent) would and should suggest.

Now let's say you've soured on General Mills for one reason or another. Those Cheerios just don't seem to taste as good as they used to; these days you're eating more Froot Loops and would just as soon buy stock in Kellogg (K) instead. Your dividend total return for 2006 may have been 11.6 percent, and the fact that it was a bit higher than the 10 percent you expected is certainly a plus. But as you approach the market to sell, you'll need to distinguish the *expected return* based on dividend yield and growth and the *realized return* you will record once you've sold the stock.

As it happens (and this is almost always the case), the market price of General Mills did not rest at precisely $53.67 at the end of 2006. In fact, the price rose faster than the dividend—closing out the year at $57.60. Instead of matching the 8.8 percent increase in the dividend, the price gained a hefty 16.8 percent. Delighted with your gain, you sell and tote up your winnings:

$138 of income ÷ $4,932 investment = yield of 2.8%

+ $828 capital gain ÷ $4,932 investment = capital gain of 16.8%

= $966 total profit ÷ $4,932 investment = total return of 19.6%

	Beginning Stock Price	Ending Stock Price	Capital Gain/(Loss)	Initial Yield	Realized Total Return	Dividend Total Return	Better/ Worse
Valuation Drops (Yield Rises)	49.32	40.00	−18.9%	2.8%	−16.1%	11.6%	−27.7%
Valuation Unchanged	49.32	53.67	8.8%	2.8%	11.6%	11.6%	0.0%
Actual 2006 Performance	**49.32**	**57.60**	**16.8%**	**2.8%**	**19.6%**	**11.6%**	**8.0%**
Valuation Rises (Yield Drops)	49.32	65.00	31.8%	2.8%	34.6%	11.6%	23.0%

Figure 2.6   General Mills: 2006 Realized Return Scenarios

Even though your dividend total return was 11.6 percent, your *realized* total return was a much higher 19.6 percent. The extra capital appreciation— the fact that General Mills' share price rose almost twice as fast as the dividend rate—put an extra $393 in your pocket. Turns out that Mr. Market was in a generous mood this time around.

Of course, nothing—not even the dividend increase—forced Mr. Market to be so generous. In any single year, we can assume that an individual stock is almost as likely to go down as it is to go up. Considering a potential range for General Mills' year-end stock price, we see that your realized total return might have been higher—but it might have been a lot lower, too. (See Figure 2.6.)

Nevertheless, the capital gain (or loss) is not the only action in General Mills' stock. No matter what the realized capital gain was, the total return was higher. I can't resist stating the obvious: Dividends are always, everywhere, and only a positive contributor to the shareholder's total return.

But even as your relationship with General Mills has just come to a highly profitable end, someone else's—the investor who bought your 100 shares—is just beginning. What can the buyer expect? In a word, less. (See Figure 2.7.)

When a stock's market price rises faster than its dividend rate, its yield declines, and vice versa. In General Mills' case, that extra capital appreciation in 2006 that made your investment so rewarding trimmed the stock's yield

	Dividend Yield	Growth Rate	Prospective Return
Year-End 2005	2.8%	7.2%	10.0%
Year-End 2006	2.6%	7.2%	9.8%

Figure 2.7   General Mills: Return Prospects, 2005 versus 2006

	Ending Stock Price	Ending Div. Rate	Ending Yield	Expected Growth	Projected Return
Valuation Drops (Yield Rises)	40.00	1.48	3.7%	7.2%	10.9%
Valuation Unchanged	53.67	1.48	2.8%	7.2%	10.0%
Actual 2006 Performance	**57.60**	**1.48**	**2.6%**	**7.2%**	**9.8%**
Valuation Rises (Yield Drops)	65.00	1.48	2.3%	7.2%	9.5%

Figure 2.8   General Mills: Dividend Return Scenarios for 2007 and Beyond

from 2.8 percent to 2.6 percent. If the dividend growth rate of 7.2 percent hasn't changed, this lower yield means the buyer of your shares can't expect to earn the 10 percent dividend total return that you once did; he or she can only look for a slightly lower 9.8 percent.

The same observation holds for the wider range of hypothetical year-end market prices for General Mills shown in Figure 2.8. A lower price directly implies a higher yield and projected total return; higher prices point to lower future returns.

In the short term, stock prices aren't set solely on the basis of dividend yield, growth, and required returns. From day to day, the stock market is simply a popularity contest: Buyers outnumber sellers for what is deemed beautiful at the moment, and prices rise; when sellers outnumber buyers, prices fall. This is nothing more than the basic law of supply and demand at work.

Furthermore, this popularity contest is only rarely framed in terms of dividends. Earnings per share and price/earnings ratios are the standard terms of discussion and disagreement—even though corporate earnings, as I discuss in Chapter 3, are not the dollars that shareholders actually get. Even when investors debate the relative merits of a stock on the basis of dividends (a debate you can often hold in a phone booth without the phone), different investors can and will come to very different conclusions about future growth prospects and required returns. At any point in time, market prices reflect who is winning or losing these debates.

But even if Wall Street largely ignores dividends, a rising dividend stream can hardly help but put upward pressure on the market price. For companies with steady business prospects, dividend rates and share prices will move in tandem—a correlation that grows tighter as time passes. (See Figure 2.9.)

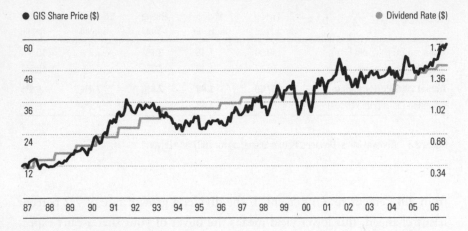

Figure 2.9   General Mills (GIS): Share Price and Dividend History

We can also observe that while General Mills' dividend growth has fluctuated in the past 20 years, its yield has stayed in a relatively narrow band between 2.5 and 3.5 percent. (See Figure 2.10.)

This provides me with my final point: The difference between prospects for dividend total return and actual realized returns is explained by changes in yield. There is no perfect yield for a stock, not even for a steady business like General Mills. Note how the years in which dividend growth was low (or nonexistent) seem to correlate with higher yields. When the dividend wasn't

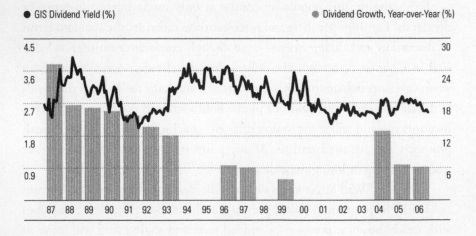

Figure 2.10   General Mills: Dividend Yield and Growth History

growing—even though it could and almost certainly would in the future—investors became more cautious and required a higher current yield.

As long as short-term changes in yield cancel out (more or less) between the time you buy a stock and the time you sell it, dividend yield and dividend growth are clearly the primary drivers of share price appreciation. There are many reasons a stock's yield might have to change in the long term, of course. Growth prospects could shrink or investor return requirements could rise; in such cases realized total returns would fall short of dividend total returns. If you can buy a stock at a relatively high yield for its future growth prospects—one where the market price doesn't properly appreciate the dividend growth potential of the business—realized returns can easily exceed dividend returns. But the longer you hold a stock, and the more dividend income you accumulate, the relevance of yield fluctuations on realized return ought to diminish, if not disappear.

The Bottom Line

Understanding the basic drivers of investment returns—specifically the concept that future returns are driven by the sum of current yield and future dividend growth—is essential to grasping the rest of the story. But thus far I've assumed that dividends and growth come out of thin air. Just where dividends come from is the topic of Chapter 3.

Chapter 2: Rules and Plays

▶ Stocks, like any other investment, only have value because of their ability to return cash to their owners—if not now, then eventually.

▶ The total return potential of a stock is equal to its current dividend yield plus its future dividend growth potential.

▶ All else being equal, as a stock's price falls, its future return potential rises—and vice versa.

3

Corporations: Dividend Machines

CORPORATIONS PERFORM MANY useful tasks in modern society. We look to them to deliver the bulk of our basic necessities and virtually all of our luxuries. Corporations provide most of the American workforce with gainful employment. They pay taxes that help support vital government services. Their scientific research efforts advance the bounds of human knowledge and improve everyday life in a million different ways.

But from the shareholder's point of view, a corporation is simply a machine for turning investment capital into dividends. Capital is the shareholder's contribution to the enterprise; his reward is the promise of dividend income in return.

The basic source of dividends is profits (also referred to as earnings) that come from the corporation's ongoing business activities. Every corporation performs this function in its own way, and some are better at it than others. But these machines have certain aspects in common—levers, if you will. If you understand the business concepts in this chapter, you're well on your way to finding great dividend-paying companies.

Capital and Profits

Most people think of profits as revenue minus expenses; an eight-year-old can grasp that concept from sitting behind the counter (or, more likely, the folding table) of her first lemonade stand. While that is true, an even more relevant connection is the one between profits and capital. It takes money to make money; any owner of a business, large or small, will confirm this nearly universal fact. If I want to sell lemonade, I have to buy lemons first. If I want to earn some interest on my savings, I need to deposit that cash in the bank. Even if all I want to do is win the lottery, I have to buy a ticket.

This same principle holds for corporate assets. You may not think of steel mills, retail display racks, and paper clips as income-generating investments, but they are. In each case, these assets enable a corporation to turn a profit on its business activities, directly or indirectly. There is no savings account at a corporation's core, but there is an equally important concept: shareholders' equity.

Shareholders' equity, also known as *net worth* or *book value*, can be viewed in two equally valid ways, as demonstrated in Figure 3.1.

First, equity is the value of a corporation's assets after subtracting all liabilities. Successful corporations—most of them, anyway—have lots of left-over value in this exercise. Grocery chain Safeway (SWY), for example, had $16.3 billion in assets at the end of 2006: inventories, buildings, delivery

Assets		Liabilities and Shareholder's Equity	
Cash and Equivalents	216.6	Accounts Payable	2,464.4
Receivables	461.2	Short-Term Debt	831.5
Merchandise Inventories, net	2,642.5	Other Accrued Liabilities	1,305.5
Prepaid Expenses and Other	245.4	**Current Liabilities**	**4,601.4**
Current Assets	**3,565.7**		
		Long-Term Debt	5,036.6
Land, Buildings, and Improvement	9,664.1	Other Liabilities	968.9
Fixtures and Equipment	7,199.0	**Total Liabilities**	**10,606.9**
Property Under Capital Leases	777.4		
Less: Accumulated Depreciation	(7,867.2)	Common Stock and Paid-In Capital	3,817.3
Total Property, Net	**9,773.3**	Treasury Stock	(4,188.7)
		Accumulated Other Comprehensive Incm	94.8
Goodwill	2,393.5	Retained Earnings	5,943.5
Other Assets	541.3	**Total Shareholders' Equity**	**5,666.9**
Total Assets	**16,273.8**	**Total Liabilities and Equity**	**16,273.8**

Figure 3.1   Safeway: Balance Sheet at Year-End 2006 (Numbers in Millions)

trucks, and the like. The firm also had liabilities totaling $10.6 billion, nearly half of which were owed to bondholders. The difference between the two, $5.7 billion, represents shareholders' equity.

Second, this equity account can be viewed as the sum of all the capital Safeway shareholders have invested in the company, plus accumulated profits, less the sum of dividends paid to shareholders (and share buybacks; more on this later). Looking more closely, we find that shareholders have put in some $3.8 billion, retained earnings total $5.9 billion, while cumulative share repurchases total $4.2 billion. Other accounting odds and ends are in a subtotal called "accumulated other comprehensive income"; after rounding, these factors indeed add up to $5.7 billion.

Using shareholders' equity as a starting point, a corporation makes investments in anticipation of earning a certain rate of return. Factories and office buildings and even paper clips are purchased with these funds to enable profitable business transactions to take place. The logic is no different than that of the savings account, except that corporations generally expect a return on their assets a lot higher than the 5 percent a savings account might offer. A savings account is liquid—the deposit can be converted to folding money anytime I care to visit the bank and make a withdrawal. It's much harder to convert a $10 million piece of complicated machinery back to cash, so the buyer has every reason to expect a much higher profit as a percentage of the investment. This brings us to a key statistic known as *return on equity*.

Evaluating Profitability: Not All Profits Are Created Equal

Consider two business enterprises that, for the time being, we'll call Fat Company and Thin Industries. In 2006, Fat Company took in just over $1.6 billion of revenue and turned a $165 million profit. For every dollar of revenue, it kept 10.3 cents. (Expressed as a percentage, Fat Company's net margin is 10.3 percent.) This 10 cents on the dollar might seem impressive; the average nonfinancial corporation in America earns something like 5 cents. Thin Industries took in almost $34 billion on its way to earning an $868 million profit. While its much larger volume allowed it to earn more than Fat Company, Thin kept only 2.6 cents of each dollar in revenue as profit. On this basis, we might judge Fat to be nearly four times as profitable as Thin. (See Figure 3.2.)

	Fat Company	Thin Industries
Profits	165	868
Divided by: Revenues	1,606	33,888
Net Margin (%)	**10.3**	**2.6**

Figure 3.2   Comparing Profitability with Profit Margins (Numbers in Millions)

However, investors don't supply the businesses they own with revenue; we provide corporations with capital. What we really want to know is how much profit is earned with each dollar we've invested. Fat's average equity capital during 2006 was $1.5 billion, while Thin's average net worth was $2.9 billion. Here we call a different indicator of profitability into action: return on equity (ROE). Where profit margins relate profits to sales (profit margins are sometimes called *return on sales*, in fact), return on equity measures profit relative to the equity required to earn it. (See Figure 3.3.)

Once our view switches to ROE, Thin Industries suddenly looks much more profitable. For every dollar shareholders had invested in Thin at the beginning of 2006, the firm earned more than 29 cents. Fat Company collected only 11 cents. From an investor's point of view, Thin is almost three times as profitable as Fat.

Just who are Fat Company and Thin Industries? Fat is actually Westar Energy (WR), the largest utility providing electric power in Kansas. Thin Industries is Sysco Corporation (SYY), the largest wholesaler of food-service products to North America's restaurant and hospitality operators. But while returns on equity might be interesting, what does it really mean? Aren't all dollar bills the same shade of green? Isn't a dollar of profit at Westar worth the same as a dollar for Sysco?

Actually, some corporate profits are much greener than others. The key variable is growth. (See Figure 3.4.) If neither Westar nor Sysco is expanding its operations, both profit streams are equal: A dollar is a dollar is a dollar. But when we introduce growth into the equation, Sysco is the much better prospect.

	Fat Company	Thin Industries
Profits	165	868
Divided by: Average Shareholders' Equity	1,499	2,948
Return on Equity (%)	**11.0**	**29.4**

Figure 3.3   Comparing Profitability with Return on Equity (Numbers in Millions)

	Equity Capital Invested	×	ROE	=	Profit Growth
Sysco	$34 million	×	29.4%	=	$10 million
Westar Energy	$91 million	×	11.0%	=	$10 million

Figure 3.4   The Cost of Earnings Growth

Assuming Westar's ROE on future investments will also be 11 percent, the company has to invest some $91 million to increase its annual profit by $10 million. Sysco, with a 29.4 percent ROE, has to invest only $34 million to score the same $10 million gain in earnings.

This is no small point. Successful corporations need to keep up with the growth of the American population and economy as a whole. A lower ROE makes it more expensive to fund the growth of a business, which either leaves fewer dollars available for dividends today or diminishes the potential for dividend growth in the future.

An Expanded View of Profitability

The real-world process of turning shareholders' equity into profits is naturally more complicated than simply multiplying shareholders' equity by ROE. Fortunately, a simple set of formulas known as DuPont analysis can help us evaluate this process. In a way, DuPont analysis mirrors the three steps necessary for a business to turn seed capital into earnings.

1. *Financial leverage.* Not all of the assets a business needs to operate will come from shareholders. Some assets are financed with liabilities—bond issues, bank loans, accounts payable, and the like. These debts magnify the amount of assets a corporation's equity can support, a concept known as financial leverage.

$$\text{Financial Leverage} = \frac{\text{Assets}}{\text{Equity}}$$

2. *Asset turnover.* The assets of a business allow it to generate revenue, the dollars hauled in by selling products or services to consumers or other businesses. Asset turnover measures how much revenue is generated for each dollar of sales. This is one way to measure a firm's productivity; all else being equal, a higher volume of revenue for each dollar of assets will lead to higher profitability.

(continued)

$$\text{Asset Turnover} = \frac{\text{Revenues}}{\text{Assets}}$$

3. *Net margin*. Revenue is not enough to turn a profit. In addition to capital, a business requires other expenditures to operate. Whatever revenue is left over after these expenses represents profit. Expressed as a percentage of sales, we find a firm's net margin. While this is a less comprehensive measure of profitability than ROE, it plays a major supporting role in the ability of a business to generate a return on its equity.

$$\text{Net Margin} = \frac{\text{Profits}}{\text{Revenues}}$$

The elegance of this three-statistic set is that multiplying all three factors together will yield return on equity. With a bit of algebra, the revenue and asset figures cancel out, leaving profits divided by shareholders' equity (return on equity) as the final product.

$$\text{Return on Equity} = \frac{\text{Assets}}{\text{Equity}} \times \frac{\text{Revenues}}{\text{Assets}} \times \frac{\text{Profits}}{\text{Revenues}}$$

OR

$$\text{Return on Equity} = \text{Financial Leverage} \times \text{Asset Turnover} \times \text{Net Margin}$$

Let's see how Sysco and Westar stack up on these measures.[1]

$$\frac{\text{Assets}}{\text{Equity}} \times \frac{\text{Revenues}}{\text{Assets}} \times \frac{\text{Profits}}{\text{Revenues}} = \text{Return on Equity}$$

$$\frac{5,333}{1,499} \times \frac{1,606}{5,333} \times \frac{165}{1,606} = 11.0\%$$

OR

$$3.56 \times 0.30 \times 10.3\% = 11.0\%$$

The figure that jumps off the page in this case is asset turnover. Utilities like Westar are notoriously capital-intensive. To generate $1.6 billion in annual revenue, the firm

[1]Since it takes assets and equity over the course of an entire year for a firm to earn a year's worth of profits, I've averaged the beginning and ending stats for both balance sheet statistics. Also, because Sysco's fiscal year ends in June, I've used calendar-year figures from the company's quarterly reports.

had to place more than $5 billion worth of assets (generating stations, transmission towers, power poles, and so forth) into service. Westar was able to borrow much of this money, but shareholders were still obliged to commit almost a year's worth of revenue in equity capital to support the firm's asset base. Furthermore, because a utility holds a natural monopoly, state regulators limit returns on equity to a relatively low level to protect consumers from abusive pricing. No wonder Westar's return on equity is so low.

$$\frac{\text{Assets}}{\text{Equity}} \times \frac{\text{Revenues}}{\text{Assets}} \times \frac{\text{Profits}}{\text{Revenues}} = \text{Return on Equity}$$

$$\frac{9,038}{2,948} \times \frac{33,888}{9,038} \times \frac{868}{33,888} = 29.4\%$$

OR

$$3.07 \times 3.75 \times 2.6\% = 29.4\%$$

A peek at Sysco's balance sheet shows more than $9 billion in average assets, mostly inventory, warehouses, and trucks. For every dollar of assets, Sysco generated $3.75 in sales. Westar, by contrast, hauls in only about 30 cents for each dollar of assets. With such productive assets, Sysco can charge tiny markups and make it up in volume. It helps, too, that Sysco's profits aren't restrained by any regulatory regime; the company can charge whatever its customers will bear.

The only DuPont metric that is roughly similar for these two firms is financial leverage. Sysco has $3.07 in assets for every dollar of equity; Westar, $3.56. The math shows us how important financial leverage is to each firm's return: With no borrowed funds, Sysco would earn only 9.6 percent on its equity; Westar, just 3.1 percent. This statistic, *return on assets*, shows how profitable a firm would be in the absence of leverage.

Financial leverage can boost a firm's ROE, but it also has two other effects:

1. Most borrowed money does not come free. Vendors who allow customers a few months to pay (coal suppliers for Westar, food manufacturers for Sysco) generally do not charge interest, but bondholders and banks certainly do. Interest expense is part of the firm's operating costs, and thus reduces profits and net margin.
2. Financial leverage has a way of exaggerating changes in profitability. A company's liabilities and interest costs are generally fixed, even as the revenue, profits, and value of assets fluctuate. If a firm's net margin declines in a bad year, the effect on ROE will be even harsher. And a loss—a negative net margin—will result in an even greater negative ROE.

Long-Term ROEs: Competition Counts

In the short run, variations in profit margins and other factors will lead directly to changes in profits and therefore in ROE. Looking at the returns of a business enterprise over a longer stretch of years, however, we discover a much larger force at work: competition.

Competition is the defining feature of free-market capitalist economies and arguably the intrinsic state of nature as well. Competition in business drives down prices and, by so doing, limits profits and returns on equity.

In a purely competitive market, returns tend to be very limited. Think of the gas wars that break out every so often in your neighborhood. When the product is an indistinguishable commodity, price is the sole defining characteristic. Since a station's markup on a gallon of gas is tiny, the temptation to grab additional volume is huge. So when a particular station owner decides he isn't getting his fair share of passing traffic, he cuts the price by a few cents a gallon—maybe by a nickel or even a dime if he's desperate.

That kind of business strategy will work for about three minutes. The managers of nearby stations need only to look out the window to learn that their prices are no longer competitive. Before long, all three stations will again be charging the same price, only now at much lower profits. If this process of slicing prices goes on long enough, eventually all three stations will be selling gasoline below cost. Losing money is hardly a sustainable business strategy. As economist Herb Stein said, if something is unsustainable, it tends to stop.

Now recall that profitability isn't solely a function of revenue minus costs; it is profit relative to capital that counts. No one would own a gas station unless he figured he could earn a return on his capital at least equal to what he could get on comparable investments elsewhere. If the owner of a $2 million gas station is earning just $100,000 annually—a piddling 5 percent return—he may well decide to give up, sell his station to a real estate developer, and invest his money elsewhere. With less supply relative to demand, the surviving stations should be able to increase their gas markups and restore profits to a worthwhile level.

On the flip side, let's say the closure of one of those gas stations makes other station managers greedy. They raise prices again and again and seem to get away with it. Customers grumble but profits skyrocket, as do the stations' returns on equity. Lo and behold, the real estate developer who just bought the land under the closed gas station runs the numbers and discovers the best use of that location is—you guessed it—another gas station. With a new competitor, prices and profits fall back.

This kind of logic applies to every business enterprise on some level. If every business faced the same dreadful competitive dynamic of a gas station, we wouldn't find firms like Sysco earning a 29 percent return on equity when nascent competitors might be willing to perform identical services for a 20 percent or 10 percent return on their investment. Some other combination of factors has to explain why a business can earn more than the minimum return some group of rivals might seek. Those factors are wrapped up in a concept called *sustainable competitive advantage*. That phrase being a bit clumsy, the estimable Warren Buffett has termed the phenomenon an *economic moat*.

Economic Moats

Moat refers to the water that once surrounded medieval castles to keep the barbarians at bay. Twenty-first century nobility (corporations) have no real need for water to protect the front office, but to succeed, they have to find ways to prevent competitors from eroding their returns.

The factors leading to an economic moat can be categorized in a number of ways. Morningstar's approach breaks them into the following four broad categories.

Intangible Assets

Intangible assets allow a firm to create a differentiated product or service without encountering direct competition. The patent on Pfizer's (PFE) cholesterol-lowering drug Lipitor falls into this category. Nothing stops the scientists at Bristol-Myers (BMY) or Merck (MRK) from analyzing Pfizer's pill to discover the formula, but because of the patent, the government will stop those firms from ripping off Pfizer's research. Pfizer will be able to sell Lipitor without direct competition for the term of its patent (usually 17 years in the United States). Thus it may charge whatever price customers will bear without worrying about peers offering a cheaper version. Anyone who pays cash for an expensive prescription can understand this concept.

Brands and government licenses are two more examples of intangibles. Anyone can create a cola-flavored beverage, but only the Coca-Cola Company (KO) can call it Coke. Anyone with the requisite millions could build a casino, but only the lucky holders of a limited number of government permits are allowed to.

As a side note, you'll often see *intangible assets* or *goodwill* listed as an asset on a firm's balance sheet. These intangibles are mere bookkeeping entries that arise as the result of acquisitions. The presence of real intangible assets shows up not on the balance sheet, but in the firm's return on equity after excluding intangibles.

Economies of Scale

As hundreds of empty downtown shopping districts across America can attest, size equals strength. Largely by virtue of its size, Wal-Mart Stores (WMT) can buy merchandise and transport it to thousands of stores cheaper than anyone else. This allows Wal-Mart to charge lower prices and still earn higher profit margins and returns on equity than smaller chains and independent merchants.

Mere heft does not automatically convey this advantage. This phenomenon only applies to firms whose size relative to competitors allows them to lower costs without lowering selling prices in concert. Very few airlines, no matter how large, are capable of generating decent returns. ExxonMobil (XOM) and Ford Motor (F) are two of the largest companies in the world, but while ExxonMobil's size enables it to find, extract, and refine oil very cheaply, Ford's massive size today is more of a curse than a blessing.

Switching Costs

A useful example of this phenomenon comes from the retail propane industry. When a homeowner signs up for new propane service, a distributor like AmeriGas Partners (APU) customarily offers her a free tank to be buried somewhere on her property. Nice, huh? Well, there's a catch: AmeriGas won't let just anyone fill that tank. If another propane supplier in town offers a better per-gallon price, AmeriGas will gladly come with a backhoe and rip up her yard to retrieve its tank. Few homeowners are willing to have their properties destroyed to save a few bucks, so there's a strong tendency not to switch suppliers on the basis of price. When customer switching costs are present, competitors in a particular field can charge higher prices than they otherwise could, and the benefit lands squarely in the firms' pockets. (Who knew Hank Hill had it so good?)

Banks like Wells Fargo (WFC) benefit from a similar phenomenon; when was the last time you changed checking accounts without moving? So do software makers like Microsoft (MSFT); who wants to learn a whole new spreadsheet program that might render existing Excel documents unreadable?

Network Effects

This one is interesting in part because it's so rare. Imagine you're looking to sell some rare stamps from your ample and well-cared-for collection. Where do you want to go? Wherever the most buyers are to be found, of course. Selling them at a garage sale, you'd be lucky to get more than a buck even for a rare treasure. Sell them on eBay (EBAY), and you'll find more buyers than anywhere else in the world. Other knowledgeable collectors will bid against one another to provide you with the best price, and eBay gets a nice piece of the action.

The network effect arises when a business can provide a service that becomes more beneficial the more people use it. Microsoft, too, benefits from the network effect; the more people who use its Word and Excel programs to create and exchange computer files, the more people who are more or less obliged to go on using Word and Excel.

Evaluating Moats

A business may find itself naturally endowed with any of these four types of moats, or it may—with great effort—be able to dig itself a moat over time. The unifying factor is the influence a moat will have on return on equity. Companies with low ROEs find growth difficult and expensive, forces that are sure to show up in weak dividend growth prospects. By contrast, firms with high ROEs get the maximum bang for the reinvested dollar, leaving plenty of cash to return to shareholders.

Not every company with a history of high ROEs has a moat, however. Only sustainable, structural competitive advantages count toward an economic moat; temporary advantages can't be relied on. Think of mall-based fashion retailers like Aeropostale (ARO) and American Eagle Outfitters (AOS). They've had some monstrous ROEs, with 30 percent not uncommon. But their ability to generate high returns is contingent on staying ahead of fashion trends, an almost impossible task over any length of time. Gap (GPS) once had a record like that, but just a couple of fashion miscues several years ago trashed profitability to a level from which the retailer still hasn't recovered.

When evaluating moats, it's necessary to look at current profitability as well as the structural state of the business. A good rule of thumb is to assume a company doesn't have a moat unless proved otherwise. Regardless of how high ROEs might be right now, it is only when the economic characteristics of the business line up with one or more of the four moat factors previously listed that we can have confidence in the sustainability of high ROEs. In other words, the key is not just to seek firms with high ROEs, but to know why those ROEs are high and should stay high into the indefinite future.

The Jump from Profits to Dividends

ROE describes how a corporation turns the shareholder's investment into earnings, but dividends require another step. For example, 3M Company (MMM) earned a profit of $3.9 billion in 2006, or $5.06 for each of its 761 million outstanding shares. It happens that one of the model portfolios I manage for *Morningstar DividendInvestor* owned 55 shares of 3M during this period, so its share of the company's profit was $278.30. Yet of this profit, only $101.20 found its way back to the *DividendInvestor* account in cash. What gives?

In this we find something of a conflict between a corporation and its shareholders. All else being equal, shareholders would just as soon receive larger dividends. Corporations, however, have interests of their own; virtually all feel the need to expand. By keeping a portion (or all) of profits inside the corporation, management can purchase additional assets, hire more people, develop new products, and—it hopes—generate still greater profits in the future. If capital is the ultimate source of dividends, then retained earnings is the principal engine of dividend growth.

Some of these efforts at growth are perfectly legitimate; if 3M can sell more Post-it Notes (to cite just one of its 55,000 or so products) in 2007 than it did in 2006 and earn higher profits as a result, it might make sense for 3M to pay smaller dividends than it could otherwise afford so it can expand the Post-it plant. However, CEOs and other corporate executives may attempt to grow in ways that don't benefit shareholders. Large mergers and acquisitions are a perennial use (or misuse) of retained earnings. They often deliver less than a dollar's worth of business value for each dollar spent. But a bigger business tends to pay its CEO more, regardless of whether the business has become a better one in the process.

The critical variable standing between earnings and dividends is the *payout ratio*, the proportion of earnings being paid out to shareholders on an annual basis. This statistic is a simple one:

$$\text{Payout Ratio} = \frac{\text{Dividend per Share}}{\text{Earnings per Share}}$$

During 2006, 3M paid out dividends totaling $1.84 per share. Dividing this sum by earnings per share of $5.06, we find that 3M had a payout ratio of 36 percent.

This raises two additional questions:

1. *What is a good payout ratio?* Higher payout ratios imply larger dividends for shareholders, but a payout ratio that is too high leaves little margin for error—a slight drop in profits could leave the firm with insufficient earnings to cover the dividend. (You'll find much more on this topic in Chapter 6.)
2. *What happens to the earnings that aren't paid out?* The dividend machine actually has two outputs: dividends and future dividend growth. Growth is a (usually pleasant) fact of life for most firms. As more consumers are born and enter the country every day, and as the American public grows wealthier over time, firms in trade need to gear up to handle the additional demand.

The key variable is growth. When a corporation turns a profit, that profit results in a higher net worth; the value of the shareholders' equity account grows. And if the ROE stays the same, a higher equity balance will lead to higher earnings.

Reinvested Income and Growth

The basic mechanics of shareholders' equity and return are similar to those of a savings account. If I deposit $1,000 in an account that earns a 5 percent rate of interest, my profit for the first year will be $50. If I don't make a withdrawal, my year-end account balance will rise by $50, to $1,050. The following year, I'll have a higher balance working in my favor, and my interest income will rise as a result. (See Figure 3.5.)

	Beginning Balance	Interest Income	Growth (%)	Ending Balance	Growth
Year 1	1,000.00	50.00	—	1,050.00	5.0
Year 2	1,050.00	52.50	5.0	1,102.50	5.0
Year 3	1,102.50	55.13	5.0	1,157.63	5.0
Year 4	1,157.63	57.88	5.0	1,215.51	5.0
Year 5	1,215.50	60.78	5.0	1,276.29	5.0

Figure 3.5   Balance Growth of a Savings Account

Every year my savings account balance grows 5 percent, and so does each year's interest income. Yet I haven't benefited directly from this growth, because I haven't taken any money out of the account. You might say I haven't paid myself any dividends out of the account. The payout ratio is zero; my benefit is all growth and no dividends.

But what if I decide to reward myself at the end of each year by withdrawing half of my interest income out of the account—that is, to pay myself a dividend with a payout ratio of 50 percent? Figure 3.6 illustrates the results.

	Beginning Balance	Interest Income	Income Growth (%)	Withdrawal	Yield on Beginning Balance	Ending Balance	Balance Growth
Year 1	1,000.00	50.00	—	−25.00	—	1,025.00	—
Year 2	1,025.00	51.25	2.5	−25.63	2.5	1,050.62	2.5
Year 3	1,050.62	52.53	2.5	−26.27	2.5	1,076.88	2.5
Year 4	1,076.88	53.84	2.5	−26.92	2.5	1,103.80	2.5
Year 5	1,103.80	55.19	2.5	−27.60	2.5	1,131.39	2.5

Figure 3.6   Balance Growth with Withdrawals

By lifting $25 out of the account at the end of the first year (tantamount to paying yourself a dividend yield of 2.5 percent), the balance available to earn interest in the following year drops by the same amount. This cuts the growth of my account balance in half, but I'm also benefiting from a little extra money in my wallet. I'm getting a mix of dividends (withdrawals) and growth.

A formula called the *sustainable growth rate* can suggest how much earnings growth we can expect, given constant ROEs and payout ratios. Because the payout ratio is presumably fixed, earnings and dividends increase at equal rates. Here's the calculation:

Sustainable Growth Rate = (1− Payout Ratio) × Return on Equity

Using this statistic, let's run some numbers on our previous examples.

Of the three stocks depicted in Figure 3.7, Westar had the highest yield—a bit over 4 percent on average over the course of 2006. Yet with the lowest ROE and the highest payout ratio, its sustainable growth rate is the lowest of the group. With lower payouts and higher ROEs, Sysco and 3M can offset lower yields (about 2 percent) with higher growth.

For businesses with high ROEs, a lower payout ratio may seem to make sense. The dollars paid out to shareholders as dividends might be able to earn 10 percent or thereabouts over the long run if reinvested in other stocks, but the dollars retained can earn a much higher return.

If we could invest on this basis—using the simple sustainable growth rate formula to project dividend growth—life would be very good indeed. A 24 percent dividend growth rate for 3M in perpetuity represents the kind of opportunity one might sell a kidney to buy. Unfortunately, the sustainable

Company	2006 Dividend	2006 Earnings Per Share	Payout Ratio (%)	2006 Return on Equity (%)	Sustainable Growth Rate (%)
Westar WR	1.00	1.87	53.5	11.0	5.1
Sysco SYY	0.68	1.39	48.9	29.4	15.0
3M Company MMM	1.84	5.06	36.4	37.8	24.1

Figure 3.7   Payout Ratios, ROEs, and Sustainable Growth Rates

growth rate formula has a few key drawbacks. For one thing, it assumes constant payout ratios and ROEs, when these factors can and do change over time. Much more important, however, is how challenging it can be for a corporation to live up to its sustainable growth potential.

Sustainable Growth, Meet Achievable Growth

Let's take another look at this formula using United Parcel Service (UPS) as an example. During 2006, UPS earned an ROE of 25 percent, roughly equal to its average over the preceding couple of years. That figure alone tells us that UPS has a tremendous opportunity to grow by retaining a large portion of its earnings to buy more trucks, planes, and distribution centers. If UPS could maintain this 25 percent return on equity *and* retain all of its earnings, the sustainable growth rate tells us its earnings will grow at a 25 percent annual clip.

But UPS is much too large to maintain a 25 percent growth rate. The company did more than $47 billion worth of sales in 2006 with a global workforce of 428,000 workers; a 25 percent growth rate would oblige UPS to nearly double those figures every three years. In the real world, UPS can't possibly reinvest all of its earnings into the business and translate those retained earnings into 25 percent annual profit growth.

But since UPS pays a dividend, its sustainable growth rate is less than 25 percent. If the firm paid out 70 percent of its earnings, the sustainable growth rate falls to a much more realistic 7.5 percent. From this we can draw a very important observation:

> The optimal payout ratio for a corporation is one that provides for a realistic rate of growth at a high return on equity, with the rest of profits returned to shareholders.

Still, UPS's dividend in 2007 was running at only about 40 percent of earnings per share—enough to suggest a 15 percent growth rate for earnings that it can't realistically achieve over any meaningful stretch of time. The earnings that (1) aren't paid out as dividends and (2) can't realistically be reinvested in the core business must still be going somewhere.

Indeed they are: acquisitions and share buybacks.

Acquisitions: Growth at Retail Prices

A corporate acquisition is the purchase of one business by another business. The assets, liabilities, revenue, and earnings of the acquired business are folded into those of the acquirer. A well-chosen, properly priced acquisition stands to add directly to the earning and dividend-paying power of the acquirer.

However, it's very difficult for companies to earn the same kind of ROEs on acquisitions that they can harvest from their existing operations. The sellers of the acquired company generally have a good idea of what it is worth—and they want to be compensated properly for the profitability and growth potential of their business. Instead of buying growth wholesale (the investment opportunities within a firm's existing operations), acquisitions carry full retail prices.

While 3M, UPS, or Sysco might be able to earn ROEs of 25 percent and up within their existing moat-protected business opportunities, it can be hard to earn even 10 to 15 percent ROEs on acquisitions. Even though the acquirer can often slash the operating costs and better utilize the growth potential of the acquired business, those lofty price tags invariably lead to lower returns. That doesn't necessarily make acquisitions a bad investment of the acquirer's retained earnings, but it's neither as profitable nor as predictable as internally generated growth.

Share Buybacks

UPS makes acquisitions every now and then (and, frankly, its recent track record is not that great), but these purchases don't absorb much of the firm's retained earnings. Instead, UPS is disposing of the bulk of its retained earnings in another fashion: share buybacks.

Begin with the premise that each share of stock represents an equal portion of ownership in the corporation. If there are 100 shares outstanding and you own 10 shares, then you own 10 percent of the firm. If the corporation buys back and retires 20 shares of stock, then only 80 will remain outstanding. You still have your 10 shares, only now they represent an ownership stake equal to 12.5 percent of the total. If the earnings of this miniature corporation haven't changed, then earnings per share—and with it, dividend-paying capacity on a per-share basis—will also increase by 2.5 percent.

The real world is more complicated. One obvious point is that share buy-backs represent an outflow of cash—capital that was probably contributing to earnings in some fashion before the buyback (even if it was simply cash that was earning interest). Share buybacks have become very common in recent years, but the effects on shareholder value relative to cash dividends are not very well understood.

Let's say that UPS is trading at $75 a share, paying dividends of $1.68 out of expected earnings of $4.17 per share—roughly the circumstances of mid-2007.

▶ Assuming that the company can reinvest 30 percent of its earnings at a 25 percent ROE, total earnings should grow at 7.5 percent annually (25 percent multiplied by 30 percent).

▶ The other 70 percent of earnings ($2.92 a share) is available to split between buybacks and dividends, and we already know that $1.68 is being paid out as dividends.

▶ The remaining earnings—$1.24 a share—can be spent on buybacks.

How much stock can the company buy back? At $75 a share, $1.24 a share worth of buybacks is enough to retire 0.017 share for each share outstanding—or 1.7 percent of UPS's total shares outstanding. This reduction in the number of shares outstanding adds directly to UPS's ability to raise its dividend rate. If total earnings are growing at 7.5 percent annually, and UPS buys in 1.7 percent of its stock each year, these buybacks boost UPS's rate of earnings per share growth to 9.2 percent.

The sad reality of buybacks is that they don't increase the total return for shareholders one bit. Consider the scenarios in Figure 3.8.

If UPS paid out all of the earnings it didn't need for investment in its existing operations, it could afford to pay $2.92 a share. That would boost the stock's yield from a so-so 2.2 percent to a handsome 3.9 percent, at least by current standards. However, UPS's dividend growth potential drops by an identical amount: The total return remains unchanged. The same relationship would hold for a much smaller dividend rate: UPS could afford to buy back many more shares and thus increase per-share earnings and dividends faster, but the additional growth is offset precisely by the drop in dividend yield.

	Status Quo	High Dividend	Low Dividend
Earnings Available for Payout	2.92	2.92	2.92
Dividend	1.68	2.92	0.50
Stock Price	75.00	75.00	75.00
Dividend Yield (%)	**2.2**	**3.9**	**0.7**
Core Earnings Growth (%)	7.5	7.5	7.5
Effect of Share Repurchases (%)	1.7	0.0	3.2
Total Dividend Growth (%)	**9.2**	**7.5**	**10.7**
Total Return (Yield + Growth) (%)	**11.4**	**11.4**	**11.4**

Figure 3.8   United Parcel Service: Payout Scenarios

Returning Cash to Shareholders? Which Ones?

Companies with big share-buyback announcements love to claim how they're returning millions or billions of dollars to shareholders. The press releases announcing acquisitions contain just as much fanfare, if not more. But step back for a second: Yes, the company is returning cash to shareholders. The question is, which ones?

Share buybacks return cash to shareholders, all right: *former shareholders*. In addition to dividends of $1.68 a share in 2007 (a total payout of about $1.7 billion), UPS appears set to buy back another $2.5 billion or thereabouts worth of stock. Including these buybacks, the total cash UPS will pay out to shareholders might run north of $4 for each UPS share. But these additional payouts aren't going into my pocket; the cash actually goes to UPS shareholders who are selling their shares back to the company. In other words, the cash goes into the pockets of the least loyal, least confident, and least dividend-oriented shareholders of the firm. Me, I just get my $1.68 a share.

Acquisitions are also returns of cash to shareholders—the *shareholders of other companies*. If UPS can buy a good business at a reasonable price and build it into a great one, I benefit. But if UPS merely wants to get bigger rather than better and more profitable, dividend returns for shareholders will probably suffer.

This is why I'm not a big fan of share buybacks, and I'm not particularly enthusiastic about acquisitions, either. Assuming the total return remains the same, I'd just as soon have more cash flowing into my pocket—even if it means slightly less dividend growth potential. By contrast, most management teams would rather not raise the dividend to a level that maximizes shareholder dividends. Buyback plans, however well intentioned, can be suspended at any time if the company sees some other use for its earnings (acquisitions, more likely than not).

That doesn't mean I'd like to see UPS pay out every available dollar. Doing so would raise UPS's payout ratio substantially and leave the dividend with less protection should earnings drop in the future. But somewhere in between a very high payout ratio with no buybacks and a low payout ratio with gobs of buybacks is a happy medium—one that provides adequate and well-protected dividend income as well as good growth, both for the corporation's existing business operations and for my future dividend stream.

The Bottom Line

As we head back up to 30,000 feet, we find that the corporate dividend machine has one basic input (capital) and two basic outputs (current dividends and dividend growth). All else being equal, a corporation with a high ROE is going to do a better job of increasing its dividend than one with a low ROE, so evaluating and monitoring a company's competitive position (economic moat) is essential. In Chapter 7, I provide additional details and a simple model for incorporating these factors into a growth forecast.

Before turning to these forecasting tools, let's take a look at dividend insight—how to read the signals sent by a corporation through its dividend payments.

Chapter 3: Rules and Plays

▶ From the shareholder's standpoint, a corporation is simply a machine that turns today's investment capital into tomorrow's dividend income.

▶ In the long run, return on equity—a direct influence on a corporation's dividend-paying potential—is a function of the corporation's economic moat.

▶ These dividend machines have two outputs: current dividend income (a function of profits and the dividend payout ratio) and future dividend growth (attributable to the reinvestment of retained earnings into existing business opportunities, acquisitions, and share buybacks)

Dividend Insight

THE STOCK MARKET never seems to get the respect it deserves. It either gets too much credit (partying like it's 1999, so to speak) or too little (the bear market of 2001–2002). As far as I can tell, this chronic problem stems not from the stocks themselves but from the way people choose to obtain their returns—and the way corporations have adapted to provide them.

Among other things, Wall Street is obsessed with quarterly corporate earnings reports. A company that announces earnings that exceed Wall Street expectations can see its stock price rise 5 or 10 percent in minutes. A firm that fails to measure up, sometimes by just a penny a share, can get clobbered by even larger proportions.

These earnings reports receive much more attention than dividend announcements, which are also made at roughly three-month intervals. Earnings releases are long and chock-full of interesting details and figures. Dividend announcements may contain no more than a paragraph focusing on just two pieces of information: how large the dividend is and when it will be paid. Dividend announcements also tend to be fairly routine; most of them contain nearly identical information quarter after quarter, year after year.

But even if earnings releases make much more interesting reading, dividends speak louder than earnings. A company's pattern of dividend payments—its dividend record—can offer valuable clues to underlying corporate performance, clues just as valuable as those provided by earnings reports and other financial data, and definitely more useful than the conclusions someone might draw from looking at a three-month stock chart. Dividends are more than mere information; they provide insight that any investor can use to make successful investments.

The Uses of Dividends

The appeal of a 6 or 7 percent current yield is obvious to someone who is looking for income. But what can we say about a stock with a yield of 1 or 2 percent? Is its dividend useless? As it turns out, a pattern of steady dividend growth—even when yields are low—can be an equally profitable driver of total return.

Ask anyone who's owned Johnson & Johnson (J&J, stock symbol JNJ) for a while. J&J hasn't appeared to be the kind of stock an income investor would grasp at; on average, it provided a current yield of just 2 percent between 1977 and 2007, and even at the stock's lowest price it never offered much more than 4 percent. (See Figure 4.1.) It would be only too easy for a

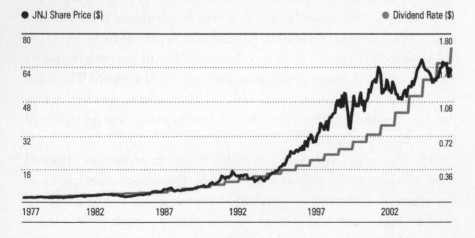

Figure 4.1   Johnson & Johnson (JNJ): Share Price and Dividend History

dividend seeker to pass on such a paltry yield—that is, until one checks out what subsequently happened to the dividend.

In May 1977, an investor could have bought 100 shares of Johnson & Johnson for $65 apiece, a total investment of $6,500. Back then, J&J paid dividends at the rate of $1.40 per year for a yield of 2.2 percent. That wasn't the kind of yield that appealed to income seekers then any more than it does now.

But in the succeeding 30 years, J&J managed to increase its per-share dividend rate an average of 14.4 percent annually. Compounded over three decades—a long time, but less than the average investor's career—the annual income from that original 100 share investment rose more than 50-fold, from $140 to $7,968. The dividends paid by those 100 shares over 30 years totaled $56,784, nearly nine times the value of the original investment.

No less majestic is what happened to J&J's share price. Between 1977 and 2007, J&J split its shares five times, turning an original 100-share stake into 4,800 shares. At the end of May 2007, J&J closed at $63.52, making those shares worth $304,896—a compound annual rate of appreciation of 13.7 percent. As the dividend rate rose, the shares couldn't help but keep pace.

Dividend reinvestment provides the icing on the cake. I estimate that an investor who used her dividends to buy more J&J shares along the way ended up not with 4,800 shares, but slightly more than 8,900—a stake worth about $563,000 at the end of May 2007. This made for a compound average annual return of 16 percent. (See Figure 4.2.)

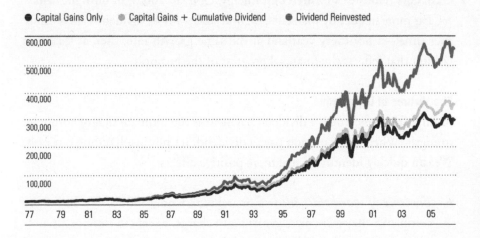

Figure 4.2   Johnson & Johnson: Cumulative Total Returns

Had one predicted how fast J&J's dividend would grow, this spectacular compound return would not have been a surprise. Johnson & Johnson's initial dividend yield of 2.2 percent plus subsequent growth of 14 percent annually would have suggested an annual return of 16.2 percent; at a realized 16.0 percent including reinvested dividends, J&J is only barely off this projection.

Durable success on the scale of Johnson & Johnson's is rare, but the basic mechanics are not. Relatively few investors hold a stock for even three years, let alone three decades. Nevertheless, those original 100 shares in May 1977 provided these returns to whoever happened to own them, for whatever reason. Dividend yield plus dividend growth equals long-term total return; what more can I say?

Sticky Dividends

Dividend rates are not stable the way a bond's fixed interest payment is. Given sufficient time, dividends either grow or decline, much in the manner of the corporations that pay them. I can cite companies paying the same dividend rate year after boring year; the utility industry provides abundant examples.

Midwestern electric utility Ameren (AEE) has paid the same $0.635 a share every quarter for almost a decade now; New Jersey–based Public Service Enterprise Group (PSEG, stock symbol PEG) went 12 years between dividend increases, while Southwest Gas (SWX) went just shy of 13 years. Long periods of flat payments end in either increases (as they did for PSEG and Southwest Gas), cuts (Houston's CenterPoint Energy, CNP, in 2002), or outright halts.

Far more frequently than cuts, we find stocks whose dividends rise steadily over time—if not every year and at the same growth rate, then at least in a fashion that reflects the financial progress of the business.

The Virtues of Dividends

As far as I'm concerned, a dividend payment is the ultimate sign of corporate strength. When a corporation pays a dividend, it's not just handing out cash. We can quickly identify several more positive effects:

▶ *Evidence of shareholder interest.* Shareholders only indirectly control the companies they own; management is in charge. Except in extreme circumstances of executive malfeasance, it's hard for shareholders to step in and require companies to pay dividends or make other shareholder-friendly moves. And since no corporation is required to pay cash dividends, it's well within the reach of management to hold on to the cash generated by the business while it calls 100 percent of the shots. By contrast, when management pays a dividend, it's showing direct interest in—and providing a direct return to—the ultimate owners of the business.

▶ *Evidence of financial strength.* It takes cash to pay a dividend. When the money shows up in your mailbox or brokerage account, the corporation has proved that, at the very least, it has cash available to pay. Financially troubled or fraudulent corporations rarely have the resources to pay meaningful dividends.

▶ *A firm basis for value.* Once a corporation establishes a reliable dividend record, it helps investors appraise the value of the stock with more confidence than current earnings or book values can.

▶ *Corporate self-discipline.* Let's say a corporation turns a $1 million profit. It also has two investment opportunities that would cost $500,000 apiece. One can provide a 25 percent return on equity, the other just 8 percent. If the company doesn't pay a dividend, chances are pretty good the firm will make both investments, even though the 8 percent prospect is probably not a good use of shareholder's money. If the business has a $500,000 dividend in place, however, the corporation has to maximize the value of the cash that's left, and chances are that only the 25 percent project will actually be funded.

▶ *Better shareholders.* Unless you happen to own 100 percent of a corporation's stock, you're not in the business alone. Hundreds, thousands, or millions of other shareholders are essentially your partners in the business. Where the stock's story is all about the share price, you're bound to find many of these partners treating your investment as if it were a racetrack ticket. But steady cash payments—and the higher, the better—attract a better class of shareholder. Folks who are in a stock for income over the long haul are less likely to overreact to temporary difficulties—or temporary gains.

Virtues and Profits

Wherever you find dividends, you're likely to find a better business, a better management team, and higher overall total return prospects than in nonpaying stocks. Not all dividend-paying stocks will do well by their shareholders, but in the aggregate, you're much better off sticking to dividend payers than not.

This observation is borne out in past investment performance. Let's look at the past decade—an era that hasn't offered much by way of dividends.

Between June 1997 and June 2007, the S&P 500 returned a mediocre average of 7.1 percent annually. The S&P 500 is a capitalization-weighted index, which means that the influence of individual stocks is proportional to the company's market value. In plainer terms, General Electric (GE), with its market value of $380 billion, carries much more weight in the index than General Motors (GM) at about $30 billion.

In 2005, Morningstar created an alternative index, the Morningstar Dividend Composite. Rather than weighting companies by market value, the influence of individual stocks is proportional to the total amount of dividends they pay out. In this index, Microsoft (MSFT) gets roughly the same amount of influence as Wells Fargo (WFC). Even though Microsoft's market value is more than 2.5 times as large, its annual dividend payouts are similar; Wells Fargo offers a much richer yield. A stock like Cisco Systems (CSCO), a very valuable corporation that chooses not to pay a dividend, doesn't get counted at all.

Between June 1997 and June 2007, this Dividend Composite Index beat the S&P 500 by an average of 2.5 percentage points per year. Though this is just one set of data, it begins to suggest that dividend-paying stocks beat nonpayers, not only with regard to income, but also in terms of total return. A second index that focuses only on a group of higher-yielding stocks, the Morningstar Dividend Leaders, generated double the return of the S&P 500. (See Figures 4.3 and 4.4.)

But is a decade a long enough stretch of time to draw firm conclusions? How about this: Data analyzed by Standard & Poor's showed that dividend-paying stocks provided total returns an average of 1.9 percentage points greater each year

Index	Annualized Total Return, 6/1997–6/2007
S&P 500 (with Dividends Reinvested)	7.1
Morningstar Dividend Composite	9.6
Morningstar Dividend Leaders	14.2

Figure 4.3   Index Comparisons: Richer Yields Boost Returns

● S&P 500 Total Return Index   ● Morningstar Dividend Leaders   ● Morningstar Dividend Composite

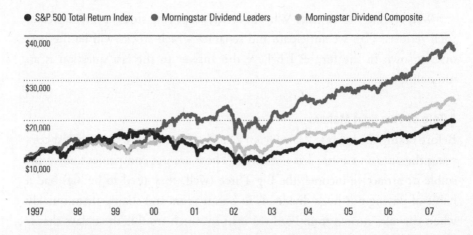

Figure 4.4   Value of the Morningstar Dividend Indexes versus the S&P 500

between 1980 and 2003—again, this being a time when yields were falling, dividend growth was nothing special, and the great masses of equity investors were chasing capital appreciation rather than income.

Still not satisfied? In a book I cannot recommend highly enough—*The Future for Investors: Why the Tried and the True Triumphs Over the Bold and the New* (Crown Business, 2005)—Professor Jeremy Siegel found that from 1958 to 2003, the 100 highest-yielding stocks in the S&P 500 returned an average of 14.3 percent annually while the index itself generated 11.2 percent annual gains. (The lowest-yielding quintile earned just 9.5 percent per year.)

Academic studies like these (and many others) are not necessarily useful simply because they illustrate hefty dividend-driven returns in the past. One such study, in Dimson, Marsh, and Staunton's *Triumph of the Optimists: 101 Years of Global Investment Returns* (Princeton University Press, 2002), showed that nearly half of the total return of American stocks in the twentieth century came from dividends. If that holds true in the next century—starting with a 2 percent yield—then we're looking at 4 percent annual returns from stocks.

Instead, I cite performance data like these because they illustrate a very important fact: *As a group, dividend-paying stocks are better and more profitable to own than nonpayers. Period.* I would even go so far as to say this: There's no good reason an investor needs to own any nonpaying stocks at all.

Why should this be true? Why do dividend-paying stocks provide greater total returns? Can we anticipate and separate which stocks will be the best ones to own in the future? I believe the answer to the last question is an unqualified yes.

A Tale of Two Seat Makers

Before taking the helm at *Morningstar DividendInvestor*, I was an analyst covering the auto and auto parts industries. These are not companies known for stable or attractive income; the Big Three (well, they used to be big) had a habit of paying out huge dividends in boom years and slicing them quickly when car sales turned sour. Ford (F) is in so much trouble these days that it isn't paying a dividend at all. Even though several parts suppliers are in better shape than their customers, good yields are hard to come by.

Yet two companies from the auto parts industry provide two of my favorite examples of the role of dividends in business and shareholder results: one that is very good, and one that is pretty bad.

One of the great growth stories of the automotive industry in the 1990s came in, of all places, the driver's seat—and all other seats as well. General Motors, Ford, and the other domestic manufacturers were starting to move the assembly of seats out of their car factories to supplier shops, where the work could be done more efficiently (and at a much lower cost of labor). Two companies dominated this emerging industry from day one: Lear (LEA) and Johnson Controls (JCI). Lear had been carved out of a larger conglomerate through a leveraged buyout and was saddled with heavy debt. Johnson Controls, by contrast, was already a 100-year-old company by that point; its founder had invented the thermostat in 1883. It entered the automotive seating business by acquiring Hoover Universal in 1985.

Both businesses grew rapidly, but when Lear came public in 1994, it might have looked like the better of the two. It was focused strictly on automotive parts, while Johnson Controls had other businesses (batteries, building controls, even plastic soda bottles). What Johnson Controls had back then, and Lear did not, was a dividend.

Despite comparable growth potential and profitability, a $10,000 investment in Lear in April 1995 was worth only $16,117 a decade later. That represents an annualized total return of just 3.9 percent, less than half of what an

S&P 500 Index fund would have earned; heck, that's less than a money market fund! The same investment in Johnson Controls, with dividends reinvested, grew to $89,153: an annualized total return of 18.9 percent. (See Figure 4.5.)

What accounts for this gaping difference? Numerous factors can be considered. For one, Johnson Controls had a more attractive roster of customers from the start. Its earliest customer, Toyota (TM), was already on its way to quadrupling its share of the North American vehicle market, and it did significant business with Nissan (NSANY) and Honda (HMC), too. Lear captured a greater share of the business from Detroit—GM, Ford, and Chrysler—only to watch those manufacturers drop from 80 percent of the market to little more than 50 percent. That's a huge factor, one that an analyst certainly wouldn't want to shortchange. Also, Johnson Controls owned some other businesses that included its traditional building climate control unit as well as the country's largest manufacturer of automotive batteries. Lear only made auto parts.

In my view, the important factor explaining the different outcomes for each firm is visible in their capital-allocation practices. In the mid- and late 1990s, Lear spent billions of dollars, almost always provided by junk bonds and other high-yield debt, to purchase just about any auto parts supplier that made interior components. Johnson Controls made some big acquisitions too, but its deals were generally smaller and quickly paid for through operating cash flow.

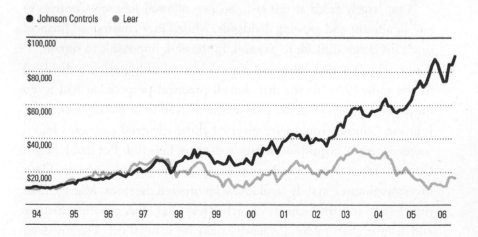

Figure 4.5   The Value of a $10,000 Investment: Johnson Controls versus Lear

One other point: In its first nine years as a public company, Lear never paid a dividend. Johnson Controls paid a dividend in every quarter over this stretch, lengthening a streak of continuous dividend payments going back to 1887—a fact that the press releases announcing the firm's dividends never fails to mention.

Lear didn't pay even a penny's worth of dividends until 2003, and even that change of stripes couldn't survive the auto industry's ongoing bath. Unable to generate enough cash flow in early 2006 to meet its debt obligations and pay for a costly restructuring of its business, Lear eliminated its dividend. Shareholders received only 10 quarterly payments totaling $2.25 a share before the dividend rate returned to zero. Meanwhile, Johnson Controls went on raising its dividend; in early 2007, it paid dividends at an annual rate equal to 11 percent of its share price in April 1994.

This story raises a good question: Are the respective dividends paid by Johnson Controls and Lear an *effect* of the fate of each business, or were dividends also part of the *cause*?

I believe the answer is yes to both.

▶ *Effect.* Johnson Controls clearly did a superior job of allocating capital in a very competitive and arguably dysfunctional industry. It partnered with better customers, made fewer and better acquisitions, and used much less debt while running a much tighter ship overall.

Lear largely failed at this task. Success allowed Johnson Controls to pay significant and growing dividends, while Lear's constrained finances made dividends difficult to pay and, in the end, impossible to sustain.

▶ *Cause.* The fact that Johnson Controls was already paying a dividend in the early 1990s meant that, for all practical purposes, it had to go on paying it. Dividends are paid at the discretion of management, and Johnson Controls could have diverted those dividend payments into a more aggressive acquisition strategy, the way Lear did. But had Johnson Controls taken this path and cut or eliminated payments to shareholders, investors almost certainly would have hammered the stock. Management thus had to run the business in such a way that both growth initiatives and regular shareholder dividends could be maintained. The dividend forced intense discipline on the management of Johnson Controls.

Moreover, Johnson Controls had established a practice of raising its dividend every year, with a streak of consecutive annual increases going back to 1975. Not only did Johnson Controls' shareholders require that current dividends would be maintained as virtually sacrosanct, they expected consistent annual growth. This made the discipline imposed on Johnson Controls' management even tighter. The company's spending on new factories and acquisitions had to be funded with the cash flow left over only after dividends were paid, and those investments had to generate ever higher levels of cash flow in future years. (See Figure 4.6.)

Lear didn't pay a dividend during the 1990s and, without a record suggesting that it should, no one ever expected it to. Freed from this financial constraint, Lear was able to spend the cash it generated internally—plus billions more from borrowing—in pretty much whatever way management thought best. Lear built an empire with $18 billion in annual sales, but the profitability of that empire has been dismal.

I strongly suspect that had Lear paid a meaningful dividend during the 1990s, it never would have made some of the acquisitions that subsequently caused so much pain. Not only would shareholders have had more money in their pockets, having collected cash from their investment over those years, but the company itself would have been healthier, wealthier, and possibly wiser.

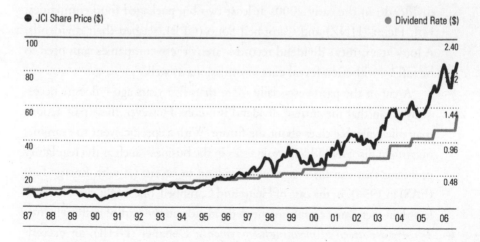

Figure 4.6   Johnson Controls (JCI): Share Price and Dividend History

The folks at Johnson Controls and Lear made their choices, and now they'll have to deal with the consequences (fame and fortune for the former, pain for the latter). But investors had a choice all along. They could listen to management's stories, look at earnings, and watch backlog growth and acquisitions; no doubt these two rivals were always trying to top each other. However, even a cursory look at dividend prospects would have steered the outsider to the more profitable stock.

Dividend Records: The Trend Is Your Friend

Stock charts may be interesting, but for my money, there is no better indicator of a company's past performance than its dividend record—the history of dividend payments over a long stretch of time.

When reviewing a dividend record, I like to use as much data as possible—at least the preceding decade's worth of information if the stock has paid dividends for that long, and ideally as many years' worth of information as I can find. Most firms are good enough to post their dividend records on their investor relations Web sites and provide similar data in their annual reports.

Among the factors I consider are these:

▶ *Have there been dividend cuts?* If the record reveals a reduction or elimination of dividend payments, that probably says a lot about the nature of the business. It isn't just the Fords and GMs of the world that trim or omit dividends; in the early 2000s at least two big packaged food companies, H.J. Heinz (HNZ) and Campbell Soup (CPB), slashed their dividends. A look at a utility's dividend record—aren't these companies supposed to be safe?—will often reveal cuts or omissions as well.

A cut in the past—especially more than five years ago—doesn't necessarily mean that the current dividend is unsafe. However, these past actions may offer valuable clues about the future. With a specific event to examine, one might discover hidden weaknesses in the business, such as the regulatory problems that can force a utility's dividend to be cut (as with Energy East (EAS) in 1994). In the case of Heinz and Campbell, one might also observe a less-than-sacrosanct commitment to dividends on the part of management.

▶ *Is there a pattern of meaningful payments?* Danaher (DHR), an exceedingly well-run industrial conglomerate by all accounts, had raised its yearly dividend payments faithfully for the 12 years through 2006. An average growth rate of 16 percent looks pretty attractive, too. But at no point over this stretch did Danaher offer a yield greater than 0.6 percent, and in mid-2007 Danaher's dividend rate was just 0.2 percent— representing a payout ratio of roughly 3 percent. This isn't exactly a dividend stream that interests me—sounds like the firm's doing just enough to claim a history of dividend growth without sharing cash flow of any consequence.

Danaher might be worthy investment for any one of a variety of good reasons; I myself am a big fan of its extremely efficient manufacturing disciplines. With the 2 or 3 percent yield Danaher could afford to pay, I could see owning its shares. But if the past is any indication, Danaher's dividend is no reason to own the stock.

▶ *Is there a pattern of meaningful increases?* Consistency—when you can find it—can be a very valuable asset for the shareholder. Companies that raise their dividends every year tend to be very proud of their records, and they aren't likely to sacrifice these records on a whim. It takes 20 long years to build a record of 20 straight years of dividend growth. If Coca-Cola (KO) were to hold its dividend flat in 2008, it would take until 2062 to rebuild its current record. Even though a firm's management team might find it convenient to hold on to a bit more cash in a given year, maintaining the record is probably going to take precedence.

Increasing the dividend every year is not enough; these increases need to add up to worthwhile long-term growth. MGE Energy (MGEE), parent of Madison Gas and Electric in southern Wisconsin, has raised its dividend every year since 1976. This fact is noted proudly on the company's investor relations web site. But it also says, without a hint of irony, that the dividend has more than doubled over the past 31 years, from $0.53 a share to $1.39. These increases add up to a growth rate of only 3.2 percent—less than the 4.3 percent rate of inflation in the same period. More recently, the dividend has advanced at a rate that would make a snail shake his head: just 0.9 percent between 2001 and 2006, one third of the inflation rate. The stock price has risen much faster, but only because investors have been willing to accept continually lower current yields—a process that can't go on forever. (See Figure 4.7.)

Year	Div Rate	Growth %	Price	Yield	Year	Div Rate	Growth %	Price	Yield
1986	1.013	—	15.44	6.6	1999	1.313	0.8	20.13	6.5
1987	1.049	3.5	14.56	7.2	2000	1.323	0.8	22.63	5.8
1988	1.102	5.1	13.78	8.0	2001	1.332	0.7	26.45	5.0
1989	1.138	3.2	15.78	7.2	2002	1.343	0.8	26.77	5.0
1990	1.156	1.6	14.89	7.8	2003	1.353	0.7	31.45	4.3
1991	1.173	1.5	20.45	5.7	2004	1.367	1.0	36.03	3.8
1992	1.213	3.4	21.67	5.6	2005	1.380	1.0	33.91	4.1
1993	1.240	2.2	22.50	5.5	2006	1.393	1.0	36.58	3.8
1994	1.253	1.1	21.67	5.8					
1995	1.266	1.1	23.33	5.4	**Averages**		Div Growth %		Yield
1996	1.280	1.1	20.25	6.3	1986–2006 (20 yrs)			1.6	5.8
1997	1.293	1.0	23.00	5.6	1996–2006 (10 yrs)			0.9	5.1
1998	1.303	0.8	22.75	5.7	2001–2006 (5 yrs)			0.9	4.3

Figure 4.7   MGE Energy: Dividend Record

Madison Gas and Electric is one of the strongest utilities in the country, and dividend growth certainly could be higher in the next five years than it's been in the past five. It had better be, or else shareholders are looking at a total return prospect in the neighborhood of 5 percent: less than they might get from a certificate of deposit.

Another good resource for dividend information (though not nearly as useful as the raw data itself) comes in the form of a book called *Mergent's Dividend Achievers* (Wiley & Sons, quarterly). Though this guide doesn't provide more than a few years' worth of actual dividend data, it does report how long a stock's streak of dividend increases is and a 10-year compound average growth rate. The guide includes every stock with 10 or more years of consecutive dividend increases; this alone makes it a good place to prospect for ideas.

Yet I wouldn't want to limit my portfolio to the stocks that make the *Achievers* list; others may offer similarly attractive potential even if they don't make the cut. For one thing, companies with dividend histories shorter than a decade—however much merit the dividend stream might offer—by definition will not make the list. Compass Minerals (CMP), which came public in December 2003 and commenced paying large dividends immediately, is just such a case. I think it's likely that Compass will make the *Achievers* list in 2014.

A couple of years of flat dividends followed by a burst of growth doesn't necessarily bother me either. Cruise operator Carnival (CCL) left its dividend unchanged through three difficult years (2000–2002) before proceeding to increase it more than threefold by early 2007. After these increases, Carnival's yield had risen from an undistinguished 1 percent or thereabouts to a healthy 3 percent. (See Figure 4.8.)

Year	Div Rate	Growth %	Price	Yield	Year	Div Rate	Growth %	Price	Yield
1988	0.100	—	3.88	2.6	2000	0.420	0.0	30.81	1.4
1989	0.100	0.0	4.97	2.0	2001	0.420	0.0	28.08	1.5
1990	0.120	20.0	3.53	3.4	2002	0.420	0.0	24.95	1.7
1991	0.130	8.3	6.56	2.0	2003	0.500	19.0	39.73	1.3
1992	0.140	7.7	8.19	1.7	2004	0.600	20.0	57.63	1.0
1993	0.140	0.0	11.84	1.2	2005	1.000	66.7	53.47	1.9
1994	0.150	7.1	10.63	1.4	2006	1.100	10.0	49.05	2.2
1995	0.180	20.0	12.19	1.5					
1996	0.220	22.2	16.50	1.3	**Averages**			Div Growth %	Yield
1997	0.300	36.4	27.69	1.1	1988–2006 (18 yrs)			14.2	1.6
1998	0.360	20.0	48.00	0.8	1996–2006 (10 yrs)			17.5	1.4
1999	0.420	16.7	47.81	0.9	2001–2006 (5 yrs)			21.2	1.8

Figure 4.8   Carnival Corporation: Dividend Record

Year	Div Rate	Growth %	Price	Yield	Year	Div Rate	Growth %	Price	Yield
1986	0.088	—	4.10	2.1	1999	0.560	12.0	46.63	1.2
1987	0.105	20.0	4.68	2.2	2000	0.640	14.3	52.53	1.2
1988	0.125	19.2	5.33	2.3	2001	0.720	12.5	59.10	1.2
1989	0.145	16.0	7.42	2.0	2002	0.820	13.9	53.71	1.5
1990	0.170	17.1	8.97	1.9	2003	0.960	17.1	51.66	1.9
1991	0.200	17.6	14.31	1.4	2004	1.140	18.8	63.42	1.8
1992	0.230	15.0	12.63	1.8	2005	1.320	15.8	60.10	2.2
1993	0.260	13.0	11.22	2.3	2006	1.500	13.6	66.02	2.3
1994	0.290	11.5	13.69	2.1					
1995	0.330	13.8	21.38	1.5	**Averages**			Div Growth %	Yield
1996	0.380	15.2	24.88	1.5	1986–2006 (20 yrs)			15.3	1.8
1997	0.440	15.8	32.94	1.3	1996–2006 (10 yrs)			14.7	1.6
1998	0.500	13.6	41.94	1.2	2001–2006 (5 yrs)			15.8	1.8

Figure 4.9   Johnson & Johnson: Dividend Record

Yet there's nothing quite like a consistent and long record of dividend increases to inspire confidence in one's investment. The dividend momentum of a stock like Johnson & Johnson speaks for itself. (See Figure 4.9.)

Introducing the Dividend Drill

Evaluating a stock's dividend record is an accessible, fast, and necessary first step toward making an overall appraisal of the company. Yet if momentum is a powerful force, it isn't an unstoppable one. A stock's dividend record, however favorable, can only go so far toward justifying an investment.

In some cases, the trend will get better, but more often the trend will deteriorate. As companies grow larger, they can begin to run out of opportunities to invest for growth at high returns on equity. This spells a declining growth rate, which will inevitably be felt through reduced dividend growth. This is particularly true for firms with very high (12 percent or more) past rates of dividend expansion. A firm whose earnings growth slows from 12 to 8 percent might be able to maintain those 12 percent dividend hikes for a while by gradually increasing the payout ratio. US Bancorp (USB), which raised its dividend 21 percent at the end of 2006, has been raising its dividend faster than earnings for a few years now. At some point, however, the payout ratio will flatten out—the company will have to retain at least some earnings for growth. When this happens, dividend growth will converge back toward the earnings trend line.

Furthermore, the market—its collective attention focused elsewhere—doesn't do a particularly good job of evaluating dividend prospects and valuing them accordingly. Piedmont Natural Gas (PNY) and WGL Holdings (WGL) are both gas utilities that raise their dividends every year, and both stocks tend to have similar yields. In the 10 years ending in 2006, Piedmont's average yield was 4.3 percent; WGL's a slightly higher 4.6 percent. But over this stretch, Piedmont's per-share dividend rate grew at an average of 5.2 percent annually, while WGL's rose a puny 1.7 percent. For a 0.3 percentage point trade-off in average yield, the Piedmont shareholder got triple the growth. Disparities like these are everywhere.

I know the vast majority of stock investors think they're buying a stream of earnings, not dividends—but let's get real: What are these businesses actually putting in the shareholders' pocket? I'm more than willing to let other folks buy stocks solely on the basis of profits, asset values, growth rates, and other financial statistics that can't be cashed at the bank. Their misplaced attention only creates more opportunities for dividend-focused investors like me.

The Bottom Line

With these bits of dividend insight as a backdrop, I've developed an analytical framework designed to answer three simple questions about a stock, centered entirely on its dividend prospects.

1. Is this dividend safe?
2. Will this dividend grow?
3. What does this dividend stream stand to return to me as a shareholder?

These are the topics of three chapters to come. But before we enter the discipline of single-stock analysis, let's see what insights dividends can provide for the stock market in general.

Chapter 4: Rules and Plays

▶ Dividends are more than just income; each payment sends a signal about the current performance and future potential of the business.

▶ Companies with meaningful, reliable, and sustainable dividend payments are simply better investments than companies that pay little or nothing out to shareholders.

▶ The dividend record provides key insights into past performance that can help you project future trends, but a forward-looking analysis is still required.

5

Dividends Past, Present, and Projected

IF YOU'RE THE kind of person who reads the fine print of newspaper or television advertisements, you're probably familiar with the phrase, "Past performance is no guarantee of future results." Behind Wall Street's marketing messages to Main Street, this line is seen just about everywhere.

The subtext of the message is something like, "We racked up these stellar returns in the stock market long before you heard of us, back in the days we had nothing to crow about, but rest assured that if you blame us for the mediocrity to come, at least our fees will be safe." Yet investors set expectations and make investment decisions based on past performance all the time, without regard to what may have changed.

A better way to project investment returns is to take the past for what it's worth—studying and understanding the underlying trends—and then consider what forces may change these trends in the future. But the most important statistic an individual stock has to offer requires no history whatsoever: dividend yield, where what you see (assuming the dividend is reliable) is what you get. That single figure is the starting point for estimating future return potential and, as we already know, it changes every time the stock price does. Unless dividend growth potential is changing, a higher yield implies higher total returns, while a lower yield strongly suggests the opposite.

These principles that work for individual stocks also apply to the market as a whole. Using these same dynamics of dividend yield and dividend growth, we can develop a high-quality forecast for future return expectations—one that doesn't rely solely on past performance.

I'm using the S&P 500 Index—the market's agreed-upon standard, if not quite a comprehensive one—for my analysis. And it is true that the market, as measured by the S&P 500, has been fairly generous in the past. Between 1960 and 2006, the market returned an average of 10.5 percent annually. A view of 1981–2006, which captures two bull markets of virtually unprecedented proportions, reveals an even more favorable 13.2 percent annual return.

What will change in the future? Here are the basics of what we know, at least as of mid-2007.

▶ The yield of the stock market is a bit under 2 percent.
▶ The likely growth rate of future dividends is likely to run in a range between 5 and 7 percent.
▶ Therefore, a good expectation for the future total return from stocks is between 7 percent (2 percent + 5 percent) and 9 percent (2 percent + 7 percent).

Before proceeding to the details of this forecast, let's take a brief look at the implications. They won't be pretty for the millions of investors who expect a lot more.

The Difference between 7 Percent and 11 Percent

This kind of forecast—7 to 9 percent from stocks?—will prompt some double takes. Why should the future be any different than the past? What about the late 1990s, when the S&P 500 gained more than 20 percent a year for five straight years?

The implications of this question couldn't be more critical for investors of all ages. Whether you're 23, 43, or 83 years old, if you own stocks, the broad market environment is the basic benchmark for what you can expect to earn and accumulate over long stretches of time. Albert Einstein is said to have described compound interest the most powerful force in the universe—and he knew a thing or two about powerful forces.

Consider Figure 5.1. An investor takes $1,000 at the beginning of each year and invests it at a market return, and in succeeding years adds another $1,000 in today's dollars (at a 2 percent rate of inflation) to the account.

In the first 10 years, the differences are clearly visible: the account earning 7 percent is worth 20 percent less than the 11 percent earner. This gap grows ever larger in the succeeding years. Fifty years hence, a 7 percent investment account is worth less than one fourth of its 11 percent counterpart. Even the 9 percent earner is worth less than half of the 11 percent investment by then.

Still, these are some pretty impressive numbers 40 or 50 years out. I dare say that a lot of investors could retire comfortably on $443,000, as long as the house and the cars are paid for and Social Security is still alive and kicking. But while I increased each year's account contribution by 2 percent to reflect inflation, the numbers in Figure 5.1 are nominal values—I haven't hit the output with inflation yet. Those values, hit with 2 percent annual inflation, are shown in Figure 5.2.

Annual Return	Year 5	Year 10	Year 15	Year 20	Year 25	Year 40	Year 50
7%	6,248	15,040	27,371	44,665	68,921	217,582	443,091
9%	6,623	16,844	32,571	56,768	93,998	375,030	904,723
11%	7,017	18,876	38,858	72,529	129,267	657,443	1,885,691

Figure 5.1   Compound Value of a $1,000 Investment Plan

Annual Return	Year 5	Year 10	Year 15	Year 20	Year 25	Year 40	Year 50
7%	5,659	12,338	20,337	30,058	42,010	120,121	221,561
9%	5,999	13,818	24,200	38,203	57,295	207,043	452,386
11%	6,356	15,485	28,872	48,810	78,792	362,955	942,898

Figure 5.2   Purchasing Power of a $1,000 Investment Plan

Ouch! Someone on this simple savings plan for 50 years might still be able to retire on the results of an 11 percent annual return with 2 percent inflation, but if the return is lower—or you don't have 50 years left to invest—excessively optimistic investment assumptions are a path to disaster. People who assume the market will shower them with double-digit gains will naturally save less, figuring the stock market will make up the difference. These are the folks whose ultimate retirement question might consist of, "Would you like fries with that?"

A Brief History of Dividend Yield

The market's current yield is a known factor. Tote up all the dividends being paid by the S&P's 500 member stocks in mid-2007, divide it by the index's value, and you get something in the neighborhood of 1.8 percent. If dividends don't rise, and stock prices don't either, you may as well tuck your nest egg into savings bonds.

This has not always been the case. The yield on the S&P 500, just like the yields on individual stocks and other basic business and investment indicators, has changed over time. (See Figure 5.3.) If we turn the clock back far enough, we'll find an era in which stockholders actually required higher yields from stocks than from bonds—precisely because dividends lacked the guaranteed payments conservative investors crave. This naïve view of stocks ignored the potential for dividend growth, and it took a long time for the true total return profile of stocks to become widely known. Only in September 1958 did

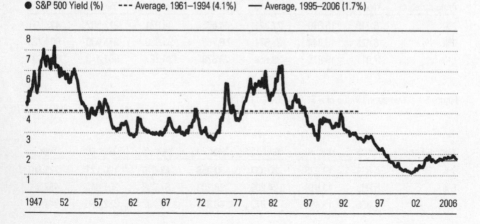

Figure 5.3   Dividend Yield of the S&P 500: 1947–2006

the dividend yield of the S&P 500 fall below the yield of long-term Treasury bonds for good.

Figure 5.3 reveals two fairly distinct eras for dividend yields. During the first, from 1947 to 1994, stocks provided an average yield of 4.1 percent. That's an amazing figure: a stock considered high-yield today would have been merely average a generation ago. From 1995 to 2006, the S&P's average yield was just 1.7 percent.

Canny market observers also took valuation clues from these figures; since the price moves inversely to yield, higher average yields—those above 5 to 6 percent—tended to signal that stocks were undervalued. The final throes of the 1970s bear market resulted in a 6.3 percent yield in August 1982, marking a multigenerational top for yields and bottom for stock prices.

At the other end of the spectrum, 3 percent was considered to be something of a floor. Yields in the past hadn't gone any lower, which in turn suggested that stock prices couldn't go much higher. Time after time, an average market yield just under 3 percent signaled imminent trouble ahead: 1961, 1965, 1972—even 1987.

So when the 1990s bull market yield again flirted with 3 percent between 1992 and 1994, people wondered if the prices had gone too far. Would a falling yield hold stocks back? Would poor dividend returns slay the bull? I remember reading this kind of discussion in the *Wall Street Journal* and elsewhere at the time, and as a fan of history, I couldn't help but agree with the heavy hand of mean reversion.

You may already know what happened. The S&P 500 yield flirted with 3 percent for a while, and then yields plummeted—2.5 percent in the summer of 1995, 2 percent by year-end 1996, and the all-time low of 1.09 percent in August 2000. Despite a modest comeback in yields (attributable first to collapsing stock prices in 2001–2002, then to rapid dividend growth from 2003 to 2006), the S&P 500 still offers less than 2 percent of its value in annual income.

A Brief History of Dividend Growth

The dividend yield of the S&P isn't the only thing the stock market has going for it. The dividends paid by S&P 500 companies have grown steadily over time, from $0.68 per S&P share to more than $25 by the end of 2006. (See Figure 5.4.)

● Dividend Rate per S&P 500 Index Unit ($)

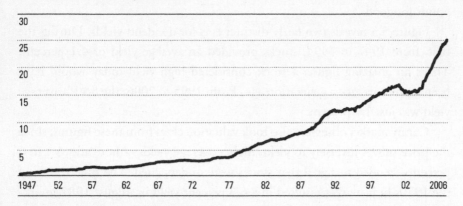

Figure 5.4   Dividend Rate of the S&P 500 Index

From year to year, the growth rate of this dividend stream fluctuates. It was a whopping 28 percent in 1950 and negative 6 percent in 2000. This correlates fairly closely to trends in the economy and inflation: Booms or rapid inflation result in faster dividend growth, while recessions or disinflation have led to slower growth or outright declines. Measured over 10-year rolling periods, this growth rate has run in a range from 8.3 percent (the decade that ended in 1981) to 2.3 percent. For the entire 49-year range of this study, per-share dividend growth averaged 6.2 percent annually. (See Figure 5.5.)

● Y/Y Dividend Growth (%)   ● 10-Year Rolling Average (%)

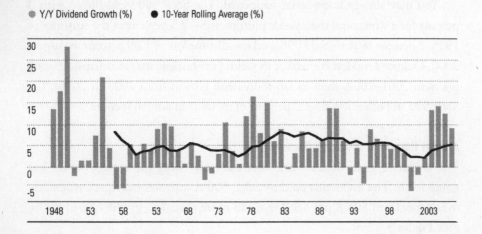

Figure 5.5   Dividend Growth of the S&P 500 Index

These dynamics of yield and growth provide a sound basis for future return projections. For example, had we known at the end of 1960 that our dividend stream would grow 5.8 percent annually from that point forward, we could have added that to a then-current yield of 3.4 percent and projected annual returns of 9.2 percent. But between 1961 and 2006, the S&P 500 actually generated annual total returns of 10.5 percent annually—1.3 percentage points higher. Why? Because stock prices rose faster than dividends—7.2 percent annually instead of the 5.8 percent growth rate of dividends. By paying more and more for each dollar of dividend income, new stock buyers made the older ones richer.

This observation is even starker if viewed between 1981 and 2006. The initial yield was a very handsome 5.6 percent, and subsequent dividend growth ran at 5.3 percent, resulting in an indicated total return of 10.9 percent. The S&P 500 actually returned 13.2 percent—an extra 2.3 percentage points. But as stock prices rose faster than dividend rates, yields fell and fell, hitting 1.8 percent at the end of this stretch.

Today's low yields leave us with a lot less to expect from the future. If we are to take our cues solely from history (a dividend growth rate of 6.2 percent) and current prices (an S&P 500 that yields 1.8 percent), then the sum of these two figures, 8 percent, gives us a pretty poor outlook for stocks.

There's more to dividend growth than just the raw figures of the past, however. Rather than relying solely on history, let's look at three of the drivers behind past growth to see what we may be able to learn about the future:

1. Inflation.
2. Dividend payout ratios.
3. Corporate profits, expressed as earnings per share for the S&P 500.

Inflation

In the big picture, there's more to dividend growth than just reinvested earnings; inflation also plays a role. When inflation rises, many corporations can raise prices faster; when these price hikes match or exceed any increases in operating costs, profits and cash flow will rise faster as well. It's a basic part of the economic backdrop whose influence is felt everywhere.

It turns out that past rates of dividend growth around 6 percent have benefited from a faster pace of inflation than we're currently experiencing. In fact, since inflation has averaged 3.8 percent annually since 1947, more than half

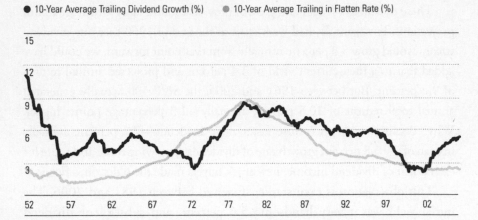

● 10-Year Average Trailing Dividend Growth (%)   ● 10-Year Average Trailing in Flatten Rate (%)

Figure 5.6   Dividend Growth versus Inflation

of the historical rate of nominal dividend growth has been lost to inflation. Real dividend growth—that which marks genuine gains in the purchasing power of the market's dividend stream—has run at a rate of just 2.4 percent. (See Figure 5.6.)

This is one of the dirty little secrets of dividends, at least for the market as a whole: They don't always keep pace with inflation. Although Figure 5.4 shows a relatively steady uptrend in nominal dollars, the S&P 500's inflation-adjusted dividend rate is much less compelling. (See Figure 5.7.) Instead of rising from

● Dividend per S&P 500 Index Unit, Real ($)

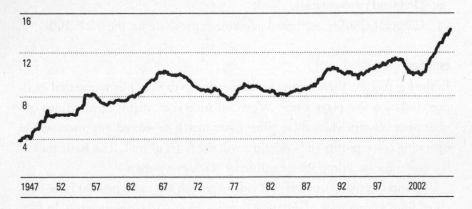

Figure 5.7   Inflation-Adjusted Dividend Rate for the S&P 500

$0.68 to $25.35 between 1947 and 2006, the value of the S&P 500's dividend stream in 1947 dollars is just $2.69—roughly one-tenth of the nominal figure. (And as if to add injury to insult, the real dividend rate of the S&P hit a peak in 1966 that wasn't surpassed until 1989—a 33-year drought!)

A better use of the past, in this case, is to add the historical rates of real dividend growth (2.4 percent) to the current level of inflation (about 2 percent). If we take our cue solely from the past, a 4.5 percent rate of dividend growth is about all we should expect.

Dividend Payout Ratios

Using dividends to evaluate the prospects for individual stocks, and for the market as a whole, is a minority discipline. Most of the wags on Wall Street are looking at earnings per share, not dividends. Since 1960, earnings per share for the S&P 500 have grown at 7.3 percent annually, ahead of the 5.8 percent growth rate for dividends, but an almost perfect match with the S&P's 7.2 percent average pace of price appreciation. But if profit growth exceeds dividend increases, that means payout ratios are falling— and indeed they have, to record lows. (See Figure 5.8.)

As with the S&P's dividend yield, payout ratios appear to have experienced two distinct eras. Between 1960 and 1994, companies paid out an average of 53 percent of their earnings. Since then, the average has run at 42 percent. At the end of 2006, this figure was only 32 percent.

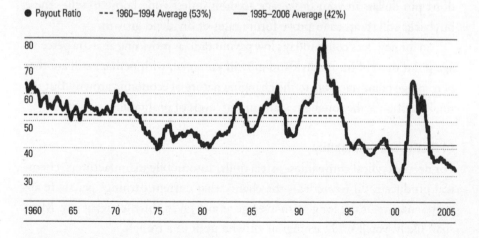

Figure 5.8   Payout Ratio of the S&P 500: 1960–2006

Leaving all other considerations aside for a moment, today's low payout ratios certainly suggest that American corporations could afford to be a bit more generous with their dividend payments. If the S&P's 500 member firms increased their collective payout ratio from 32 percent to the old average of 53 percent, dividends per S&P share would rise by nearly two thirds, which in turn would improve the yield of the index from 1.8 percent to nearly 3 percent.

Furthermore, corporate America is less capital-intensive than it used to be. In the 1950s or 1960s, economic growth meant building more steel mills, car factories, and oil refineries. If firms like these turned a $10 million profit, but then had to reinvest $7 million to acquire more of these costly kinds of assets, only $3 million was left for shareholder dividends. Today, however, economic growth is much more likely to be knowledge-based: scientific research, new product development, marketing, and the like. These investments don't create assets in the balance-sheet sense of the word, so whatever a business spends on these activities is deducted from current profits. This in turn means that the earnings that the shareholder sees are much closer to what she actually stands to benefit from. So returns on equity—especially if we exclude the accounting entries necessitated by acquisitions—are noticeably higher than they once were.

In the meantime, it's fair to ask where all these retained earnings are going—the 68 percent of profits that aren't being fed back into shareholders' pockets via dividends. Regrettably, the bulk of these funds aren't being reinvested in core business activities that generate high returns on equity. Most are going toward share buybacks. While not tantamount to dividends—they don't put dollars in your brokerage account unless you choose to sell—these buybacks still stand to improve future rates of dividend growth.

So for now, let's count today's low payout ratio as providing an extra percentage point or so of future dividend growth potential, with perhaps still another percentage point traceable to the changing nature of economic growth. But the final question is the toughest: Can current levels of profitability persist?

Of Profits and Profitability

For deeply cyclical companies—steel mills, automobile manufacturers, chemical producers, oil refineries—the chance that current earnings per share are representative of the long-term average at any given time is pretty low. More than likely, you'll find earnings at either a peak or a trough.

We can ask this same question about the market in general: Are corporate profits closer to the bottom, the top, or merely average? One way to consider this question is to look at after-tax corporate profits as a percentage of national income (an economic statistic similar to GDP), as depicted in Figure 5.9.

Historically, after-tax corporate profits have claimed 4.9 percent of the nation's income. The rest goes mainly to employee compensation, taxes, and other areas of the economy. This figure, too, has changed over time, but it's had a tendency to revert to the long-term mean. When this share is well above average, pressures of one kind or another (higher wage demands by employees, slackening economic growth, higher taxes) push it lower. When it is below average and business investments are less profitable, corporations stop investing in new capacity until the economy recovers and they can use existing resources more efficiently.

Since we're starting our forward-looking analysis in 2006, the fact that this profit share is well above historical averages doesn't bode well. Claiming 6.4 percent of the national income in 2006, corporate profits are some 30 percent above average. That has been a boon for recent stock price action and dividend growth, but only if the current level of corporate profitability can be sustained can we claim that current payout ratios leave room for improvement. There's not a one-to-one correlation between the S&P's earnings per share and this statistic;

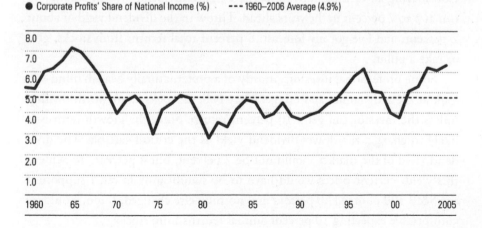

Figure 5.9   Corporate Profits' Share of U.S. National Income

a number of other factors are at work. But if we make the simple assumption that S&P profits are also 30 percent above normal, then the sustainable payout ratio of the market is not 32 percent today but 42 percent—a level that leaves a lot less room for future dividend increases.

The Bottom Line

Let's sum up where our projection for dividend growth lies:

▶ Historically, dividend growth for the market as a whole has run at 6 percent annually.
▶ If we look at the pace of real dividend growth—roughly 2.5 percent—and add the current rate of inflation (2 percent), this backward-looking indication falls to 4.5 percent.
▶ If we give the market credit for low payout ratios and rising returns on equity, knowing that a lot of the earnings not being distributed as dividends are going toward growth-boosting share buybacks, we can lift our dividend forecast by 2 or 3 percentage points—bringing our estimate up to about 7 percent.
▶ If we further assume that corporate profits as a percentage of national income are unsustainably high, we can easily knock a final percentage point off our forecast.

Considering all of these moving parts, I figure dividend growth is likely to run at 5 to 7 percent in the years ahead. Throw in the dividend yield of about 2 percent, and I've got my forecast: 8 percent total returns from stocks, give or take a point.

Some professional investors, mostly of a preternaturally bearish mind-set, look at these dynamics and cringe. They believe stocks aren't worth owning unless the investor can get a 10 percent return. Since the growth term isn't likely to change, that leaves dividend yield as the critical variable: The dividend yield of the market should not be 2 percent, but 4 percent. To achieve this yield, current prices would have to be significantly lower. I suppose if the S&P 500 plunged 50 percent and nothing else changed, I, too, would be comfortable expecting 10 percent annual returns from stocks.

Yet I don't agree with the conclusion that stocks are overvalued. An 8 percent return from stocks seems entirely reasonable, given the low rate of inflation and the lack of attractive fixed-income alternatives. Instead, I believe the great masses of America's shareholding class should curb their enthusiasm and expect to be satisfied with less.

For the investor who wants to stick with stock mutual funds tied to the S&P 500, the implications of this forecast are obvious: Spend less and save more. On the other hand, it's not necessary to own the entire market, or to tie one's goals solely to what the market is capable of providing. By definition, half of all stocks will underperform the market, while the other half will do better. Dividends are the single best tool I know of for separating the stocks capable of beating this 7 to 9 percent prospect for the market as a whole.

That's what this book's central analytical tool—an approach I've termed the Dividend Drill—is all about.

Chapter 5: Rules and Plays

▶ Dividend yields for the market in general are a lot lower than they used to be—a fact that bodes ill for future total returns.

▶ Dividend growth prospects—even after considering recent changes to corporate dividend policies, profitability, and inflation trends—don't look to run much better than 5 to 7 percent annually in the years and decades to come.

▶ Investors should not expect more than 7 to 9 percent annual returns for the stock market as a whole. Fortunately, you don't have to own the whole market: Dividend insights can reveal those stocks that are poised to generate better-than-average returns.

6

Is It Safe?

MANY INVESTORS—PARTICULARLY those looking for income to meet living expenses—get excited when they uncover stocks offering yields of 8 percent, 10 percent, or more. With prevailing interest rates on fixed-income investments running at perhaps half this level, who can blame them? And every so often, a stock will be quoted with a yield of 25 or 50 percent. A stock that will return half of your purchase price in just one year? How can it lose?

Believe me, it can—and it probably will. In my 15-plus years of investing, both personally and professionally, nothing seems to signal trouble like a double-digit yield. There are exceptions, of course—a depressed stock price may foreshadow a quick rebound in financial results and large capital gains in addition to income. But the chances that any particular 10 percent yield—especially in the income-crazed markets of today—will turn out to be a bargain are very, very low. I call these securities sucker-yield stocks.

New Century Financial (NEWCQ), a mortgage broker catering to subprime residential borrowers, was one such sucker-yield stock. Management had been frustrated by the low price/earnings ratio investors were willing to award its stock. So in early 2005, this firm increased its quarterly dividend rate from $0.23 a share to $1.50, or $6.00 on an annualized basis. With the stock then trading around $60, this payout resulted in a 10 percent yield. New Century raised its quarterly payment by a nickel in each of the next eight quarters. In December 2006, it declared a dividend of $1.90 a share ($7.60 annualized).

Yet even as the dividend rose quarter after quarter, the stock drifted lower. The stock's average yield during 2006 was an incredible 17.7 percent.

You might already know the end of this story. The loans New Century was making were the very definition of dubious, a fact management should have been aware of. Not content to simply make these loans and resell them to unwitting investors elsewhere, New Century borrowed billions of dollars to hold some of these mortgages on its own account. When delinquencies surged and nervous bankers wanted their money back, the dividends came to a screeching halt and New Century went bust. The stock price dropped to less than a buck in early 2007. (See Figure 6.1.)

While it was hardly obvious in 2005 or 2006 that New Century would soon go belly-up, the instability of its dividend was entirely clear. Despite my observation that New Century had an innovative business model, the mortgage industry is an incredibly tough one in which to dig an economic

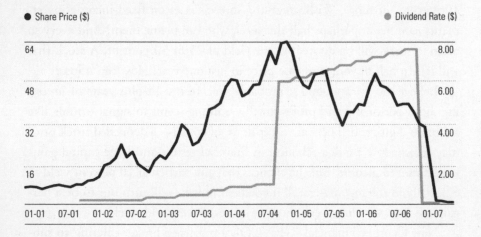

Figure 6.1   New Century Financial: Share Price and Dividend History

moat and earn sustainable returns. A surge in charge-offs, whenever it finally occurred, was sure to clobber earnings and damage New Century's ability to fund dividend payments. The fact that its bankers could cash in their chips almost at will prevented New Century from navigating through a tougher business environment. Yet the interested investor didn't need to know all of these problems to have avoided the stock; yields of 12, 15, and 20 percent spoke clearly enough.

That's why I put New Century on *Morningstar DividendInvestor's* "Payouts in Peril," the red-flag watch list, long before the bust. Even as those quarterly dividends kept rising—an indication that in most cases suggests underlying financial strength—a ridiculous yield combined with an inherently vulnerable business model sent ominous signals of doom. New Century's shareholders suffered terribly, so I can't say I take any pleasure in being right in this case. But the underlying signs were all too clear: Dividend investors beware!

These sucker yields aren't always limited to obviously high yields. ConAgra Foods (CAG), a stock whose story I describe later in this chapter, turned out to be a sucker-yield stock too, even though its shares yielded only 5 percent before the cut.

What we want—indeed, demand—is a dividend rate that we deem safe for the foreseeable future. Income streams that fluctuate or disappear at the first sign of trouble are unlikely to provide us with the steady returns of cash we seek.

My process for evaluating dividend safety is relatively straightforward.

1. Are earnings *sufficient* to cover the dividend?
2. Are earnings *stable* enough to cover the dividend amid short-term variations? If not, does the company have access to other resources to fund the dividend?
3. Are earnings *durable* enough to cover the dividend for the foreseeable future?
4. Is management not only able but *willing* to maintain current dividend payments when the going gets tough?

If you can't resolve these four questions to your satisfaction, avoid the stock. Even if the dividend alone seems to make the investment a tantalizing prospect, don't be afraid to chuck the idea into the "too tough" file. But using these guidelines, there are hundreds, if not thousands, of dividend streams we can deem safe.

Earnings: The Capacity to Pay

Dividends are sticky, that much we know. Implicit in a given dividend rate is a strong indication—though well short of a promise or guarantee—that the corporation will go on paying at least that much into the indefinite future. But dividends have to come from somewhere, and that is earnings.

Earnings? What about Cash Flow?

Some folks may question my assertion that dividends come out of earnings. Dividends are paid in cash, right? A company might be able to generate (or manufacture) substantial earnings on paper while taking in very little cash. Rapidly growing or capital-intensive companies may even lay out more cash than they take in, reporting positive earnings all the while.

This is a fair point to make, but let's look at the definition of earnings: an increase in the net worth of a business that arises from its business activities. If net worth increases, this creates the capacity for the firm to distribute cash to shareholders. Even if that cash doesn't come directly from operating activities, the corporation will have the option of borrowing or selling assets to fund dividend payments. As long as dividend payments do not exceed earnings, the firm's net worth will continue to grow.

That isn't to say that cash flow doesn't count; it certainly does. For complicated businesses—the type I tend to avoid anyway—the cash flow statement can provide key insights into the business. In the vast majority of cases, however, earnings are a fair proxy for cash flow.

For simplicity's sake, I and other investors and analysts prefer to look at earnings on a per-share basis (net income divided by the number of shares outstanding). Fortunately, historical data on earnings per share (EPS) are everywhere—in company press releases, Securities and Exchange Commission (SEC) filings, and at Morningstar.com and other Internet sites. Unfortunately, raw EPS data are rarely the best place to begin.

► Last year's EPS, or the sum of the most recent four quarters, tells you what happened in the past. Whether I am considering buying a stock for its dividend or I already own it, I'm naturally more interested in the future.

► Accounting figures for earnings, though certainly comprehensive, do not always provide an accurate representation of ongoing earning power. Stated figures necessarily include unusual gains (usually related to one-time sales of assets) and unusual losses (most often related to restructuring activities). While these may be relevant when considering a company's overall earnings prospects, they, too, happened in the past.

For the purposes of dividend safety analysis (and, in the next chapter, dividend growth), we want to look forward with a figure that will exclude any unusual, nonrecurring events. Here again we have several choices, ranked in declining order of appeal:

► *Management guidance.* Since management is in touch with the state of the business every day, it surely knows more about current earnings prospects than I can. Its outlook is therefore my preferred source. If management provides a range instead of a point estimate, then I use the midpoint of that range.

► *Wall Street consensus.* Not every company provides a forecast for earnings per share, but almost all large companies are followed by professional analysts at investment banks and brokerage houses, who publish estimates for earnings. The average of these figures—known as the *consensus estimate*—is available free in many places on the Internet (including Morningstar.com.)

► *Trailing earnings.* If the company doesn't provide guidance and neither do any Wall Street analysts, then this is about all that is left. Before using the reported figure, however, you'll want to see if there are any unusual gains or expenses—most companies break these out in their descriptions of the business—and exclude their effects. As long as the most recent information doesn't suggest earnings have started to fall, assuming the status quo will persist isn't an unreasonable basis for safety analysis.

► *My own forecast.* Failing all else, I might make my own earnings estimate. How to build a short-run earnings estimate is a topic that could easily take up a book on its own, but if you're familiar with how the business works, you might be able to make a forecast on your own.

Estimates for future EPS have drawbacks, too. The future is always an unknown, and estimates—whether obtained from Wall Street analysts, company management, or a forecast you build yourself—are subject to a range of error. As far as I'm concerned, however, any look forward—even if it is by definition flawed—beats the look back. What's behind us will have its uses, but drivers and investors alike are better served looking through the windshield rather than at the rearview mirror.

To start pondering the matter of dividend safety, I'll call on an old friend of mine, Compass Minerals International (CMP). From the name, you might assume that Compass digs for gold or oil; instead, this is North America's largest miner of salt—mostly for deicing highways, but another 10,000 or so uses as well. This is a remarkably profitable business. As the owner of the two largest salt mines in the nation, Compass can get salt out of the ground and transport it more cheaply than its competitors. Furthermore, the industry itself is quite concentrated. Just three competitors mine almost all the salt on the continent, and all three firms treat their salt mines as they should be treated: as cash cows.

However favorable these economics may be, Compass is forced to contend with one major variable: the weather. The consumption of deicing salt is a function of how much snow and ice there is to melt. Long, cold, and wet winters in the upper Midwest may be depressing for the region's inhabitants (I can attest to that), but at Compass's headquarters in Kansas City, they'll be breaking out the champagne. Short, warm, dry winters call for lots of coffee.

Because of variability in the weather, Compass prefers not to provide annual outlooks for EPS. It's up to Wall Street to do that; at mid-2007, the full-year consensus estimate called for earnings of $1.88 a share.

Special Math for REITs and Energy MLPs

I wrote earlier that earnings are the best indicator of a corporation's dividend-paying capacity in most cases. Two big exceptions apply for real estate investment trusts (REITS) and energy master limited partnerships (MLPs). It's not unusual for these firms to have payout ratios substantially in excess of 100 percent, yet their fat cash distributions go on and on.

For example, Kinder Morgan Energy Partners (KMP), one of the nation's largest energy logistics firms, paid cash distributions of $3.23 per unit in 2006, even though reported profits totaled just $2.04 per unit. Knowing that corporations don't like to set dividends at levels that might force an embarrassing cut down the road, what gives? Different though they might seem, REITs and energy MLPs have one factor in common: Reported earnings systematically underestimate the amount of cash they generate. The key factors are depreciation (a noncash expense) and capital spending (a nonexpense outflow of cash). Because REITs and energy MLPs provide some of the best yields out there, I devote much additional discussion of their prospects—including the math behind their true dividend-paying capacity—in Appendixes 5 and 6.

Lately some other kinds of companies, including some rural telephone utilities and newspaper chain GateHouse Media (GHS), have attempted to use similar figures to justify very high dividend rates. I tend to be a bit more skeptical of these other cases, however; the cash flows of a newspaper aren't nearly as predictable as those of an office building or pipeline.

Payout Ratios: The Sufficiency to Pay

If Compass appears set to earn $1.88 a share this year, how does that prospect relate to the dividend? That's what the *payout ratio*, first mentioned in Chapter 3, will tell us.

Historical payout ratio data are usually calculated on the basis of the profits earned and dividends paid out during the year in question. Since we're taking a forward-looking view, we will alter these statistics slightly:

$$\frac{\text{Current Dividend Rate}}{\text{Forecast Current-Year Earnings Per Share}} = \text{Forward Payout Ratio}$$

Compass' dividend rate at mid-2007 was $1.28 a share. Dividing this into $1.88 in anticipated EPS, Compass' forward payout ratio is 68 percent.

The most obvious implication of this ratio is that Compass's earnings appear sufficient to fund its current dividend rate. A stock whose payout ratio is above 100 percent—particularly if there is no easily identifiable reason that earnings will soon rebound and provide more adequate coverage for the dividend—could very well be headed for a dividend cut.

Most forward payout ratios are substantially below 100 percent. In Compass's case, however, we already know that earnings can fluctuate substantially in response to weather conditions. Could a couple of warm years in a row—good for Midwesterners, bad for Compass—threaten this $1.28 a share dividend rate? What we need in this case is margin of safety: room for earnings to fall short without forcing Compass to cut its dividend.

The forward payout ratio provides us with a good approximation of what this margin of safety is, albeit in a backhanded way. Consider how Compass's payout ratio will change if it earns $1.60 in 2007 instead of $1.88, a shortfall of 15 percent: the payout ratio will be 80 percent, not 68 percent. With EPS of $1.40, the payout ratio shoots past 90 percent. With the $1.88 consensus estimate as a starting point, just how far could Compass fall short? The following formula tells us:

$$100\% - \text{Payout Ratio} = \text{Payout Margin of Safety}$$

The margin of safety for Compass's dividend is 32 percent—that's how far actual earnings could fall short of estimates while leaving the dividend fully funded.

All else being equal, a lower payout ratio implies a safer dividend than a high payout ratio—but only rarely is all else equal. What would represent a relatively low payout ratio for a regulated natural gas utility (say, 60 percent) would be very high for a commodity chemical producer. The safety margin we should require—that is, how low of a payout ratio—rests on the stability of the underlying earnings stream.

A common, if not always useful, shortcut is to look at a particular stock relative to industry standards. Among regional banks, for example, payout ratios are typically in the 30 to 50 percent range. Food, beverage, and consumer product companies are often in the same neighborhood. Utilities, whose earnings are perceived to be more stable, often pay out 60 to 80 percent of earnings. Sometimes, however, these guidelines will let you down—as averages, they can't capture company-specific factors that a company-specific investor would want to investigate further. And outside of a handful of industries, there are no standards. With just three major players, only one of which (Compass) is publicly traded, there's no salt industry peer group to compare Compass's 68 percent payout ratio with.

In point of fact, payout ratios are meaningful only when considered in the context of the stability and durability of earnings. Rather than using a one-size-fits-all approach to payout ratios, I prefer to look at companies on a case-by-case basis. If the payout ratio is above 100 percent and there aren't clear short-term explanations to suggest this state is temporary, I drop the idea and move on. If it's below 100 percent, I proceed to the factors that affect dividend safety directly.

Earnings Stability

No company, no matter how conservative or defensive, can generate a perfectly stable stream of earnings; real-world results are lumpy, whether investors like it or not. Among the key drivers of variability in the short run are these:

▶ *Revenue fluctuations*. Every business encounters some variation in its revenue stream, even if that business is protected by an economic moat. Some businesses face much wider swings than others. In a recession, the sales of a steel mill or automobile manufacturer are likely to drop much further than those of a grocery store or a natural gas utility. In boom times, the reverse is true—heavy industries and consumer cyclicals will see larger upswings in sales while more defensive industries continue to plod along.

▶ *Operating leverage*. The cost structure of a business always contains a mix of variable and fixed costs. Variable costs are tied to the level of revenue. At your local grocery store, for example, most of the costs (that is, the groceries themselves) are variable. If revenue drops, the cost of merchandise sold will drop by a nearly identical amount. By contrast, a steel mill may have to employ 1,000 workers whether the annual output of the plant is worth $200 million or $1 billion. High fixed costs greatly magnify the effect of revenue changes on the bottom line.

▶ *Financial leverage*. Businesses with large debt loads are obliged to pay interest and principal when due. Lenders expect to be paid on time and in full, whether operating profits are large or small. Since interest expense doesn't vary with revenue and operating profits, it's simply another fixed cost: Interest magnifies the effect of changing revenue on earnings.

More on Financial Leverage

Consider the fate of two firms with $100 million in operating profit. One has only $5 million in interest expense and reports $95 million in pretax earnings; the other has $75 million in interest costs and just $25 million in pretax income. A 10 percent decline in operating income will be unpleasant for the first firm; its pretax income will fall by a slightly larger 10.5 percent (from $95 million to $85 million). But that 10 percent decline will be downright painful for the second firm; its pretax earnings will plunge from $25 million to $15 million, a drop of 40 percent. (See Figure 6.2.)

	Low Financial Leverage			High Financial Leverage		
	Before	After	Change	Before	After	Change
Operating Profit	100	90	−10.0%	100	90	−10.0%
Interest Expense	−5	−5	—	−75	−75	—
Pretax Profit	**95**	**85**	**−10.5%**	**25**	**15**	**−40.0%**

Figure 6.2   Financial Leverage Illustrated (Dollars in Millions)

One way to evaluate this leverage directly (for nonfinancial firms) is to look at the company's *interest coverage ratio:* How large are operating profits relative to interest expense? This ratio is calculated as follows:

$$\frac{\text{Operating Profit}}{\text{Interest Expense}} = \text{Interest Coverage}$$

Looking to a sample of utilities—one mostly electric, one gas, and one telephone— let's interpret some of the results by referring to Figure 6.3.

	2006 Operating Profit	Interest Expense	Coverage
MGE Energy MGEE	79.0	15.0	5.3
Southwest Gas SWX	209.2	95.0	2.2
FairPoint Communications FRP	61.4	39.7	1.5

Figure 6.3   Evaluating Interest Coverage Ratios (Dollars in Millions)

I mentioned in Chapter 4 that MGE Energy—despite a distinct lack of dividend growth—was one of the strongest utilities in the country, financially speaking. Its operating profits covered interest expense 5.3 times in 2006. Southwest Gas is clearly more leveraged than MGE, with interest coverage of just 2.2 times—relatively low by industry standards, but still within the range of respectability. But FairPoint Communications has very little room for error—interest expense was covered only 1.5 times in 2006. A modest drop in profits will be greatly magnified by the time it reaches the bottom line. On the basis of this single data point, I'd be nervous about buying FairPoint for its dividend.

While the interest coverage ratio illustrates the most direct impact of debt on a company's ability to fund its dividend payments, it's not the only indicator. Financial leverage looms just as large on the balance sheet. A business funded almost entirely with equity generally has a hard time going bust; you can't go bankrupt if you don't owe anybody money. But a capital structure consisting of 80 percent debt and 20 percent equity leaves borrowers with much less margin for error, and if borrowers get hurt even a little in the event of default, chances are shareholders will be wiped out.

A standard metric for balance sheet leverage is the debt/total capital ratio, or just debt/capital. This expresses how much of the company's long-term funding is comprised of debt.

$$\frac{\text{Total Debt}}{\text{Total Capital (Debt + Shareholders' Equity)}} = \text{Debt/Capital}$$

Turning back to the three aforementioned utilities, refer to Figure 6.4.

From 2006 Year-End Data	Debt	Total Capital	Debt/Capital (%)
MGE Energy MGEE	309.3	684.6	45%
Southwest Gas SWX	1,413.9	2,315.3	61%
FairPoint Communications FRP	608.3	833.0	73%

Figure 6.4   Evaluating Debt/Capital Ratios (Dollars in Millions)

Note the close correlation—MGE's high interest coverage ratio is tied to a low (by utility standards) debt/capital ratio of 45 percent. FairPoint's funding is 73 percent debt. If FairPoint's earnings start to decline—as may well happen someday—the wolf will be that much closer to its door.

(continued)

Many companies are willing to borrow as much as 50 percent of their total capital (debt plus equity). For most businesses, this doesn't seem to be particularly abusive or risky. After all, cheap debt will increase a company's return on equity. Other firms—almost always ones with very high returns on total capital and stable profit streams, like Hershey (HSY)—are able to carry high debt/capital ratios because operating profits are so much larger than interest payments. But these situations are relatively rare among high-yield stocks; if the debt/capital ratio is high, dividend coverage is likely to be poor.

Both the interest coverage and debt/capital ratios have drawbacks; in some cases, other measures of operating profit (such as earnings before interest, taxes, depreciation, and amortization) or equity (market value of assets instead of book value) may be appropriate. Further, acceptable levels of financial leverage vary widely by industry. Companies with very steady earnings streams—utilities are a prime example—can afford to make large interest payments without introducing unacceptable variability to profits. But for deeply cyclical companies, financial leverage only magnifies an already volatile situation, and makes their dividends that much less reliable.

These three factors account for the bulk of short-run changes in earnings—affecting maybe just one year at a shot, or a couple of years in economically sensitive industries. Working in tandem, however, they can introduce substantial volatility to a company's profit stream.

It's hard to generalize what constitutes acceptable levels of revenue variability, operating leverage, and financial leverage. But the more you study a business, observing past changes in revenue and earnings, the more likely you are to recognize a bad situation when you see it. Any one source of variability may be manageable: Genuine Parts GPC, parent of the NAPA chain of auto parts stores, has a lot of fixed costs, but its revenue is very stable and debt load quite modest. A propane distributor like Suburban Propane Partners (SPH) may see wide swings in revenue depending on the price of propane, but most of its costs are variable and debt is manageable. But a firm with wide fluctuations in revenue, high fixed costs, and mountains of debt—General Motors (GM) comes to mind—will see extreme swings in profits. (Deeply cyclical companies generally aren't worthwhile dividend payers in the first place; they're of little use to income investors anyway.)

These change factors naturally influence how low a stock's dividend payout ratio must be for us to consider it safe. Let's see how Compass Minerals stacks up on these considerations:

▶ *Revenue fluctuations.* Compass's sales of deicing salt are going to fluctuate from year to year. Over the past five years, annual sales have run as low as $459 million (2002) and as high as $742 million (2005). Of course, these figures don't mean much unless you read the details behind them. In Compass' case, 2005 included very favorable weather conditions (for the firm, at least) in the first and fourth quarters; in 2006, deicing salt sales were abnormally low in both. (See Figure 6.5.)

▶ *Operating leverage.* At the operating profit level, percentage changes from year to year have been even larger than the fluctuations in revenue—evidence of the relatively high fixed costs you'd expect from a mining concern. (See Figure 6.6.)

▶ *Financial leverage.* At first glance, Compass's balance sheet looks dreadful: Liabilities actually exceed assets! (See Figure 6.7.) As it happens, this is more of a historical accident than a sign of insolvency. Mines and equipment that Compass bought long ago—assets that generate substantial earnings today—are recorded at original cost minus decades' worth of depreciation.

For most firms—including Compass—the interest coverage ratio is a better proxy for financial leverage. Among other benefits, it directly reflects the impact of the firm's debt burden on profits. For nonfinancial

	2001	2002	2003	2004	2005	2006
Revenues	481.5	459.0	553.5	639.9	742.3	660.7
Y/Y Change (%)	—	−4.7	20.6	15.6	16.0	−11.0

Figure 6.5   Compass Minerals: Annual Revenue 2001–2006 (Dollars in Millions)

	2001	2002	2003	2004	2005	2006
Operating Profit	53.4	72.1	91.2	118.8	142.9	119.4
Y/Y Change (%)	—	35.0	26.5	30.3	20.3	−16.4

Figure 6.6   Compass Minerals: Annual Operating Profits 2001–2006 (Dollars in Millions)

Cash and Cash Equivalents	7.4	Accounts Payable	73.0
Receivables, Net	114.0	Current Long-Term Debt	3.1
Inventories	146.1	Other Current Liabilities	42.9
Other Current Assets	16.3	**Current Liabilities**	**119.0**
Current Assets	**283.8**		
		Long-Term Debt	582.4
Land, Buildings, and Improvement	783.0	Other Long-Term Liabilities	70.0
Less: Accumulated Depreciation	−408.4	**Total Liabilities**	**771.4**
Total Property, Net	**374.6**	**Shareholders' Equity**	**−65.1**
		Total Liabilities and Equity	**706.3**
Goodwill	47.9		
Total Assets	**706.3**		

Figure 6.7   Compass Minerals: Balance Sheet as of December 31, 2006 (Dollars in Millions)

companies, an interest coverage ratio of less than 2 makes me nervous; however, Compass has cleared this hurdle every year since it came public in 2004. (See Figure 6.8.)

Let's take a look at how all of these factors have combined to influence Compass's bottom line in the past. (See Figure 6.9.)

It appears there are good doses of revenue fluctuations, operating leverage, and financial leverage at work with this firm. Compass's earnings from year to year, at least relative to most companies with 60 to 70 percent payout ratios, are not terribly stable. In any one year, we probably can't rule out the

	2001	2002	2003	2004	2005	2006
Operating Profit	53.4	72.1	91.2	118.8	142.9	119.4
Interest Expense	−12.1	−39.8	−53.7	−59.0	−61.6	−53.7
Interest Coverage Ratios	**4.20**	**1.81**	**1.70**	**2.01**	**2.32**	**2.22**

Figure 6.8   Compass Minerals: Interest Coverage 2001–2006 (Dollars in Millions)

	2003	2004	2005	2006
Earnings per Share (Ex-Unusuals)	0.85	1.35	1.62	1.69
Dividends per Share (since IPO)	—	0.94	1.10	1.22
Payout Ratio (%)	—	**69**	**68**	**72**

Figure 6.9   Compass Minerals: Earnings and Dividends 2003–2006

possibility that earnings might fall short of the dividend, even with a payout ratio well below 100 percent indicated at mid-2007. If I compare the firm's 68 percent payout ratio only with the potential for short-run earnings short-falls, I might have to conclude that a 68 percent payout ratio doesn't provide an adequate margin of safety.

Earnings Durability

By this point, you might decide you would just as soon look for more obviously secure dividends elsewhere. (That's what makes the Compass example worth considering.) But before we condemn this salt miner to the realm of questionable dividends, let's reconsider two basic dividend insights: (1) Dividend rates are sticky and (2) dividends send signals. These points raise a key question: Why would Compass pay dividends at the rate of $1.28 annually if it couldn't always earn that much?

The stability of earnings from one year to the next is certainly a relevant issue for dividend safety, especially for companies with very high debt loads (much higher than Compass). If a bad year happens to coincide with major debt maturities or some other call on cash, the dividend may be slashed.

But if stability is relevant to dividend safety, durability—the ability of average earnings to cover dividend payments over the long run—is much more so. Durability implies that the firm can take a financial punch in one year and come back swinging the next. Durability implies an earnings stream that, if not quite predictable in any one year, can be relied upon over a series of years, during which short-term fluctuations should average out.

My durability checkpoints are less quantitative than those for earnings stability, but if anything they're easier to appraise.

The first is *sustainable competitive advantages*, also known as economic moats. As I discussed in Chapter 3, an economic moat enables a business to generate returns on equity well above the required return on that capital. In doing so, an economic moat also shields a company's earnings and cash flow from competitive pressures.

Let's revisit United Parcel Service's (UPS) dividend in this context. With a dividend rate of $1.68 a share annually and a book value of $14.52 per share, UPS would have to earn a return on equity of at least 11.6 percent ($1.68 divided into $14.52) just to fund its dividend. If competitors could flood the market with blue, yellow, and purple trucks to run UPS's brown ones off the road, they would—probably at returns much less than the 25 percent or so UPS generally earns. But they can't; UPS's competitive advantages are simply too strong. We find that economic moat doesn't just enable large returns on equity; it shields shareholder dividends from competitive threats as well.

I require an economic moat around every business in which I invest for income. To do otherwise would be to leave my dividend stream subject to the unfavorable acts of competitors, a risk I'd just as soon avoid. Over the long term, an eroding competitive position can threaten a dividend whose payout ratio once appeared reasonable.

My second durability checkpoint is *long-term demand*. Even as the economy grows overall with time, some industries fail to participate. Demand for wire-line telephone connections, to cite one example, grew rapidly in the 1990s as households added extra lines for dial-up Internet modems, faxes, even phones for the kids. Then came the advent of cellular phones, DSL Internet service, and cable services of all kinds. Traditional wireline connections are now declining at a single-digit clip. Even though these firms' competitive standing hasn't eroded to the point where their moats have disappeared, falling demand will invariably lead to falling profits.

Finally, I look at *liquidity*. A company's liquidity—the cash it has plus any cash it has ready access to—is always relevant to the payment of dividends. Earnings and cash flows will fluctuate from quarter to quarter and year to year, and a pile of existing cash or ready access to credit can help smooth out those variations. But if a company lacks liquidity, the stability of earnings becomes much more important than long-term durability.

From an earnings durability point of view, Compass stacks up surprisingly well.

▶ There's no doubt the firm has an economic moat—its existing mines are just short of irreplaceable assets, and it's highly unlikely that any substitute product will come along that is cheaper or more effective at getting rid of ice.

▶ While Compass's earnings could fall more than 32 percent in a given year—and we can't rule out a couple of dry or warm years in a row—would mere weather patterns change the firm's ability to earn acceptably high profits in a normal year? Of course not; not only does the firm's economic moat protect its profit-making potential in a normal year, but when it does snow, the highway department has no choice but to send out the salt trucks.

Compass's management is extremely well aware of the impact of weather on its business. Even though management is reluctant to offer an EPS outlook for any particular year, the firm regularly discloses estimates of the impact of above- or below-average weather trends on revenue and operating profits during the winter quarters. Using these figures, it's relatively easy to ascertain where the average earning power of the business is at any point.

▶ In addition to its cash balances, Compass has access to as much as $125 million in short-term borrowings through a revolving credit line, only $28.5 million of which was drawn at the end of 2006. This borrowing capacity would be sufficient to pay about nine quarters' worth of dividend payments with no earnings at all. No major debt maturities are on the horizon, either. (Better yet, Compass will soon have the option of refinancing some of its high-rate debt early, probably at much lower interest rates.)

Were we to focus solely on short-term earnings stability, Compass's payout ratio of 68 percent might seem too high. By definition, a lower payout ratio always implies greater dividend safety than a higher one. But a broader look at the durability of long-term earning power confirms the signal that management is sending through the dividend itself: Compass may not be a gold mine, but salt mines just might be more profitable.

All things considered, Compass's 68 percent payout ratio looks entirely appropriate. We've got a margin of safety for short-term earnings instability, but the long-run profit stream is a highly durable one. I recommended these shares to *Morningstar DividendInvestor* subscribers in April 2005 and haven't regretted it. (How could I? Since then Compass has raised its dividend twice by an average annual rate of 7.9 percent.)

Compass's high payout ratio sends one additional signal: Management is determined to use shareholders' funds wisely. In a cash-cow business, the temptation to make acquisitions and increase assets and revenue quickly is enormous, even if these moves would almost certainly prove a poor use of retained earnings. Taken in isolation, the fact that Compass has adopted a high-payout policy may or may not imply an insecure dividend stream, but it speaks volumes about the firm's devotion to rewarding shareholders.

The Willingness to Pay

The natural stickiness of dividends implies that temporary challenges—even if they force the payout ratio above 100 percent—shouldn't force a dividend cut. The firm will probably opt to borrow or sell assets (if necessary) to make up a short-term shortfall, especially if the absolute dollar amount of the gap is small.

Earlier I mentioned ConAgra as having been a sucker-yield stock even though its dividend yield (before the cut) was only about 5 percent. You wouldn't think of a food manufacturer as a risky business, but the firm's economic moat has been shrinking for years. Still, something even worse failed investors in this case: management's willingness to pay.

For nearly three decades, ConAgra's board had increased the dividend for the November payment. As the core business deteriorated amid heavy competition (ConAgra's products tend not to be market share leaders) and rising costs, the firm's dividend increases grew smaller and smaller until finally, in September 2005, the board opted not to raise the dividend at all.

Going into that fall's dividend announcement, I was considering buying the stock. The yield was already above 4 percent—very high by food industry standards at the time—but new management looked to finally be addressing the firm's weak competitive position. I figured ConAgra had two choices. It could embark on a serious cost-cutting and asset sale campaign that would, if anything, increase cash flow and provide better protection for the dividend. Or management might decide to slash payments to shareholders in order to invest more heavily in marketing initiatives with dubious potential for payback—a real problem, given ConAgra's weak competitive stance.

With these potential outcomes, I decided to let the September dividend announcement make my decision for me. Either management would reaffirm its commitment to the dividend rate by raising it, or it would signal a future cut by leaving it unchanged. The latter is exactly what happened. ConAgra left its quarterly dividend unchanged for November 2005. Not only did I pass on buying the shares, I predicted a cut to *Morningstar Dividend Investor* subscribers. Six months later, ConAgra cut its payout by a third, from 27.25 cents per share to 18 cents.

I believed then, and still believe, that ConAgra could have maintained its dividend. A year later, earnings trends were improving, though I seriously doubt the dividend had to be chopped for ConAgra's financial performance to rebound. Dividends represent a commitment by a company to its shareholders—a commitment that many of those shareholders are counting on for income. In this case, management gave shareholders a pay cut rather than hack away at expenses elsewhere.

Variable Dividends

Some types of companies—energy royalty trusts, for example, and certain specialty financial firms—make no pretense of promising steady dividends. As earnings rise and fall, even on a monthly basis, so does the shareholder's income. San Juan Basin Royalty Trust (SJT), which does nothing but collect royalties from natural gas wells on land it controls, illustrates this phenomenon. (See Figure 6.10.)

When the market price for natural gas rises, San Juan's monthly distributions shoot higher. When prices fall, so does the investor's income. These wide fluctuations also have a predictably large effect on the market price of the shares. This variability makes it very difficult to forecast dividends with any reliability.

There's nothing inherently wrong with a business that chooses to structure its dividend policy in this manner, but these stocks are for speculators, not long-term investors. The fact that their yields can be (and often are) very high does not make them an attractive source of income.

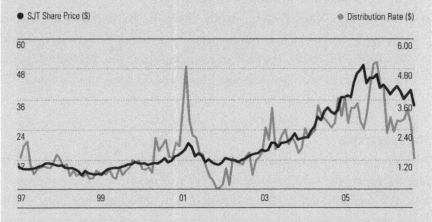

Figure 6.10   San Juan Basis Royalty Trust (SJT): Share Price and Cash Distribution History

Warning Signs

In the past few years, I've predicted a number of high-profile dividend cuts, warning *Morningstar DividendInvestor* subscribers not to rely on these stocks for income. Some of these were easy, such as retailer Pier 1 Imports (PIR), which eliminated its dividend in 2006 amid a good deal of red ink. In other cases, I missed calls that only seem obvious in hindsight.

Many of these situations had conditions in common:

▶ *Unsustainable earnings sources.* Equity Office Properties, which was the nation's largest landlord before it was taken private in a leveraged buyout, managed to pay out dividends that exceeded cash flow for several years by selling off properties. This was a finite source of income, and at the end of 2005, this otherwise rock-solid REIT slashed its dividend 34 percent. This same dynamic—payouts that couldn't be maintained from sustainable earnings—has led to dividend cuts for several other REITs as well.

▶ *Excessive debt or pension obligations.* General Motors (GM). Need I say more?

▶ *Legal problems.* In 2005, Fannie Mae (FNM) and Marsh & McLennan (MMC) both faced significant legal and regulatory issues. Even though core operating earnings—as best an outsider could tell—remained intact, these conditions forced significant dividend cuts. I correctly called the cut at Marsh, but I missed it at Fannie Mae.

▶ *Peer pressure.* When Ford cut its dividend in several steps to zero, this did not bode well for General Motors—and indeed GM cut its dividend 50 percent in 2006. And if there was trouble at the top, pain was felt down the food chain as well; suppliers Dana, Delphi, and Visteon (VC) all eliminated their dividends.

The Bottom Line

Adequate and appropriate payout ratios, healthy balance sheets, durable earnings—these are the basic building blocks of a secure income stream for investors. For me, however, the safest dividend is the one that's just been raised. Recall the signals that dividends send: When making the decision to raise the dividend, management knows that investors will expect higher payouts into the indefinite future. If it can't afford to raise the dividend now, it won't. But if it can, that sends a very positive signal of dividend safety.

True, New Century increased its quarterly dividend only months before filing for bankruptcy. But in almost every other case I can think of, dividend increases provide the best possible evidence of dividend safety. Analyzing a dividend's safety is critical in understanding where future dividends will come from and whether they can be relied upon.

DividendInvestor Case Study: Dividend Safety

While a very high yield (8 to 9 percent or more) usually signals trouble, on occasion it may herald a rare opportunity for both high dividend total returns and substantial capital appreciation as well. Conversely, what may seem like a decent payout ratio to begin with can rise quickly in a rapidly deteriorating situation. Homework, as usual, is the key.

In August 2005, I recommended AmeriGas Partners (APU), the nation's largest propane distributor, for its 7.3 percent yield and decent (if not terribly high) potential for distribution growth. I had a pretty good handle on current industry conditions: Warm weather, plus high propane prices that prompted consumers to turn down their thermostats, was acting as a temporary drag on profits, even though AmeriGas's cash distribution remained well covered.

Another propane distributor, Suburban Propane Partners (SPH), faced the same industry conditions but appeared to be in much worse shape. Not only had propane volume been light, but Suburban's smaller fuel oil delivery business was in deep trouble. Propane suppliers own their customers' tanks, making it hard for homeowners to shop around on price. Fuel oil tanks are owned by homeowners, which mean the lowest-price supplier gets the business, whether there's any margin in it for the winning supplier or not. To prevent customer switching, fuel oil distributors offered—get this—a per-gallon price cap for the season. And when the price of crude oil surged past all the old record highs in the 2004–2005 heating season, fuel oil suppliers could choose to either honor the contracts and risk insolvency, or renege on the caps and lose customers (or run the risk of being sued). One of Suburban's closest peers, Star Gas Partners (SGU), wound up in a liquidity crisis. This forced the sale of Star Gas's attractive propane assets, leaving it with a perilously weak balance sheet and only the dubious fuel oil business to support it.

Suburban's fuel oil business was much smaller than its propane business, but this didn't stop Suburban from taking a big hit from these price caps. Cash flow was clobbered, and Suburban's trailing payout ratio soared to 139 percent. The price of the units fell from $35 to $25, putting Suburban's yield close to 10 percent. At this price, investors were pricing the units for a steep cut in cash distributions.

This seemed like exactly the kind of situation that I'd warned investors away from, yet I had a feeling that homework might suggest there were diamonds in Suburban's lump of charcoal. Management made no secret of the fact that the fuel oil caps were going away—permanently— and if fuel oil buyers still wanted them, they could buy their fuel oil from somebody else.

(continued)

DividendInvestor Case Study: Dividend Safety *(continued)*

It quantified the hit of the fuel oil caps in dollar terms ($21.5 million, to be precise). Adding this one-time expense back to Suburban's 2005 results made it clear that without the caps, the payout ratio would have been a much more tolerable 100 percent. Management was trying to tell its story to anyone who would listen; the fact that almost nobody did opened up a big opportunity.

I recommended the units at $25.20 and devoted *Morningstar DividendInvestor's* January 2006 cover story to explaining my logic. In the absence of the fuel-oil price caps, cash flow would improve sharply, making the safety of Suburban's distribution obvious once again. Not only that, but (unbeknownst to me at the time) Suburban's management was executing deep cuts in operating costs. Cash flow skyrocketed; less than eight months later Suburban began raising its per-unit cash distribution rate. (See Figure 6.11.)

Not only had I locked in an initial yield of 9.7 percent, but the market price went back to $35. By mid-2007, Suburban's distribution rate was $2.80 a unit (up 14 percent in less than two years) and the market price had nearly doubled, to $48.

But if changing circumstances can quickly reduce a sky-high payout ratio to more sustainable levels, so can an ill-chosen situation deteriorate in a hurry. In May 2006, I recommended the shares of specialty retailer Tuesday Morning (TUES) at a yield of 5 percent, a cash return well above average for the industry. The company had just instituted a generous dividend policy that seemed well met for a business with limited long-term growth potential. I crunched the numbers, met with the management, and came to the conclusion that with a payout ratio a bit above 50 percent, the dividend was not only well covered but poised to grow. I recommended the stock at slightly under $16.

In hindsight, this was wishful thinking at best (or, I should say, at its worst). Same-store sales—a key metric of a retailer's performance—had been negative for seven straight quarters when I

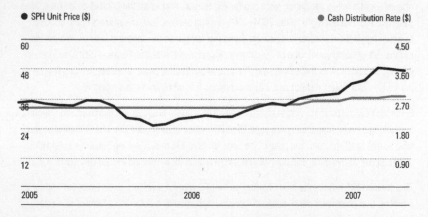

Figure 6.11   Suburban Propane Partners (SPH): Recent Share Price and Dividend History

made my purchase. I deluded myself into believing that these negative trends just made future comparisons easier, and I believed management's rosy projections for a turnaround. Up to that point, Tuesday Morning had been able to hang on to high profit margins and returns on equity—indications, at least on the surface, of an economic moat. But Tuesday Morning's basic business model—selling closeouts of name-brand department store–type merchandise at prices 50 to 80 percent off—became less and less relevant as the big department store chains themselves began offering similar markdowns. And as same-store sales continued to fall, it turned out that costs had already been slashed to the bone; there was nothing left to cut. The earnings stream was no longer a durable one (if in fact it ever had been).

What I thought was a 50 percent forward payout ratio soon rose to 60 percent, then 70 percent, then 90 percent. A trend of negative same-store sales I thought had run its course was actually accelerating into the red. By late 2006, I wasn't even sure the company would be willing to maintain its $0.80 annual dividend (even though it had no long-term debt). In January 2007, I sold—at a modest gain, amazingly enough, though the stock soon dropped to $11. In March 2007, the company declared its $0.80 annual dividend out of earnings that just barely covered it. (See Figure 6.12.) But I still wouldn't rule out a cut in the future.

What distinguished Suburban Propane from Tuesday Morning? More important than their respective payout ratios were their economic moats. Suburban clearly had one, while Tuesday Morning's moat was largely a figment of my imagination. These underlying competitive advantages (or lack thereof) had direct implications for future earnings stability and growth, which in turn was reflected in dividend safety, dividend growth, and—eventually—market price.

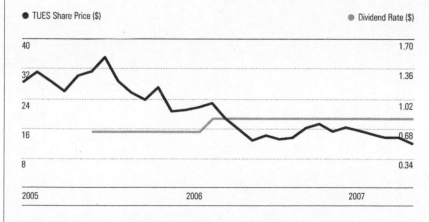

Figure 6.12   Tuesday Morning (TUES): Recent Share Price and Dividend History

Chapter 6: Rules and Plays

▶ Even though dividend rates are sticky, not all dividends are safe. Be especially wary of those that offer extra-high current yields, as they may be cut or eliminated in the future. Fortunately, dividend cuts can be anticipated and thus avoided.

▶ A stock's payout ratio should always be less than 100 percent on a long-term basis. However, it must be viewed in context of the stability of the underlying earnings stream, as well as the willingness of management to maintain the dividend through times of temporary difficulty.

▶ The safest dividends, in almost all cases, are the ones that continue to grow over time.

Will It Grow?

ONE OF MY favorite publicly traded businesses is a firm whose products touch millions of consumers every day, almost always without their knowing: Neenah, Wisconsin–based Bemis Company (BMS). While not affiliated with a better-known manufacturer of toilet seats under the same name, Bemis makes flexible plastic packaging used to hold and preserve thousands of consumer products, more than $3 billion worth a year. Ever buy Oscar Mayer bacon? (I buy, and eat, probably a bit more than I should.) That comes in a Bemis package. How about 12-packs of Pepsi? Bemis makes the printed plastic wrapping that holds the bottles together. Del Monte Fruit To-Go? Those easy-peel covers are from Bemis, too.

This enterprise got its start in 1858 as a maker of cotton sacks for flour and similar products. Since then, the company has successfully navigated the transition from cloth to paper and then to plastic. That's a trick equal to a buggy whip maker converting itself into a leader in steering wheels. Through constant innovation, Bemis has dug itself a nice economic moat. There's not a lot food manufacturers can do to improve on bacon, but if Bemis can make it more convenient, attractive, or less expensive to pack, then Oscar Mayer can charge premium prices for what would otherwise be a commodity product. Since Bemis comes up with the ideas, it, too, gets to charge higher prices and earn healthy profit margins. Best of all, Bemis has paid out hundreds of millions of dollars in dividends along the way, with payments made to shareholders every year since 1922. An increase in early 2007 lengthened the company's streak of continuously rising dividends to 24 years in a row.

In mid-2007, Bemis was trading at about $34 a share and paying quarterly dividends at the rate of $0.84 annually, giving the stock a yield of about 2.5 percent. I have no doubts about Bemis's ability to go on paying at this rate; it looks to be only about 40 percent of this year's earnings. Since Bemis is supplying packaging mostly to industries that don't depend much on the state of the economy, cash flows have a history of stability through thick and thin. Debt is manageable—possibly even a little bit on the low side. But a 2.5 percent yield alone isn't going to make Bemis a worthwhile investment. What we need from Bemis is dividend growth—lots of it.

In this chapter we consider the following indicators of future dividend growth:

▶ What does the firm's dividend record suggest about the future?
▶ How fast can a company grow, and how much will it cost in terms of retained earnings?
▶ On the basis of a company's current yield and potential for dividend growth, what kind of total return can we expect?
▶ Will the capacity for dividend growth translate into actual dividend increases, or will reluctant management stand in our way?

The Dividend Record

Let's see what insights we can glean from the most recent 20-year chunk of the firm's long history by referring to Figures 7.1 and 7.2.

Any cuts? No, only increases. Check.

Meaningful payments? The long-term average yield has run right around 2.2 percent. Check.

Meaningful increases? Yes, every year, even if they have been a bit lumpy. Check.

Year	Div Rate	Growth %	Price	Yield	Year	Div Rate	Growth %	Price	Yield
1986	0.075	—	3.53	2.12	1999	0.46	4.5	17.44	2.64
1987	0.09	20.0	4.80	1.88	2000	0.48	4.3	16.78	2.86
1988	0.11	22.2	5.81	1.89	2001	0.50	4.2	24.59	2.03
1989	0.15	36.4	8.59	1.75	2002	0.52	4.0	24.82	2.10
1990	0.18	20.0	7.41	2.43	2003	0.56	7.7	25.00	2.24
1991	0.21	16.7	10.25	2.05	2004	0.64	14.3	29.09	2.20
1992	0.23	9.5	12.56	1.83	2005	0.72	12.5	27.87	2.58
1993	0.25	8.7	11.81	2.12	2006	0.76	5.6	33.98	2.24
1994	0.27	8.0	12.00	2.25					
1995	0.32	18.5	12.81	2.50	**Averages**		Div Growth %		Yield
1996	0.36	12.5	18.44	1.95	1986–2006 (20 yrs)			12.3	2.18
1997	0.40	11.1	22.03	1.82	1996–2006 (10 yrs)			7.8	2.27
1998	0.44	10.0	18.97	2.32	2001–2006 (5 yrs)			8.7	2.23

Figure 7.1   Bemis Company: Dividend Record

Going beyond this 20-year look at the data, Bemis said in its February 2007 dividend announcement that the year would mark the 24th consecutive year of giving shareholders a raise. This might seem like a minor distinction, but I like to see companies with good dividend records tell shareholders as often as possible. Doing so prompts me to believe that management is strongly committed to maintaining and increasing the dividend.

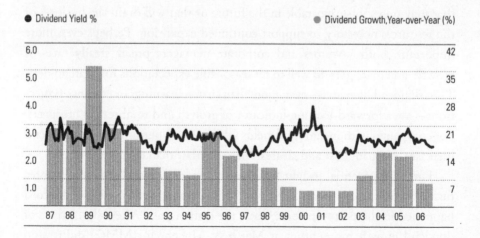

Figure 7.2   Bemis Company: Dividend Yield and Growth History

When looking at a dividend record—or any record of financial performance—it makes sense to look at trends over a series of years (I use five-year average growth rates) and to weight more recent information more heavily than older trends.

▶ If I could believe that the next 20 years would mirror the past 20, over which time Bemis churned out dividend increases averaging 12.3 percent annually, the stock would be poised to provide total returns pushing 15 percent annually. I'd be positively giddy over the stock's prospects.

▶ This record also reveals that the dividend rose much faster in the first five years (1986–1991) than it did in any subsequent five-year period. At the other end of the spectrum, Bemis's dividend rose at an average of 4.9 percent annually in the five years from 1998 to 2003. From Figure 7.2, we might infer a generally declining rate of dividend growth—an unfavorable sign, especially as the yield has remained roughly constant between 2 and 3 percent.

▶ The most recent data—an 8.7 percent rate of growth from 2001 to 2006 and a 10.5 percent increase in early 2007—are probably the most representative of the firm's current prospects.

As I described in Chapter 4, dividends send important signals about the state of a business and the trajectory it is on. Dividends being sticky and cuts relatively rare, corporate boards are reluctant to raise their dividends to levels that may prove unsupportable in the future or that will drain the business of the resources necessary to support continued expansion. Perhaps even more important, both investors and corporate managers prefer steady rates of growth, and managers do well to set reasonable expectations for shareholders. Thus dividend increases—even more than current earnings or earnings projections—are a forward-looking indicator of growth and total return prospects. For companies with meaningful yields (above 2 or 3 percent), I take dividend increases as the loudest and clearest messages that management can send.

For all its potential insight, a favorable dividend record cannot guarantee future performance. Everything I've described about Bemis's dividend record happened in the past—in some cases, the distant past. After all, 43 years of dividend growth momentum at Marsh & McLennan (MMC) didn't stop that company from halving its dividend in early 2005. Just as we can't take a stock's dividend yield entirely for granted, we must look forward to provide a solid estimate of future growth potential.

Introducing the DDRM

In Chapter 3, I discussed the various levers that make a company's total return prospects tick: internal growth potential, acquisitions, the returns on equity earned on incremental investments, payout ratios, and changes in the share count (buybacks and new issues). I've developed a model that takes all of these factors as inputs and churns out estimates of dividend growth and total return. I call it the Dividend Drill Return Model, or DDRM.

I've seen dozens of different ways to analyze companies, value their shares, and (if only implicitly) forecast the total return the prospective shareholder can expect. Almost all of these take the form of intricate spreadsheets, sometimes hundreds or thousands of lines long, with dozens of different factors to consider—everything from accounts receivable to deferred taxes. For all the rigor such models can provide, the analyst too often winds up drowning in the details and missing the big picture. Usually the number of truly relevant factors can be counted on one hand. The DDRM has just five inputs, two of which are not even estimates but merely describe the current state of the stock.

1. *Current stock price.* This is available from brokerage offices, newspapers, and a hundred Internet sites (including Morningstar.com).
2. *Current dividend rate.* Ditto, as long as you're getting a pure regular dividend rate, unsullied by special payments, currency fluctuations, or bad data.
3. *Earnings per share.* This takes a bit more effort to obtain and evaluate, but here I have good news: We'll be using the same figure that we used in Chapter 6 for dividend safety analysis.
4. *Core growth rate.* This figure will require the most thought. How fast can the business increase its annual profits? Past performance can provide a good starting point, but after that we'll still have a lot of thinking to do in order to come up with a good estimate.
5. *Return on equity.* Few types of growth are free. Most of the time, a corporation will need to commit additional capital to the business in order to grow. In a backhanded but logical manner, this estimate will incorporate the cost of growth into our dividend growth and total forecast.

How the DDRM Works

The DDRM breaks a stock's prospective total return into three factors: the current dividend yield, the total amount of profits available to pay dividends, and any changes in the number of shares receiving dividends. By combining the effects of the last two factors, the DDRM generates an estimate for dividend growth.

In Chapter 3, I suggested that one way to estimate a company's growth potential was through the sustainable growth rate (SGR):

$$(1 - \text{Payout Ratio}) \times \text{Return on Equity} = \text{Sustainable Growth Rate}$$

In some cases, the SGR will provide a realistic estimate for growth, but more often than not it will overstate the case—perhaps greatly. For companies requiring external funding to grow (namely in the form of new equity issues), the SGR will understate the case. The theory behind this simple formula, sound enough on paper, falls apart in practice.

Consider Hershey Company (HSY), which earned an outstanding ROE of 68 percent in 2006—a tribute to both its wide economic moat and a fairly aggressive use of debt to juice returns on equity. Hershey, a terrific company by any standard, today accounts for less than 1 percent of America's $500 billion annual outlay for packaged foods. But if Hershey retained 100 percent of its earnings and then attempted to increase equity and earnings at 68 percent annually, that strategy would imply replacing America's entire food budget with Hershey-branded chocolate in less than a decade. Much as I appreciate the Take 5 bar, that's not going to happen.

Hershey pays a respectable dividend by food company standards; the stock's indicated payout ratio in mid-2007 was 44 percent (a dividend rate of $1.08 divided by earnings of $2.46 a share). This dividend drops Hershey's SGR from 68 percent to 38 percent, but in the big scheme of things, 38 percent is no more attainable as a rate of long-term expansion than 68 percent is. We're going to have to look at Hershey's growth prospects independent of the SGR.

Later on, I'll provide a wider look at how to ascertain a company's growth rate. But for now, let's reckon that Hershey won't be able to expand its overall business any faster than 5 percent annually. If earnings per share and dividends track this figure, we can add this 5 percent growth rate to Hershey's yield of about 2 percent and count on a 7 percent total return.

However, linking net income growth directly to dividend growth misses two important factors:

1. We haven't yet ascertained how much earnings Hershey must retain for a 5 percent annual growth rate.
2. To the extent that Hershey has earnings left over after paying dividends and funding growth, what happens to those dollars?

We can flip the SGR around to tell us how much of Hershey's profit must be retained to fund annual growth. By making the growth rate one of the SGR formula's inputs and establishing the payout ratio as the output, we find:

$$100\% - \frac{\text{Core Growth Rate}}{\text{Return on Equity}} = \text{Optimal Payout Ratio}$$

For Hershey:

$$100\% - \frac{5\%}{68\%} = 93\%$$

The SGR is telling us that Hershey could conceivably pay out 93 percent of earnings and still grow at a 5 percent annual rate. The inverse of the payout ratio, which measures the proportion of earnings not being paid out as dividends, is the retention ratio.

$$100\% - \text{Payout Ratio} = \text{Retention Ratio}$$

If Hershey can afford to pay out 93 percent of its earnings as dividends, the retention ratio tells us that only 7 percent of earnings (7.35 percent, to be precise) needs to be retained to support a 5 percent core growth rate.

Using this notion, let's turn to Hershey's actual earnings. In mid-2007, Hershey was expected to earn $2.46 a share. Of this profit, 7.35 percent of it needs to be retained to support a 5 percent core growth rate. That translates to $0.18 per share. In essence, this is the cost of Hershey's growth on a per-share basis.

Core Growth ÷ Return on Equity × Earnings Per Share = Cost of Growth
Per Share

For Hershey:

$$5\% \div 68\% \times 2.46 = 0.18$$

Among other things, this analysis shows how inexpensive it is for a company with a very high ROE to grow. It also adds to our ability to project where Hershey's earnings are going.

From earnings per share of $2.46, we can now deduct the dividend rate ($1.08 a share) and $0.18 per share for Hershey's cost of growth. That still leaves $1.20 of per-share earnings unaccounted for. These additional earnings, a term I refer to as the *funding gap*, must have some value for shareholders.

Earnings Per Share − Dividend Rate − Cost of Growth Per Share = Funding
Gap

For Hershey:

$$2.46 - 1.08 - 0.18 = 1.20$$

What becomes of this remainder? Let's check Hershey's cash flow statement to see what the company is actually doing. As it turns out, Hershey is using the dollars in this funding gap to buy back its own shares. Between 2002 and 2006, Hershey repurchased nearly $2 billion worth of its own shares; the average number of shares outstanding declined from 269 million to 234 million—a drop of 13 percent. Since dividends are paid on a per-share basis, a smaller number of shares allows the same total dividend payment to rise on a per-share basis.

As I illustrated in Chapter 3, these buybacks add directly to the growth of Hershey's core business to provide total dividend growth potential on a per-share basis. At a share price of $52, a funding gap of $1.20 a share enables Hershey to buy in 2.3 percent of its outstanding shares annually. This provides us with yet another key statistic, *share change*.

Dividend Rate ($)	1.08	Funding Gap ($)		1.20
Divided by: Share Price ($)	52.00	Divided by: Share Price ($)		52.00
Current Yield (%)	**2.1**	**Share Change (%)**		**2.3**
Core Growth Estimate (%)	**5.0**	Core Growth (%)		5.0
Divided by: Return on Equity (%)	68	Plus: Share Change (%)		2.3
Multiplied by: Earnings per Share ($)	2.46	**Total Dividend Growth (%)**		**7.3**
Cost of Growth ($)	**0.18**			
		Plus: Dividend Yield (%)		2.1
Earnings per Share ($)	2.46	**Projected Total Return (%)**		**9.4**
Minus: Dividend	(1.08)			
Minus: Cost of Growth ($)	(0.18)			
Funding Gap ($)	**1.20**			

Figure 7.3   Hershey Company: Dividend Drill Return Model

$$\text{Funding Gap} \div \text{Share Price} = \text{Share Change}$$

For Hershey:

$$1.20 \div 52.00 = 2.3\%$$

We started with the premise that dividend total return was equal to yield plus dividend growth. Dividend growth, in turn, breaks down into core growth (the rate of growth for total profits) plus share change (the shrinkage in outstanding shares due to share buybacks). By placing all of these parts into a logical worksheet, the DDRM now looks like Figure 7.3.

The DDRM Applied

The DDRM, like any model, has drawbacks, and I discuss some of those in a bit. But the biggest drawback of the DDRM (again, like any model) is its dependence on high-quality inputs. You may have heard the phrase "Garbage in, garbage out." Whether calculated using Microsoft Excel or pen, parchment, and an abacus, this applies to the DDRM. We know the stock price and the current dividend rate; the other three estimates are just that—estimates.

Thinking about Earnings per Share

The earnings per share figure we use will be the same as what we use to evaluate dividend safety—a forward-looking estimate for earnings. In some cases, like property real estate investment trusts and pipeline operators, we'll want to use a cash flow statistic that better represents ongoing cash generation and dividend-paying ability (more on these in Appendixes 5 and 6).

However, an estimate I might use for 2007 or 2008 may not represent a stable level of future earnings. It helps greatly when the company has an easily identifiable economic moat and a history of stable profits, but you wouldn't want to use 2007 earnings projections for Caterpillar (CAT) or Nucor (NUE), with their profits near or at boom-time highs. If you're considering an investment in a cyclical stock for its dividend, you'll want to develop enough knowledge about those cycles and what the true long-term average earning power of the business is.

Thinking about Core Growth

Since the core growth figure flows directly into a stock's dividend growth forecast and, by extension, its total return forecast, getting this figure into a reasonable ballpark range is critically important. This is especially important for stocks with low yields and firms with high returns on equity.

I like to use a building-block approach to generate an estimate for internal growth. Think about the basic drivers of all businesses: volume and price. Volume is a function of how many people are buying how much of a product. Price is influenced by inflation, though some firms are much better at passing price hikes through than others. Wherever possible, I try to tie my expectations to broader trends—the growth of the U.S. population, inflation, regional economic growth, and so forth—whatever might be influencing the expansion potential for the business at hand.

▶ For a food company like Kraft (KFT), I might figure it can raise prices 2 percent a year—just equal to inflation—but since population grows only 1 percent a year, 3 percent is probably the best it can do for top-line growth.

▶ At Johnson & Johnson (JNJ), chances are fairly good it will be able to grow a couple of percentage points faster than the economy when both volume and price are considered; 7 percent or even 8 percent seems realistic.

▶ When it comes to banks, a deposit taker in Texas like Cullen/Frost (CFR) is probably going to grow a lot faster—maybe 6 or 7 percent annually—than the 2 to 3 percent that Rust Belt–centric National City (NCC) has in store.

When forecasting core growth, I prefer to stick with internal growth prospects only. Acquisition-led growth can be hazardous to forecast, and it's even harder to assume that the acquirer will be able to generate high ROEs as a result. Only when a company has demonstrated a pattern of making modest-size acquisitions on a regular basis would I fold some acquisition-derived growth into my estimate.

Thinking about Return on Equity

The projected return on equity will also have a significant impact on the DDRM, if not quite as large an effect as core growth. Here I believe the past can provide a very useful guide. I usually wind up using either the most recent year's ROE or, if ROE has fluctuated widely in the past, a 5- or 10-year average.

However, it's still important to take a forward-looking view. The most important factor governing long-term returns on equity is the company's economic moat: Is it getting wider or narrower over time? Sears (SHLD) was once America's dominant retailer, but as Wal-Mart (WMT) and other discounters figured out better ways to do business, Sears' competitive advantages diminished and eventually disappeared. By contrast, a business like Johnson & Johnson, with an ever-accumulating and deepening base of scientific knowledge, has a widening moat. And in some cases, growth requires very, very little retained earnings. Think about Microsoft (MSFT): when it wants to expand, it hires more programmers. The cost of this growth that can be traced to retained earnings—a computer and a cubicle—is negligible.

The *type* of core growth you're forecasting should be reflected in your ROE forecast as well. A core growth estimate that includes heavy doses of acquisitions should naturally have a lower ROE than one that relies on internal growth only. But if you're only counting on internal growth, you might discover that past ROEs will overstate the cost of growth: Past acquisitions can easily weigh these figures down. In such a case, you may want to calculate ROE on a tangible basis, excluding goodwill and other intangible assets from the shareholders' equity account. As a case in point, Bemis earned a 12.5 percent ROE in 2006 on a book basis, but if we exclude goodwill and intangibles—assets that don't need to be replaced or added to when the company only expands internally— the implied return on equity nearly doubles to 24.7 percent. (See Figure 7.4.)

	Book	Tangible
Tangible Assets (Inventories, Property, etc.)	2,295.2	2,295.2
Goodwill and Intangibles	696.4	0.0
Average Total Assets	**2,991.6**	**2,295.2**
Average Total Liabilities	1,580.8	1580.8
Average Shareholders' Equity	**1,410.8**	**714.4**
Net Income, 2006	176.3	176.3
Return on Equity, 2006	**12.5%**	**24.7%**

Figure 7.4   Bemis Company: Book ROE versus Tangible ROE (Dollars in Millions)

With these thoughts on making estimates, let's turn the DDRM full blast on Bemis and see what we can reasonably expect.

▶ *Stock price.* In mid-2007, Bemis was changing hands around $34 a share. Though the price fluctuates every business day, I'll use this as a rough approximation. (The total return estimate the DDRM produces won't change much if I actually wind up paying $33.50 or $34.25.)

▶ *Dividend rate.* Bemis declared a $0.21 per share quarterly dividend in February 2007 and the same again in May. Annualized, this dividend rate is $0.84.

▶ *Earnings per share.* From recent press releases, I find that management expects earnings of $1.98 to $2.08 per share in 2007. This range excludes some restructuring charges, but these expenses are just about over, and the company has no history of spoiling itself with nonrecurring charges year after year. I'll give Bemis the benefit of the doubt and use the midpoint of $2.03 for the DDRM.

▶ *Core growth.* Revenue has more than doubled over the past decade, growing 8.2 percent a year on average. About half of this growth has come from acquisitions, with the rest generated internally. Bemis is a much bigger company than it was a decade ago, which means that successful new product launches and small acquisitions will have less of an impact than they once did. Then again, 8 percent growth isn't that much faster than the U.S. economy as a whole (about 6 percent). It isn't as if the company has outgrown its ability to expand further. Internal growth potential of 3 to 4 percent a year probably hasn't changed; if anything, these prospects are made more solid by recent growth in Europe and South America, as well as a rapidly expanding effort into pharmaceutical and medical device packaging. And with a strong balance sheet, Bemis can afford to make larger acquisitions in the future. With all these things considered, I'll use 8 percent for my core growth estimate.

▶ *Return on equity.* Bemis's ROE over the preceding decade averaged a bit under 16 percent, but the past couple of years has been on the weak side of average—just 12.5 percent in 2006, including the hit from restructuring. Management's guidance implies a rebound to 14 percent in 2007, and its longer-term outlook calls for a reduction in capital spending (good for asset turnover) and additional cost savings from the restructuring efforts in 2006 (good for margins). A return to the 16 percent ROEs of the past doesn't seem unreasonable.

Dumping these three estimates (earnings per share, core growth, and ROE) into the DDRM, along with the stock's current price and dividend rate, I figure Bemis can raise its dividend 8.5 percent annually—pretty much in line with the past. That, plus a 2.5 percent current yield, suggests an 11 percent total return. (See Figure 7.5.)

Dividend Rate ($)	0.84	Funding Gap ($)	0.18
Divided by: Share Price ($)	34.00	Divided by: Share Price ($)	34.00
Current Yield (%)	**2.5**	**Share Change (%)**	**0.5**
Core Growth Estimate (%)	**8.0**	Core Growth (%)	8.0
Divided by: Return on Equity (%)	16	Plus: Share Change (%)	0.5
Multiplied by: Earnings per Share ($)	2.03	**Total Dividend Growth (%)**	**8.5**
Cost of Growth ($)	**1.02**		
		Plus: Dividend Yield (%)	2.5
Earnings per Share ($)	2.03	**Projected Total Return (%)**	**11.0**
Minus: Dividend	(0.84)		
Minus: Cost of Growth ($)	(1.02)		
Funding Gap ($)	**0.18**		

Figure 7.5   Bemis Company: Dividend Drill Return Model

Capital Consumers and the DDRM

Corporate profits are in abundance these days, enabling thousands of firms to pay dividends, reinvest for growth, and buy back large quantities of stock—a triple play of gain for investors. However, this isn't the case across the board.

I've already observed that a low return on equity effectively makes it more costly for a company to grow. This is the case at Great Plains Energy (GXP), an electric utility serving Kansas and Missouri. Its dividend yield of 5.7 percent is relatively high for a utility, as is its payout ratio of 90 percent. If it weren't for the fact that the company's regulated subsidiary (Kansas City Power & Light) generates stable earnings, I might even question the safety of this dividend.

Great Plains doesn't have a great dividend record, either. It cut the dividend in 1986, and those expecting income growth more recently have had to live through a nine-year dry spell; the quarterly dividend of $0.415 a share hasn't been raised since the summer of 1998.

What Great Plains does have, in addition to an above-average yield, is pretty good growth potential by utility standards. The region is running out of electricity, giving Great Plains the ability to grow by building new generating stations. When these new plants throw the switch and start turning coal into electricity, earnings should grow substantially.

Let's run a quick DDRM on Great Plains:

- *Stock price:* About $29 in mid-2007.
- *Dividend rate:* $1.66 a share.
- *Earnings per share:* Wall Street analysts' average forecast for 2007 was $1.85 at midyear.
- *Core growth:* Management says it should be able to expand at 10 percent annually for the next five years, a very fast pace for a regulated utility. Thereafter, growth should return to a more traditional 2 to 4 percent annual rate.

  This presents a challenge: The DDRM can't incorporate two different stages of growth separately. I could build out a much more detailed forecast (and I would, if I actually planned to buy the stock), but as a shortcut, I'll estimate a core growth rate of 6 percent—roughly the midpoint between near-term potential of 10 percent and a longer-term 3 percent.

Dividend Rate ($)	1.66	Funding Gap ($)	(0.92)
divided by: Share Price ($)	29.00	divided by: Share Price ($)	29.00
Current Yield (%)	**5.7**	**Share Change (%)**	**−3.2**
Core Growth Estimate (%)	**6.0**	Core Growth (%)	6.0
divided by: Return on Equity (%)	10.0	plus: Share Change (%)	−3.2
multiplied by: Earnings Per Share ($)	1.85	**Total Dividend Growth (%)**	**2.8**
Cost of Growth ($)	**1.11**		
		plus: Dividend Yield (%)	5.7
Earnings Per Share ($)	1.85	**Projected Total Return (%)**	**8.6**
minus: Dividend	(1.66)		
minus: Cost of Growth ($)	(1.11)		
Funding Gap ($)	**(0.92)**		

Figure 7.6 Great Plains Energy: Dividend Drill Return Model (totals may not add up due to rounding)

▶ *Return on equity:* To limit the potential abuses of a utility's monopoly in a given area, state regulators limit returns to a modest level. Given what we know about Great Plains' investment plan, a 10 percent ROE looks reasonable.

With these inputs, Figure 7.6 depicts what the DDRM has to say.

As I anticipated, it's going to be very expensive for Great Plains to grow: $1.11 a share. But at Great Plains' current dividend rate, it is retaining earnings equal to just $0.19 a share. The funding gap term is *negative* to the tune of $0.92 a share.

Does this mean that Great Plains will have to slash its dividend by $0.92 a share? I know of one utility that, faced with large capital expenditures for its growth initiatives, did force shareholders to take a pay cut: Wisconsin Energy (WEC) sliced its dividend by nearly half in 2000. However, low-return, capital-intensive businesses like these have another option: raising capital by selling more shares. Fortunately for Great Plains' shareholders, that appears to be management's plan.

There is a trade-off, though. Newly issued shares have the opposite effect of share buybacks; they dilute the growth rate for future dividends. If the funding gap term is negative, then the share change term will be negative as well—a drag on growth. So even as Great Plains stands to increase total earnings at 6 percent annually, it will be issuing 3.2 percent more shares every year. Net dividend growth for the shareholder falls to just 2.8 percent, not much faster than inflation.

Great Plains Energy might not be a bad investment at an 8.6 percent long-term total return prospect. But in the real world, I'm willing to bet that until those new power plants are built and earnings grow to where Great Plains' payout ratio reaches a more normal 60 to 70 percent, dividend growth will remain just beyond the horizon.

Premises of and Limitations to the DDRM

Like most financial models, the DDRM is theoretically complete—subject to certain limitations.

The biggest of these limitations overlaps with the primary flaw in the *dividend yield plus dividend growth* assumption itself—its status as a perpetuity. To work, one must presume that the current dividend is sound and the dividend growth rate will remain stable into the indefinite future. However, if the stock price rises at roughly the rate of the dividend over time, we can use this approach to forecast total returns over time horizons shorter than forever. I generally use a five-year view.

Unreliable inputs will lead to a faulty total return estimate, of course. Two of the DDRM's inputs—dividend rate and stock price—are time-specific certainties; the stock price is what it is, and (as long as the current dividend is sound) we know the dividend rate, too. Unfortunately, the other inputs are susceptible to wider ranges of error:

▶ *Earnings per share.* For the model to produce a good estimate of future total return, the earnings figure we use needs to be reasonably representative of long-term earnings power. If we use an earnings estimate that will collapse if there's a recession next year, the DDRM will not generate a high-quality total return projection.

▶ *Core growth.* In many cases—especially for lower-yielding stocks—this estimate has the largest single impact on dividend growth and total return. Depending on the ROE assumption, the contribution to total return may be negligible (for low assumed ROEs) or huge. Where the impact of core growth on total return is close to a one-to-one ratio, be conservative.

▶ *Return on equity.* The ROE a company is earning today may or may not be representative of the returns available on future investments of retained earnings. If Hershey for some reason decides to pay down debt rather than buy back stock, ROE will almost certainly decline. When ROE is very high or otherwise unconnected to the returns the company can expect on future investments with retained earnings, we may need to use estimates unconnected to past return performance. In any event, I'm often reluctant to use ROEs of more than 25 to 30 percent when projecting future returns; anything higher than this, and you're projecting an awful lot of bang for a buck of retained earnings. (Note that knocking Hershey's 68 percent ROE in Figure 7.3 down to a more realistic 30 percent reduces the stock's total return forecast from 9.4 percent to 8.9 percent.)

▶ *Free growth.* Not all earnings growth requires reinvestment. A few businesses are in the sought-after position of being able to increase prices without commensurate increases in costs or the need to add additional capital, and those price hikes can flow directly to the bottom line. We may then, on occasion, need to include a *free growth* term to the model. Like core growth, it adds directly to dividend growth and total return; unlike core growth, we presume no additional capital is required to achieve it. Such examples are relatively rare, but for property-owning REITs (to take one example), contractual increases in rental rates can lead to annual earnings gains of perhaps 2 percent without additional capital investments.

These limitations are one reason I like to run multiple scenarios before settling on a set of estimates. In the real world, my core growth estimate, return on equity forecast, and even my earnings per share estimate are unlikely to be perfect. Short-term variations will wash out—these are long-term forecasts, after all—but it still makes sense to see what Bemis's prospects would look like under alternative scenarios for core growth and ROE. (See Figure 7.7.)

	7% Growth	**8% Growth**	9% Growth
14% ROE	10.0%	10.6%	11.1%
16% ROE	10.4%	**11.0%**	11.6%
18% ROE	10.6%	11.3%	12.0%

Figure 7.7 Bemis Company: DDRM Scenario Analysis

Because Bemis doesn't have a volatile past, I opted for a relatively narrow range of scenarios—growth between 7 percent and 9 percent, ROE between 14 percent and 18 percent. This seems to me to encompass the range of likely possibilities based on what I know about the business. Fortunately, the gap between my best guess and a more conservative set of assumptions (7 percent core growth and a 14 percent ROE) is just one percentage point. If I wind up being off by that much, I might be disappointed, but far from devastated.

The DDRM is relatively simple, but that doesn't mean analyzing a business and forecasting its prospects is just as easy. Studying the gears and levers that make Bemis tick and developing these forecasts was a process that took many hours over a period of several weeks. But this research is time well spent; the better you understand what you own, the greater the likelihood of your success.

Means versus Motive

With solid, reasonable inputs for companies with predictable earnings streams, the DDRM does a good job of forecasting dividend growth potential. But while the model is designed to forecast dividend growth directly, implicit in the DDRM is an earnings per share forecast as well. The DDRM assumes a constant payout ratio, and at a constant payout ratio, earnings and dividends rise (or fall) in tandem.

In the real world, payout ratios—if generally stable—are not necessarily constant. Not every company will choose to raise its dividend, even when it can. The means are not enough; management must also be motivated to return more cash to shareholders as the business expands.

As I see it, real-world dividend growth potential falls into one or more of three categories: trend, incentive, and hope.

Trend

When a company has a long history of predictable dividend increases behind it, management can and should be reluctant to tinker with the trend. Associated Banc-Corp (ASBC), having raised its dividend for 37 years in a row, probably isn't going to break the chain just because earnings growth has temporarily stagnated. Instead, it will raise the dividend (as it has) to reassure investors that long-term earnings and dividend growth potential remain intact.

Not all companies have long trends in place, and I don't mean to suggest that a 20- or 30-year run of annual dividend increases should be necessary before making an investment. Occasionally I run across promising firms that appear determined to build a favorable trend, such as UAP Holding (UAPH). After announcing plans to pay dividends at the rate of $0.50 annually in the prospectus for its 2004 initial public offering (that itself being a highly unusual act), this distributor of agricultural supplies proceeded to raise this rate 80 percent in less than two years. A short trend here, combined with clear signals from management regarding the importance of its dividends, may be sufficient for the investor to rely on.

Incentive

Some companies—I'm thinking here mostly of energy master limited partnerships and real estate investment trusts—may not have a favorable trend of growth under their belts, but can still be relied on to expand their dividends over time. Real estate investment trusts (profiled in depth in Appendix 5) are required to pay out at least 90 percent of their taxable profits. That doesn't mean that the payout ratio, based on funds from operations, can't fall well below this figure if funds from operations are growing and the dividend does not; but at some point, taxable profits will rise to where dividend increases are not just encouraged, but required by law.

A better example of this phenomenon comes from propane distributor AmeriGas Partners (APU). When I recommended the units in August 2005, AmeriGas had just issued its first cash distribution increase since going public in 1995—and that just a measly 1.8 percent. With a yield on the units of 7.3 percent, I was going to need more dividend growth (at least 3 percent) to make this investment work over the long term. But AmeriGas, like most master limited partnerships (which are profiled in depth in Appendix 6), had a built-in incentive for more and faster distribution growth. A utility called UGI Corporation (UGI) controls AmeriGas as its general partner, and as such, it is entitled to a rising share of total cash distributions as the payouts to the publicly traded limited partnership units rise over time. I would not be disappointed: In 2006, AmeriGas raised the distribution rate 3.6 percent and set a public target of 3 percent annual growth in the future. In 2007, AmeriGas proceeded to increase the distribution an even larger 5.2 percent.

Direct incentives like these are relatively rare. On occasion, you'll find a case where the founder, CEO, or other key shareholders are compensated primarily through dividend payments. For their income to grow, so will yours—specialty lender CapitalSource (CSE) and energy MLP Kinder Morgan Energy Partners (KMP) are prime examples in this case. But where you can identify clear incentives for dividend growth, they can easily make up for the lack of a long trend. (And where you find both attractive trends and obvious incentives at work—such as with Kinder Morgan—dividend growth in line with the progression of earnings is virtually assured.)

Hope

In the absence of clear trends or clear incentives, hope is about all that's left. In early 2005, I recommended shares of Sonic Automotive (SAH), a chain of new-car dealerships, which had started to pay dividends just six quarters earlier. The trend, in essence, had just two data points: the first $0.10 quarterly dividend in September 2003 and an increase to $0.12 one year later. The yield on the shares was just 2 percent, so I was counting on (that is, hoping for) a lot of dividend growth. On Wall Street, two data points are often interpreted as a line and therefore a trend, but in this case there was no trend, only hope. Sonic didn't raise its dividend in September 2005—a critical disappointment. I asked management about it and learned that steady dividend growth had never been part of its financial plans. Recognizing my error, I sold.

Human nature being what it is, I've bought into a few more growth hope plays since, including Tuesday Morning (TUES), whose purchase and subsequent sale I discuss in Chapter 6. I also bought Microsoft (MSFT) because I figured the firm was capable of doubling or tripling its regular dividend to provide a meaningful yield. Instead, Microsoft management opted for the more familiar share-buyback route for its billions and held dividend growth to a low-double-digit pace. In the aggregate, these hope plays haven't worked out well at all—especially compared with the clear trend and incentive stories.

For most other investors, mere earnings growth or a rising stock price might provide an adequate reward. But I'm looking to obtain lots of income first, increase that income second, and then let the capital gains piece take care of itself. It's hard to make this kind of strategy work when the dividends aren't delivering the income and income growth you want.

The Bottom Line

The building blocks of our total return prospect are dividend yield and dividend growth. Chapter 6 gives us the first figure, if we can establish the dividend is safe. This chapter has provided the tools necessary to forecast dividend growth. By this stage in the Dividend Drill, we've developed the basis for dividend total return projections.

But knowing this figure doesn't make a stock a buy. The final step—asking "What's the return?"—is the process of judging whether a stock's prospective return is sufficient to make an investment worthwhile.

DividendInvestor Case Study: Dividend Growth

It would be easy—oh, so easy—to invest solely on the basis of historical trends in dividend growth. But a changing situation can easily render the past irrelevant.

One of my biggest disappointments to date has been my August 2005 buy recommendation of First Horizon National (FHN), a regional bank based in Memphis, Tennessee. This bank, which is not terribly large, operated in four rather distinct areas:

1. The dominant commercial and retail banking franchise in its home state of Tennessee.
2. A mortgage origination business that operates nationwide.
3. A small investment bank (FTN Financial) that caters, oddly enough, to other banks.
4. A batch of retail bank branches in Atlanta; metropolitan Washington, D.C.; Dallas–Fort Worth; and Houston.

If all there was to First Horizon was First Tennessee, this would have been (and probably would still be) a very attractive bank. First Tennessee is the only large bank still based in the state, and as other regional banks (most notably Regions Financial, RF) acquired their way into the state, First Tennessee was only too happy to cherry-pick the best employees, customers, and depositors annoyed with the acquired banks' changes in management. I couldn't really see the 15 percent average dividend growth of the previous five years continuing, but with a payout ratio of 50 percent and an ROE north of 20 percent, it was pretty easy to see the dividend rising at least 8 percent in the years to come.

However, the underlying challenges of First Horizon's other three businesses—where sustainable competitive advantages were either questionable or nonexistent—were being covered up by the mortgage boom. When conditions in the mortgage industry began to sour amid rising short-term interest rates, First Horizon's earnings and ROE dropped substantially. At the end of 2005, First Horizon raised its dividend just 4.7 percent, not 8 percent; in 2006, it didn't raise the dividend at all. (See Figure 7.8.)

From where I sit in mid-2007, dividend growth seems all but out of the question for First Horizon. My key DDRM inputs—earnings per share and ROE—were unreliable and therefore deeply

(continued)

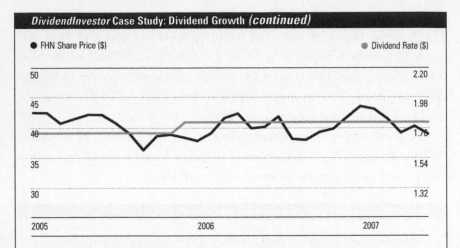

Figure 7.8   First Horizon National (FHN): Recent Share Price and Dividend History

flawed. I'm still inclined to think that earnings will eventually rebound, and that the stock is therefore undervalued, but with a payout ratio now approaching 75 percent, there's little reason to believe First Horizon will or should raise its dividend until this uncertain earnings recovery takes shape—possibly several years away. In the meantime, I'm probably stuck with a flat dividend stream and only a vague hope for capital appreciation. (There being better banks around, I may even look to replace this holding at some point.)

Now contrast this with Wells Fargo (WFC), another mortgage-centric bank I recommended in November 2005. Like First Horizon, Wells Fargo's dividend record is impressive, but its underlying business is more stable and much better run. In this case, my initial projection for 8.5 percent annual dividend growth has been almost exactly correct: Wells Fargo's next two annual dividend increases averaged 9.1 percent. (See Figure 7.9.)

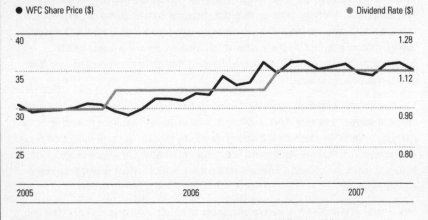

Figure 7.9   Wells Fargo Company (WFC): Recent Share Price and Dividend History

What distinguishes Wells Fargo from First Horizon? I think it comes down to quality. Seemingly similar in terms of profitability, growth potential, and valuation two years ago, Wells Fargo turned out to be a much more durable business than First Horizon. Quality can be difficult to ascertain from numbers alone, but evaluating the individual pieces of First Horizon more closely would (or at least should) have kept me from buying the stock.

Chapter 7: Rules and Plays

▶ In almost every case, future dividend growth is necessary for a stock to provide an adequate total return.

▶ Using the DDRM, we can forecast future dividend growth by considering current earnings and dividends per share, the stock's current price, future growth potential of the business, and the returns on equity that the business will earn on new capital investments.

▶ It's not enough that a company *can* increase its dividend. You should also consider whether or not the company's management actually *will*.

What's the Return?

THE DIVIDEND DRILL is a three-step process. In the first two steps, the questions "Is it safe?" and "Will it grow?" combine to provide an estimate of a stock's future total return. But this estimate alone won't give us a thumbs-up or thumbs-down on a particular stock. We need a standard against which to measure if a given return estimate is high enough to warrant an investment.

I'd like to provide a surefire answer to what is enough, but this is largely in the eye of the beholder. Anyone will agree with the premise that riskier stocks should offer higher prospective returns, but quantifying risk is even harder than estimating returns.

For example, Consolidated Edison (ED)—whose dividend record I noted in Chapter 2—has many thousands of shareholders who must be satisfied with their investment. The yield of 4.5 percent is comparable to what you'd find from a money market fund, and the dividend is growing, albeit at a paltry 1 percent annual rate. Some folks would be willing to settle for a total return like that, but I would demand more, much more—at least 9 percent.

While dividend prospects can't tell us whether a stock is worth owning, they can—with the help of a broader perspective on the risks and rewards of owning stocks in general—provide us with some guidelines. In this chapter I offer:

▶ A framework for looking at investment risk.
▶ Suggested return thresholds for stocks based on yield.
▶ A way to value a stock using the DDRM.

The Standard Approach to Risk

Risk. Everywhere you look in the stock market, you're guaranteed to find at least some of it. But do you know what it is?

The most common way to measure a stock's risk is to measure the volatility of its market price relative to the stock market as a whole. Yet these statistical formulas suffer from a number of shortcomings, most notably their focus on a stock's past performance, even though real-world investors are naturally interested in the future. When people still thought of Enron as a natural-gas pipeline operator in 1996, the look back over the preceding five years might have suggested the stock was a conservative pick. By the end of the next five years, Enron was bankrupt.

The biggest problem with this view is the idea that volatility is the same as risk; it's not. Real-world risk is the chance that an investor might one day be forced to sell shares after earning poor returns or losses. This risk can be a function of paying too much for a stock (accepting a prospective total return that is too low) or actual business performance that falls far short of expected results. Volatility is just a measure of how much the stock price flops around from day to day. Volatility is perhaps a good proxy for risk among investors who trade every day, but for long-term investors, it isn't up to the job.

The Dividend Approach to Risk

I look at risk through the same prism I use to evaluate a stock—its dividend stream. A strong, well-funded dividend payment that rises over time forms the basis for an investment that should provide a decent return with only a modest probability of long-term loss. A shaky dividend stream suggests the opposite—subpar returns and a significant chance of loss.

The top risk I associate with a stock is the chance that its dividend might be cut or eliminated. This is of particular concern for stocks with yields of 6 percent and up, where payout ratios tend to be high and the current dividend is likely to provide half or more of future returns. Mortgage REIT Annaly Mortgage Management (NLY) sliced its quarterly dividend in multiple steps from $0.68 a share in December 2002 to a dime in December 2005. Not only did shareholders lose 85 percent of their dividend income, but the stock fell from more than $20 to less than $12. Volatility aside, that's an example of risk that anyone can appreciate.

Lower-yielding stocks are less susceptible to dividend cuts, but a nearly equally insidious risk applies—weak dividend growth or none at all. Eastman Chemical (EMN), which manufactures plastic bottles, among other things, might have appeared to provide a decent return prospect at the end of 1996 at a price of $55.25 a share. The economy was healthy, demand for plastic bottles was growing rapidly, and Eastman offered a dividend of $1.76 annually for a yield of 3.2 percent. But in the next 10 years—a full decade, folks—Eastman's dividend rate did not budge. By the end of 2006, the stock had risen just 7.3 percent, to $59.31 a share. (See Figure 8.1.)

Total return over this stretch: just 3.5 percent per year, almost all provided by dividends. In those 10 years, the S&P 500 returned more than 8 percent

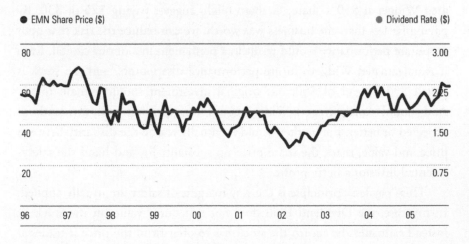

Figure 8.1   Eastman Chemical (EMN): Share Price and Dividend History

a year on average, even with a big bear market thrown in. Eastman just barely kept pace with inflation, which ticked along at 2.5 percent annually. Downside to dividend growth is clearly a threat to returns as well.

Good, solid research restricted to moat-protected businesses (which Eastman and Annaly were definitely not) can help minimize the chances of subpar investment results, but we have another tool at our disposal: a principle known as a margin of safety.

Margins of Safety

I first mentioned the concept of a safety margin in Chapter 6 when discussing dividend safety and payout ratios. In most cases, I don't want to see a dividend taking up 100 percent of current earnings; I wanted some room for earnings to fall short without threatening my income. This same concept—room for error—can be applied much more broadly. After all, no matter how much time, diligence, information, and effort the investor brings to bear on a set of stocks, he is going to make mistakes. Reality does not play out according to anyone's script, and I've certainly made my share of bad calls.

The basic margin of safety principle is to pay less for a stock than it is worth. Benjamin Graham, the father of value investing, coined this invaluable insight in his books *Security Analysis* (1934) and *The Intelligent Investor* (1949). If we could reasonably value the assets and prospects of Amalgamated Widget at $50 a share, Graham might suggest paying $25 or $30. By paying far less than the business was worth, we can reduce the risk that poor corporate performance would result in a permanent loss of our capital. Even if Amalgamated Widget's future performance disappoints, and the stock is worth $35 instead of $50, our original investment should remain intact. And should Amalgamated Widget churn out earnings and dividends as expected or better, the market would eventually realize the disparity between price and value, mark the share price up substantially, and hand the safety-oriented investor a hefty profit.

This "pay less" principle is the way margins of safety are usually applied. In my case, the Dividend Drill does not spit out a value on the stock; it instead estimates the return the stock has to offer from the price it trades at today. For our purposes, a margin of safety isn't a matter of price versus value.

Instead, *we should require a higher total return from the stocks we buy than we might settle for otherwise.*

Requiring an Adequate Return

A good place to start is to begin with the return potential for the market as a whole. On the basis of the numbers I crunched in Chapter 5, a total return of 7 to 9 percent annually is about all we can expect. For someone prepared to accept an 8 percent return and exert no additional effort to earn it, the best option might be a low-cost mutual fund that tracks the S&P 500 Index. Regarding this, I have two observations:

1. This simple strategy, however respectable if used over a long period, isn't going to generate much income. Most of the return will come in the form of lumpy and unpredictable capital gains. If someone needs only $30,000 a year worth of income and happens to have $1.5 million to invest, fine. For someone with savings of $500,000 looking for the same income, this indexing strategy isn't going to cut it.
2. While the return for the market might average 8 percent, some stocks will do better and some will do worse. Some will turn out to be the Microsofts (MSFT) and Amgens (AMGN) of the future, generating high-double-digit returns year after year. Other companies will be like General Motors (GM), slowly declining by providing dismal returns over long stretches of time. A small handful will be the WorldComs and Enrons of tomorrow, creating massive losses.

When we take up the task of selecting individual stocks, we can hope to craft a portfolio of conservative, stable, predictable stocks that stand to beat the 8 percent bogy with larger quantities of income. Research—using the first two steps of the Dividend Drill—will get us most of the way there. The final step is establishing an appropriate margin of safety—and here again, dividends will be our guide.

In theory—and more often than not, in practice—there is a trade-off between dividend yield and dividend growth. The typical stock with a 2 percent yield might be paid by a company retaining 60 or 70 percent of its earnings for reinvestment and growth. Another stock that offers an 8 percent yield might be paying out all or nearly all of its earnings, providing little or no prospect for dividend growth.

In the context of an 8 percent total return from the market overall, we find the dividend yields and dividend growth prospects of individual stocks in the market moving in opposite directions. All else being equal, at least for the purposes of this illustration, this trade-off looks like Figure 8.2.

In this highly simplified example, we find that the market's 1 percent yielders are pricing in growth rates of 7 percent in perpetuity. At the other end of the yield spectrum, the market judges the dividend of a stock yielding 10 percent to be at risk and likely to shrink over time.

Whatever combination might make up that 8 percent total return, it's not enough. Were we buying an index fund, the variations among individual stock returns within the index (some higher than average, some lower) would cancel out, more or less. But looking at any individual company, there's no averaging to make up for flawed analysis or subsequent disappointments. Ah, but if we increase our return requirement to a figure greater than 8 percent, we will have some room for error as different scenarios play out:

▶ We might project an above-average 10 percent return from a given stock and wind up with only 8 percent, but that margin of safety of 2 percent-age points enabled us to still earn an average return.

Dividend Yield (%)	+	Dividend Growth (%)	=	Market Return (%)
1		7		8
2		6		8
3		5		8
4		4		8
5		3		8
6		2		8
7		1		8
8		0		8
9		−1		8
10		−2		8

Figure 8.2   Total Return Trade-Offs

▶ Were we to have settled for an 8 percent return initially and the business came in at 6 percent, we've fallen behind.

▶ If we project 10 percent and get 10 percent, not only was our investment safer and more prudent at the outset, but we are rewarded with an above-average return.

So how much additional return should we require to obtain an adequate margin of safety? Let's head back to the yield/growth trade-off shown in Figure 8.2.

▶ At one end of the spectrum, we find stocks with 1 percent yields needing to deliver annual dividend growth of 7 percent into the indefinite future to make for a worthwhile investment. But with our total return relying overwhelmingly on this uncertain growth figure, the 1 percent yielder might not be able to increase its dividend as fast as we need it to.

▶ At the other end, with stocks yielding 10 percent, this approach suggests that the market expects the dividend to drop over time. Though not every stock yielding 10 percent at 2007 prices faces heavy risks of dividend cutbacks, investors—voting with their buy and sell orders—are implying that could well be the case.

▶ In the middle—the yields between 4 percent and 7 percent—I find the sweet spot. Given an 8 percent return prospect for stocks overall, the idea of getting at least half of that return in the form of dividend income is quite attractive. As we move toward 7 percent, our growth potential drops to 1 percent, but we stand to get 88 percent of our total return on the more reliable terms of steady dividend income.

With these observations in mind, I add a varying margin of safety to my projected market return of 8 percent based on the stock's initial yield. This provides us with the minimum return we should require from each and every stock we buy: the *hurdle rate*. (See Figure 8.3.)

In the 4 to 7 percent sweet spot for yields, I'd be willing to settle for an extra percentage point of prospective return for 9 percent overall. Why just one percentage point?

Dividend Yield	+	Dividend Growth	=	Total Return	+	Margin of Safety	=	**Hurdle Return**	Memo: Implied Dividend Growth
1		7		8		4		**12**	11
2		6		8		3		**11**	9
3		5		8		2		**10**	7
4		4		8		1		**9**	5
5		3		8		1		**9**	4
6		2		8		1		**9**	3
7		1		8		1		**9**	2
8		0		8		2		**10**	2
9		−1		8		3		**11**	2
10		−2		8		4		**12**	2

Figure 8.3   Market Return + Margin of Safety = Hurdle Rate

▶ In addition to adding a margin of safety, I think an investor who takes on the work required to select and evaluate individual stocks (or pays someone else to do so) is entitled to expect more than the 8 percent the market hands out.

▶ In general, these 4 to 7 percent yielders provide enough current income to mute the short-term relevance of market prices, but they don't have yields so high that dividend safety is likely to be the dominant issue.

▶ A one-percentage-point differential may look small, but the difference between an 8 percent return and 9 percent adds up over time. A $1,000 investment compounded over 20 years at 8 percent produces an ending value of $4,661. At a 9 percent annual return, that investment is worth $5,604, a sum 20 percent larger.

At the extremes—very low yields and very high yields—I might want as much as 4 percent more on an annual basis to justify an investment. Rapid dividend growth is less certain than modest rates, and lofty yields are almost always less secure than lower ones, so a higher hurdle rate for investment is generally appropriate.

Also note that these hurdle rates force all stocks, even high-yielding ones, to provide a dividend growth rate of at least 2 percent. Why would I want to buy a stock whose dividend can't grow at least as fast as inflation, where the purchasing power of my income is shrinking over time? And not only does this requirement compensate us for inflation, it also forces us to seek growth—and as I observed at the end of Chapter 6, a growing dividend is much more likely to be a safe one.

Hurdle Rates in Action

In Chapter 7, I ran DDRM total return projections for three stocks: Hershey (HSY), Bemis (BMS), and Great Plains Energy (GXP).

▶ I estimated a 9.4 percent total return prospect from Hershey, composed of a 2.1 percent current yield and 7.3 percent dividend growth potential. This low yield implies I should hold out for an 11 percent total return; unless I'm significantly underestimating Hershey's core growth potential (the ROE of 68 percent almost certainly isn't an understatement!), I'm not likely to be satisfied with an investment in Hershey on the basis of its dividend prospects.

▶ For Bemis, a yield of 2.5 percent implies a hurdle rate somewhere between 10 percent and 11 percent. I like the company, so I may go ahead and buy, but not before I consider other, potentially higher-returning opportunities for my capital first (more on this approach in Chapter 10).

▶ Even if I set aside my doubts that Great Plains Energy will raise its dividend at all in the next couple of years, the indicated total return of 8.6 percent isn't enough to clear my hurdle. I'd be willing to settle for less from Great Plains than I would from the lower-yielding Bemis—the hurdle rate is just 9 percent—but Great Plains doesn't appear likely to top this even if regular dividend increases were already under way.

I have to confess the obvious: my hurdle rates are somewhat arbitrary. There's a solid, logical process behind them: I figure the market in general can return 8 percent; I have to require a margin of safety in addition to that figure; and that margin of safety should be greater if I'm relying on either a high (and therefore unpredictable) dividend growth rate or a very high (and possibly unsafe) dividend yield. But you may look at my hurdle rates and decide they are too high or too low, so feel free to set your own. The more important lesson I mean to convey is this: Whatever hurdle rate you use, make sure you use one!

Valuing a Stock with the DDRM

While the Dividend Drill Return Model's main output is a total return forecast, we can use the dividend growth it estimates, the stock's dividend rate, and our hurdle return to calculate the maximum price we would be willing to pay.

This exercise calls back to the Gordon Growth Model that I described in Chapter 2. The Gordon Growth Model doesn't work particularly well for companies with low dividend yields (less than 2 percent), high dividend growth rates (greater than 7 percent), or firms with a wide range of potential growth rates. But for mature businesses with safe, decent yields and predictable growth, this formula can work very well indeed.

Let's turn to Piedmont Natural Gas (PNY), a stock I would love to recommend and own. This firm has to rank among the best-managed and best-positioned utilities in the country. Piedmont has paid dividends every year since 1956 without a single reduction, and not since 1978 has it failed to pay a higher per-share dividend than the year before. (See Figure 8.4.)

Over the past five years, shareholders' paychecks have risen an average of 4.5 percent annually. Piedmont's record is so steady that running the DDRM hardly seems necessary, but I'll do so anyway, using the following inputs:

▶ *Share price*: $25.
▶ *Dividend rate*: $1.00 a share.
▶ *Earnings per share*: Wall Street expects $1.45 a share for fiscal 2007.
▶ *Core growth*: 6 percent annually. This is quite high for a utility, but Piedmont's operations in southeastern states have pretty good demographic characteristics. Better yet, the company has been a steady and capable acquirer of smaller natural-gas utilities in the region. This 6 percent is more or less comparable to the growth of Piedmont's net income over the past decade.
▶ *Return on equity*: 11 percent, equal to what Piedmont earned in 2006. This is a bit lower than the average of the past 10 years, but I figure that ongoing acquisitions (and the goodwill picked up in the process) will probably keep this figure a bit on the low side. (See Figure 8.5.)

Year	Div Rate	Growth %	Price	Yield	Year	Div Rate	Growth %	Price	Yield
1986	0.30	—	5.66	5.30	1999	0.69	6.2	15.06	4.58
1987	0.33	10.0	4.84	6.81	2000	0.73	5.8	19.09	3.82
1988	0.37	12.1	6.09	6.08	2001	0.77	5.5	17.90	4.30
1989	0.40	8.1	7.03	5.69	2002	0.80	3.9	17.68	4.52
1990	0.42	5.0	7.34	5.72	2003	0.83	3.7	21.73	3.82
1991	0.44	4.8	8.34	5.28	2004	0.86	3.6	23.24	3.70
1992	0.46	4.5	9.63	4.78	2005	0.92	7.0	24.16	3.81
1993	0.49	6.5	10.06	4.87	2006	0.96	4.3	26.75	3.59
1994	0.52	6.1	9.44	5.51					
1995	0.55	5.8	11.63	4.73	**Averages**		Div Growth %		Yield
1996	0.58	5.5	11.69	4.96	1986–2006 (20 yrs)			6.0	4.71
1997	0.61	5.2	17.97	3.39	1996–2006 (10 yrs)			5.2	4.01
1998	0.65	6.6	18.00	3.61	2001–2006 (5 yrs)			4.5	3.96

Figure 8.4   Piedmont Natural Gas: Dividend Record

Dividend Rate ($)	1.00		Funding Gap ($)	(0.34)
Divided by: Share Price ($)	25.00		Divided by: Share Price ($)	25.00
Current Yield (%)	**4.0**		**Share Change (%)**	**−1.4**
Core Growth Estimate (%)	**6.0**		Core Growth (%)	6.0
Divided by: Return on Equity (%)	11.0		Plus: Share Change (%)	−1.4
Multiplied by: Earnings per Share ($)	1.45		**Total Dividend Growth (%)**	**4.6**
Cost of Growth ($)	**0.79**		Plus: Dividend Yield (%)	4.0
Earnings per Share ($)	1.45		**Projected Total Return (%)**	**8.6**
Minus: Dividend	(1.00)			
Minus: Cost of Growth ($)	(0.79)			
Funding Gap ($)	**(0.34)**			

Figure 8.5   Piedmont Natural Gas: Dividend Drill Return Model

It turns out that Piedmont's past growth rate of 4.5 percent is almost identical to the 4.6 percent that the DDRM predicts. The overall total return projection of 8.6 percent is not bad, yet it's still a bit shy of my 9 percent hurdle rate for companies with 4 to 5 percent yields.

How can I get 9 percent so this wonderful little utility can meet my standards? On one hand, Piedmont's dividend growth potential could exceed the 4.6 percent pace my DDRM projects. However, I have no sound basis for making that leap of faith at present. (It isn't as if I can manufacture a higher return simply by making aggressive or unrealistic estimates.) But dividend growth is not the only variable here. Piedmont's $1.00 dividend rate may be fixed (at least until the next increase), but the stock's yield changes every time the stock price does. If the price dropped, the yield would rise. And if the yield rose, the projected total return would, too.

How low of a price should I hold out for? What should my hurdle price be? There are two ways to figure this out.

1. One approach would be to fiddle with the stock price input until the DDRM projects a 9 percent total return. (Because the share price influences both the dividend yield and share change terms in the DDRM, this is actually the more accurate way.)
2. The other approach is to draw my dividend growth estimate from the DDRM and let the simpler Gordon Growth Model do the rest of the work. (While not quite as accurate, the difference isn't likely to be significant, and the Gordon Growth Model is both faster and more useful for illustrating the impact of hurdle rates on prices.)

$$\frac{\text{Current Income}}{(\text{Required Return} - \text{Growth Rate})} = \text{Present Value}$$

For Piedmont Natural Gas:

$$\frac{\$1.00}{(9.0\% - 4.6\%)} = \$22.73$$

If I'm going to demand a return of at least 9 percent from Piedmont, I need to hold out for a price of $22.73 a share—about 9 percent below where the stock traded in mid-2007. At $22.73, Piedmont's dividend yield would be 4.4 percent. With 4.6 percent growth, this makes a total return just high enough to clear my 9 percent hurdle—in other words, $22.73 is my hurdle price. (Yet again, we see that key investment principle at work: As price falls, future return potential rises.)

If I opt instead to fiddle with the stock price in the DDRM, my spreadsheet's "goal seek" function tells me to hold out for $22.25. The stock's yield would be a bit higher (4.5 percent), but dividend growth falls slightly (from 4.6 percent to 4.5 percent) as a lower stock price suggests Piedmont will have to issue more shares to fund its growth. While the gap between this $22.25 and the Gordon Growth Model's $22.73 is negligible, the roughly 10 percent gap between these hurdle prices and Piedmont's current level of $25 seems to me large enough to merit holding out. Whatever Piedmont's future dividend growth turns out to be, the more I pay for the shares today, the less I'll earn in the future.

As much as I would like to participate in Piedmont's steady returns, I'm going to wait. Looking at Piedmont's 52-week price range, I find that $25 is already pretty close to its low for the year, and it hasn't seen a price with a $22 handle since late 2005. If I'm lucky, I may find Piedmont meeting my price requirements one day. If it doesn't, well, there are other stocks on the market that should be able to.

You might be willing to settle for a bit less from Piedmont or any other stock than I would. But remember: The more you pay for a stock, the less you stand to earn—and the greater the probability that its future returns will fall short of your expectations.

Final Reality Check: Yield History

Before you push that "buy" button, there's one more reference you may want to consult: the stock's past yield. My hurdle rates are defined in terms of absolute returns, and these are returns I'm willing to be very patient to collect in cash. That doesn't mean that other investors will be so patient.

The best example I can think of is one all too familiar to millions of investors: General Electric (GE). Historically, GE offered a dividend yield in the 2 to 4 percent range with an excellent (and generally stable) history of handsome dividend growth, double digits in most years. But in the late 1990s—as with so many other stocks—the market price got way ahead of GE's dividend potential. The stock's yield plunged to a low under 1 percent in late 2000. (See Figure 8.6.)

Someone looking at GE at its peak price in 2000 might have been able to justify the 1 percent yield by counting on many more years of 10 to 15 percent dividend growth ahead. But this simply wasn't realistic—GE was and is already one of the largest companies on earth. GE might be capable of

Figure 8.6　General Electric (GE): Historical Dividend Yield and Growth

delivering 8 to 10 percent dividend growth in the future, but at a 1 percent yield, there was no way GE was worth buying for its dividend stream.

The ultralow yield was a very clear warning sign: The stock price was way too high. This irrational exuberance couldn't have come at a worse time; GE's dividend growth rate would soon drop to 5 percent for 2002 and 2003 before recovering. The stock price naturally got crushed, and seven years later, it remains well below the 2000 high.

I don't hold the opinion that past ranges for yields necessarily provide good buy and sell signals. If a firm's dividend growth rate is accelerating, paying a price that carries a yield at the low of past ranges might make sense. Meanwhile, a historically high yield for a stock whose dividend isn't growing—or may actually be at risk—may be flashing a sell signal, not a buy. Taken in isolation, an evaluation of past yields alone will lack the forward-looking view provided by DDRM return projections.

Instead, I use a stock's yield history as a framework for considering where my analysis might be wrong. There are all kinds of factors one could cite to justify a marked-up stock price and rock-bottom yield: a drop in interest rates, a rosy reassessment of risk, maybe just sheer price momentum. Looking back from mid-2007, this has been the case for utilities and, at least until very recently, real estate investment trusts. But a yield that is low by historical standards forces you to ask some useful questions.

▶ *Have dividend growth prospects changed materially for the better?* Between 1996 and 2004, AmeriGas Partners' average yield was nearly 10 percent, and never less than 7.4 percent. When the distribution wasn't growing, these yields reflected an entirely rational assessment by the market. But once AmeriGas started to raise its distribution, a double-digit yield was no longer necessary for investors to earn a double-digit total return. (See Figure 8.7.)

▶ *Were past yields clearly too high for subsequent dividend growth potential?* In hindsight, this was the case for Realty Income (O), Vornado Realty Trust (VNO), and many other blue-chip REITs in the late 1990s. But this observation doesn't apply to most regulated utilities, whose potential for dividend growth have scarcely changed.

By contrast, a historically high yield prompts similar questions:

▶ *Has the dividend become unsafe?* ConAgra's (CAG) market price clearly signaled a dividend cut well in advance. Even though its yield was only 5 percent—not exactly what you'd call a sucker yield—this was easily the highest yield on ConAgra shares in the previous 20 years. ConAgra's yield came back down, of course: right after the dividend was cut by a third.

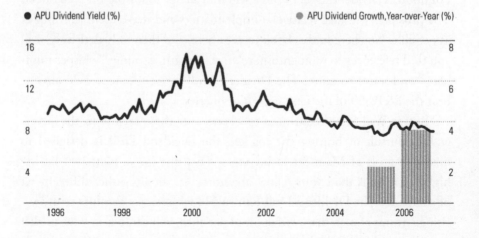

Figure 8.7   AmeriGas Partners (APU): Historical Distribution Yield and Growth

▶ *Is dividend growth over?* Even if the dividend remains safe, investors should naturally require an extra-high yield if growth has come to a halt. Ditto for a material drop in future growth prospects.

Stuffing the "Too Tough" File

Don't be afraid to look at a stock, do your homework, make the best estimates you can, and then give up. One of the critical factors for investment success is to *know what you own.* If you can't really figure out how the company makes money, how it grows, and how it might change over time, don't buy it. Warren Buffett and his partner Charlie Munger have passed on all kinds of potential opportunities because the businesses were too complicated, or there were factors at work they couldn't quite comprehend or project. I'm sure at other times they found businesses that they would have loved to own at a lower price, but the stock was never cheap enough to meet their standards.

There are plenty of other investments out there. The easiest decision you can make is to choose *not* to buy something you don't already own. Make the most of these easy calls! Having a "too tough" file that overflows out onto the floor can only improve your investment results.

What's *Your* Return?

I doubt this Dividend Drill of mine will find a large following on Wall Street. The pros prefer to take relatively simple matters and make them as complex as possible. Nowhere in this book (except here, and then only derisively) will you find references to momentum, relative strength, earnings "whisper numbers," and sector rotation. The Dividend Drill is not meant to help anyone beat the S&P 500 in the next month or quarter.

But as Wall Street continues to obsess over these factors in the never-ending pursuit of beating the market, the Dividend Drill is designed to meet the goals of Main Street investors. This isn't just a matter of having higher standards than your fellow investors—it's an altogether different set of standards. The Dividend Drill Return Model forecasts absolute returns—rising streams of cash that, with a bit of patience, you can put in your pocket regardless of Mr. Market's mood swings.

DividendInvestor Case Study: Total Return

The "What's the return?" question should never be about which stocks are merely good _enough_, but rather which are good in an absolute sense as well as compared to what other stocks stand to provide.

When I recommended Cleveland-based National City (NCC) in January 2005, its yield of 3.8 percent was rather high by bank standards. (As I write this, a 3.8 percent yield is actually below average for a bank of this size.) The bank's history of decent ROEs in a tough area of the country made its shares appear underappreciated and underpriced, yet its dividend had grown at only a 4.9 percent annual clip over the previous five years. Mortgage profits were dropping, and the bank's basic footprint—concentrated in the slow-growing, cyclical Rust Belt—did not bode well for the future. Drawing from dividend growth rates of the more distant past, I went out on a limb and projected faster dividend growth in the years ahead, of 8 percent rather than 5 percent. But even if the dividend only grew at 5 percent, an indicated total return of 8.8 percent sure seemed to beat holding on to money market funds that, at the time, paid only about 1 percent.

As I came to learn the hard way, a low return on cash is a rotten reason to buy a stock, much less a perennial also-ran like National City. Admittedly, I bought the stock a few months before I developed the Dividend Drill Return Model, much less my explicit hurdle rates for the _DividendInvestor's_ Dividend Portfolio. By mid-2005, I understood the banking industry better, and what had seemed at first to be respectable performance now seemed shabby by comparison. Yet even then—with every indication that National City's return profile was mediocre and likely to stay that way—I didn't sell the shares until January 2007. Sure, the dividend continued to grow, but, as shown in Figure 8.8, the growth rate dropped each year: 5.7 percent in 2005, 5.4 percent in 2006, and 5.1 percent in 2007 (the last increase took place after I sold).

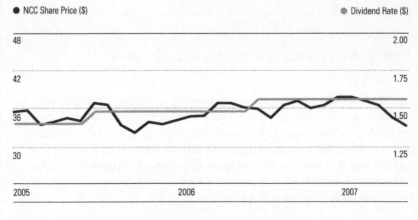

Figure 8.8   National City (NCC): Recent Share Price and Dividend History

(continued)

DividendInvestor Case Study: Total return *(continued)*

By the time I sold, the bank industry's average dividend yield was a lot higher, so National City's middling dividend growth had created no real market value. My selling price of $37 a share was virtually identical to the average of $36.34 I'd paid two years earlier.

Now contrast this with my (first) purchase of Realty Income in July 2006. Rather than making a good enough investment from a point of weakness (that is, with cash burning a hole in my pocket), I watched Realty Income for 19 months before its price came down to a level I was willing to pay. When I bought around $22, Realty Income yielded 6.4 percent. Furthermore, I was highly confident that the company would build on its five-year average dividend growth rate of 4.5 percent—I didn't need to hope for improvement, I could rely on the existing trend. I could have bought sooner at higher prices, but I'd held out for a nearly 11 percent indicated return. And the company itself did not disappoint: a year after I bought, Realty Income's dividend had grown 8.7 percent. (See Figure 8.9.) Growth had accelerated when I didn't need it to, where National City's growth fell shy of my return requirements.

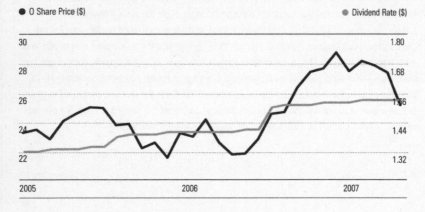

Figure 8.9   Reality Income (O): Recent Share Price and Dividend History

National City had been striving mightily for mere mediocrity, while Realty Income was (and is) absolutely at the top of its game. But what really separated these two were their easily ascertainable total return prospects. Even though I initially thought National City was a solid bank, the indicated total return should at least have prompted me to hold out for a lower price and higher yield. If anything, I ought to have been willing to settle for an even lower (say, 9 or 10 percent) return from so steady a dividend payer as Realty Income, but because I held out for more, I've earned much higher returns as a result.

Chapter 8: Rules and Plays

▶ Require a margin of safety for your purchases by requiring a forward-looking total return prospect higher than you might be willing to accept if the future was certain.

▶ Stocks whose yields are either low (less than 4 percent) or high (greater than 7 percent) should require higher margins of safety than reliable stocks with reliable 4 to 7 percent yields.

▶ If a stock's total return prospect is unattractive, or attractive but subject to a wide range of error, seek alternative opportunities elsewhere.

Independence

I HAVE GREAT NEWS FOR YOU! Wall Street continues to ignore the role of dividend income, much less dividend growth, in long-term total returns. Patiently collecting a yield of 3 percent or 5 percent hardly sounds like a winning strategy when any individual stock can go up or down that much in a single day. Sometimes dividends will be in vogue; between 2003 and 2006, higher-yielding segments of the market like utilities and real estate investment trusts boomed. But were institutional buyers really in these stocks for their yields? Perhaps at first, but after the first year or two, their capital gains were built primarily on price momentum, not income and income growth.

This oversight of dividends creates opportunity.

▶ Even if it pales in comparison with the short-run fluctuations of stock prices, collecting a 3 percent or 5 percent yield puts between one third and one half of an average year's return from stocks in the investor's pocket.

Over any longer stretch of time, total returns from the market at large converge toward the average. To the extent the dividend seeker obtains a large share of that total return through dividends, his returns will be less volatile and probably no smaller than the market at large.

▶ Because of this, stocks with above-average yields are less likely to be grossly mispriced (either over or under) than their low- or no-yield peers. A stock with a secure $1 dividend may fall from $30 to $25 after an unexpectedly bad earnings report, but it's not going to $5. Long before that, we dividend seekers will swoop in and buy the stock just for the steady income.

▶ Dividends provide better signals to investors than short-run profit reports or economic indicators do. When a company's earnings fall but the board still raises the dividend, that act expresses confidence in future results—confidence that is payable in cash.

But dividends provide more than income, and more than insight. Dividends give the investor independence, a very rare state on Wall Street.

The Wall Street Way

I see only two ways for an investor to generate superior results: One must have access to either superior information or superior insight.

What about superior information? If you've got it, you might be able to make a lot of money. Should you share an elevator ride with the CEO of BigMouth, Inc., and overhear his plans to take the company private at a large premium to the current stock price, you might be able to make a 25 percent or 50 percent profit overnight. This extreme example presents certain drawbacks, such as the possibility of jail time.

Knowledge doesn't need to be inside information to provide a shot at superior returns. Small, publicly traded companies are required to make the same comprehensive SEC disclosures that huge ones do, and what they say about themselves in routine filings may go overlooked by other investors (or at least until such matters affect quarterly earnings directly). Other times, you might learn about a company's prospects from sources completely unrelated to the stock market. It isn't inside information to chat up a retail clerk and discover that sales at that store are soaring; to the extent that it might be part of a larger trend unanticipated by the market price, a healthy pop could be in the offing.

As a rule, however, few companies can do or say much without the news being quickly and widely disseminated through the marketplace. For one thing, the SEC's Regulation FD forces publicly traded firms to make material information available to all market participants at the same time, via press release, conference call, or SEC filing. For another, the edge that fresh information can provide is so great, and the competition for an edge so severe, that the market's gunslingers will move the stock price before ordinary investors have a chance to react. Only by looking at tiny firms—those with market values of $100 million or less—is an ordinary individual investor likely to stumble across information she can truly call her own. (There aren't many dividend payers down there, by the way.) I won't say that this can't be achieved, but I will say that as a strategy, acquiring and acting on superior information is very difficult.

Yet this focus on short-term information flows is the basic modus operandi on Wall Street—never mind that short-term results that are exceedingly difficult to predict, let alone capitalize upon. When General Electric (GE) reports quarterly results, earnings per share of $0.43 when the Street is looking for $0.41 or $0.42 might prompt a 3 percent or 4 percent one-day gain in the share price. With hundreds of analysts attempting to forecast GE's earnings, these folks still can't always nail the number. Only in spreadsheet forecasts do revenue, earnings, and cash flow follow predictable patterns. Within a certain range of error—and it's wider than people seem to think—the difference between $0.43 and $0.41 is random.

The tragedy for those spending so much time on next quarter's or next year's earnings is that they will miss the big picture. In five years, GE's stock price will be a function of earnings and dividends five years out; quarterly variations will cancel out. GE's dividend has risen at an 8 percent annual pace for more than 50 years; I'm willing to bet that it will continue to rise at a similar rate even as earnings growth wiggles above and below the trend. If anything, longer-term performance for well-established firms is easier to forecast than short-term developments.

It turns out that the big money on Wall Street doesn't have all the advantages you might imagine. Overwhelmingly compensated based on short-term performance, these men and women have to beat the index day after day, month after month, or they're out on the pavement. Mr. Market wields a terrible sword over their heads; as they attempt to master his next move, they become slaves to his every whim.

A more workable alternative to seeking superior information is to develop superior insight. Are you focusing on data that move markets from minute to minute, or do you pick and choose the information that is relevant to long-term dividend safety and dividend growth? Does bad news or a one-day drop of 5 percent force you to dump at a loss, or do you step back and calmly assess the new information? Are you in stocks for instant gratification or long-term total return?

Can you think, act, and meet your goals independent of the market? With dividends, I'll bet you can.

Stepping toward Independence

As an individual investor, what difference does it make whether you beat the S&P 500 this year? After all, you have no one to report to but yourself and possibly your spouse. If the index rose 16 percent last year and your portfolio gained only 11 percent, you're not going to fire yourself; you have nothing to be ashamed of! You're not one penny poorer than you were before checking the S&P. Unlike your suspender-clad competitors on Wall Street, Beacon Street, or LaSalle Street, you're free: free to pursue returns independent of short-term market trends; free to focus on long-term performance rather than tomorrow's or next week's capital gain; free to keep costs low; free to pay attention to factors—dividend safety and dividend growth—that the market tends to ignore.

Even before we consider the temperamental advantages dividends provide, there are a number of ways to separate yourself from the rest of the marketplace.

Go Long-Term!

By stretching one's time horizon beyond that of the pros, by eschewing any attempt to beat the market over the short term, and by focusing on absolute rather than relative return, any investor—regardless of strategy—can put himself on a better footing than the pros. In a way, I feel sorry for Wall Street's professional investors; except for a handful of true long-term money managers (who follow guidelines much as I've described), these folks are charged with almost impossible tasks. To the extent the professionals' irrational goals lead to irrational stock prices, individual investors can benefit.

Invest, Don't Speculate

According to Benjamin Graham, an investment is an operation that promises adequate income and safety of principal. Anything else is speculation. Amen to that! Even though it's easy to think of stock shares as lottery tickets, a view subtly popularized by those who benefit from rapid trading (brokerage firms), those shares represent very real, tangible ownership in an actual business enterprise. Treating stocks as short-term bets doesn't do right by the companies themselves; they deserve better owners.

Fortunately, nothing stops the long-term investor from viewing himself as a partner in a real business enterprise. The entrepreneurs who own America's successful private businesses (or the overwhelming majority of them, at least) can't be in the game for a profit measured over minutes or months. They don't have a multitrillion-dollar sea of liquidity quoting them an updated price every 10 seconds. Their return consists of income they collect and the business value they can build through profitable growth. A true long-term investor in stocks is in no different a position.

So don't buy a stock—particularly a dividend-paying stock—with the next hour, day, or month in mind. Take high-quality, income-producing stocks off the Street and give them good homes. After all, it is only in hindsight (or on television) that quick rewards from trading are abundant. Trying to guess which stock will hit tomorrow's list of biggest winners is an almost futile exercise, and it's certainly no goal for income investors to dwell upon.

Minimize Trading Costs

With stock trades often offered by brokers at $10 or less, it's easy to imagine stock trading as cheap. This is true for folks who hold their trading activity to a minimum, but for the market overall, cheap trades have not been a plus.

If you doubt me, look at the revenues and profits of Charles Schwab (SCHW) or TD Ameritrade (AMTD), to say nothing of the big investment banks. Though I can't criticize Schwab's slate of offerings (this is where I hold my personal accounts and have received excellent customer service), it isn't as though these brokers have suffered as a result of low commission rates. Discount and full-service brokerages have prospered beyond the wildest dreams of their forebears. Back when commissions were set by the stock exchanges (and often ran to 2 percent or more of a small trade's total value), 10 million shares was a busy day on the New York Stock Exchange. By slicing commissions in the post-1975 deregulated environment, plunging costs created bigger incentives to trade—and boy, has Wall Street ever made it up on the volume. Today, the NYSE handles 2 billion shares on an average day, with 2 billion more on the NASDAQ (the latter barely existed when commissions were fixed).

Commissions aren't the only costs that factor into trading. Among less-liquid stocks, bid-ask spreads can be more expensive than commissions. A 500-unit trade of small-cap Crosstex Energy LP (XTEX), for example, might garner $36.00 for a seller while a buyer pays $36.20, maybe more. The dealer's take in this trade—$100—easily surpasses the $10 in commissions each side of the trade paid its brokerage firm.

The biggest cost of trading often comes in the temptation to trade itself. Cheap commissions encourage exactly the kind of short-term mentality that so often proves fruitless, if not outright damaging to investors' wealth. I can't say that the pre-1975 regime of fixed commissions and limited competition was a good thing. All else being equal, there's nothing to admire about paying $50 or $100 to buy $2,500 worth of stock. However, high commissions at least required investors to carefully consider their moves beforehand. A $10 trade might well be the financial equivalent of a no-fault divorce: Making it easy to get out of a stock diminishes the thought required before getting in. I can't be certain, but I strongly suspect that trading costs are in fact a much bigger drag on investor returns today than they were when per-trade costs were many times higher. Entry and exit barriers are not always bad things.

Mind Your Opportunity Costs

Let's say your portfolio is entirely in money market funds that yield just 4 percent. Perhaps you just retired with a six-figure lump-sum payment, or you rolled over a 401(k) from work into an individual retirement account. Knowing that stocks are the best place to invest, you're looking to dump the money market as fast as possible in favor of individual stocks. After all, stocks return much more, right? Not so fast! When your money is earning only 4 percent, it's easy to let your standards slip.

Don't forget that cash is always worth 100 cents on the dollar—and stocks are not. If you buy the first 20 stocks you look at, chances are you'll be highly disappointed with the results. Even a stock like Consolidated Edison (ED) with a prospective return below 6 percent (as of this writing), might look good enough when the alternative is a 4 percent money market fund, but other stocks will almost certainly outperform both figures.

Dividends: The Ultimate Psychological Advantage

These mental advantages can work for individual investors regardless of their underlying strategy. One might, for example, seek emerging growth stocks in hopes of identifying the next Microsoft (MSFT) or eBay (EBAY). One might also invest in turnarounds, dogs with darling potential. Morningstar's general investment philosophy is essentially agnostic toward income, instead looking to exploit wide differences between market price and business value, wherever and however they may arise.

Still, these attitudes and strategies can be very difficult to deploy in real-world investing activities. The media sure don't help, with big swings in the market reported and hyped almost everywhere you turn. And even if you manage to ignore the hype and hope to focus on real business fundamentals, seeing your account balances rise and fall in a volatile market can test even the most even-minded temperament.

In times of market turbulence, the investor who relies solely on advancing stock prices to justify and validate her picks is sure to come down with headaches, heartburn, or worse. But what dividends provide, and stock prices do not, is an emotional anchor for your investment's value.

You might do all the necessary homework and estimate that the business prospects of Google (GOOG) make the shares worth $600 apiece. If the stock is trading around $500, you've got some upside and even some room for error. You may be exactly right on your $600 estimate of value, but only if and when Mr. Market chooses to agree will you realize your return.

So what happens when Google's revenue growth comes up a couple of percentage points short in the next quarter, and the stock drops to $450?

What happens if the market goes into correction mode and the market price plunges to $400? Google doesn't pay a dividend, so a rising stock price is the only way you can obtain a return on your investment. As it falls, the very fellow you're counting on to prove you right—Mr. Market—is telling you you're wrong. It takes tremendous courage to stare down Mr. Market and hold on to a stock that is moving against you.

Now compare this with a stock whose value and prospects are firmly rooted in dividends, like Genuine Parts (GPC), parent of the NAPA chain of auto parts stores. For such a steady business, it amazes me how hard Mr. Market tried to whipsaw investors. Between early 1998 and late 2000, the market price of Genuine Parts was cut in half, even though the dividend continued to rise every year. (See Figure 9.1.)

To be fair, whoever paid $38 a share for Genuine Parts in March 1998 didn't get a very good deal. The yield of 2.6 percent at the time was too low for the company's subsequent dividend growth, making the shares overvalued in hindsight. When the stock hit bottom in September 2000, a $10,000 investment from March 1998 would have been worth roughly $5,500, even with dividends reinvested.

However, Genuine Parts' yield at the bottom was nearly 6 percent. The stock had gone from being overvalued to deeply undervalued. With no reason to believe the company would cut or halt its payments, the dividend

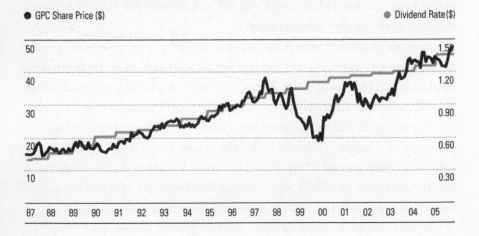

Figure 9.1   Genuine Parts (GPC): Share Price and Dividend History

provided firm evidence that, at the very least, Genuine Parts wasn't going out of business. Without the constant reassurance of quarterly dividend payments, it would have been tough for even the hardiest long-term investor to hang on. But with a dividend that continued to rise, one could at least be assured that Genuine Parts was going to stick around.

These dividends also encouraged a perseverance that eventually resulted in a decent reward. By the end of 2006, that $10,000 investment from March 1998 was worth nearly $17,000 with dividends reinvested—an annualized return of 6.2 percent. Even if a bit disappointing, this still beat the S&P's average return of 4.6 percent over the same stretch. Far more dramatic is the rebound from the bottom: Rather than taking a 45 percent hit, the patient and courageous holder more than tripled the value of her investment from the bottom.

Independence in Action

To take this illustration one step further, the folks who relied on Genuine Parts' dividend for the income it provided were never disappointed at all. The company never failed to pay a dividend on time and never failed to raise it in the manner it always had. There was no reason for shareholders—especially those who had owned the stock for a long time already—to take their cues from Mr. Market. Obtaining this stream of steadily rising income was the purpose, the key indicator of success, and the success itself: all paid in cash.

If this frame of mind can prove useful for holding a single stock, it works even better within the context of an entire portfolio. I manage the two model portfolios in *Morningstar DividendInvestor* solely on the basis of cash flow: How much income are they generating, and how fast is that income stream growing?

What might an approach such as this look like? Look no further than the first of *DividendInvestor's* two model portfolios: the Dividend Builder, designed to deliver a 3 to 5 percent current yield and an 8 to 10 percent annual growth rate in income. (The other, the higher-yielding Dividend Harvest, is described in more detail in Chapter 10.) On June 30, 2007, here is what the portfolio looked like, excluding cash: about $111,500 worth of stock at market prices throwing off $3,720 worth of income annually at present dividend rates. (See Figure 9.2.)

Company/Ticker	Jun-07 Price	Shares Held	Market Value	Div. Rate	Annual Income	Div. Yield	Est'd DivGr	**Est'd Return**
3M Company MMM	86.79	55	4,773.45	1.92	105.60	2.2	9.0	**11.2**
Associated Banc-Corp ASBC	32.70	215	7,030.50	1.24	266.60	3.8	7.5	**11.3**
Bank of America BAC	48.89	200	9,778.00	2.24	448.60	4.6	8.0	**12.6**
BB&T BBT	40.68	200	8,136.00	1.84	368.00	4.5	8.0	**12.5**
Bemis BMS	33.18	150	4,977.00	0.84	126.00	2.5	8.5	**11.0**
Coca-Cola KO	52.31	100	5,231.00	1.36	136.00	2.6	8.0	**10.6**
Compass Minerals CMP	34.66	270	9,358.20	1.28	345.60	3.7	8.0	**11.7**
Crosstex Energy Inc. XTXI	28.73	330	9,480.90	0.88	290.40	3.1	15.0	**18.1**
Diageo PLC ADR DEO	83.31	85	7,081.35	2.45	208.25	2.9	7.5	**10.4**
First Horizon National FHN	39.00	100	3,900.00	1.80	180.00	4.6	8.0	**12.6**
Johnson & Johnson JNJ	61.62	150	9,243.00	1.66	249.00	2.7	10.0	**12.7**
Microsoft MSFT	29.47	165	4,862.55	0.40	66.00	1.4	10.0	**11.4**
Sysco SYY	32.99	130	4,288.70	0.76	98.80	2.3	10.0	**12.3**
United Parcel Service UPS	73.00	100	7,300.00	1.68	168.00	2.3	10.0	**12.3**
US Bancorp USB	32.95	275	9,061.25	1.60	440.00	4.9	8.0	**12.9**
Wells Fargo WFC	35.17	200	7,034.00	1.12	224.00	3.2	8.5	**11.7**
Totals			**111,535.90**		**3,720.25**	**3.3**	**8.9**	**12.2**

Figure 9.2   The Dividend Builder Portfolio as of June 30, 2007

Some folks might look at this portfolio and yawn. A bunch of banks, some big-cap blue chips, a couple of small-caps that few people have heard of. What makes this portfolio special?

Answer: Every single one of these stocks was chosen on the basis of the safety of its dividends and those dividends' long-term growth prospects. I don't buy stocks on the basis of being able to sell at will; if the market were to close for the next five years (a thought experiment I floated back in Chapter 1), I don't think I'd make many changes, if any at all.

What gets me excited is not the chance for short-term gain, even though I believe a number of these stocks are deeply undervalued on the basis of their dividend potential. Instead, I look 5, 10, and 20 years into the future and see an ascending, accumulating, compounding flow of cash. If I do nothing, I'm sure some of these firms' dividend growth will disappoint, while others will grow faster than I expect today. But in the aggregate, this portfolio is designed to build earning power. Its paper value at any point is merely an afterthought.

Assuming I can reinvest the future dividends in this account on equally attractive terms, Figure 9.3 shows the cash flows I project:

This is not magic—except for the magic of dividend yield, dividend growth, and compounding. I'm merely paying attention to what dividends have to say and investing my funds accordingly.

I suppose I could be taking the more conventional view of dividends: a concept I call "deals with a yield." I might buy and recommend stocks whose current yields were decent, but where I really expected a big runup in the price. This would certainly be a more active strategy, swapping stocks with Mr. Market every few months or so in pursuit of capital gains. But why not let the companies themselves do the bulk of the work? Why not sit back and just let the cash roll in? Why not arrange for my portfolio paychecks first and let these stocks' market values take care of themselves?

I don't present the portfolio holdings and projections to make permanent endorsements of these stocks. However well-intentioned these recommendations appear today, I'm sure some of them will prove disappointing, with dividend growth falling short or the dividends themselves falling into jeopardy. Other companies will surprise me on the upside with dividend increases larger than what I presently expect. And new candidates will come along to supplant the old, offering better dividend return prospects than the ones I hold now. But when I trade, I'm not merely exchanging one stock for another as variable stores of value, but rather swapping from a low-return dividend stream into a higher-returning one. At the end of the month, year, or decade, I will evaluate my progress on the basis of the dividends I've collected, how fast they've grown, and how fast I may continue to expect them to rise in the future.

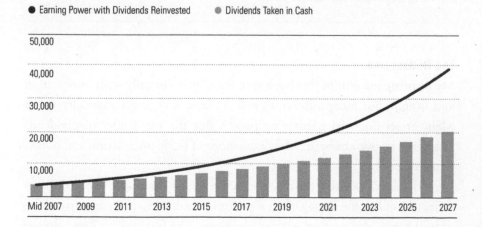

Figure 9.3   Dividend Builder Portfolio: Cash Flow Forecast

But What about Beating the Market?

You may still be wondering: Can this dividend strategy of mine beat the market? Over the short run—and I'd define *short run* as any interval of less than five years, maybe longer—I can only say that I have no idea whatsoever. I do know I'll be collecting a lot of cash, and I know that stream of cash will rise, but I see little point in projecting market values when the moods of Mr. Market are as inscrutable as ever.

Still, I'll grant the basic point: If a low-cost index fund can return 8 percent annually—even if it's not consistent, even if it doesn't include much cash—why bother with dividends?

Let me recall some of the points made earlier in the book. In Chapter 5, I made the case that the stock market in general—as measured by the S&P 500—probably can't return more than 7 to 9 percent on an average annual basis in the future. Building on this observation in Chapter 8, I suggested investing only in those stocks that could meet a hurdle rate of at least 9 percent, and possibly much more for stocks with very low or very high yields. This hurdle return should apply not just to a portfolio as a whole, but to every individual stock within it.

As time passes, some stocks that are selected with the Dividend Drill approach will certainly return less than originally expected—maybe even less than 8 percent. Some others, however, will doubtless return more. Even within a relatively concentrated portfolio, a lot of these hits and misses will average out over time. But if you've set a minimum return that exceeds the market prospect of 8 percent, and your stocks merely perform in line with your expectations, I am quite confident in projecting that, yes, you and I both will beat the market.

The Bottom Line

My ultimate mission in this book is to equip you not only with information and insight, but independence as well. Today's Wall Street mentality serves Main Street financial needs very poorly. But the availability of dividends allows the investor to bypass the fluctuations of fickle price action and obtain returns directly.

If dividends can help the investor hang on to any individual stock through times of trouble, the aggregation of multiple dividend streams in a diversified portfolio provides an even greater advantage. The final act of *The Ultimate*

Dividend Playbook is to assemble a portfolio of well-chosen, dividend-rich stocks that can deliver the income and growth you seek. The process I prescribe for creating a portfolio is all about delivering on the investment goals you set for yourself—rewards independent of the forces afflicting Wall Street in general.

Chapter 9: Rules and Plays

▶ Just because Wall Street pursues short-term capital gains while ignoring dividends doesn't mean you have to. In fact, this irrationality creates opportunities for dividend seekers to earn high returns in cash.

▶ A long-term, low-turnover, value-oriented strategy can help anyone improve his odds of investment success. But only dividends—which provide constant positive feedback even when share prices don't—stand to provide most of us with the psychological fortitude necessary to ride out volatile market environments.

▶ The ultimate state of independence belongs to the investor willing to arrange his portfolio solely on the basis of current and future income while letting market values take care of themselves.

10

Managing a Dividend Portfolio

IF BUILDING A PORTFOLIO seems like a complicated endeavor full of unpalatable trade-offs and fuzzy concepts like diversification, dividends—as in every other way—stand ready to provide invaluable assistance. Dividends are the ultimate tool for matching stocks with their appropriate owners. Do you need 3 percent of your portfolio's value every year for living expenses? Put a portfolio together that generates 3 percent of its value every year in dividends. Need 5 percent? Then go for a mix of stocks that yield 5 percent as a group. No need for cash from your portfolio today, but looking for maximum earning power a decade or two down the road? Then you've got maximum flexibility.

In this chapter, I look at the process of creating a portfolio driven by dividend income and growth. I'll let others attempt to turn portfolio management into rocket science. As I see it, building a portfolio begins with two simple questions—questions that only the investor can answer:

1. How much income do I need from my stocks for living expenses?
2. What are my tax circumstances?

From there, we'll consider how to create an opportunity set, which stocks to buy, and how to manage the portfolio thereafter. The key to all of these concepts is that dividends—not just market prices—are the underlying drivers of all decisions.

I have a real-world example to share. From *Morningstar DividendInvestor's* launch in January 2005 through the end of 2006, its centerpiece was its $100,000 real-money model portfolio. While I might say good or bad things on any number of stocks in any one issue, this portfolio provided a venue for clear buy and sell recommendations, whose subsequent performance was then laid bare for all to see. But one portfolio just wasn't enough; some subscribers were looking for low yields with high growth rates, while others preferred stocks offering much higher current income. That's why, at the end of 2006, we added a second model account—the Dividend Harvest Portfolio—with a mission to obtain the maximum level of current income possible without sacrificing safety or the long-term purchasing power of its income. In the process, I found myself with a fresh $100,000 lump of cash to invest. How I went about setting goals for this account, and the stocks I chose to buy, provides a useful illustration of my portfolio strategy in practice.

Question 1: Target Yield

Your personal need for cash from your investment portfolio should set the minimum yield of your portfolio. As I demonstrated in Chapter 1, attempting to live off fickle capital gains can be hazardous to your wealth. If you need $1,000 a month to supplement other sources of income, design a portfolio that generates at least $1,000 a month in income over the course of a year. If you need $2,000, then go for $2,000. In other words, arrange for your portfolio paycheck first!

Of all the issues involved in building a portfolio, this is the one I'm least able to answer from afar. I can't tell you how much money to live on. What

Number of Choices by Minimum Yield Requirement

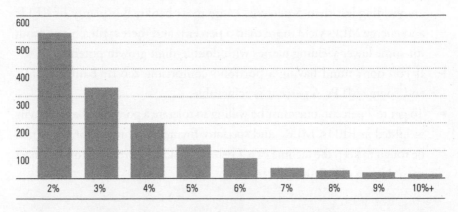

Figure 10.1   Morningstar's Coverage: Dividend-Paying Stocks Sorted by Yield

I can do is describe how much income is available from stocks. Drawing from Morningstar's coverage list of more than 1,900 stocks in mid-2007, Figure 10.1 shows how many choices are available at increasing minimum thresholds for current dividend yield.

It's clear that restricting one's choices to only those stocks yielding 3 percent and up will quickly shrink the number of stocks the investor has to consider. At the extreme—yields of 9 percent and up—very few offer dividends that I would consider safe. Excluding these outliers, however, this is actually a high-quality set of investment opportunities. With dividends signaling durable earnings, financial strength, and shareholder-friendly management teams, this stands to be highly fertile ground.

Now for the big question: What's the highest yield an investor can expect to earn from a reasonably well-diversified portfolio? This, too, is a matter of trade-offs. From where I write today:

▶ An average yield of 4 percent isn't hard to extract from current markets. There are lots of banks, utilities, real estate investment trusts (REITs), and energy master limited partnerships (MLPs) to pick from in this range, and a 4 percent portfolio average is low enough to include some 2 percent and 3 percent yielders from other stocks like Johnson & Johnson (JNJ) that offer much faster dividend growth than their high-yield kin.

▶ Five percent is a bit more of a stretch, but still reasonable. Most utilities are yielding less than 5 percent, as are most banks. But plenty of REITs and energy MLPs yield more than 5 percent, and there's still a bit of room for some lower-yielding names with double-digit growth potential.

▶ If you don't mind having a portfolio comprising mostly banks, REITs, and energy MLPs, 6 percent is achievable.

▶ To get to 7 percent, one must be willing to tolerate a portfolio that is heavily weighted in REITs, MLPs, and specialty financials. Furthermore, it would be tough to keep the income of a 7 percent-yielding portfolio growing faster than the rate of inflation.

Expecting a portfolio of equities to deliver more than a 7 percent average yield—at least from where we stand today—is not a good idea. Up in this rarefied air, the stocks you'd be stuck owning would almost certainly include some whose dividends are likely to be cut at some point, or at the very least offer no prospect of keeping pace with inflation over the long run.

This 7 percent yield limit that I suggest is certain to change as inflation, Treasury yields, and the yields offered by low-quality, high-yield corporate bonds all fluctuate over time. (It's worth noting that these junk bonds are natural competitors for investment dollars that might otherwise flow into stocks, even though the income paid by junk bonds is fixed, while high-yield stock dividends can and do grow over time.)

The concept of a yield limit presents an obvious problem to the investor of limited means. From where I write today, someone who needs $25,000 in annual income from a $250,000 account is extremely unlikely to find safe yields in this range. I'd go so far as to say it is impossible. Rather than court high risks to your future income, it's better to scale down your lifestyle or find another way to supplement your income. Painful and inconvenient as these options are, such choices are preferable to a portfolio that reaches for yield by taking too much risk, or one that sells off stock to fill the gap, diminishing future income in the process.

For the Harvest Portfolio, I considered the range of available yields with acceptable levels of safety and growth and set a target yield range of 6 to 8 percent.

Question 2: Tax Status

All else being equal, there's no reason to pay taxes on income that you don't plan to spend. How this affects your investment choices is a function primarily of where your money is held. While there are many different titles a brokerage account might take, they all fall into two basic categories.

Tax-Deferred Accounts

This catch-all category includes traditional individual retirement accounts, Roth IRAs, 401(k) plans, Keogh plans, and profit-sharing plans. Older folks tend not to have much money in these accounts, since tax-deferred accounts came along too late for most of today's octogenarians to accumulate sizable assets in them. But for those in their 50s and 60s, tax-deferred accounts can easily represent the bulk of their retirement wealth.

These accounts share one key benefit: Investment income—whether dividends, capital gains, interest, or whatever—is not taxed when it is earned. Only when money is withdrawn from the account does the investor owe tax—except for Roth IRA and Roth 401(k) accounts, where even withdrawals are tax-free! This is a huge advantage: They allow the investor to reinvest 100 percent of dividends and capital gains, no tax drag involved. Compounded over decades, this is a huge boon for long-term wealth accumulation. A $10,000 investment returning 10 percent annually will bloom to nearly $1.2 million in 50 years. That same investment, if clipped annually for 15 percent of its returns in taxes (for an after-tax return of 8.5 percent), ends up being worth only half that. Nor does it take 50 years for an appreciable gap to show up: Even after 10 years, a similar tax-paying account would be worth only 87 percent of what a tax-deferred account is.

However, there are several trade-offs involved. For one thing, withdrawals from a tax-deferred account (except Roth accounts) are taxed at higher rates than are dividends and long-term capital gains in a taxable account. Another drag, one that is particularly important for investors seeking maximum yields, is the fact that tax-deferred accounts are effectively prohibited from owning certain types of stocks. Most of these prohibited stocks are master limited partnerships, which are otherwise quite attractive high-yield securities to own. For those seeking 5 to 7 percent yields from a tax-deferred account these days, the inability to buy MLPs creates a diversification problem (more on this later).

If your portfolio is in a tax-deferred account, it doesn't matter how high your target yield is, as long as it exceeds your need for withdrawals. If you prefer higher yields for the greater certainty of a safe yield relative to dividend growth, the extra income can simply be reinvested.

Taxable Accounts

To provide the maximum range of choices, including MLPs, I treat the Harvest Portfolio like a taxable account.

Whatever money isn't in a tax-deferred account is, by definition, taxable. When the investor cashes a dividend check or sells shares at a gain, the government gets part of the profit. For investors who are still in accumulation mode, the obligation to pay taxes on investment income that is reinvested will be a drag. However, this is much less of a problem for investors who are in withdrawal mode. The tax rates on income earned in taxable accounts are generally lower than on withdrawals from tax-deferred accounts. A taxable account also has the flexibility to own anything, including potentially lucrative high-yield MLPs.

Are taxes on reinvested income to be minimized at all costs? Hardly. Taxes should be just one of many factors to consider when buying an individual stock or managing a portfolio. For one thing, the reinvestment of income is a simpler and more reliable path to compounding wealth than the pursuit of capital gains. For another, capital gains are also taxed whenever one sells a stock at a gain.

Yields, Taxes, and Choices

Let's say for the time being that 7 percent is the market's yield limit. Our friend Bernie has $500,000 to invest in stocks, so he could structure his portfolio to provide as much as $35,000 in annual income. As it happens, Bernie only needs $20,000 of income from his stock portfolio after taking Social Security and other sources of income into account.

Naturally this is a wonderful problem to have. Three basic choices come to mind:

1. Bernie could go for the maximum amount of income and boost his lifestyle a notch or two—throw a new Lexus into his spending plans every few years or maybe an annual trip to Europe.
2. If he takes a thriftier route, Bernie could invest for a 7 percent yield target and simply reinvest the extra income, which would add directly to his wealth and future earning power.
3. Bernie also has the luxury of targeting a 4 percent yield for his portfolio and choosing to earn more of his total return through dividend growth.

The first choice is up to Bernie, but if asked to choose between reinvestment and dividend growth, I'd suggest the latter. By tilting his total return goal toward dividend growth, Bernie will probably wind up owning stocks with safer dividends than would otherwise be the case. Furthermore, if his investments are in taxable accounts, a mix of lower yields and faster dividend growth will reduce his annual tax bills.

Building Your Opportunity Set

Before starting to buy stocks for the Harvest, I created a list of about 100 names that yielded at least 5 percent. The more names you look at, and the more businesses you get to know, the better your final selections will probably be.

There are two basic ways you can build an opportunity set like this: Either let the stocks come to you or go looking for them. Letting stocks come to you isn't at all a bad strategy; in fact, I heartily recommend it. Some of my most profitable investments have been those that wafted into my brain unexpectedly—a citation in a book, an article in the *Wall Street Journal* or the *New York Times,* maybe a press release that was linked to a different company I was considering at the time. When one of these random stocks looks promising, even if it's not at all worth buying immediately, I add the ticker symbol to one of my long-term watch lists. Some new development down the road—a baseless drop in price or a big dividend increase—might then prompt me to take a closer look. But while a watch list approach like this can bear a lot of fruit over time, it's hard to populate a portfolio quickly this way.

Another way to have stocks come to you is to pay someone like me to bring worthwhile ideas to your attention. The newsletter I edit, *Morningstar DividendInvestor,* presents new dividend stock ideas every month as well as updates on the two model portfolios I manage—including clear buy and sell recommendations. I also monitor the broader universe of high-yield and high-dividend-growth stocks, commenting on whatever opportunities or perils may arise as markets and business fundamentals evolve. If that's not enough, consider a subscription to Morningstar.com. As of this writing, Morningstar covers nearly 2,000 stocks around the world, more than 1,000 of which pay dividends. (Thus ends my advertisement.)

The other approach is to go looking for stocks—most likely by screening for high yields. I still buy a copy of *Barron's* every so often to go through its thousands of listings by hand. Because they're sorted by alphabetical order, however, I have to look at a lot of names that don't offer meaningful yields before collecting a handful of names worthy of further investigation. Database screens offer instant gratification: I can perform a search for stocks that yield more than 5 percent and shrink a cast of thousands into hundreds or possibly dozens. I might then exclude all firms with no history of raising their dividends, those that inhabit industries I find unattractive, those with excessively high payout ratios, and so on. If you're a subscriber to Morningstar.com, our highly valuable economic moat ratings are easily added to your queries—something I do every time.

Once I had my list of Harvest candidates, I began ranking their dividend safety characteristics and potential return prospects. I had the benefit of years of experience: I understood most of these firms' basic prospects already. Of course, a group of 100 stocks may be too many for you to research thoroughly, so let me suggest three basic organizing tactics for this list.

1. *Ditch the least likely prospects quickly.* To me, low-grade prospects have several attributes in common.
   - ▶ Payout ratios in excess of 100 percent. (This rule, applied with database screening tools, may exclude virtually all high-yield MLPs and REITs. For these firms, you'll have to perform dividend safety analysis by hand.)

▶ A history of variable dividends, which is common among mortgage REITs, Canadian energy trusts, shipping firms, and other firms whose profits tend to come and go.

▶ An obvious lack of an economic moat. This will cut out chemical stocks, auto stocks, and a number of other unreliable dividend-paying prospects.

▶ A lack of past dividend growth that at least matches inflation. (If the business appears attractive anyway, you can always go back and revisit the story later.)

2. *When seeking a certain yield, look for maximum dividend growth.* From the standpoint of an income investor, growth is often a two-for-one deal. Not only does a rising income stream increase a stock's total return prospects, but an underlying cash flow stream that is rising effectively lowers the stock's payout ratio, which in turn suggests a more durable dividend payment.

3. *When seeking a certain rate of growth, look for maximum current yield.* Certain companies—even whose stocks offer similar yields—will be able to increase their dividends faster than their peers. This may be due to a higher return on equity, a higher natural core growth rate, or both. In mid-2007, both National City (NCC) and US Bancorp (USB) were trading with yields around 5 percent. But while National City is probably looking at many more years of 4 to 5 percent dividend growth, US Bancorp should be able to churn out 8 percent annual dividend increases and possibly more. Similarly, both First Potomac Realty Trust (FPO) and Senior Housing Properties Trust (SNH) were yielding in the mid-6 percent range, but while the former is capable (at least by my estimates) of raising its dividend 8 percent annually, Senior Housing's dividend growth is unlikely to exceed 3 to 4 percent. That doesn't make Senior Housing an inferior opportunity in absolute terms, but judged by relative prospects, I'd rather own First Potomac.

After winnowing the weakest candidates from my initial list of 100 or so, I'd shrunk my range of choices to about 25 stocks. From there, I ran my Dividend Drill research process on each. Between the end of December 2006 and June 2007, I invested all of the Harvest's initial $100,000 cash balance into a group of 13 stocks, as shown in Figure 10.2.

What did all of these stocks have in common that the rejects did not? In each case, I was satisfied that their dividends were adequately covered with long-term sustainable earning power. In each case, the prospective dividend returns beat my hurdle returns based on yield (the same hurdles I described in Chapter 8).

On this basis alone, I could probably have bought 20 stocks instead of 13, so I ranked their prospective dividend returns in two ways:

1. *Quantity.* This might go without saying, but I prefer higher indicated returns to lower ones.
2. *Quality.* This is a fuzzier concept, but I'd rather own a class act like Realty Income (O) with an 11 percent dividend return than a me-too retail REIT at 12 percent. Scenario analyses help in this regard (lower-quality and less-reliable firms have wider ranges of potential returns), as does an understanding of the relative attractiveness of the assets of each business. All else being equal—including indicated return—I'd still rather own a

Company/Ticker	Jun-07 Price	Shares Held	Market Value	Div. Rate	Annual Income	Div. Yield	Est'd DivGr	Est'd Return
AmeriGas Partners APU	36.15	250	9,037.50	2.44	610.00	6.7	3.0	**9.7**
Biovail BVF	25.42	300	7,626.00	1.50	450.00	5.9	2.0	**7.9**
Buckeye GP Holdings BGH	33.28	250	8,320.00	0.96	240.00	2.9	8.0	**10.9**
Buckeye Partners BPL	51.32	175	8,981.00	3.20	560.00	6.2	4.0	**10.2**
CapitalSource CSE	24.59	325	7,991.75	2.40	780.00	9.8	4.0	**13.8**
Crosstex Energy LP XTEX	35.31	170	6,002.70	2.24	380.80	6.3	8.0	**14.3**
First Potomac Realty FPO	23.29	400	9,316.00	1.36	544.00	5.8	8.0	**13.8**
Kinder Morgan Energy KMP	55.19	200	11,038.00	3.32	664.00	6.0	6.0	**12.0**
Lloyds TSB Group ADR LYG	44.72	140	6,260.80	2.67	374.41	6.0	6.5	**12.5**
MuniMae LLC MMA	24.38	350	8,533.00	2.07	724.50	8.5	4.0	**12.5**
Realty Income O	25.19	500	12,595.00	1.53	766.50	6.1	4.5	**10.6**
Suburban Propane SPH	47.87	150	7,180.50	2.80	420.00	5.8	3.5	**9.3**
TEPPCO Partners TPP	44.36	145	6,432.20	2.74	397.30	6.2	7.0	**13.2**
Totals			**109,314.45**		**6,911.51**	**6.3**	**5.0**	**11.3**

Figure 10.2   The Dividend Harvest Portfolio as of June 30, 2007 (excludes cash but includes capital appreciation to end of period)

regional bank based in North Carolina (such as BB&T, BBT) than one in Ohio (Fifth Third, FITB)

Finally, in every case but one (which I describe a little later), a steady trend or incentive suggested that my income would indeed rise at the long-term rate I anticipated. The market didn't stand still as I was buying—in fact, the account's value rose nearly 10 percent by the end of June 2007—but I was well pleased with the results: An account that started with $100,000 in cash had been converted into a dividend stream providing nearly $7,000 in annual income that stood to grow at 5 percent annually.

Diversification

Once the account was fully invested, the Harvest Portfolio held seven energy MLPs, two specialty financials (MuniMae, MMA, and CapitalSource, CSE), a high-yield foreign bank (Lloyds TSB Group, LYG), two REITs, and one oddball (Biovail, BVF).

The true disciples of diversification would look at this portfolio—52 percent of its value in energy MLPs?—and laugh. The received wisdom on Wall Street is that more diversification is always better. Owning just 8 or 10 stocks is risky; owning 80 or 100 is much less so, and an index fund that takes a bite of every stock listed in the market is as well diversified as you can get.

But this approach to diversification carries a very real cost. Even professionals can't know the details of 100 stocks through and through, so what chance does the part-time stock picker have at obtaining such a wide breadth of knowledge?

My opinion on the topic mirrors that of Marty Whitman of Third Avenue Funds: "Diversification is only a surrogate, and usually a [expletive deleted] poor surrogate, for knowledge, control, and price consciousness."

Knowledge and price consciousness—that is, investing with a margin of safety—are disciplines available to anyone willing to do his homework. I'd much rather own 10 or even 5 companies I know very well, and which I've bought at objectively attractive prices, than own 500 stocks whose ticker symbols I might not even be able to recall at will.

As for control, it depends on how you view the concept. Granted, it's very hard for the buyer of 100 or 1,000 shares of stock to obtain control of a corporation. Management can completely ignore your suggestions about how the business should allocate capital or fix the problems that crop up. But companies that pay large dividends are in fact ceding control over part of their assets and earnings. You may receive only 2, 4, or 7 percent of your investment's value in cash each year, but once that cash hits your account, you're in control of its future use!

Intelligent diversification also means owning stocks from more than just one industry or area of the economy. A portfolio consisting entirely of stakes in 40 different REITs or 30 different utilities is not diversified; if those industries go south, the common economic forces applying to them will lead to common pressure on dividend safety and growth. But a portfolio with, say, two or three REITs, three or four banks, an MLP or two, and a handful of consumer staples firms might make for an appropriately diversified dividend stream.

My Hope for Biovail

There's no reason to buy a stock just to add diversification. Biovail Corporation International (BVF) is a Canadian specialty pharmaceutical company with a decent business, though growth (getting new drugs approved by the Food and Drug Administration) is much more difficult to estimate. To compensate shareholders for the ups and downs of the new drug research and approval process, management instituted a hefty dividend policy at the end of 2006, giving the stock a yield above 7 percent.

My Dividend Drill analysis suggested that while Biovail's dividend was safe, its growth potential was maybe only 2 percent or thereabouts until a batch of new drugs stood to come to market later in the decade. Until then, I didn't have much confidence that the dividend would actually rise. In hindsight, I can see that the chief appeal of this stock was the fact that it wasn't a financial or energy concern. It was hope, not clear trends or incentives, that formed the basis of my dividend growth expectations. I'm reluctant to sell; the stock is cheap on just about any metric you care to name, and that fat yield remains intact. But under trend/incentive/hope framework for evaluating dividend growth, I'm not sure I would buy Biovail again.

By contrast, the stock with the clearest management incentive for income growth—Buckeye GP Holdings (BGH)—doubled in just the first six months I owned it. When

I bought it for $16.49, it offered a 5 percent yield: this for an enterprise capable of increasing its cash distributions by at least 8 percent annually and probably much faster. This growth potential was almost completely ignored when I bought, but once the word got out, the market quickly repriced the units. Another lesson learned, this time an eminently positive one.

Nevertheless, the higher your target yield, the more difficult it becomes to diversify across even two or three industries. As I mentioned earlier, a 6 or 7 percent yield target these days restricts your range of choices to a relative handful of banks, REITs, and energy MLPs. This places extra emphasis on the need for each individual holding to pass the Dividend Drill's tests for dividend safety. Don't be tempted to reach for additional yield from stocks whose dividends may not be safe.

As for how much of each stock to own within a given yield target, I look to dividend safety rather than indicated dividend returns. I made Realty Income my top holding because I consider its dividend extremely safe. But even within a range of dividends we can reasonably consider safe, some are less safe than others. This is why I spread my capital a bit more thinly at the other end of the spectrum (CapitalSource and Biovail, for instance).

One final suggestion: Buy slowly. Don't feel obliged to put all of your money to work overnight. Holding cash while doing additional research or waiting for better prices naturally leads to better decisions.

What about Risk?

This is a natural concern for all investors: What kind of downside volatility might I encounter with a portfolio of high-yield stocks?

The answer depends on how you're defining risk. If you're concerned solely about short-run changes in market value, I can't promise that dividend-paying stocks won't drop when the market does. Furthermore, high-yielding stocks tend to be sensitive not only to the broad economic forces affecting stock prices in general, but especially to changes in interest rates. If you've crafted a portfolio that pays an average of 6 percent and bond yields start shooting up over a series of days or weeks, don't be surprised if all or almost all of your stocks fall in tandem (and vice versa).

However, if your investment goals revolve around income, the nature of risk changes significantly. The real threat is that one or more of your holdings might subsequently cut their dividend rates, or that your portfolio's income growth fails to keep pace with inflation. A short-term shock to interest rates should not affect the actual quantity of dollars your portfolio is throwing off, as long as you've chosen businesses capable of maintaining their dividends even if their interest expenses increase.

Tracking Your Progress

Most people evaluate success or failure on the basis of changes in the market value of their accounts. In other words, they're looking to Mr. Market to validate their choices and provide their rewards. I prefer a dividend-based approach, even for evaluation purposes. Indeed, I believe it is essential for a dividend portfolio's long-term success. If you sell stocks just because they're down—especially if the drivers of dividend growth haven't changed significantly—you won't be around for the eventual rebound. In the long run, market values will reflect dividend prospects. But even in the short run, dividend metrics—a portfolio's income yield and income growth—provides a much more valuable look at underlying performance than mere market value.

Portfolio yield is a pretty easy metric to track. In a portfolio that isn't receiving new cash on a regular basis or seeing withdrawals in excess of the income it generates, it's simply total dividend income divided by the initial value of your portfolio. A portfolio that begins the year with $400,000 of market value and throws off $20,000 worth of income has generated a 5 percent average yield. (This calculation only becomes more complicated if you're adding more money to the account over the course of the period, or if you make withdrawals in excess of the income the portfolio has thrown off. In that event, you might want to use an average portfolio value for the year in the denominator rather than the initial value.)

Portfolio income growth—specifically the portion we're interested in, which can be traced to dividend increases rather than portfolio buying and selling—can be a little tougher to calculate. My approach, however, is far from opaque.

1. Sum up your annualized portfolio income from the beginning of a period (most likely a calendar year) by multiplying the number of shares you owned by their then-current dividend rates.

2. Subtract the annualized dividend income of the positions you sold during the period. For example, let's say you owned 100 shares of Southern Company (SO) paying a $1.49 per share dividend, for $149 worth of annualized income. If you sell your Southern shares during your evaluation period, subtract this figure from your beginning income run rate.

3. Then add the annualized income of any stocks you bought using the dividend rate at the time of purchase. You might, for example, have swapped your Southern shares out for a stake in AmeriGas Partners (APU). This act increases your income relative to your annualized income after the Southern sale, but it hasn't come from dividend increases—it's merely a swap of one investment for another. (If you happen to buy more shares of a stock you already own, you'll want to count the income of those additional shares separately.)

Adding these three figures will provide a same-stock base of annualized income, similar to the same-store performance metric used by retailers. Finally, sum up the annualized dividend income of your portfolio at the end of the period. Divide this figure (which we hope is higher) into the first figure you toted up—the same-stock income base—and subtract 1. This percentage change is your same-stock dividend growth.

To illustrate these formulas with hard numbers, Figures 10.3 and 10.4 give the amounts for *Morningstar DividendInvestor's* original model portfolio in 2006. My recommendations generated dividend income equal to 4.7 percent of the account's value (excluding cash) at the beginning of the year, and over the course of the year its annualized income stream rose 6.9 percent from dividend increases.

This approach paints a fairly accurate portrait of the underlying return your investments are providing regardless of market prices. As long as you keep trading to a minimum, then your long-term capital appreciation (over three- to five-year measurement periods) ought to tick along at a similar rate.

2006 Dividend Income Received	4,639.65
Market Value of Stocks (12/31/05)	98,926.00
2006 Portfolio Yield (%)	**4.7**

Figure 10.3   Dividend Portfolio: Yield in 2006

Annualized Income (12/31/05)	4,346.53
Less: Income of Stocks Sold	−765.94
Plus: Income of Stocks Purchased	1,255.90
Same-Stock Base Income	**4,836.49**
Annualized Income (12/31/06)	5,172.20
Same-Stock Income Growth Rate (%)	**6.9**

Figure 10.4   Dividend Portfolio: Same-Stock Dividend Growth in 2006

In 2006, the market value of the *Morningstar DividendInvestor* model portfolio actually rose quite a bit faster than its annualized income, producing a total return of 21.9 percent. In 2005, share prices lagged dividend growth; in 2007, the same lag showed up again. I have no idea where the market value of this model portfolio will be one week or even one year hence. But I have a very good idea of how much income it will generate and how fast this income will grow. As its income-generating potential rises, I have little doubt that its market value will as well—but I'll let Mr. Market take care of that.

Monitoring Existing Holdings

I'd love to say that dividend-paying stocks can be bought with the Ronco approach: "Set it and forget it!" But in the real world, business prospects and their impact on dividend safety and growth can and will evolve.

It's a good idea to rerun the Dividend Drill on your existing holdings every so often; unless conditions change radically, once a year should do the trick. Among key factors to monitor in between full reviews:

▶ *Dividend growth.* Is the dividend rising at least as fast as you originally projected? That's obviously a good sign, the kind of performance that can put you at ease. I haven't had to spend much time thinking about *Morningstar DividendInvestor* recommendation Coca-Cola (KO) because its dividend growth is ticking along almost exactly as I anticipated. But when TC Pipelines (TCLP) failed to raise its cash distribution on schedule in 2005 and 2006, a much deeper explanation of the forces at work was required. Growth could be slowing, returns could be falling, management's view toward rewarding shareholders might be changing for the worse. In an extreme case, a severe slowdown or stop in dividend growth may hold more ominous signs for the stability of the dividend itself.

▶ *Payout ratio.* Even if the dividend is rising, if its growth exceeds the growth rate of earnings, the payout ratio will rise, possibly rendering the dividend less secure. At the very least, a rising payout ratio may diminish growth opportunities as fewer dollars are left inside the business to support core growth. There's little point in obsessing over short-term earnings misses relative to Wall Street analyst expectations, but a pattern of such disappointments may indicate diminishing competitive strength or falling core growth rates.

These kinds of checkups aren't required on a daily or monthly basis, but I would suggest you keep a diary of your original dividend growth expectations and any changes to your forecasts over time. If the core growth, return on equity, and earnings per share inputs are deteriorating, you may find better uses for your capital. If these metrics are improving and the share price hasn't yet reacted with a steep markup, you may even want to buy more.

When to Sell, When to Swap

If the decision to buy a stock can be difficult, at least the goal is simple: to latch on to the highest-quality and most rewarding stream of dividends available. Selling is much tougher; the stock price may have changed dramatically (up or down), which messes with your head. It could just be that the market is wrong; then again, you might be wrong. And selling involves not just one but two decisions: you have to figure out what to do with the proceeds.

Yet again, dividends show up in a timely and useful fashion: Let the dividend prospects tell you when to trade.

The most obvious reason to sell is where the dividend safety is deteriorating. To date, I haven't bought a single stock for either *Morningstar Dividend-Investor* model portfolio that has gone on to cut its dividend. The principles behind the question "Is it safe?" have been invaluable in this regard. But at some point, I may make a mistake, or find that the company can't live up to my expectations. When my basic "Is it safe?" analysis starts to suggest one of my holdings' dividends is at risk, I start looking—quickly—for alternative uses of my capital.

Hopefully, you'll take note of a deteriorating situation before the rest of the firm's shareholders and get out. In the real world, this won't always be the case—the stock price might already be down 20 or 30 percent. Should you still sell? Yes, probably. It's very hard to know how low the dividend might go (you rarely see a dividend trimmed by just 5 or 10 percent; 50 percent is closer to normal) or how the market price will react. Better to bail on an uncertain situation, particularly if you can replace your existing income stream by buying another stock with the sale proceeds.

But what if a cut comes as a complete surprise? I haven't had this happen yet—and I hope I never will—but I think I'd go back to square one: Rerun the Dividend Drill with the new, lower dividend rate. If the new dividend rate is still safe, then at least you'll have additional time and perspective to make a rational decision. I've noticed that stock prices sometimes bottom either right before or right after dividend cuts, as was the case for Deluxe Corporation (DLX) in 2006. When the underlying business remains solvent—the dividend cut is just a matter of an unsustainably high payout ratio—the stock price may rebound sharply once your fellow income investors have fled. If it does, and your market value recovers, you'll have a much easier time replacing your original income stream.

Focusing on dividend safety comes in especially handy when the market hits a banana peel and market values drop. Look at your income: Is it still there? Is it still safe? An important key for long-term success is to react to fundamental business developments, not changing market prices alone. Even if this is an emotional exercise more than a financial one, it may well prevent you from dumping otherwise worthy holdings at low prices.

With the exception of these safety sales, all other potential trades can be viewed in context of opportunity costs. Does another stock offer a materially higher dividend return prospect than the one I might be looking to sell? These swaps fall into two camps:

1. *Can I trade up in yield?* As much as I like owning AmeriGas Partners with a 7 percent yield and a 3 percent growth rate, it's possible that I'll discover another stock (be it another propane supplier or a completely different business) that offers the same 3 percent growth rate but an

8 percent current yield. If I make a swap like that, I can increase my income immediately without giving up future growth potential.

2. *Can I trade up in growth?* This mirrors the yield trade-up: I might be happy as a clam to own AmeriGas for a 7 percent yield and 3 percent growth, but if another 7 percent yielder comes along with high-quality prospects for 6 percent growth, I can increase my future income and wealth faster without my current rate of income taking a hit.

The second point—trading up in growth—comes in especially handy when a stock you bought a year or two ago goes on to increase its dividend more slowly than you expected (or not at all). For instance, you might buy a stock with a 3.4 percent yield and a reasonable estimate of 8 percent growth, only to see the dividend grow just 5 or 6 percent and fall short of your hurdle return. This is exactly what happened with my original recommendation of National City in early 2005. Even though its yield had risen a bit by January 2007—a product of that modest dividend growth and a flat market price—it still didn't look capable of meeting my return requirements. Just about any bank looked to provide a higher future return. Nevertheless, any new purchase should be justified on two counts:

1. *Relative.* If a new purchase doesn't look capable of returning at least a percentage point or two more than your least-attractive existing holding (the stock you're probably looking to sell), there's probably not much benefit in making the swap.

2. *Absolute.* It isn't enough for the new stock merely to beat the old one; it should also top the hurdle returns I suggested in Chapter 8. If you have a stock that needs selling (whether because of diminished dividend security or a poor indicated return) and there are no obvious and easily justifiable buys, you might as well hold cash until something better comes along.

Not all purchases will require sales elsewhere. Sometimes you'll have new cash to invest—perhaps from regular savings or some unexpected windfall. You might also have excess dividend income to put to work. But when you have new money to invest, your first act shouldn't be to search for brand-new holdings. If you've already assembled an attractive portfolio, the best stock to buy with fresh capital might be more shares of something you already own.

These simple trading strategies can, when sparingly applied, add incremental income and growth potential to a dividend portfolio over time. But don't feel compelled to trade. As long as your existing holdings perform according to your expectations—their dividends remain safe and grow at the rate you expect—there's no need to continually search for the bigger, better deal. And the longer you own a stock, the better you'll understand it, and the easier it will be to own.

Dividend Reinvestment: Active versus Passive

I've mentioned before that reinvesting dividends—especially into stocks whose dividend rates are rising over time—can be a terrific strategy for accumulating wealth and future income-generating power. Dividend reinvestment plans (DRIPs, profiled in greater detail in Appendix 1) are a convenient, low-cost (or no-cost) way to roll dividend income into new shares, especially when those individual dividend payments are relatively small.

Within a good-size portfolio, however, DRIPs have a drawback: Each dividend payment will be reinvested in the stock that paid it, regardless of whether that stock offers the best dividend return (or even a merely adequate return) at that time and price.

In an active dividend reinvestment strategy—the one I employ for *Morningstar DividendInvestor's* model portfolios—I take my dividends in cash and allow them to accumulate in the brokerage account over a period of months. When this cash balance has grown to the point where a new purchase transaction is economical (maybe $1,000 or thereabouts, given a $10 discount commission rate), I'll select just one existing holding—the one that offers the best future total-return prospects—and roll all of my accumulated dividends into it. This may require more effort than a DRIP, but by concentrating my funds in the best available return prospect at the time, it should enhance my portfolio's income and future growth potential.

The Bottom Line

When managing a dividend portfolio, it's vital to place primary emphasis on the income that your account is generating rather than its market value. Mr. Market is going to try his best to shake your confidence: Dividend-paying stocks, while generally less volatile than the market in general, will occasionally enter periods of wild fluctuations. Sometimes a falling market price will signal genuine trouble—declining growth prospects or new risks to the current dividend rate—but more often than not, 10 or 20 percent price drops are just a matter of Mr. Market's mood swings.

So don't let Mr. Market get the better of you. He doesn't know the secrets of dividend yield and growth, much less how to price these prospects appropriately and rationally. You do!

Chapter 10: Rules and Plays

▶ The basic organizing principle of a dividend portfolio is its target yield. This should reflect your need or preference for income, be it for living expenses or dividend reinvestment.

▶ Within a given target yield, go for as much growth as possible. Not only will it add substantially to your portfolio's total returns, but growing dividends are likely to be safer than flat ones.

▶ Let dividends tell you when to trade. Consider selling when a stock's dividend is no longer safe; beyond that, use opportunity costs (the prospective dividend returns of new ideas relative to existing holdings) as your guide.

The Future of Dividends

ONE OF THE key themes in this book is the idea that dividends, through both yield and growth, enable investors to meet real-world financial needs directly with their portfolios. Fickle capital gains (green today, red tomorrow, endlessly unpredictable) do not. The more this fact is repeated, and the broader the word spreads, the more popular dividends will become. Throw in the demographic realities to come over the next few decades—80 million new retirees or thereabouts—and dividends could very easily be to the next 25 years of investor experience what capital appreciation has been to the past quarter century.

The problem, at least for tomorrow's dividend-seekers, is that there may not be enough to go around. American corporations may be doling out about $300 billion in dividend income annually, but there's still a lot of sand crunching through the gears of the market's dividend machine. A number of companies (banks, real estate investment trusts, utilities—you know the names by now) are paying out substantial dividends, but elsewhere in the stock market, companies representing the bulk of the stock market's value continue to withhold earnings that by all rights should be going back to shareholders as dividends.

This problem has three roots: indefensible tax policies, poor corporate governance, and shareholder passivity. Fortunately, there are solutions to each of these problems, and in the end, shareholders can and will call the shots.

Dividend Taxes: No Fair!

Until very recently, long-term capital gains have almost always been taxed at lower marginal rates than dividend income. Dividend income was lumped in with other ordinary income, taxed at the taxpayer's top marginal tax rate. Capital gains got a break—at times, a massive break. (See Figure 11.1.)

One might claim that the tax code *should* favor capital gains over dividends, since capital gains reflect growth, and growth is good for the economy. As this pertains to individual companies, this is hogwash! I'll be the first to agree that public policy ought to encourage savings and capital formation, as these lead to economic growth, more and better-paying jobs, and a higher overall standard of living. However, there is no necessary link between the dividends corporations pay out to shareholders and how much I, as a shareholder, choose to spend. If I own General Motors (GM) and I don't need my dividends for living expenses, I'll reinvest them. And not only will I reinvest

Figure 11.1   Top Federal Tax Rates for Dividends and Capital Gains
Source: Citizens for Tax Justice

my dividends, but I'll have the option of reinvesting not only in GM but in any one of 10,000 other publicly traded stocks. Where it regards GM at least, chances are my capital will find much more productive uses outside the company than inside it.

Providing incentives for corporations to hold on to their excess earnings and invest them in unproductive ways surely inhibits economic progress rather than enhancing it. The market is not just a group of 10,000 CEOs, but a class of 100 million investors. Why not let all of our voices be heard?

The 2003 tax act helped greatly by reducing the tax rate on dividend income to a maximum of 15 percent from 38.6 percent previously. Along with a smaller rate reduction in capital gains (from one half the regular rate to a maximum of 15 percent), the act also—finally!—brought the tax rate on dividends back into line with that paid on capital gains.

Fiddling with tax rates alone can't correct the tax code's inherent unfairness toward dividends, however. The problem seems to lie with the nature of taxes: It's easy to tax something that objectively occurs, like the receipt of a dividend payment (plenty of paper trail there) or the sale of a stock at a gain (a bit bulkier for the Internal Revenue Service to track, but far from impossible). Unrealized capital gains—buying a stock at $15 that goes to $30 but continuing to hold—would be exceedingly difficult to lay a levy upon.

This is bad for two reasons: First, it penalizes investors who opt for a high-income, low-growth strategy. Never mind that these folks are providing capital just as faithfully (perhaps much more faithfully) to enterprises that generate commerce, provide jobs, and pay taxes the same way low- and no-dividend companies do. But by passively receiving the bulk of their rewards through dividends, these shareholders are simply an easier target for the IRS to tax.

Second, and perhaps much more damaging, the built-in tax bias against dividend income gives corporate managers a reason—actually, more of an excuse—to withhold dividends.

Dividend Battleground: Shareholders versus Management

Theoretically, the net worth of a corporation—including its future earning capacity—belongs to shareholders. Legally and practically, this is not true. From a legal point of view, a corporation exists as an entity separate from its shareholders. Just because you might own 1 percent of the stock in a tiny retail chain doesn't mean you can walk into a store, count the cash in the till, and lift 1 percent of it out for yourself. There's a term for that, and it's not a dividend; it's called theft. Only the board of directors can decide if, when, and in what exact amount shareholders receive cash directly from the corporation. If you don't like the board's dividend policy, you can vote against the directors in the next election. That being an almost nonexistent way for small investors to effect change, selling shares on the open market is your only recourse.

Judging from the behavior of many corporations, CEOs and directors might as well be the legal owners of the entire enterprise. With few direct restraints, they're capable of controlling assets, dictating strategies, and paying themselves whatever they please. Only when managers behave badly enough to force the share price down to ridiculously low levels can their hold be shaken. Well-heeled private-equity funds or industry rivals are capable of summoning the resources to acquire control of the corporation and fire the bad actors. The humble owner of 100 shares has virtually no voice, let alone any control.

I look at this situation the same way I look at government action. When a government passes a law, enacts a tax, or spends money, the act usually transfers something of value (money or rights) from one group of citizens to another. Most of the time, the benefits are concentrated in the hands of a few, while the costs are widely dispersed. The beneficiaries know exactly who they are and are well-organized, vocal, and willing to stuff cash into campaign chests—these are the special-interests groups that every elected official claims to be fighting. Those bearing the costs are unorganized, largely unheard, and rarely even aware of what they're missing.

Now consider corporate actions in the same light. An acquisition has targeted beneficiaries—the managers of acquiree, and usually the acquirer, stand to cash in big-time. Meanwhile the costs (in the form of excessive acquisition premiums) are widely dispersed among thousands or even millions of individual shareholders. Same thing with eight- or nine-figure CEO salaries: These payouts are usually a tiny percentage of the corporation's overall profits; shareholders aren't poorer by more than a rounding error. But the beneficiary—the CEO—might vault himself into the Forbes 400.

Cash dividend payments turn this normal state of human affairs on its head. The benefits are spread widely—every shareholder gets an equal bite—while a few executives give up control of dollars they could otherwise leverage to their benefit, either directly (via bigger pay packets) or indirectly (by expanding the asset base and obtain more compensation as magistrates of a larger empire).

This isn't to say that CEOs, directors, and other top managers don't have a vested interest in the market performance of their shares; in most cases, they do. Not only would a low stock price threaten management's independence, but often very large chunks of these managers' wealth is tied up in stock option grants. If the share price rises, the CEO cashes in. These options are generally the source of the nine-figure executive payouts that make headlines every so often.

So it should come as no real surprise that CEOs and directors all too often opt for share buybacks, acquisitions, and dubious growth initiatives meant to pump up the stock price. These riskier venues for channeling total return through per-share growth rather than dividends can create all kinds of abhorrent behavior:

▶ Share buybacks can be good for shareholders, but only if the cost of the repurchased shares is less than their intrinsic business value. When a business overpays for stock—even its own stock—it is destroying shareholder value. Everybody knows this, but I have yet to see any CEO admit he's overpaying for his own stock. Unfortunately, the investment decision rests with the individuals whose appraisal of the stock's value is likely to be the highest.

▶ Acquisitions—returning cash to other companies' shareholders, so to speak—are hardly a panacea. Academic studies have shown that perhaps two-thirds of all acquisitions destroy value for the shareholders of the acquiring firm—value usually tossed out the window by paying too much. Only the shareholders of the firm being acquired benefit. But acquisitions are just too tempting for CEOs; last time I checked, CEO pay was linked most closely to the size of the company being run, rather than its return to shareholders. So CEOs overestimate cost savings, project "revenue synergies" that rarely exist, and roll the dice with shareholders' money.

▶ Every business has a natural rate of growth that optimizes the profitability of retained earnings. Few companies, and very few that are already giants, have expansion potential that can sustain double-digit growth for any length of time. For the great mass of America's corporations, natural growth rates are no higher than the nominal growth rate of the U.S. (or possibly global) economy as a whole: maybe 5 to 7 percent, depending on their presence abroad. Attempting to grow at 8, 10, or 20 percent necessarily means picking expansion projects outside the firm's core competency that inevitably offer higher risks and lower rates of return. Consider Microsoft (MSFT). Even though its core business is strong enough to cover up a lot of mistakes, Microsoft has laid billions of dollars into businesses that are only tangentially associated with operating systems and office software (such as MSN.com and Xbox, to name just two losers). When companies feel the heat to deliver total return through growth rather than dividends, overall returns on equity often suffer.

▶ A stock whose entire value proposition to shareholders is growth will have few friends when the growth doesn't pan out—even if the situation is only temporary. This can't help but create an incentive, no matter how perverse, to tinker with the numbers in order to avoid disappointing the Wall Street analysts and their lemminglike followers.

In some cases, the natural growth rate of a firm is negative, such as it's been for the old optical camera and film industry. Faced with an unpleasant reality, such firms ought to slowly and patiently liquidate their assets and pay out as much in dividends as possible, since one day those dividends and the earnings that support them will cease. But doing so would naturally deprive many a CEO, director, and consultant of hefty compensation, so companies like Eastman Kodak (EK) instead invest billions in initiatives designed to reinvigorate growth. Rather than increase its dividend to truly maximize shareholder value, in 2003, Kodak slashed its per-share dividend from $1.80 a year to just $0.50 so it could invest in emerging technologies. (See Figure 11.2.) Any average Joe or Jane on Main Street could correctly identify this strategy as throwing good money after bad. The results have been predictable.

By contrast, a dividend never hurts shareholders. The cash that goes in their pockets is there to stay—the value passed into their hands can't vanish

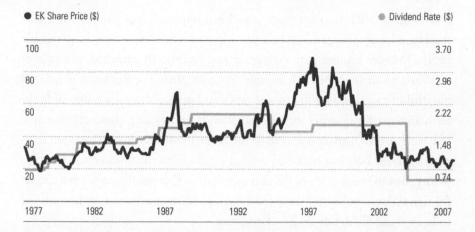

Figure 11.2   Eastman Kodak (EK): Share Price and Dividend History

because of an earnings miss or a market correction. But take a look at the impact of dividends on the holders of stock options:

▶ Only stockholders receive dividend payments. Owning an option entitles the holder to purchase stock at a given price by some future date, but owning an option doesn't allow its holder to receive any cash from a dividend payment.

▶ Furthermore, stock prices automatically adjust downward on the ex-dividend date to reflect the payment of the dividend. In that moment, shareholders are no worse off, but option holders suffer.

▶ Higher-yielding stocks also (but not always) tend to be less volatile than low- or no-yield stocks. Raw volatility makes options more valuable because there is a greater probability the options will be in the money when the holder wants to exercise. Lower volatility—an obvious plus for outside investors like us—is actually a negative for option holders.

With these conditions as a backdrop, one might easily wonder why *any* corporation pays a dividend. After pondering the question for years, it seems to me mostly a matter of tradition. Certain companies have been expected to pay significant dividends—utilities and banks being the prime example. Ditto for consumer product firms and traditional telecom companies like AT&T (T) and Verizon (VZ). In other cases, it's all but required: Real estate investment trusts are legally obligated to kick out big dividends when they have taxable profits. Master limited partnerships, if not technically required, are at least expected to so investors will be able to cover their tax liabilities. And in a handful of cases, you'll run across firms that have cultivated a group of long-term investors by paying out nice dividends and raising them consistently. If I were a CEO, these are exactly the kind of shareholders I'd want: folks who wouldn't bolt just because I missed third-quarter earnings estimates by a penny. But to break a 30- or 40-year streak of higher payments sends a dreadful signal that would send these folks fleeing. Momentum and pride combine to keep these dividends alive and growing.

Elsewhere, it's largely a matter of trust. Corporations that don't pay dividends are naturally expected to reinvest those funds at high rates of return and maintain high growth rates for earnings per share and stock prices. A company like rural phone utility CenturyTel (CTL)—a slow-growing business at best that has stubbornly refused to raise the yield on its shares north of 1 percent—had better find ways to reinvest its ample excess cash flow in productive ways. If it neither raises the dividend nor finds some other way to grow, shareholders will vote with their feet.

Shareholders Who Should Know Better

The dividend problem is a three-legged stool. The unfairness of the tax code and the self-interest of management couldn't have led yields to record lows all by themselves. The final leg is critical: shareholder apathy.

There was a time when most shares in American companies were held directly by individuals. Defined-benefit pension plans owned some stocks and so did a few insurance companies and banks, but for the most part, the corporate wealth of the United States was owned directly by individual investors. Some of these shareholders (the short-term trader types) have never cared about dividends; these penny-ante payments just mess up their recordkeeping. For the rest, however, income provided a critical reason to own stocks. Those that didn't pay a dividend—whether earnings could permit such payments or not—were regarded with suspicion.

Over the past few decades, the vast majority of corporate stocks have migrated into the concentrated hands of intermediaries, mostly mutual funds.

Again, we find conflict between the interests of the ultimate shareholder (the mutual fund investor) and the fund's manager. Fund managers are almost always paid fees as a percentage of assets. More assets means more fees. And to get more assets, most managers believe they have to beat the S&P 500 or some other index. Worst of all, such funds have to beat their bogeys consistently—if not every quarter, then every year. So as a group, these managers can't help but chase capital gains. Dividends may be fine for those with long time horizons, but they simply take too long to accumulate to have a meaningful impact on quarterly or even annual performance. These managers, who control trillions of dollars' worth of stock, certainly have the power to band together and demand higher dividends. But until recently, they simply didn't care—and even now, real dividend pressure is rare.

What of those hardy individual stock pickers? If we can judge from the success of discount brokerage firms, plenty of Americans still own stocks directly. But many of their holding periods are measured in months, if not minutes. (Do you really think a $5 or $10 trade is cheap? Try day-trading for a year and you'll find out. Believe me, these guys make it up in the volume, the same way a casino can claim 90 percent-plus payouts on the slots and still wind up with all the gamblers' money in the end.) True long-term stock pickers may not have died out as a breed, but they definitely belong on the endangered species list. There aren't enough of them to exert real pressure on even small companies, let alone a Google (GOOG) or Cisco (CSCO).

What a pathetic state of affairs! But hang on: These dark clouds might—just might—be lifting. Remember those widely dispersed shareholders, whose ranks are growing with each passing year of baby boom retirements? An investor like Sally (from Chapter 1) might have been able to accumulate a nice nest egg from stock funds invested without any specific regard to dividends, but if the last bear market didn't teach her peers that capital gains are a poor way to obtain retirement income, the next bear market—whenever it happens—almost certainly will.

It's no wonder that investors are starting to vote with their feet, marching steadily toward the smaller group of stocks that offer large and predictable dividends. Wall Street—no slouch when it comes to identifying and capitalizing upon fads—has responded with a slew of mutual funds, exchange-traded funds, and other investment vehicles designed to kick out higher yields. These products have already accumulated tens of billions of dollars' worth of assets, but this is more than a fad; it's a bona fide trend.

This demographic makes me highly optimistic that the growing popularity of dividends will force changes in the tax code, management behavior, and even fund manager strategies.

Solutions for the Tax Bias

As of this writing, even the current tax treatment of dividends is at risk. Presumably to keep long-term deficit projections from spiraling out of control, large portions of the 2003 tax act come with expiration dates attached. The 15 percent maximum federal rate on dividend income has already been extended once, from the end of 2008 to the end of 2010, but with control of Congress passing from right to left in November 2006, the prospect of additional extensions—much less making the tax changes permanent—has diminished.

Some politicians and academics would like to see the tax rate on capital gains and dividends cut to zero. Others see no reason that investment income should be taxed at rates lower than wages and salaries. All I ask for is basic fairness: Whatever the rate, tax dividends and capital gains equally, but do so when these two forms of income are *spent,* rather than when they are earned. This need not take the form of a radical overhaul of the tax code, such as the often-proposed replacement of the income tax with a consumption tax or national sales tax. A ready blueprint already exists: the individual retirement account.

An IRA is directly favored by the tax code, either by allowing a deduction when funds are contributed (traditional IRAs) or by permitting withdrawals that are tax-free (Roth IRAs). What if we drop the direct tax subsidies and apply the advantage provided by both types of IRAs: deferral of investment income? Allow folks to put money into brokerage accounts, invest however they choose, and tax gains only when they are withdrawn and spent. Whatever returns are earned in the meantime, whether dividends, capital gains, or interest, can then compound on equal terms. Corporations would feel much freer to return cash through dividends, investors could identify the best uses for those dollars, and the government could still collect tax when investment dollars are withdrawn and spent. I know this sounds too good to be true, but

I can't help but throw it out there as a near-perfect solution anyway. Perhaps some congressman or senator will read this book and mull it over. After all, the senator who came up with the Roth IRA (William Roth of Delaware) got his name on it; what a branding opportunity for an erstwhile presidential contender! (And what sitting senator isn't?)

Another potential solution is to give investors credit for the income taxes paid on dividends at the corporate level. If we subscribe to the notion that corporate profits are taxed twice, why not do what the Australians do: Have dividends carry a tax credit that the investor can use to offset any tax she might owe on her dividend income. This is called an *imputation* system, and it's used in several other countries. No doubt this helps explain why Australia's stock market has one of the highest dividend yields in the world.

At any rate, today's investors face the prospect of higher tax rates on their investment income as soon as 2011. The proponents of the 2003 tax act honestly believe that their tax cuts helped the stock market rebound, though I imagine the end of the 2001 recession and the subsequent boom in corporate profitability had a much more relevant impact. It's much harder to argue with the likely effect of a big tax increase; whether it influences the overall level of the stock market or not, it will definitely punish investors, particularly those who hold stocks with high dividends.

An important tenet underlying economic theory is that investors are in the market seeking after-tax returns. To the extent that a particular shareholder expects an 8 percent annual return after taxes, higher tax rates will force investors to demand higher pretax returns. And how does one obtain a higher pretax return? By paying a lower price for the shares. I have little doubt that the industries most favored by today's tax policy—qualified dividend payers like utilities, banks, and consumer staples firms—will see investors depart and stock prices fall if tax rates revert to their pre-2003 level.

Moreover, the 2003 tax breaks will be competing with other fiscal problems—most notably the escalating punitive effects of the alternative minimum tax and the skyrocketing cost of Medicare—for the government's available resources. The 15 percent maximum tax rate for both dividends and capital gains doesn't have to be raised—something that would take the development of legislation and force congressmen and senators to go on the record in favor of doing so. An act of inaction, simply letting the 2003 tax rates expire, may be exactly what happens.

However, whether Democrats or Republicans are ascendant in Washington come 2010, I seriously doubt either party wants to be responsible for a massive tax increase that is felt not just by billionaires but by millions of small investors. Let's be honest: These folks vote in proportions much higher than the citizenry at large. The more retirees who come to rely on dividend and other investment income for living expenses, the more politically costly inaction will prove to be. So instead of seeing the current 15 percent maximum tax rate simply expire, I expect even a Democratic Congress or administration to reaffirm these reduced tax rates for investors of average means. Bill Gates's tax rate might go up, but it seems to me unlikely that John Q. Retiree will suffer from a tax bite on the dividends from his 100 shares of Microsoft.

While acknowledging the potential for higher tax rates and their likely negative impact on stock prices in 2010, I'm confident that dividend investing will not go out of style or cease to work. Even as top marginal tax rates have fluctuated wildly over the past century, dividend-paying stocks as a group have distinguished themselves by providing superior returns. What's more, investors have other tools at their disposal to maximize after-tax returns: tax-deferred accounts and the choice to own lower-yielding but reliably fast-growing streams of dividends.

Solutions for Corporate Conflicts

Whether investors like Sally look to own dividend-paying individual stocks or prefer to find high-yield equity mutual funds, their collective buying pressure will change the market's landscape. The stocks of corporations that pay significant dividends and bear high yields will rise; those that don't will lag far behind. That's how the free market's price-signaling system works. We've already seen this phenomenon emerge in a number of ways: the rapid buildup of assets in dividend-oriented fund products, the rising valuations of utilities and REITs, and—here and there—aggressive new dividend policies from a few individual corporations.

As a case in point, rural telephone companies all tended to trade at pretty low multiples of earnings and cash flow back around 2003. Token or nonexistent dividends were largely the rule, but growth prospects were somewhere between inflation at the high end and negative single-digit growth at the low end. Then two firms—Alaska Communications (ALSK) and Citizens Communications (CZN)—broke ranks by initiating enormous dividends. Their valuations soared as investors responded to the opportunity to participate directly in these cash cows. Meanwhile, the aforementioned CenturyTel stuck to its payout ratio of less than 10 percent, and its stock has barely budged. CenturyTel is larger than Alaska or Citizens and a better operator on just about every metric. But its stubborn resistance to paying out more cash has cost its shareholders' pockets—and management's reputation and option values—dearly by comparison.

Another case in point: newspapers. Most newspaper chains have long histories of paying dividends, albeit tiny ones. Yields rose only when their stock prices started to fall. Then, as with the telecom industry, one player broke ranks. GateHouse Media (GHS) came public in 2006 offering a yield around 6 percent, easily triple the industry average. GateHouse's approach is to dish out as much cash as possible; if it wants to make more acquisitions, it will seek fresh debt and equity financing instead of funding deals from retained earnings. Even if GateHouse's policy is flaky by industry standards, its example created pressure felt even in the hallowed halls of industry leaders New York Times Company (NYT) and Gannett (GCI). The Times increased its dividend 31 percent in 2007; Gannett raised its quarterly payout 29 percent. Their yields are still well below GateHouse's; then again, GateHouse's dividend policy is so aggressive one might have cause to doubt its long-term sustainability. Nonetheless, peer pressure is having an effect.

The more investors demand dividends, whether through individual stocks or mutual funds, the more pressure there will be on corporations to respond. One way or another, the yield on stocks will rise—but managers have a choice. Dividend yield, after all, is the dividend rate divided by the stock price. A rising numerator will raise the yield, but so will a falling denominator. CEOs and their boards can either get with the times and raise their dividend rates to levels that properly balance payout ratios with internal growth opportunities, or they can watch their stock prices decline until the yield becomes attractive. Where corporations are throwing off more cash than can be profitably reinvested in the business (and I don't mean share buybacks here), the choice is theirs to make.

I suspect that as time goes on, more corporate boards will opt for higher dividend rates. Where stock option grants—an obvious form of compensation expense—were once excluded from earnings as if they didn't exist, these economic costs are now buried in the income statement where they belong. Grants of restricted stock—which do participate in dividends—are becoming more popular relative to options. Finally, we may be entering an age where management and shareholder interests are more properly aligned—and higher dividends will be the avenue through which this new environment takes shape.

One final point: I can't claim that much higher dividend rates for the market as a whole would necessarily lead to higher stock prices or future returns, but it most certainly would increase the *quality* of those returns. Within the context of an 8 percent long-run total return prospect, a 3 or 4 percent market yield—implying dividend rates 50 to 100 percent higher than those found today—would necessarily diminish the pace of share buybacks and therefore future dividend growth potential. But I'd take that growth-for-income swap in a heartbeat, and I have little doubt that many millions of soon-to-be retirees would as well.

What It Is, Rather than What I'd Like It to Be

The silver lining to today's markets is that there are still plenty of high-yield and high-dividend-growth stocks to pick from. You may not get much from the technology or industrial sectors, but effective diversification doesn't mean having one toe stuck into every pie. Diversify among what works for your financial circumstances and what can be bought with attractive total return prospects.

The manager-shareholder conflict can be overcome by choosing firms whose commitment to dividends (by tradition, trust, or regulation) is sacrosanct. Hoping for dividend growth from low-yield stocks doesn't seem to pan out well. The status quo can and sometimes does change, but where we don't find momentum driving the dividend, we may as well assume inertia is the default state of affairs.

As for taxes, the way some people talk about the subject can be such a shame. You'd think they'd be happier if they could just find a way to avoid earning income so they wouldn't have to pay taxes. Their rhetoric belies their self-interest, of course—they're fully invested like the rest of us. Yet I've met a few investors who put all their money in municipal bonds; that way they can grin about how their 3 percent and 4 percent returns are putting one over on Uncle Sam.

Me, I don't *have* to pay taxes, I *get* to. (Try not to draw the obvious conclusion about my political leanings.) I suppose I could quit my job and stuff my savings in the mattress to avoid paying any and all income taxes, but that's no way to live one's economic life. When I make a gain, even a taxable one, I have to cheer: I'm still ahead, even after taxes. I also remember that when I mess up and take a loss, the IRS shares in my pain.

Tax minimization and tax avoidance are distinct strategies. The latter goes so far as to avoid income in order to avoid tax. The former merely judges investments on the basis of their after-tax potential. If you don't need your dividend income for current living expenses, focus on low-yield, high-growth dividend payers whose income will swell as you head toward retirement. If you can own these stocks in a qualified account, you don't need to worry about the tax drag at all. And if you do need income from your portfolio for living expenses, craft a portfolio that generates that income and leaves the rest of your total return prospect in dividend growth.

Whatever the futures of taxation and corporate governance may hold, I expect reliable dividend-paying stocks to become more attractive over time. More people will want them; their valuations will rise as a result; that will create pressure for more generous dividends elsewhere; and so on. The kind of companies we are looking to buy today are exactly the ones who stand to benefit from these trends—no further effort required.

Chapter 11: Rules and Plays

▶ An unfair tax code, self-interested corporate managers, and passive shareholders continue to conspire against dividends.

▶ In the future, more favorable forces (led by new retirees' need for steady income) may align to encourage American corporations to adopt more dividend policies that better suit shareholders' interests.

▶ Whether these things happen in the future or not, there's little doubt that the kind of dividend-rich stocks we seek today will become more desirable in the future.

Epilogue

Rules and Plays

I HAVE TO admit that the stock market, even for as passionate a stock picker as me, can be highly annoying at times. I look around and see my fellow investors focusing on all the wrong things: tomorrow's economic data, next week's Federal Reserve meeting, next quarter's earnings per share, next year's presidential election. They're looking to beat the market, not pay the bills or build cash earning power for the future. Dividends don't appeal to these kinds of investors and possibly never will.

Fortunately, no one is forced to invest his hard-earned dollars on this basis. Dividends—particularly the large and growing ones—put cash in our pockets regardless of the fads and failings of Wall Street. There are more than enough worthwhile businesses for Main Street investors to pick from.

By way of a summary, here are some guidelines I think you might find useful as a checklist.

The Ultimate Dividend Rules

▶ Capital gains are an unreliable source of income. If you need income from stocks, get it from dividends instead.

▶ Dividends are the ultimate source of a stock's value for shareholders.

▶ Current dividend yield plus dividend growth indicates a stock's future total return prospects.

▶ Avoid stocks with unsafe dividends.

▶ Past rates of dividend growth are a useful guide, but a forward-looking estimate is much more relevant.

▶ The real world is unpredictable, so demand a margin of safety by requiring a higher total return prospect than you might otherwise settle for.

▶ Start your portfolio planning with a target yield; then buy a group of stocks that, as a group, can deliver the income you seek.

▶ Growing dividends are usually safer dividends as well. Within your target yield, seek as much growth as possible.

▶ The more companies you evaluate before buying, the better your eventual portfolio will look and perform.

▶ Consider selling when a stock's dividend no longer looks sustainable.

▶ Beyond that, let opportunity costs be your guide. Unless a new candidate offers a materially higher prospective return than the least attractive stock you already own, you should feel no need to trade.

The Bottom Line

I suspect that one day, investors will come back to basics and learn to rely on the income, insight, and independence that dividends provide, rather than capital gains alone. That would mark a real improvement in market efficiency, which in turn couldn't help but benefit investors, the corporations in which they invest, and our economy in general.

For now, though, I feel as if I've got a secret—albeit one that I've been more than willing to share with you through this book. Let others chase capital gains, tote up their statement values at the end of every trading day, and beat the market if they can. Dividends may not be the only path for an individual investor's success, but if there's a better one, I have yet to find it.

By the time you read this, the current economic boom may have gone bust. The Dow Jones Industrial Average might be at 16,000, 10,000, or anywhere in between. I can't say for sure that underlying dividend fundamentals for my existing model portfolio holdings (or any of the stocks mentioned in this book) won't change in 2008 or the years beyond. If they do, I'll take John Maynard Keynes' advice to heart: "When the facts change, I change my mind. What do you do, sir?"

But the kinds of facts I'm watching—income, growth, and dividend return potential—are timeless. I have complete confidence that my portfolios' income will grow, accumulate, and compound. I'm investing for the long haul, and I'm investing for cash. Let Mr. Market have his games. With the dividends providing the right income, the right insight, and a truly independent frame of mind, you can do the same.

Appendix 1

The Nuts and Bolts of Dividend Payments

DIVIDEND PAYMENTS ARE not always as straightforward as they seem. The exact terms and conditions under which the shareholder receives these parcels of cash can vary in a number of ways that the well-informed dividend investor needs to be aware of. In this appendix, we take a closer look at the types of dividends that companies pay and the process through which they are paid.

Let's Get Paid: The Dividend Payment Process

Bonds and bank accounts make earning income fairly easy. Even though interest may be paid only at monthly, quarterly, or semiannual intervals (the last predominates in the case of bonds), both investments accrue interest every day. If you cash out a savings or money market account, or sell a bond in the open market, whatever interest the investment has earned will be part of the proceeds. When buying a bond that is already issued, accrued interest is included as part of the purchase price.

Because dividends are not legal obligations the way bond or bank interest is, stocks do not accrue income between dividend payments. Only when a corporation's board of directors declares a dividend does the firm become legally required to pay. For this reason, dividends carry specific dates. Own the stock before a certain date passes (the ex-dividend date), and you'll receive the dividend a week or a month later (the payment date).

Let's look at the dividend paid by Coca-Cola Company (KO) in the first quarter of 2007. We'll be looking for four key pieces of information: the declaration date, the record date, the payment date, and the per-share dividend rate. From this data we'll be able to infer the two most important pieces of information regarding the dividend:

1. *The ex-dividend date.* This is the most important date in the dividend payment process. Oddly enough, it is not to be found in Coke's press release or most other firms' dividend announcements. This is the date on which the stockholder becomes legally and technically entitled to the dividend.
2. *The annualized dividend rate.* Dividends can be paid at several types of intervals; to make comparisons among firms, we standardize their dividends on an annualized basis.

The process begins with a regularly scheduled meeting of Coke's board of directors. Since Coke makes a practice of paying a dividend roughly every three months, a discussion of the dividend shows up on the board's agenda at regular intervals.

On Feb. 15, the board holds just such a meeting. It has been about a year since Coke last raised its dividend; with 44 straight years of dividend increases behind it, investors are doubtless looking for an increase. While we outsiders aren't generally privy to the details, we can assume that corporate officers offer board members their outlook for profits, cash flow, capital expenditures, and so forth. Depending on the managers' views and the opinions of individual board members, perhaps some debate breaks out. At some point the chairman calls for a vote, and the board votes in favor of paying a dividend of $0.34 a share.

After the meeting is adjourned, someone from the corporate communications office is called in, and a press release is assembled. It's released the same day, and it reads as follows:

> ATLANTA, February 15, 2007—The Board of Directors of The Coca-Cola Company today approved the Company's 45th consecutive annual dividend increase, raising the quarterly dividend 10 percent from 31 cents to 34 cents per common share. This is equivalent to an annual dividend of $1.36 per share, up from $1.24 per share in 2006. The dividend is payable April 1, 2007, to shareowners of record as of March 15, 2007.

The directors' statement goes on to say that the increase reflects their confidence in the company's long-term cash flow, and to praise the firm for having returned billions of dollars to shareholders in the previous five years, over which time the per-share dividend rate grew at an annual average of 11 percent. The real meat in the release, however, is the information conveyed in the first paragraph.

The date of the press release, Feb. 15, is the *declaration date*. By voting to pay the dividend, the corporation is obligated (except in extreme circumstances) to make the specified payment to shareholders.

The press release also tells shareholders how much they can expect for each share they own—in this case, $0.34. A mythical holder of 100 shares, Jane Q. Beverage, can expect a check in the mail (or a deposit to her brokerage account) of $34.

But who will receive the dividend? This brings us to the *record date*. On the average trading day, 10 million shares of Coke change hands; those $0.34 dividend payments can't go to both the buyers and the sellers. Thus, while February 15 brought good news, simply owning the stock as of that date doesn't entitle any particular shareholder to the dividend. Only those who are the legal owners of shares at the opening of business March 15—the record date—are entitled to receive the dividend. Those folks who sell before the record date, or buy after the market opens March 15, are out of luck.

Also, it takes time to process those dividend payments—to print and mail checks in an earlier era, and today to discover whose electronic bits and bytes entitle them to the dividend. The payment is thus made about two weeks later, on April 1.

As I mentioned earlier, the most important date—the *ex-dividend date*, or simply *ex-date*, is not found in the press release. With investors swapping millions of shares in Coke (and billions overall) among themselves on a daily basis, it takes time to process that paperwork, too. When Jane purchases shares of Coke on, say, March 7, she's the owner immediately from a *practical* standpoint, but she won't become the *legal* owner for two more business days. Only on March 9 will the cash in Jane's brokerage account move to whoever sold her the shares and those shares transfer back to her account. From a practical standpoint, then, an investor needs to have held shares at least two business days before the record date to become eligible for the dividend. In Coke's case, this results in an ex-dividend date of March 13. To collect a dividend, Jane must have purchased shares no later than the market close March 12.

Free Money? Not Quite

One more event takes place on the ex-date, this one of equal parts short-term importance and long-term irrelevance. When a corporation pays a dividend to shareholders, the net worth of the company declines by the exact amount of the dividend. With 2.31 billion shares issued, this one quarterly dividend payment amounts to the impressive sum of $785 million. Coke's net worth, roughly $18 billion before the dividend is declared, drops to about $17.2 billion immediately afterward—a decline representing the exact sum of cash that is transferred from the corporation to its shareholders. Presumably this is only a momentary and temporary drop, with incoming earnings and cash flow steadily increasing the value of the firm in the months preceding the dividend payment. Indeed, Coke earned a profit of $1.3 billion in the first three months of 2007. Nevertheless, some adjustment is in order to reflect the outflow of cash.

Therefore, before the market opens on the ex-date, the New York Stock Exchange reduces the opening price of Coke shares by the amount of the dividend. All else being equal, Coke shares that ended trading on March 12 at $47.95 a share would begin March 13 at $47.61—$0.34 less. But if the market value of Coke shares has fallen, our intrepid shareholder Jane is no worse off: she'll receive $0.34 for each of her 100 shares in just over two weeks.

Once this adjustment is made, the normal market forces of supply and demand take over; with more sellers than buyers lined up at the beginning of March 13, Coke begins the day with a trade at $47.35 (down $0.34 because of the dividend and another $0.26 because of an influx of orders to sell).

As a side note, these ex-dividend adjustments make collecting dividends a poor strategy for short-term investors and traders. Buying the stock at the last minute of business on March 12 for $47.95 will indeed entitle another Coke shareholder, Jack X. Trader, to a payment of $0.34 a share April 1—even if he sells immediately at the open March 13. However, the prearranged decline in the market price will wipe out this seeming gain.

Nevertheless, strategies abound (what dubious notion *isn't* available on the Internet these days?) that suggest rapid-fire trading strategies can capture the dividend by buying right before the ex-date and selling shortly thereafter. Jane, with her 100 shares, would be lucky if the $34 dividend covered trading costs, even if the price didn't automatically adjust downward. Even for very large special dividends, long-term investors interested in income would do well to avoid such attempts; the market is rigged against them.

Regular Beats Special: Dividend Types

Coke (like most dividend-paying corporations) hands out dividends on a regular quarterly basis. The calendar of dividend payments is consistent from year to year, as are the per-share rates. Having received a payout of $0.34 a share on April 1, Jane Q. Beverage can expect another $0.34 a share on July 1. With Coke's long history of raising the dividend, Jane can also expect an increased dividend ($0.37, perhaps $0.38) in the first quarter of 2008. Enforced by well-founded investor expectations and market tradition, consistent income at predictable intervals is the rule for most dividend-paying corporations in the United States. Breaking with tradition courts shareholder fury and a nasty reaction in the market price.

Still, nothing prevents a corporate board from choosing to pay dividends at some other time interval. Knowing this interval is key to determining the most important figure regarding a dividend, the *annualized dividend rate*. This figure represents the total dividend income each share is likely to receive in the succeeding 12 months on the basis of the most recent dividend action. This statistic is much more useful than the trailing dividend rate, the sum of dividends paid in the previous 12 months. Since we're buying in anticipation of future results, not past performance, all of our key statistics must be forward-looking.

▶ Quarterly payers are just that: They pay dividends roughly every three months. The annualized dividend rate for Coke, for example, is $1.36 ($0.34 multiplied by 4). Coke did us the favor of performing the multiplication in its press release.

▶ A sweet handful of companies pay dividends monthly. Blue-chip landlord Realty Income (O) is a prime example; its dedication to providing shareholders with a return rich in dividend income is reflected in part through these frequent, convenient payments. Its monthly dividend rate of $0.12775 in mid-2007—admittedly a mathematical challenge—translated into an annualized dividend of $1.533 per share. (Not that a monthly dividend necessarily means a strong one. Winn-Dixie, WINN, dished out monthly dividends for decades, until it announced an 80 percent dividend cut in 2001. It filed for bankruptcy in 2005.)

▶ A tiny minority of firms, such as Expeditors International of Washington (EXPD), pay semiannual dividends. Despite the wider time interval between payments, a shareholder of these firms can reasonably expect the next dividend payment to be equal to or higher than the previous one. Paying a dividend costs a corporation a bit of money for paperwork, so less-frequent dividends typically reflect relatively small ones: Expeditors (annualized dividend of $0.22 a share) has a history of yielding less than 1 percent.

▶ A small but growing minority of corporations have opted for annual dividends. Walt Disney (DIS) adopted an annual payment in 1999; McDonald's (MCD) did so in 2000. As with semiannual dividend payers, yields among annual payers also tend to be low; I suppose if you're not going to pay a big dividend, you might as well avoid the hassle of going through the process more often.

Everything I've described thus far is a regular dividend. The press release announcing a dividend almost always clarifies whether the dividend is regular or special; regular dividends are our sole focus at this point. These dividends are characterized as such because they arrive at regular intervals and, for most firms at least, set a benchmark of how much the shareholder can expect at those intervals going forward. To fail to declare a dividend when anticipated constitutes a negative act of inaction, most likely with negative implications for the stock price. In fact, U.S. companies with their backs against the financial wall (Ford, F, comes to mind) will put out a press release announcing a halt to dividends rather than let silence speak for itself.

Whatever the dividend policy, the most recent press release describing a dividend action, combined with a look at past practices, should provide enough information to infer an annualized dividend rate. When (as is the case with some alternative corporate structures like royalty trusts) past dividends have been highly irregular, with per-share rates or payment dates fluctuating all over the place, the stock paying it is unlikely to be a suitable holding for predictable income.

Special Dividends

Some dividends are labeled *special*. In this context, special does not mean better, but rather that the dividend is a one-time event that isn't likely to be repeated in the foreseeable future. This represents a critical difference: Special dividends, except in a minuscule number of exceptional circumstances, cannot be characterized as income. Regular—not special—dividends are what income seekers should look for.

Many special dividends represent a way to get rid of excess corporate cash. In 2003, rural Pennsylvania utility Commonwealth Telephone (which has since been acquired by Citizens Communications, CZN) borrowed $300 million in a bond offering because, I suppose, it discovered that its balance sheet was healthy enough to do so. For two years it fiddled around, buying back some of its own shares while looking for other telecom businesses to buy. Meanwhile the bulk of the cash simply sat there. Unable or unwilling to invest this cash in the business—a prudent decision, given the circumstances—it decided to let its shareholders figure out a solution on their own. On May 3, 2005, Commonwealth declared a special dividend of $13 per share, an announcement that lifted the stock price from $46.72 to $50.65 in a single day.

Why the enthusiasm? For one thing, Commonwealth had a large under-used asset in that cash that acted as a drag on its profitability for shareholders.

By transferring the cash to shareholders, Commonwealth's actual operations in the telephone business emerged as more profitable and thereby more desirable. After all, investors can hold cash in their own accounts if they want to; what benefit does a massive cash pile held inside the corporation provide them? For another, the stock price was certainly aided by Commonwealth's plans to initiate a smaller but still substantial regular dividend annualizing at $2 per share.

Special dividends are governed by the same ex-date rules that regular dividends are. When Commonwealth shares went ex-dividend June 13, the market price duly dropped by almost $13 a share ($12.79, to be exact). Investors were better off than they were before the special dividend was *declared*, since management was clearly acting to enhance Commonwealth's profitability. However, they were no richer after the dividend's ex-date than they were the day before.

Special dividends themselves are thus of limited relevance for investors, and even less important as a source of income. What Commonwealth really did was hand an unproductive part of its invested capital back to shareholders. That $13 a share payment wasn't income, but a return of the capital those shareholders already had invested in the firm. When looking at returns *of* capital (in economic rather than tax terms) and returns *on* capital, investors should focus squarely on the latter.

Exceptions do exist. Truck maker PACCAR (PCAR), known for its Peterbilt and Kenworth marques, pays a special dividend almost every year in addition to its regular quarterly dividends. The heavy-truck industry is notorious for its cyclicality; profits soar when the economy booms and drop sharply during recessions. PACCAR uses these special dividends to provide extra (if unpredictable) income to shareholders without stepping regular dividends up to a cyclically unsustainable level.

Special dividends need not be paid in cash. Stock dividends (also known as stock splits) represent special dividends as well. San Francisco-based Wells Fargo (WFC) split its stock two-for-one in August 2006. For each share outstanding, the board declared a dividend of one additional share. Of course, this act did not double the value of the bank. Splitting the stock was akin to taking a 16-inch pizza divided into eight slices and cutting each of those slices in two. Sure, there are now 16 slices, and everyone at the party can have twice as many slices as they could before, but each slice is half the size. As you might imagine, the market price of Wells Fargo dropped by half on the split's ex-dividend date.

Even though they create no actual wealth for shareholders, much less income, splits are generally received as good news. You might call it an expression of goodwill by the board of directors. Wells Fargo stock traded in the low $70s before the split and the mid-$30s afterward. It would be embarrassing for its nominal price (regardless of value) to fall to, say, $15, so in splitting the stock, Wells Fargo is implying that the value of the stock has limited downside. Some companies also claim that the split will make the stock more affordable for investors, a statement that has no basis in reality. More affordable can only mean a lower stock price in relation to earnings per share, dividends, and other yardsticks of fundamental value, but the split cuts all of these statistics in half as well.

Some companies, such as Valley National Bancorp (VLY) and Tootsie Roll Industries (TR), issue small stock dividends every year. At Valley, the proud holder of 100 shares winds up with 105 after a 5 percent stock dividend, though the ex-date adjustment and proportional declines in per-share earnings and dividends ensure that this act creates no actual value. Since these dividends do not constitute income—only cash dividends, and regular ones at that, do that—a small stock dividend is an utterly useless exercise that only serves to complicate the shareholders' bookkeeping.

Finally, special dividends can take the form of stock in other companies, usually a subsidiary that a corporation wants to get rid of by spinning it off as an independent entity. Altria Group (MO), formerly Philip Morris, spent much of the 1980s and 1990s adding packaged food manufacturers to its longstanding trade in the cigarette business. Presumably engineered to dilute the taint of tobacco (a strategy that didn't exactly work), the operations gathered under its Kraft Foods (KFT) subsidiary eventually became a drag on the tobacco executives' time.

In 2001, Altria separated and sold part of Kraft in an initial public offering while continuing to hold 89 percent of the stock for itself. Then, when the threat of tobacco litigation dwindled to a level the tobacco businesses could shoulder on their own, Altria declared a dividend of 0.692 share of Kraft for each Altria share outstanding. The holder of 100 Altria shares before the ex-date received 69 shares of Kraft while keeping all 100 of his original

Altria shares (as well as a tiny bit of cash to make up for the fractional share). Since the Kraft stock already trading publicly was trading at around $30 a share, this distribution was worth about $21 to each Altria shareholder. True to ex-dividend form, Altria's stock price dropped nearly $20 the day those Kraft shares were distributed.

What You See May Not Be What You Get

Today's Internet-empowered investor has access to many different sources of information. Dividend rates and yields are often provided alongside current stock price information. But while pricing data are almost always accurate, dividend information ranges from somewhat reliable to downright sketchy. The dividend data on foreign stocks are even iffier because of the payment practices native to many other countries, to say nothing of currency effects. But even information presented on the reddest, whitest, and bluest American stocks often contains material errors.

For one thing, quoted dividend rates and yields are frequently overstated by the inclusion of nonrecurring special payouts. When Microsoft (MSFT) paid out a special dividend of $3 a share in late 2004, many data providers suggested the stock's yield was north of 10 percent. In fact, Microsoft's regular dividend of $0.32 annually put the stock's yield at closer to 1 percent.

Conversely, the full impact of an increase to a firm's regular dividend can be slow to show up in Internet data, causing the yield to be *under*stated. A common practice is to present a stock's dividend rate by adding the value of all per-share dividends paid in the previous 12 months. In December 2006, Canadian specialty pharmaceutical firm Biovail Corporation International (BVF) shifted from an annual dividend of $0.50 a share to quarterly dividends of $0.375 (a total of $1.50 annually). Yet most data providers failed to reflect this threefold increase between the time the new policy was announced and the ex-date of the new, higher quarterly dividend. With the stock then around $21, what might have looked like a current yield of about 2.4 percent was in fact north of 7 percent.

Despite the fact that the dividend rate and yield are two of the most basic data points of a stock, the dividend seeker ought to double-check both statistics with the only authoritative source: the press release describing the company's most recent dividend action. Here we will find clarification between regular and special dividends, the frequency of the dividend, and accurate per-share rates. In every case, we want the most up-to-date information available. The dividends a company has paid in the past can be useful information from a research standpoint, but when evaluating current income, our focus is solely on what we can expect going forward.

Globe-Trotting for Dividends

The choices available to American investors are hardly limited to U.S. companies. Thousands of foreign stocks are available on the U.S. markets in one form or another; the largest of these are usually listed as American depositary receipts (ADRs) or American depositary shares (ADSs) on the major U.S. stock exchanges. These ADRs and ADSs represent a convenient way to own stakes in firms abroad while still collecting dividends in U.S. dollars; the banks that administer the ADRs take care of converting the dividends from their original currencies.

Yet after several years of searching, I've found that relatively few foreign stocks present good opportunities for steady income. Canadian firms follow U.S. practices (regular dividends paid quarterly, and so on), but dividend traditions in other nations fall all over the map.

▶ British and Irish firms, such as Diageo (DEO) and Allied Irish Banks (AIB), tend to make a practice of paying interim and final dividends—the interim usually smaller than the final, and they're generally not spaced an even six months apart (a gap of four or five months between the interval and the final seems to be the rule). As with their U.S. counterparts, however, the payment amounts tend to be consistent; this year's interim payment should be equal to or higher than the interim a year ago, and ditto for the final. A few U.K. firms with large U.S. shareholdings, such as GlaxoSmithKline (GSK) and British Petroleum (BP), pay quarterly, but these tend to include a larger final payment once a year.

▶ Other European firms (French, German, Swiss, and so forth) typically pay just once a year, even when those payments and the shares' yields are high. Moreover, last year's payment provides rather less guidance as to what a shareholder can expect this year; where U.S. and U.K. companies prefer to hold dividends steady when profits encounter a temporary drop,

Continental European boards are much more willing to slice the dividend when earnings decline.

▶ Japanese corporations tend to pay in the U.K.-style interim and final format, though the payment dates for large companies are likely to be spaced at equal six-month intervals.

▶ Emerging markets' dividend practices are all over the map. I've seen Brazilian firms pay as many as five times during a year, with no pattern seeming to govern timing or amounts. I'm sure it makes sense to them, but—being spoiled by American predictability—it makes no sense whatsoever to me. In any event, keen attention to detail is required for such stocks. What you see is unlikely to be what you'll get.

Unless you're prepared to do a tremendous amount of research, I'd strongly suggest sticking with listed ADRs. Owning foreign stocks directly, though not impossible, often leads brokerage firms to charge steep fees for currency conversions. Moreover, the universe of listed ADRs provides a wide selection that generally represents the largest and most financially stable firms in countries abroad. Since they're listed on U.S. exchanges, they're obliged to file financial information and other disclosures with our Securities and Exchange Commission. If you seek racier international exposure, I'd recommend mutual funds instead. The fees global and foreign funds charge, though typically higher than their U.S.-focused kin, are often a good deal. They have access to local information that few individual American stock pickers can match, and their insights will help shield your capital from costly mistakes.

Calculating an ADR's annualized dividend rate can be complicated. Domiciled as it is in Britain, Diageo naturally pays dividends in British pounds. France Telecom (FTE) and Siemens (SI) pay in euros; Honda Motor (HMC) pays in yen. The ADR administrator will convert these dividends into U.S. dollars for you, but it can't guarantee the exchange rate. So summing the dividends paid to U.S. holders over the preceding year is unlikely to provide a reliable annualized dividend rate. Moreover, one ADR does not necessarily represent one ordinary share; many ADRs represent two or more ordinary shares of the underlying issuer.

Given the inconsistent dividend practices of differing countries, your best source for foreign dividend data is the company's own dividend announcements.

Analyzing Foreign Dividends

Let's look at Lloyds TSB Group (LYG), the largest retail bank in Britain.

Like most British dividend payers, Lloyds pays in the interim and final format. If I look at the two most recent dividends paid to ADR holders, I find a final dividend paid in March 2007 of $1.87, plus an interim of $0.80 paid in August 2006. On this basis, the annualized dividend rate looks like $2.67 per ADR. But because the British pound has been rising against the dollar, Lloyds' true dividend rate is a bit higher. Going to the press releases on the bank's web site (www.lloydstsb.com), I find that the final dividend was 23.5 pence per ordinary share (that is, 0.235 pound per share) and the interim was 10.7 pence. The annualized dividend rate is thus 0.342 pound per share. From the web site I also learn that there are four ordinary shares behind each ADR, and from another site I discover that each British pound currently translates into 1.9743 dollars. By multiplying the pound-denominated dividend rate by the number of shares in each ADR and then by the exchange rate, I figure the annualized dividend rate of Lloyds' ADRs to be $2.70 apiece.

This brings up another issue: currency risk. If I buy Lloyds for my portfolio, counting on a dividend of $2.70 per ADR, I'm implicitly betting that the British pound will at least hold steady. If the pound rallies to $2.10, I can smile—my annualized income will rise to $2.87. But if the pound falls to $1.80, I'll collect only $2.46. These exchange-rate fluctuations will have a similarly direct effect on the ADR's price as well.

While I generally require stocks to offer steady and increasing income, I'm willing to tolerate some currency risk and the fluctuations it introduces to my dividend income, as long as a falling currency doesn't also threaten Lloyds TSB Group's ability to maintain its dividend in pound-denominated terms. It's become fashionable to seek foreign currency exposure on its own merit; America's free-spending ways compared with the rest of the world certainly don't bode well for the value of greenbacks. But with plenty of investment choices at home that would benefit from a falling dollar (Coca-Cola, to name but one example, derives more than two-thirds of its operating profits abroad), I have a hard time owning foreign stocks just because they're foreign. Instead, I look for good businesses offering attractive, consistent dividends, wherever they may be domiciled.

One final hitch applies to many other countries' stocks that makes them less attractive as a source of income: foreign withholding taxes. I describe this phenomenon in Appendix 2.

Dividend Reinvestment Plans

An appendix on the mechanics of dividends could hardly be complete without paying homage to the dividend reinvestment plan (DRIP). Despite an acronym that might make homeowners and landlords cringe, these plans have allowed millions of investors to steadily accumulate wealth through dividend-paying stocks.

A dividend reinvestment plan allows the investor to have his dividends used to purchase additional shares of stock. Sponsored by dividend-paying companies and administered by their stock transfer agents, DRIPs offer a low-cost (and often free) way to let dividends compound the investor's stake. Participation generally has just two requirements.

1. The investor needs to own shares that are registered in his own name, as opposed to the more common practice of "street name" registration, in which shares are actually held in the name of the investor's broker.
2. The investor needs to let the company know that he wants dividends reinvested. A telephone call, possibly followed up by filling out a short form, will usually do the trick.

To see how this works, let's say you purchased 100 shares of Piedmont Natural Gas (PNY) at the end of 2001 for $17.90 apiece, a total outlay of $1,790. Over the next year, Piedmont paid four quarterly dividends of $0.20 apiece. Had you received these dividends in cash, you would have received four checks for $20, $80 all told. That's enough to buy a nice steak dinner for two, as long as you don't go overboard on the wine.

Over the succeeding five years, Piedmont paid a total of $4.13 a share in dividends ($413 for your 100-share stake), while its share price rose from $17.90 to $26.75 (a capital gain of $885). (See Figure A1.1.) On a stand-alone basis, Piedmont provided a total return of $1,298, or 11.5 percent on an annualized basis. Sweet!

But if you didn't need those small dividend checks for income, you could have used them to buy more shares. With even the cheapest Internet broker commissions being $7 or so, none of those quarterly checks would have been enough to buy even a single share.

Luckily, Piedmont is happy to convert these small dividend checks into additional shares at no transaction cost to you. The DRIP plan will buy and hold fractional shares, so that your entire dividend can be reinvested. Not only that, but Piedmont—like a number of DRIP sponsors—will give you as an incentive a 5 percent discount on the market price on shares purchased with reinvested dividends. With each dividend reinvested, the next quarterly dividend grows.

Date	Transaction	Market Price ($)	Dividend Received	DRIP Purchase Price ($)	Shares Bought	Shares Held	Total Market Value
12/31/01	Initial Purchase of 100 Shares	17.90	—	—	100.00	100.00	1,790.00
04/15/02	Dividend of $0.20/share	18.20	20.00	17.29	1.16	101.16	1,841.05
07/15/02	Dividend of $0.20/share	16.49	20.23	15.67	1.29	102.45	1,689.37
10/15/02	Dividend of $0.20/share	17.15	20.49	16.29	1.26	103.71	1,778.04
01/15/03	Dividend of $0.20/share	17.44	20.74	16.57	1.25	104.96	1,830.47
04/15/03	Dividend of $0.2075/share	18.10	21.78	17.19	1.27	106.22	1,922.14
07/15/03	Dividend of $0.2075/share	19.44	22.04	18.47	1.19	107.42	2,088.22
10/15/03	Dividend of $0.2075/share	19.79	22.29	18.80	1.19	108.60	2,148.74
01/15/04	Dividend of $0.2075/share	21.68	22.54	20.60	1.09	109.70	2,378.26
04/15/04	Dividend of $0.215/share	20.13	23.59	19.12	1.23	110.93	2,232.51
07/15/04	Dividend of $0.215/share	20.90	23.85	19.85	1.20	112.13	2,343.03
10/15/04	Dividend of $0.215/share	22.21	24.11	21.10	1.14	113.28	2,515.87
01/14/05	Dividend of $0.215/share	22.48	24.35	21.36	1.14	114.42	2,572.09
04/15/05	Dividend of $0.23/share	21.93	26.32	20.83	1.26	115.68	2,536.86
07/15/05	Dividend of $0.23/share	24.43	26.61	23.21	1.15	116.83	2,854.07
10/14/05	Dividend of $0.23/share	23.08	26.87	21.93	1.23	118.05	2,724.63
01/13/06	Dividend of $0.23/share	24.54	27.15	23.31	1.16	119.22	2,925.57
04/13/06	Dividend of $0.24/share	23.71	28.61	22.52	1.27	120.49	2,856.74
07/14/06	Dividend of $0.24/share	24.83	28.92	23.59	1.23	121.71	3,022.12
10/13/06	Dividend of $0.24/share	26.57	29.21	25.24	1.16	122.87	3,264.65
12/29/06	**Market Value of Investment:**	**26.75**	—	—	—	**122.87**	**3,286.77**

Figure A1.1   Piedmont Natural Gas: Hypothetical Reinvestment of Dividends

With each passing quarter, your initial holding of 100 shares grew—even if just a share at a time. But with each additional share, your quarterly dividend income rose, enabling you to buy still more shares. I estimate that this 100-share investment would have grown into a holding of 122.87 shares worth $3,287 by the end of 2006. Your total gain in value was $1,497, a 15 percent improvement on simply taking the dividends in cash. Instead of earning an 11.5 percent annualized return, this DRIP account's value has compounded at a 12.9 percent clip. (See Figure A1.1.)

Give the compounding power of a DRIP a five- or ten-year stretch in which to work its magic, and a small stake can easily grow into a large one. As for incremental effort required on the part of the investor? None at all!

Many DRIPs are accompanied by direct stock purchase plans, which enable investors to bypass brokers entirely and buy shares with no commissions directly from the company. Piedmont, for one, allows a starter stake as small as $250 through its direct stock purchase plan and will even allow shareholders to set up automatic bank drafts to acquire extra shares on a monthly basis. Most brokerage firms also sponsor low-cost dividend reinvestment for thousands of stocks, often including firms that don't sponsor DRIPs themselves—though special deals like Piedmont's 5 percent discount don't apply to these.

For all their merits, dividend reinvestment plans have two small drawbacks worth mentioning. One is taxes: The fact that you're reinvesting the dividends rather than taking them in cash and spending them matters not one whit to the IRS. Additionally, all of the tiny purchases that eventually make up a DRIP account can complicate the cost-basis accounting should you sell down the road. You won't want to throw your DRIP account statements away. Nevertheless, DRIPs are one of the best ways I can think of to accumulate wealth.

Appendix 2

Dividends and Taxes

THE TAX CONSEQUENCES of investment income is my very least favorite topic in *Morningstar DividendInvestor*, but it's a necessary one.

Corporate profits in America are usually said to be taxed twice: first on the corporate level, then again when profits are passed on to shareholders through dividends and capital gains. Whether this double taxation is fair is subject to debate; after all, corporations have to factor income taxes into their costs when making investments, and corporations—entities whose assets and liabilities are legally separate from their owners—benefit from government goods and services like ordinary citizens do.

The government has been tinkering with the tax code recently, and for once, this has been to the dividend investor's benefit. After gaining the White House in 2001, policy wonks in the Bush administration sought legislation to provide more equitable treatment for dividend income. If correcting a historical economic inequity wasn't reason enough, the recession, bear market, and corporate scandals of 2001 to 2003 provided ample reason for Congress to act. The resulting Jobs and Growth Tax Relief Reconciliation Act of 2003 created what are known as qualified dividends and sliced their tax rates to a maximum of 15 percent.

Still, a relatively high combined tax rate for a corporation and its shareholders creates enormous incentives for businesses to structure themselves in ways that minimize tax payments. For example, assets in real estate and natural resources can be structured to avoid taxes at the corporate level—presumably because the government wants to provide incentives for shareholders to invest in them. These entities are then forced, explicitly or implicitly, to pay out the bulk of their cash flow—hence high rates of income in addition to a lower overall tax burden. Then again, no loophole exists without the loop; these corporate structures have tax rates and, in the case of partnerships, paperwork requirements that run far beyond those applied to ordinary common stocks.

Whatever it is that you buy, make sure you know what you are buying. If you don't understand the tax consequences thoroughly, seek professional help first. While taxes aren't a central focus of this book, I can at least describe the basic mechanics at work.

Types of Income

From a tax perspective, capital gains are beautifully simple. Buy a stock for $20, sell it for $25, and your gain is $5. If you hold the stock for less than a year, you'll pay your ordinary tax rate on the gain. Hold it for more than a year, and you'll owe no more than 15 percent of your winnings to the Internal Revenue Service.

Investment income is not so simple; it comes in several different flavors, all with distinct tax consequences.

- *Qualified dividend income.* Here we find the lowest tax rates on investment income the IRS has to offer.
- *Ordinary dividend income.* Not all dividends are eligible for qualified treatment, and as a result, they are taxed at the investor's top marginal tax rate.
- *Partnership income.* Like ordinary dividend income, partnership income is taxed at the investor's top tax bracket. However, the amount of taxable income you receive from a partnership may bear little or no relationship to the actual amount of cash distributions you've received.

▶ *Capital gains.* Hard as it may be to believe, income received from real estate investment trusts, partnerships, and other alternative structures can include taxable income characterized as capital gains. If these capital gains come from assets held for longer than one year, this income will be taxed at the lower capital gains tax rates on the investor's tax return.

▶ *Returns of capital.* When a business hands out cash to investors that exceeds its accumulated taxable income, those payments may be characterized as a *return of capital* rather than income. Returns of capital are not immediately taxable, but instead reduce the investor's cost basis, possibly leading to larger capital gains taxes when the investment is sold.

C Corporations

By far the simplest equities to own, ordinary corporations pay taxes on their income. Accountants refer to these entities as *C corporations*, since the rules are found in Subchapter C of Chapter 1 of the Internal Revenue Code. A corporation's assets and, more important, its liabilities are completely separate from its shareholders. This doubtless accounts for their popularity; the vast majority of listed equities in the United States are organized in this way. Shareholders owe tax only on the dividends they receive, not on any taxable income the corporation might retain for other purposes. Finally, the taxable income of these dividends is reported to shareholders on the relatively simple Form 1099.

Under current tax law, almost all of the dividends being paid by C corporations are characterized as qualified dividends, which are taxed at rates no higher than 15 percent. But, as you might expect, additional rules apply. Dividends are only qualified for this reduced tax rate so long as (1) the corporation itself had paid taxes on the income it paid out to shareholders, and (2) the shareholder held the stock for at least a 61-day stretch including the dividend's ex-date. (As of this writing, these reduced tax rates are set to expire in 2010.)

On occasion, a C corporation might also pay a dividend characterized as a return of capital. This usually only applies to large, one-time special dividends that exceed the corporation's accumulated taxable income. If there are returns of capital in a C corporation's dividends for a given tax year, the individual investor's share will be broken out on his Form 1099.

Real Estate Investment Trusts

From a legal point of view, real estate investment trusts (REITs) are also corporations, but they have opted for an alternative set of tax rules in exchange for abiding by certain rules, the most important of which are (1) the requirement to invest only in certain types of real estate-related assets, and (2) an obligation to pay at least 90 percent of taxable income out to shareholders as dividends. As long as the REIT abides by these rules, it does not have to pay income taxes itself.

For shareholders, however, REIT dividends are not eligible for the reduced tax rates on qualified dividends. These dividends are taxed at the higher rates applicable to ordinary wage income. As with corporations, taxable income is reported to investors on Form 1099.

Yet the dividends paid by a REIT are not always composed entirely of ordinary dividend income. If a REIT has sold an asset for a taxable profit during the year, part of its dividend may be characterized as capital gains for shareholders. If the asset was held for more than a year and the profit thus represents a long-term capital gain, shareholders will pay a lower rate of tax on this portion of their dividends.

In many cases, REIT dividends also include returns of capital. The taxable income of most REITs reflects large noncash deductions for depreciation, even though from an economic point of view, the assets (office buildings, shopping centers, and so on) aren't actually falling in value. A REIT can thus afford to pay out dividends exceeding its taxable income, and to the extent it does, this portion of shareholder dividends will be treated as a return of capital.

Business Development Corporations

Business development corporations (BDCs) are similar to REITs in that they can avoid paying income taxes in exchange for abiding by strict limits on their business activities (a high payout ratio, asset rules, and, unlike REITs, a limit on their use of debt). These firms are typically organized to make debt and equity investments in small and midsize businesses that can't access Wall Street capital on terms as favorable as larger enterprises. A BDC must pay out 95 percent of its taxable income and, as with a REIT, those dividends are taxed at ordinary income tax rates. (Again, as with REITs, returns of capital and capital gains income might be included along with the dividend.) Allied Capital (ALD) and American Capital Strategies (ACAS) are two well-known examples of BDCs. Their high yields have attracted plenty of income-oriented investors, but as with any investment, it isn't the tax or legal form of organization that counts, but the attractiveness of the underlying business activity.

Master Limited Partnerships

Unlike a corporation, a partnership is not considered to be a separate entity from its owner, but rather a contractual pooling of assets. Publicly traded partnerships are known as *master limited partnerships* (MLPs), and their ownership is divided proportionally into units (as opposed to shares). Limited unit holders still have limited liability, though there is a theoretical risk that creditors could go after cash distributions made in an act of management fraud. But from a legal and tax perspective, what the partnership does, it does in your name, not its own.

The benefit of this form of business organization is that the partnership does not pay taxes itself. Instead, a partnership's taxable income (or loss) is divvied up among the partners and added to their individual tax returns. Each unitholder receives a Schedule K-1, a form that contains the proportional revenue, expenses, and profits attributable to his ownership. But, as with REITs, MLPs are restricted to certain types of business activities, mostly related to natural resources or real estate. The MLP structure has proved most popular among the operators of oil and natural-gas pipelines, businesses whose steady cash flows lend themselves quite naturally to large cash distributions for unitholders.

The key to understanding MLP taxation is this: Cash distributions and taxable income are completely separate concepts. Unlike REITs, which are obliged to pay out at least 90 percent of their taxable income so the government can tax shareholder dividends, the tax rules don't *require* an MLP to make cash distributions to shareholders.

In isolation, this could make owning an MLP a rather unattractive prospect. An MLP with 10 million outstanding units that earns $25 million in taxable profits will pass $2.50 per unit worth of taxable income on to its unitholders. These unit holders are then obliged to pay tax on this income, regardless of whether the MLP pays out any cash. But to protect investors from owing tax even though they haven't received any cash, the partnership agreements that govern MLPs almost always require them to pay out virtually all of their available cash flow.

The taxable income of an MLP will usually consist primarily of ordinary income, taxable at the unitholder's top marginal tax rate. But if the MLP has taxable capital gains, those will be reported separately. If the MLP has earned qualified dividend income from a taxable subsidiary or some other invest- ment, that will be reported separately. Indeed, just about everything an MLP does from a tax perspective will be reported separately on the Schedule K-1 form. The unitholder is then obliged to fold these figures into his individual tax return. Not only that, but the unitholder is technically liable for the tax- able income in the individual states in which the MLP does business. These paperwork matters can easily turn into a headache; I'll have more to say on this later on.

By contrast, all of the cash payments an MLP makes to its unitholders are characterized as returns of capital. These payments are not taxable—at least not directly. Instead, every dollar you receive reduces your cost basis in the investment.

Royalty Trusts

From a tax perspective, domestic royalty trusts are similar to MLPs. These are not dissimilar to the trusts used in estate planning; indeed, that is how some trusts like Great Northern Iron Ore (GNI) came into being. There aren't many of them on the public markets today; they only merit mention because those that exist tend to have high yields to attract investors (even though their businesses are rarely attractive to own). Most earn income derived largely on the basis of some commodity output (and therefore prices) from land they control. Like MLPs, their taxable income flows down to investors—termed *beneficiaries* or *certificate holders*—separately from any cash distributions. And, like MLPs, they pay out virtually all of their cash flow.

But unlike MLPs, royalty trusts are not presumed to exist forever. When the gas wells or iron mines owned by the trusts are no longer productive—or some other event occurs to trigger dissolution of the trust—no value will remain for investors. For this reason, you'll want to read a trust's financial documents *very* carefully; Great Northern Iron Ore, for example, will cease to exist on April 6, 2015—a fact hardly evident in its market price as of this writing.

Limited Liability Corporations

Still another type of corporation—the limited liability corporation—also brings limited liability for investors to the table, but for tax purposes it is virtually identical to an MLP. MuniMae (MMA) is an example of a publicly traded business organized as an LLC, but it kicks out a Schedule K-1 just like an MLP.

How Returns of Capital Work

With so many moving parts at work in a REIT or MLP, let me try to simplify matters a bit. From an economic perspective, what you see is what you get. Regardless of how the IRS chooses to treat the cash paid out by a REIT, MLP, or some other tax-advantaged business entity, that cash represents income—cash you're getting in return for your investment.

The key variable for these equities is your *taxable cost basis*. For ordinary C corporations, this figure almost always represents whatever you originally paid for the stock. For tax-advantaged entities, this figure changes over time.

To illustrate this, let's say that, at the very last minute of trading on December 28, 2005, you bought 500 shares of REIT First Potomac Realty Trust (FPO) at $26.36 a share. Your total cost for this purchase—your cost basis—is $13,180. Then, over the course of 2006, First Potomac paid dividends totaling $1.125 a share, a total of $562.50 for your 500-share stake.

Had this income come from qualified dividends, your tax calculation would be very simple indeed: You held the shares long enough to qualify for the 15 percent tax rate, so you'd owe $84.38 in tax. Unfortunately, your tax calculation isn't going to be quite so simple.

In early 2007, First Potomac prepared its tax returns. Its announced breakdown of income is shown in Figure A2.1.

	Per Share	Share of Total (%)
Ordinary Taxable Dividend	0.4504	40.0
Unrecaptured Sec. 1250 Gain	0.0307	2.7
Return of Capital	0.6439	57.2
Total Dividends Paid	**$1.1250**	**100.0**

Figure A2.1   First Potomac: 2006 Taxable Income

	Per Share	Your Total	Taxable Income	Tax Rate %	Total Tax
Ordinary Taxable Dividend	0.4504	225.20	225.20	28	63.06
Unrecaptured Sec. 1250 Gain	0.0307	15.35	15.35	25	3.84
Return of Capital	0.6439	321.95	—	—	—
Total Dividends Paid	**$1.1250**	**$562.50**	**$240.55**	—	**$66.89**

Figure A2.2   First Potomac: 2006 Tax Summary

Good news! More than half of your dividends represented returns of capital on which you don't owe tax, at least not yet. The other two types of income (including that inscrutable entry) are taxable at about 28 percent, assuming that happens to be your federal tax rate. Figure A2.2 shows what you'll owe on your 2006 income from First Potomac.

Those returns of capital sure have a nice effect on your tax bill. Even though you're paying a higher tax rate (28 percent instead of 15 percent) on your taxable income, the fact that 57 percent of your dividends aren't currently taxable produces a current tax liability of $66.89—$17.49 less than you'd have owed on an equal sum of qualified dividends.

However, those returns of capital are no free lunch. The difference between the $562.50 of dividends you received and the $240.55 of income on which you paid tax—in other words, the return of capital of $321.95—reduces your cost basis in the stock. Although you still paid $13,300 to buy your shares, the IRS now considers your cost basis to be $12,978.05.

This reduced cost basis comes back to bite you when you sell your shares. Let's say you sold your 500 shares on Dec. 29, 2006, exactly 365 days from your date of purchase so you can pay the reduced tax rate on long-term capital gains. (See Figure A2.3.)

Congratulations! You've just captured a capital gain of $1,375. With those hefty dividends, you've hauled in a healthy 14.7 percent total return. We know how much tax you owe on the dividends; we already figured that out. The question now is how much you will owe on your capital gains.

Even though your economic capital gain is $1,375.00, the returns of capital during 2006 that accompanied your dividends have reduced your

Sale Proceeds from 500 Shares at $29.11	14,555.00
Less: Cost of 500 Shares at $26.36	−13,180.00
Capital Gain	**1,375.00**
Dividends Received ($1.125 a Share)	562.50
Total Return	**1,937.50**

Figure A2.3   First Potomac: 2006 Total Return

	Economic	Taxable
Sale Proceeds from 500 Shares at $29.11	14,555.00	14,555.00
Less: Cost of 500 Shares at $26.36	−13,180.00	−12,978.05
Capital Gain	**$1,375.00**	**1,576.95**
Tax Payable at 15%	206.25	236.54

Figure A2.4   First Potomac: 2006 Capital Gain, Economic versus Taxable

taxable cost basis—and thus inflated your taxable capital gain. Instead of owing $206.25 in long-term capital gains tax, you'll have to pay $236.54. (See Figure A2.4.)

The bottom line is this: Returns of capital are not taxes *avoided*, but merely taxes *deferred*. Not that deferring taxes isn't a big plus. Consider these advantages:

▶ Had you continued to hold your First Potomac shares, you'd have gone on collecting dividend income with a relatively low tax burden. Only if returns of capital accumulate to the point that your taxable cost basis drops to zero—something the IRS doesn't allow—would you have to pay taxes on 100 percent of your dividend income.

▶ Furthermore, these returns of capital have shifted dividends that would have been taxed at an ordinary tax rate of 28 percent into capital gains that were clipped for only 15 percent. Your overall tax rate for the life of the investment winds up being lower than it would have been without those returns of capital.

More on MLPs

The tax math for MLP investments is even more complicated than for REITs, in three ways:

1. The taxable results of an MLP are much more likely to contain multiple sources of income, which in turn may be taxed at different rates. This is one reason a REIT can report its taxable income to shareholders on the short Form 1099, while an MLP has to use the much longer Schedule K-1.

2. The characterization of an MLP's taxable income is based on the partner's actual purchase price. When you buy units, the MLP establishes a set of tax accounting books for your specific investment. If you pay a premium to the value of the partnership's assets (which is almost always the case), the MLP writes up the value of the property and starts depreciating it for tax purposes at a much higher rate. This is both a blessing and a curse; it means your taxable income might be very low and possibly even negative at the outset, but it also makes it hard to predict just how much taxable income you'll receive.

3. The coup de grace is that returns of capital from an MLP, unlike those of a REIT, can't be shifted from the higher ordinary income tax rate to the lower capital gains tax rate; the IRS won't allow it. This phenomenon is known as *recapture of depreciation.*

I think another example will come in handy, even if I'm only estimating this time. Let's say you bought 200 units of Buckeye Partners (BPL) on December 29, 2005, for $41.92 each. Your total investment—and initial cost basis for tax purposes—is $8,384. Then, over the next 12 months, Buckeye dishes out $3.025 per unit in cash distributions, or $605 for your investment.

Then the end of the tax year comes and you receive your Schedule K-1. While difficult to predict with precision, Buckeye's management had recently indicated that newly purchased units can expect allocations of taxable income equal to roughly 30 percent of cash distributions, at least for the first year or so. For Buckeye, that implies that you'll probably be on the hook for $0.91 per unit of taxable income, a total of $182. When you file your tax return for 2006, you'll owe tax on this $182 at a 28 percent rate—a total of $50.96. (See Figure A2.5.)

	Per Unit	Total
Cash Distributions	3.025	605.00
Estimated Ratio of Taxable Income	30%	—
Estimated Taxable Income	**0.91**	**182.00**
Ordinary Income Tax Rate	—	28%
Estimated Tax	**—**	**50.96**

Figure A2.5   Buckeye Partners: Estimated 2006 Tax Liability

Considering that you took in $605 in cash distributions, paying $50.96 in tax sounds like a pretty good deal; this is an effective tax rate of less than 10 percent. Again, this seems to beat the tax rate on qualified dividends.

As I said earlier, all cash distributions from MLPs are treated as returns of capital. Your taxable cost basis is falling, just as it did with First Potomac, but much faster in this case. At year-end, before you receive your Schedule K-1, your taxable cost basis is just $7,779.

The taxable cost basis of an MLP has not just one but two moving parts. Cash distributions reduce your cost basis, but the taxable income allocated to you as an MLP unitholder pushes it back up. Adding this factor to the total, your cost basis at the end of 2006 now stands at $7,961. (See Figure A2.6.)

As you did with First Potomac, you took the opportunity to sell your Buckeye units on Dec. 29, 2006, at $46.48 per unit. First, let's see how this investment made out on a pretax basis by referring to Figure A2.7.)

Congratulations again—you've made a total return of more than 18 percent for the year. Buckeye did its part; now it's time for us to do our part and calculate the tax. As far as the IRS is concerned, you didn't receive any dividend income; your entire profit represents a capital gain. However, this capital gain will be separated into two parts: the part that came from the decline in your

Original Cost of 200 Units at $41.92	8,384.00
Subtract: Cash Distributions Received	−605.00
Add Back: Allocated Taxable Income	182.00
Taxable Cost Basis	**7,961.00**

Figure A2.6   Buckeye Partners: Taxable Cost Basis

Sale Proceeds from 200 Units at $46.48	9,296.00
Less: Cost of 200 Units at $41.92	−8,384.00
Capital Gain	**912.00**
Cash Distributions Received ($1.125 a Share)	605.00
Total Return	**1,517.00**

Figure A2.7   Buckeye Partners: Total Return in 2006

taxable cost basis (recapture of depreciation) and the piece that came from the increase in Buckeye Partners' market price.

Figure A2.8 shows that your taxable income is the same $1,517 that we calculated on a pretax basis earlier. But as we close the books on this investment, we find that the sum of allocated taxable income ($182) plus the recapture of depreciation ($423) is equal to the $605 in cash distributions we received. On both of these amounts, we had to apply the 28 percent ordinary tax rate for a total tax liability of $169.40. Only the portion that represented a true economic capital gain—the difference between what we originally paid for the stock and our selling price—is taxed at the lower 15 percent long-term capital gains rate.

As with First Potomac, the ability to defer taxes into the future is a nice bonus for investors. If we hadn't sold, we could have deferred taxes equal to 70 percent of our cash distributions. However, over time, the ratio of taxable

	Taxable Amount	Tax Rate %	Tax Owed
Sale Proceeds	9,296.00	—	—
Less: Original Cost Basis	−8,384.00	—	—
Long-Term Capital Gain	**912.00**	**15.0**	**136.80**
Sale Proceeds	9,296.00	—	—
Less: Taxable Cost Basis	−7,961.00	—	—
Less: Long-Term Capital Gain	−912.00	—	—
Recapture of Depreciation	**423.00**	**28.0**	**118.44**
Total Taxable Capital Gain	1,335.00	—	—
Plus: Allocated Taxable Income	182.00	28.0	50.96
Total Taxable Income and Tax	**1,517.00**	**20.2**	**306.20**

Figure A2.8   Buckeye Partners: 2006 Gain, Economic versus Taxable

income relative to cash distributions tends to rise—those big initial depreciation deductions will start to shrink relative to the cash distributions you're
receiving. This is especially problematic if the MLP itself isn't growing by
acquiring more assets and laying more pipe (not too likely for a growth-
oriented MLP like Buckeye). As long as your income is growing faster than
your taxable income allocation, though, you're still ahead.

Nevertheless, be warned: The longer you own an MLP like Buckeye or a
REIT like First Potomac, the further its taxable cost basis will fall—and the
more tax you'll owe when you choose to sell.

If this seems hopelessly complicated, I have wonderful news: Buckeye and
other MLPs will do all of this characterizing and calculating of taxable income
for you on your Schedule K-1. All you have to do is fold the figures from the
K-1 into your tax return. Popular tax software programs like TurboTax—to
say nothing of qualified tax professionals—are equipped to handle K-1s.

Why should we bother with these partnerships and REITs when there
are stocks out there that pay straight qualified dividends, easily tracked and
taxed? The answer lies in the realm of trade-offs: MLPs and most REITs offer
much higher current yields than most qualified dividend payers. An MLP
like Buckeye owns assets that are not unlike a steady Eddie utility, but instead
of a 4 percent yield, Buckeye routinely offers 6 to 7 percent or more. If I were
investing very small amounts—a couple of thousand dollars at a shot—the
hassle and expense of coping with Schedule K-1 forms might not be worth
the extra income. But if I can devote a more significant dollar figure to a well-
chosen MLP or two, where the extra income could easily offset any additional
tax-filing costs, these may be trade-offs well worth making.

Taxable Losses from MLPs

In 2006, Kinder Morgan Energy Partners (KMP) paid out cash distributions of $3.23 a
unit. Earnings per unit using standard accounting were $2.04 (though distributable cash
flow, a better proxy for the cash-distributing ability of an MLP, was $3.26). So while I
knew Kinder Morgan was paying out virtually all of its cash flow, even I was surprised
to see my Schedule K-1 for the 2006 tax year. The 75 units held in *Morningstar Dividend-
Investor's* model portfolio were allocated a taxable *loss* of $364, or $4.85 a unit.

(continued)

This information could trigger one of two responses.

1. *If reported profits are positive but taxable income is negative, then Kinder Morgan must be cooking the books!* Not at all: Kinder Morgan is investing heavily in new pipeline construction, creating huge tax write-offs for depreciation. The taxable loss reflects these investments—and the ample tax incentives offered for making them—but the cash flows generated by its existing assets are very real indeed.
2. *Great—I'll use this loss to offset my other income and cut my tax bill!* Sorry, but the tax rules state that taxable losses generated by MLPs can only be used to offset future gains on the same investment. We didn't owe any tax on our Kinder Morgan investment in 2006 as a result of the loss—an effective tax rate of zero—but neither could we use it to offset other forms of taxable income. Only if we sell will we be able to capture the benefit of our 2006 allocation of a taxable loss.

This phenomenon is yet another reason to be glad that MLPs do all of the tax record keeping for the investor!

Foreign Dividend Taxes

Governments look to tax income wherever and however it is earned, dividends included. Most see no reason to let their corporations' dividends go untaxed just because they're being sent abroad. So they impose withholding taxes on the dividends that accrue to U.S. and other foreign investors. The United Kingdom is notable in that it doesn't; because of a longstanding tax treaty between the two nations, whatever Lloyds TSB Group (LYG) or Diageo (DEO) pay to their domestic shareholders will go directly to U.S. investors as well. But Switzerland, for example, imposes a 15 percent withholding tax on dividends, such as those paid by drug maker Novartis (NVS). Of the $0.88 per American depositary receipt (ADR) declared by the company in 2006, only $0.75 reached America's shores.

These foreign taxes can be recovered, at least in part, through a credit on the shareholder's U.S. tax return. For each ADR of Novartis earning an $0.88 dividend, a U.S. shareholder would owe $0.13 a share in tax at the 15 percent qualified rate. The 15 percent withholding tax that stayed in Switzerland is also $0.13 a share, so this credit offsets the U.S. tax: You won't owe the IRS any additional tax on this dividend payment.

However, if you happen to collect dividends from a country with a withholding tax rate higher than what you'd owe in the United States, such as Turkey or India, you can't recover the difference, which might be 5 or 10 percent of the total dividend payment. (Although I doubt you'll find many reliable dividend payers in either of those countries.)

Because of these factors, you'll want to check out the withholding taxes of a country before you buy one of its stocks and the practices of the particular ADR in handling them. Your best resource is often to contact the company's investor relations department before buying. And if you can, try to own stocks carrying significant withholding taxes in ordinary taxable accounts (more on this in the next section).

Taxable versus Tax-Deferred Accounts

When considering the tax consequences of your investment choices, it isn't just the investment itself that matters. The type of account that will hold the investment matters as well.

In a taxable account, investors may own whatever securities they please. You'll have to file the tax return and pay whatever is owed, but there are no restrictions on what types of equities you might own. The downside is that you'll owe tax regardless of whether the income is spent or reinvested. If you're not withdrawing your portfolio income for living expenses or other uses, these incremental tax payments create a drag on your long-term accumulation of wealth.

By contrast, tax-deferred accounts—IRAs, 401(k)s, SEPPs, Keoghs, and so on—allow the investor to defer taxes on current investment income. Cash returns can be reinvested and compounded until the account holder makes withdrawals. Most of these accounts are funded with pretax dollars in exchange for the full amount of any withdrawals being taxed as ordinary income. Roth IRAs and Roth 401(k)s don't provide the investor with any tax break when contributions are made, but—at least under current tax law—withdrawals are not taxed at all: not on the original contributions nor on any subsequent gains.

While tax law prescribes few limits on the securities a tax-deferred account may own, income from MLPs or royalty trusts can create tax problems for the account itself. These firms get to exempt themselves from taxes only because those tax liabilities are being passed down to investors. In a taxable account, the IRS catches partnership income on the investor's tax return. But tax-deferred accounts are not themselves tax-paying entities; partnership income might flow in, but no tax would flow out to the IRS.

To prevent this abuse, the IRS has set a limit of $1,000 of what it calls *unrelated business taxable income* for IRAs and other tax-deferred accounts. If one of these accounts catches taxable income from partnerships in excess of this figure, the IRA itself—not you, its owner—can get whacked with a hefty tax bill that will drag down your investment's return. This $1,000 limit *could* be treated like a tax loophole by owning just enough MLP units to stay under the limit.

My advice is simply this: Don't own MLPs in tax-deferred accounts. REITs are fine, qualified dividend payers are fine, and there are still plenty of high-yield stocks to pick from. Why court a tax problem if you don't have to?

Dividend income from ADRs can present problems for tax-deferred accounts as well. Since the account isn't paying tax on the dividend income, there's no way to use the tax credit a taxable investor would receive from the foreign withholding tax. Even Canada, just barely a foreign country in the eyes of many Americans, imposes a 15 percent withholding tax on its corporate dividends. In other words, the withholding tax is an unrecoverable, deadweight loss. If you have the choice of owning a high-yielding ADR from a country with withholding taxes in a taxable account instead of a tax-deferred one, you'll stand a better chance of getting the full after-tax value of your dividend.

Appendix 3

Banks

IF I WERE to sit down with a blank sheet of paper and a pencil and attempt to create a perfect dividend machine, my sketch would look very much like the average U.S. bank.

Income investors have traditionally looked first to utilities and real estate investment trusts in search of income. In the late 1990s, bank yields of even 3 percent were relatively rare. Since then, a combination of rapid earnings growth, rising payout ratios, and generally stagnant share prices has created a wonderful opportunity for income investors. From where I sit today, banks offer the single best combination of dividend yield, dividend growth, and total return available in the marketplace. Though a bank's common stock isn't guaranteed by the government the way its deposits are, I'd much rather have money *on* the bank (that is, in its stock) than *in* the bank.

Bank Basics

Anyone with a checking account or car loan already knows the basic operations of a bank: It takes money from one group of people (depositors) and lends it to another group (borrowers). On the asset side, a bank may also own bonds and other securities.

On the liability side, a bank can issue bonds of its own or tap the short-term financing markets for additional funding.

In this way, a bank's revenue and profits are directly tied to its balance sheet, much more so than at the average business. The difference between what a bank earns on its assets and what it pays on its liabilities is called *net interest income*. The ancient creed of bankers—"Borrow at 3, lend at 6, play golf at 3"—still applies today, even if the figures themselves might be a little different.

To illustrate the basic operations of a bank—with round numbers that you won't find in the real world—I've decided to make one up. (See Figure A3.1.) Why not call it Basic Bank & Trust?

For this very simple example, we find (1) $100 million of loans throwing off $7 million in interest income (a 7 percent rate of return), and (2) $90 million of liabilities on which the bank pays a 3 percent rate of interest, $2.7 million in all. The raw difference between the interest rate the bank earns on its assets and what it pays on its liabilities is the net interest spread. With Basic Bank & Trust earning 7 percent and paying 3 percent, the net interest spread is simply 4 percent.

A bank also requires shareholders' equity to operate. One of the key features of a balance sheet—not just a bank's, but any corporation's—is that while liabilities are fixed, the value of the assets may change. If Basic Bank & Trust tried to do business without equity—$100 million in both assets and liabilities—then even a small decline in the value of its assets would render it insolvent. Equity provides both depositors and shareholders with much-needed room for error. A bank's *equity/assets ratio* is thus a key indicator of solvency and financial strength.

Summary Balance Sheet			Interest Rate %	Amount
Assets (Loans, Securities)	100,000	Interest Income	7.0	7,000
Liabilities (Deposits, Bonds, etc.)	90,000	Interest Expense	−3.0	−2,700
Shareholders' Equity	**10,000**	**Net Interest Income**	**4.0**	**4,300**

Figure A3.1   Basic Bank & Trust: Balance Sheet and Earnings (Dollars in Thousands)

Interest Rates and Banks

Most people seem to think that banks earn their spread by borrowing at short-term, variable interest rates and lending at long-term fixed rates. This conventional wisdom greatly overstates reality. Instead of simply playing the *yield curve* (the difference between short-term and long-term rates), banks tend to earn the bulk of their net interest income through *credit spreads*: the difference in rates between risk-free liabilities and risk-bearing assets.

Think of it this way: Individual depositors in Basic Bank & Trust's hometown probably wouldn't be willing to lend to businesses directly—there'd be too much risk involved with any single loan. Neither would businesses gain by borrowing from individuals in $500 or $5,000 increments; this would be complicated and costly. So Basic Bank & Trust, acting as an intermediary, steps into the breach and charges a spread for matching borrowers' needs with depositors' funds, as well as covering the risk that borrowers may fail to repay in full.

That isn't to say that banks aren't sensitive to interest rates; to some extent, every bank's profits will be affected as rates rise and fall. Some institutions—such as savings and loans that hold long-term, fixed-rate mortgages—are much more sensitive to the yield curve than ordinary commercial or retail banks. Other bank executives may decide to make overt bets on the yield curve, usually to their peril. But the broader effect of interest rates on the average bank isn't that much different than it is for the economy in general: Low interest rates encourage borrowing and allow banks to increase their assets faster; high rates have the opposite effect.

$$\text{Shareholders' Equity} \div \text{Assets} = \text{Equity/Assets Ratio}$$

For Basic Bank & Trust:

$$\$10,000 \div \$100,000 = 10.0\%$$

This equity on Basic Bank & Trust's balance sheet has another positive effect. It doesn't earn interest; shareholders will be compensated through earnings and dividends much further down the line. Because not all of the bank's assets are funded with interest-paying liabilities, there's a bit of a mismatch between the net interest spread and the best indicator of the profitability of lending activities, *net interest margin*. Instead of subtracting the average rate paid on liabilities from that earned on assets, we divide net interest income by total earning assets.

Net Interest Income ÷ Earning Assets = Net Interest Margin

For Basic Bank & Trust:

$$\$4,300 \div \$100,000 = 4.3\%$$

Thus far, Basic Bank & Trust has brought in $4.3 million of net interest income with $10 million of shareholders' equity. If life were just this simple, that would represent a whopping 43 percent return on equity. But we still have to consider few more factors.

▶ *Noninterest income.* Basic Bank & Trust doesn't just take deposits and make loans; it also charges fees for other services. Everything from overdraft charges on checking accounts to activities ranging from investment advisory and insurance brokerage goes into this figure. Adding net interest income to noninterest income represents a bank's total revenue, or *net revenue.*

▶ *Provision for loan losses.* No well-run bank wants to lend money that it can't expect to be paid back in full, with interest. But some loans, no matter how conservatively made, will go bad. When they do, these losses decrease the bank's net income.

▶ *Noninterest expense.* Tellers, clerks, loan officers, and bank presidents don't work for free. These costs, plus rent, utilities, and any other operating expenses, are also deducted from revenue.

▶ *Income taxes.* Like any other corporation, Basic Bank & Trust will have to pay income taxes on its profits.

Including these factors, Figure A3.2 shows what Basic Bank & Trust's income statement looks like.

With Basic Bank & Trust's full income statement now in view, we can now calculate two more important performance statistics:

1. *Efficiency ratio.* Banks don't express their income in terms of profit margins the way other types of companies do, but management and shareholders will naturally still take an interest in the relationship between operating costs and net revenue. The resulting statistic, the efficiency

Interest Income	7,000
Interest Expense	−2,700
Net Interest Income	**4,300**
Add: Noninterest Income	1,100
Net Revenue	**5,400**
Less: Provision for Loan Losses	−500
Less: Noninterest Expenses	−2,400
Pretax Income	**2,000**
Less: Income Taxes (40%)	−1,000
Net Income	**1,500**

Figure A3.2   Basic Bank & Trust: Income Statement (Dollars in Thousands)

ratio, is essentially the opposite of the profit margin. Unlike profit margins, where higher numbers indicate higher profitability, we'd just as soon see a bank's efficiency ratio be as low as possible.

$$\text{Noninterest Expense} \div \text{Net Revenue} = \text{Efficiency Ratio}$$

For Basic Bank & Trust:

$$\$2,400 \div \$5,400 = 44.4\%$$

2. *Return on equity.* This is the ultimate measure of a bank's success on behalf of shareholders. Calculating the ROE for a bank is no different than for any other corporation. Basic Bank & Trust earned a $1.5 million profit on $10 million of shareholders' equity, so its ROE is 15 percent.

Accounting for Loan Losses

As I said earlier, some loans will inevitably go bad—that's the way a banker's cookie will crumble from time to time. The foregoing simplified example doesn't do justice to the actual process of dealing with bad loans. Basic Bank & Trust can't just wait to take the hit when the loan is finally written off; the accounting process begins immediately. This topic may seem a bit complex, but it's very important to understand when analyzing a bank, so let's see if I can simplify it a bit.

Let's say Basic Bank & Trust has $100 million of loans outstanding. Management knows that some of these loans won't be repaid in full, but right now it doesn't know for sure which ones or, for that matter, how much it might lose on any particular loan if the borrower defaults. Nevertheless, accounting rules force the bank to make some kind of estimate.

On the basis of what it knows about its borrowers—their current financial condition, the value of the collateral backing up these loans, and historical loan losses, to name just a few factors—Basic Bank & Trust figures that by the time all $100 million worth of loans are settled, it will get only $98 million of its money back. The $2 million difference between these two figures is set aside in an account called the *allowance for loan losses*. On the asset side of its balance sheet, Basic Bank & Trust will list the gross amount of loans outstanding, the size of the reserve (a negative asset, if you will), and the net figure of $98 million. On the income statement, this allowance was reflected by provisions that reduced reported earnings long ago.

Early one morning (about 9 o'clock for bankers), the president of Basic Bank & Trust picks up the local paper and discovers that one of his borrowers, a used-car dealer, has just filed for bankruptcy. The bank lent $2 million to this clown, and now he's gone belly-up. Spewing coffee over his desk, the president proceeds to call in the officer who made the loan and chew the poor fellow out.

Not all is lost, though. The red-faced loan officer reminds the bank president (who approved the loan in the first place, by the way) that this loan is secured by the land and buildings on the used-car lot. As best he can tell, this collateral is worth $1.4 million.

The first accounting step is the *charge-off*. Because Basic Bank & Trust can't reasonably expect to get its full $2 million back, it will write the value of this loan down to the collateral's market value, $1.4 million. Only $600,000 of the loan will be charged off.

But as in physics, every accounting action has an equal and opposite reaction. Where will this $600,000 hit be felt? Not on the income statement—at least not directly, and at least not yet. (See Figure A3.3.)

For the time being, this charge-off shown in Figure A3.3 will be covered by the bank's allowance for loan losses, since this is exactly what the allowance is for. Even though a $2 million loan has gone into default,

	Gross Loans	Allowance	Net Loans
Before the Loan Goes Bad	100,000	−2,000	98,000
Charge-off	−600	600	0
After the Bad Loan	**99,400**	**−1,400**	**98,000**

Figure A3.3   Basic Bank & Trust: Loan Goes Bad (Dollars in Thousands)

the net loan figure shown on the balance sheet hasn't changed: It's still $98 million.

The bank's attorney moves quickly to repossess the property. Basic Bank & Trust doesn't want to be in the used-car business; it just wants as much of its money back as possible. A month or so later, a real estate developer offers the bank $1.4 million for the property—exactly what the loan officer figured the collateral was worth. The developer gives Basic Bank & Trust a check for $1.4 million, and the bank hands over the deed to the property. (See Figure A3.4.)

Only now has the size of Basic Bank & Trust's net loan portfolio shrunk, and only by $1.4 million—the amount of the loan actually repaid. The other $600,000 was reflected earlier by the reduction in the allowance for loan losses. Finally, the $1.4 million received is now sitting in the bank's cash account, so total assets haven't changed.

The final step comes at the end of the quarter. The bank's managers look over the rest of the loan portfolio and realize the $1.4 million balance in the allowance for loan losses account isn't enough; more loans will probably go bad in the future. On the basis of their best estimates of future loan performance, they deem a $1.9 million allowance to be appropriate. It's a bit lower than the $2 million allowance at the end of the previous accounting period, but the bank now has fewer loans outstanding, and the used-car dealer's loan was one of the riskiest; the remaining portfolio doesn't look quite as risky. (See Figure A3.5.)

	Gross Loans	Allowance	Net Loans
Before the Loan Goes Bad	99,400	−1,400	98,000
Collateral Gets Sold	−1,400	—	−1,400
After the Bad Loan is Sold	**98,000**	**−1,400**	**96,600**

Figure A3.4   Basic Bank & Trust: Recovering the Bad Loan (Dollars in Thousands)

	Gross Loans	Allowance	Net Loans
After the Bad Loan is Sold	98,000	−1,400	96,600
Adjustment to the Allowance	—	−500	−500
Final Balances	**98,000**	**−1,900**	**96,100**

Figure A3.5   Basic Bank & Trust: Adjusting the Allowance (Dollars in Thousands)

Ending Allowance for Loan Losses	−1,900
Plus: Beginning Allowance for Loan Losses	2,000
Less: Charge-offs during the Period	−600
Provision (Expense) for Loan Losses	**−500**

Figure A3.6   Basic Bank & Trust: Bad Loan's Impact on Earnings (Dollars in Thousands)

Because the allowance has gone up—at least from where it was after that used-car dealer loan was charged off—this again reduces the value of the bank's net loans. This additional provision of $500,000 is what finally shows up on the bank's income statement. (See Figure A3.6.)

This little drama plays out on the bank's second floor; as a shareholder, all you get to see is what is reflected in the financial statement. Here are some key indicators:

▶ *Past-due loans.* Between a fully performing loan and a charge-off, the borrower usually falls behind on scheduled interest and principal payments. This value will be reported in the bank's footnotes.

▶ *Nonperforming assets.* This is the total value of loans that the bank seriously doubts it will be able to collect in full. This isn't a projection of future losses—the full value of a $10 million loan might be included in nonperformers, even if that loan is secured with $9 million in cash. However, the more nonperforming assets a bank has, the greater the likelihood that the eventual losses will be higher than what has already been charged off.

▶ *Allowance for loan losses.* How large or small this figure is relative to gross loans will tell you how prepared a bank is for a deterioration in credit quality.

The *charge-off ratio* is the most important indicator and the most relevant. These are still estimates, but every time a bank is forced to confront the prospects for a bad loan, the expected loss is reflected in this figure. Low charge-off ratios suggest that the bank is doing a good job identifying creditworthy loans.

$$\text{Net Chargeoffs} \div \text{Gross Loans} = \text{Chargeoff Ratio}$$

For Basic Bank & Trust:

$$\$500 \div \$10,000 = 0.5\%$$

Evaluating Banks

Equity/asset ratios, net interest margins, efficiency ratios, charge-off ratios— all of these figures and more will influence a bank's profitability. These profits, in turn, dictate the security of a bank's dividend and its ability to grow.

Every bank is different (even though many will look more or less the same at first glance). Strategies vary widely—some focus on commercial lending, others on consumers, still others on residential real estate, specialty finance, or investment banking. A few even cling to the old thrift business model (also known as a savings and loan) and use depositors' funds to buy long-term mortgages.

Whatever the strategy, it might amaze you that banks that are merely average routinely earn ROEs of 15 percent or more. After all, money is probably the ultimate commodity. But if money is a commodity, it also never goes out of style, as Christopher Davis of Davis Advisors—a champion investor in financial services firms—has pointed out. Loans and deposits aren't subject to technological changes; sure, individual lenders or deposit takers can tweak the terms and rates offered on such products, but the basic function of these activities is timeless and utterly essential to the functioning of a capitalist economy.

The economic moats that banks use to earn these handsome returns come from a variety of sources.

▶ *Regulation.* Many industries are regulated by various levels of government; for example, utility regulators routinely step in to limit profits to prevent monopoly abuse. Banks are heavily regulated too, but there's no ham-handed ceiling on profits. Instead, regulators pay close attention to the health of a bank's balance sheet. Since the Federal Deposit Insurance

Corporation (FDIC) guarantees depositors' funds up to $100,000 apiece, the chief goal of bank overseers is to ensure that no deposit-taking institution goes bust. Regulators have a great deal of power to limit or stop what they might view as risky lending practices (risks that might jeopardize depositors' dollars), and they inadvertently shield the bank's stockholders from loss as well. It's no small wonder, then, that bank failures are very rare. In 1997–2006, only 44 banks failed in the United States out of the 10,000-plus that were in existence.

Many banks are too big to fail. If Bank of America (BAC), Citigroup (C), or JPMorgan Chase (JPM)—which are literally trillion-dollar institutions—or even one of the larger regional banks were to go belly-up, the repercussions through the rest of the financial system would be catastrophic. Regulators will step in long before such an event threatens the economy.

This doesn't mean that regulators are always friendly to banks. In 2006, the Federal Reserve raised short-term interest rates to a level that made banks' holdings of Treasury bonds structurally unprofitable, an environment that in turn led bank profit growth to slow to a crawl. Even so, returns on equity remained in that 15 to 20 percent range across the board.

▶ *Cheap funding.* The fact that the government guarantees deposits, plus the fact that checking deposits by tradition pay very little interest (if any), allows banks to fund their loans and other earning assets more cheaply than any other player in the economy. In early 2007, a time when the U.S. Treasury had to pay 5 percent to borrow short-term and 4.5 percent or more on long-term bonds, banks' average cost of funds was less than 4 percent. Making good returns on lending can be a tough business; anyone can make a loan, but only a bank can take a deposit.

▶ *Customer switching costs.* When passing a new bank branch in your neighborhood that offers a $100 bonus on new checking accounts, do you jerk the steering wheel to the right, march on in, and transfer your accounts on the spot? Of course not. Chances are you, like tens of millions of your fellow Americans, have your paychecks wired into your existing checking account, your mortgage and car payments automatically wired out, and various other financial accounts all linked back to where you currently bank. It's more than $100 worth of grief to change all those existing transactions, and in making a transition you'd run the risk of having deposits and payments assigned to the wrong account, possibly leading to bounced checks or other problems.

Even if you're just looking for certificates of deposit—where none of the problems involved with swapping checking accounts apply—sheer apathy is likely to keep your money in the same place for long stretches of time. Banks can pay less for deposits than elsewhere and charge more for services, and the vast majority of depositors will put up with it.

▶ *Economies of scale.* Bigger banks (those with $5 billion to $10 billion or more in assets) can leverage their size to spread fixed noninterest expenses, such as the costs of accounting and account servicing, over a larger base of earning assets. But even a small bank, if it pays careful attention to costs, can generate solid returns more or less like clockwork.

These factors add up to an impressive economic moat for virtually all banks. That moat translates to returns on equity well above the returns required by shareholders.

The factor that turns a great story from anyone's point of view into a near-perfect one for dividend investors is this: Expanding a bank is not easy. A certain level of growth, usually tied to regional economic prospects in the mid single digits, tends to fall into a bank's lap with little effort on the part of management. But to expand a bank internally at the kind of rates that some handsome ROEs might imply—15 percent or even 20 percent annually—is extremely difficult even for small institutions. In the end, most banks simply kick the profits they don't need for modest growth out to shareholders as dividends—a practice that bankers never gave up, even when other sectors of American industry did.

While a bank's dividend yield and historical growth rate are useful starting points for analysis, these easily obtainable statistics are no substitute for forward-looking fundamental research.

In the context of the Dividend Drill research process, here are some bank-specific factors I consider. To build up some worthwhile estimates, I'll describe

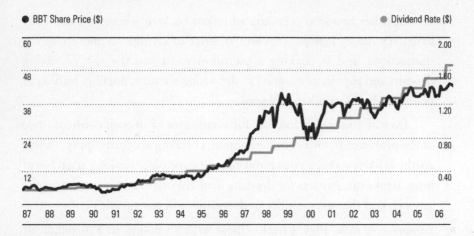

Figure A3.7   BB&T Corporation: Share Price and Dividend History

my thoughts on a bank once called Branch Banking and Trust, which is now known simply as BB&T Corporation (BBT). Like many deposit takers, BB&T has an impressive record. (See Figure A3.7.) Let's turn to what the future might hold.

Bank Dividend: Is It Safe?

Despite the favorable economic attributes belonging to almost all banks, dividend cuts can and do occur.

A wise old gentleman with decades of industry experience once told me, "Banks don't get in trouble by paying too much for deposits. Banks go bad when they make bad loans." So the first question one should consider is the bank's asset quality.

I start with the balance sheet. As you might expect, real-world bank balance sheets are not so simple as the example I showed at the beginning of this appendix. In addition to loans and securities that throw off interest income (*earning assets*), banks also have their own property (branches, computers, and so forth), as well as (in most cases) a goodly sum of goodwill and other intangible assets.

Figure A3.8 shows a summarized version of BB&T's balance sheet at the end of 2006.

Cash Due from Banks	2,024
Other Short-Term Investments	1,521
Securities	22,868
Cash and Securities	**26,413**
Gross Loans and Leases	82,911
Less: Allowance for Loan Losses	−888
Loans and Leases, Net	**82,023**
Premises and Equipment, Net	1,410
Goodwill and Other Intangible Assets	5,281
Other Assets	6,224
Total Assets	**121,351**
Deposits	80,971
Short-Term Debt	8,087
Long-Term Debt	15,904
Accounts Payable and Other	4,644
Total Liabilities	**109,606**
Shareholders' Equity	**11,745**
Loan-Loss Allowance Ratio (%)	**1.1**
Equity/Assets Ratio (%)	**9.7**

Figure A3.8   BB&T Balance Sheet as of December 31, 2006 (Dollars in Millions)

The key figures here are at the bottom.

▶ *Loan/loss ratio.* This is the allowance for loan losses divided by total loans outstanding. Since BB&T is a conservative lender with a history of low charge-offs, 1.1 percent looks okay. If the bulk of BB&T's loans were of questionable quality, this might not be nearly enough.
▶ *Equity/asset ratio.* All else being equal, the higher this figure, the stronger the bank. Looking at the bank's book figure of 9.7 percent, BB&T looks very strong indeed.

However, not all of BB&T's assets have real cash value. In the past, BB&T has made dozens of acquisitions, usually paying more for the acquired firm than its net asset value. This premium accumulates in an account known as goodwill and other intangible assets; BB&T has a whopping $5.3 billion

	Book Basis	Tangible Basis
Tangible Assets	116,070	116,070
Other Short-Term Investments	5,281	0
Total Assets	**121,351**	**116,070**
Total Liabilities	109,606	109,606
Shareholders' Equity	**11,745**	**6,464**
Equity/Assets Ratio (%)	**9.7**	**5.6**

Figure A3.9   BB&T: Book Equity versus Tangible Equity (Dollars in Millions)

worth. If we back these intangibles out of assets and equity, total assets drops a little, but equity drops a lot. (See Figure A3.9.)

Is a 5.6 percent tangible equity/assets ratio enough? We have to read this statistic in context of the bank's size and lending strategy. For conservative lenders like BB&T, equity/assets ratios of 5 percent or greater are generally fine. Large foreign banks often have equity/asset ratios lower than this, presumably because their governments stand ready to ensure they don't fail—the risk to the economy would be too large. In the United States, however, there's nothing to stop a badly run bank from wiping out shareholders or merely slicing its dividend. Adequate capital provides an all-important cushion for shareholders. But for riskier lenders or smaller banks, I might want to see a much higher tangible equity/assets ratio of 8 percent, or possibly 10 percent.

Banks and Acquisitions

This issue of tangible equity raises an interesting question: Why would BB&T pay two to three times the book value of another bank or business to acquire it? Dozens, if not hundreds, of banks are sold on these terms or even richer ones every year, so there must be some logic to it.

In accounting terms, BB&T may only be getting 30 to 40 cents worth of equity for each dollar spent on acquisitions, but it isn't really buying the acquired bank's equity; what it's after is the deposits and earnings, including the long-term growth potential of both. BB&T can also cut operating costs by eliminating overlapping back-office and administrative functions.

This doesn't mean that BB&T or any other bank might not overpay for an acquisition and destroy shareholder value in the process, but in the banking industry (unlike most), well-chosen and well-managed acquisitions can easily add to the buyer's growth— including dividend growth.

The next statistics to consider are not on the balance sheet or the income statement, but in the footnotes.

► *Charge-offs.* I'm not so interested in this figure in any one year, but over a much longer stretch of time. Almost any bank can report low charge-offs when the economy is at the peak of health; I want to know what happens when loans start going bad in greater quantities.
► Nonperforming assets. Do these, too, surge in bad times? This may seem a little redundant, since bad loans show up in the charge-off data as well. However, if the bank has to cope with many more bad loans during recessions, future performance is less predictable.

I like to see charge-offs that are low (less than 1 percent on average) and consistent. On both of these counts, BB&T looks solid, especially on the charge-off ratio—just 0.33 percent of the bank's loans have gone bad. (See Figure A3.10.) This figure has fluctuated with the economy, but the worst year between 1992 and 2006 was just 0.48 percent. Other banks making

Year	Nonperforming Assets/Total	Charge-off Ratio %	Year	Nonperforming Assets/Total	Charge-off Ratio %
1992	0.59	0.45	2000	0.36	0.27
1993	0.42	0.38	2001	0.53	0.40
1994	0.35	0.15	2002	0.56	0.48
1995	0.35	0.23	2003	0.49	0.43
1996	0.35	0.30	2004	0.36	0.36
1997	0.44	0.40	2005	0.27	0.30
1998	0.33	0.28	2006	0.29	0.27
1999	0.33	0.26	**Averages**	**0.40**	**0.33**

Figure A3.10   BB&T: Asset Quality and Charge-Off History

riskier loans—in hopes of earning higher net interest margins—can naturally expect higher and more variable charge-off ratios. This can be a profitable strategy, but I'd just as soon stick to less-exciting banks with steady credit performance.

Another safety plus is low efficiency ratios. Since most of a bank's noninterest expenses are fixed, a bank with a 65 or 70 percent efficiency ratio will naturally be more sensitive to swings in net revenue than one whose operating costs are just 45 percent of revenue. Efficiency ratios of 50 percent or below generally indicate a bank that actually is efficient, but higher ratios are not necessarily bad for banks that derive large chunks of their net revenue from noninterest income. BB&T's efficiency ratio in 2006 was 53 percent, but with 42 percent of net revenue coming from fee-based sources, high fixed costs certainly don't appear to threaten future dividend payments.

Finally, let's look at BB&T's payout ratio. With a dividend rate of $1.68 a share in mid-2007 and expected earnings of $3.33, BB&T's payout ratio comes in at 50 percent. Given the company's prudent lending strategy, this seems like more than adequate protection for the dividend.

I tend to become suspicious when a bank's payout crawls north of 60 to 65 percent. There's nothing necessarily wrong with slightly higher payout ratios, particularly if the bank in question doesn't have many opportunities to expand by retaining earnings; such is the case for Britain's Lloyds TSB Group (LYG), a stock I've recommended to *Morningstar DividendInvestor* subscribers.

I might also give a bank a break if it's having a bad year, so long as an eventual recovery is reasonable to expect and results won't be bad enough to damage the balance sheet in the meantime. For example, New York Community Bancorp (NYB) had a payout ratio north of 100 percent in mid-2007, as earnings were squeezed by a rising cost of deposits. Its asset quality is almost perfect, however, and future changes in interest rates should restore the bank's earning power. But for a bank with poor asset quality or a very low equity/assets ratio, even a low payout ratio isn't going to give me much comfort.

Bank Dividend: Will It Grow?

Remember how I said earlier that anyone can make a loan, but only a bank can take a deposit? This observation provides a neat way to evaluate the growth prospects of the banking industry. Bank deposits have historically grown about as fast as the economy, at 5 or 6 percent a year, depending on inflation. That provides a baseline for measuring the industry's prospects as a whole. Moreover, the growth of fee-based services has a record of outpacing deposit and loan growth, adding perhaps a percentage point to industry growth. Of course, with 1,000 or more publicly held banks to pick from, some institutions will perform well year after year while others fall short.

Here are the key factors I take into consideration when estimating core growth:

▶ *Geography.* Some areas—predominantly western and southern states—are growing faster than the rest of the country, and their rising population and household wealth can boost the fates of local banks. Other areas (the Rust Belt, Appalachia, certain parts of the South) lag the overall economy, making it tough for local banks to grow faster than the rate of inflation.

▶ *Strategy.* You might say there are two basic kinds of banks: Those that are trying to gather as many deposits as possible, and those that are trying to make as many loans as they can. The deposit-driven banks are my favorite; again, only a bank can take a deposit, and it's a very cheap form of funding that almost always leads to above-average profitability. Loan-driven banks that aren't equally good at gathering cheap deposits often resort to more costly forms of funding—broker-sold CDs, commercial paper, and bond issues—that narrow their margins.

▶ *Revenue sources.* I love fee income. Unlike the spread business of deposits and loans, it requires little or no equity capital for support. These activities, such as insurance brokerage and investment advice, usually carry fat margins and above-average growth rates as well. These in turn benefit ROE.

▶ *Acquisitions.* In general, I don't give banks credit for growth added via acquisitions. In the few cases where a bank is a relentless and extremely disciplined acquirer, I might add a few percentage points of core growth to its internal growth prospects. But if I do this, it will have to be reflected in my assumptions for returns on equity. Acquiring a bank is not nearly so profitable as simply expanding the operations already in place.

For BB&T, 6 percent core growth seems like a reasonable assumption. This is perhaps a bit faster than U.S. nominal GDP, but BB&T's footprint in faster-growing southeastern states as well as a lot of fee-based revenue (insurance brokerage) should give a bit of an edge.

As for ROE, I have a choice to make. In 2006, BB&T earned only 13.4 percent on its shareholders' equity, a slightly subpar figure by industry standards. However, this figure was weighed down by the $5.3 billion in intangible assets on its books. Not only that, but net income was depressed by $104 million worth of noncash expenses related to these intangibles. These intangible assets don't need to be added to when the bank expands internally, so I back both figures out of ROE. (See Figure A3.11.)

What might BB&T have in store? Let's turn to our friend the Dividend Drill Return Model, using assumptions of a 6 percent core growth rate and a 25 percent return on incremental equity. (See Figure A3.12.)

	Book	Tangible
Average Equity	11,437	6,425
2006 Net Income	1,528	1,632
2006 Return on Equity (%)	**13.4**	**25.4**

Figure A3.11   BB&T: Book ROE versus Tangible ROE (Dollars in Millions)

Dividend Rate ($)	1.68		Funding Gap	0.85
Divided by: Share Price	42.00		Divided by Share Price ($)	42.00
Current Yield (%)	**4.0**		**Share Change (%)**	**2.0**
Core Growth Estimate (%)	**6.0**		Core Growth (%)	6.0
Divided by: Return on Equity (%)	25		Plus: Share Change (%)	2.0
Multiplied by: Earnings per Share	3.33		**Total Dividend Growth (%)**	**8.0**
Cost of Growth	**0.80**			
			Plus: Dividend Yield (%)	4.0
Earnings per Share	3.33		**Projected Total Return (%)**	**12.0**
Minus: Dividend	(1.68)			
Minus: Cost of Growth	(0.80)			
Funding Gap	**0.85**			

Figure A3.12   BB&T: Dividend Drill Return Model

Bank Dividend: What's the Return?

This is where banks are truly beautiful businesses for income investors. A core growth rate of 6 percent isn't likely to attract many growth-oriented types, but when you throw in the effect of share repurchases (which boosts BB&T's dividend growth rate 2 percent annually) and an up-front dividend yield of 4 percent, BB&T looks poised to deliver annual total returns of 12 percent.

Running some different scenarios for growth and profitability, I find that even a disappointing set of inputs (20 percent ROE and 4 percent core growth) should still provide BB&T shareholders with a 10.3 percent total return. At the other end of the spectrum (8 percent core growth and a 30 percent ROE), BB&T would offer a gangbuster return prospect of 13.8 percent. (See Figure A3.13.)

Return prospects on this order are not at all uncommon as of this writing, a handsome return prospect by any measure. But while my basic hurdle rate for a stock yielding 4 percent is only 9 percent (see Chapter 8), I tend to require a little more from banks—no less than 10 percent, and that's only for the most predictable dividend growers. If you find a total return prospect below 10 percent, I can all but guarantee there's a better bank out there to buy.

Bottom Line: Banks

Banks may not be the first place most investors look for income. From where I write today, banks are still thought of as cyclical plays on interest rates, and right now, that interest rate cycle isn't at all favorable for near-term earnings growth. But in the past couple of years, many banks have raised their dividend rates and payout ratios substantially, even as their share prices have in the aggregate made relatively little progress. One day, I think even Mr. Market will wake up and realize that a bank's total return prospect isn't just about earnings growth and capital appreciation anymore; the yields are just too good to ignore.

	4% Core Growth	6% Core Growth	8% Core Growth
20% Return on Equity	10.3%	11.6%	12.8%
25% Return on Equity	10.7%	**12.0%**	13.4%
30% Return on Equity	10.9%	12.3%	13.8%

Figure A3.13   BB&T: DDRM Scenario Analysis

I'll wrap up this appendix with a list of some of my favorite banks. (See Figure A3.14.) Not all are worth buying at the prices offered at any particular moment, but these all combine low-risk business strategies with high profitability and good dividend growth prospects.

Company/Ticker	
Associated Banc-Corp ASBC	TCF Financial TCB
Astoria Financial AF	Trustmark TRMK
Bank of America BAC	**US Bancorp USB**
BB&T BBT	Wachovia WB
Cullen/Frost Bankers CFR	**Wells Fargo WFC**
M&T Bank MTB	Westamerica Bancorporation WABC
Marshall & Ilsley MI	Wilmington Trust WL
Synovus Financial SNV	

Note: Names in bold are DividendInvestor recommendations as of mid-2007.

Figure A3.14 *Morningstar DividendInvestor's* Favorite Banks

Appendix 4

Utilities

UTILITIES ARE THE traditional refuge of stock investors seeking stable income and reasonably stable share prices. Even during recessions, people have to heat their homes, take showers, and keep that TV set aglow. Neither are utilities great growth businesses, so the industry has a long history of paying out most of its earnings to shareholders. It's also one of those endlessly relatable industries, since most Americans shell out money to one or more publicly traded utilities every month. While the industry picture is more complicated than one might expect and, at least as of this writing, utility stocks are very expensive by historical standards, a well-run utility can still be a dividend seeker's best friend.

Utility Basics
Left entirely to their own devices, utilities could be hugely profitable enterprises. For starters, utilities operate under franchises that designate them as the sole suppliers of electricity, water, or natural gas in a given area. This makes sense

enough, since it's not in anyone's interest to have three or four sets of power lines crisscrossing a particular neighborhood. Even if franchise rights did not exist, the immense amounts of capital investment required to set up a water, gas, or electric network would all but prohibit competition. Running electricity or natural gas into a new subdivision might cost tens or even hundreds of thousands of dollars, but once the major grid hookup is in place, connecting individual homes costs a relative pittance. Moreover, most utilities operate with assets that are decades old—assets that would cost many times their original cost to duplicate. No one is going to start up a competing enterprise. The economic moat here is obvious.

Monopoly power invariably results in abuses, so various levels of government stepped in long ago to regulate utilities. The most important of these regulations—consumer rates charged for electric, water, and gas—are established by state agencies. In the process, a utility's earning power does not start with revenue and end with profits; instead, it is generally an allowed level of profits plus a reasonable estimate for expenses that determines a utility's revenue.

Let's imagine the state of Hometown Electric Company, a utility I just made up. Over the years, Hometown Electric has accumulated $200 million worth of utility assets—a coal-fired generating station, hundreds of miles' worth of wires and poles, transformers, trucks, meters, and so forth. Half of these assets are funded with bonds paying an average interest rate of 7 percent; the other $100 million worth of assets represents shareholders' equity. In an unregulated state, who knows just how profitable these monopolistic assets might be? In the real world, state regulators have determined that Hometown Electric will be allowed to earn no more than a 12 percent return on equity. Hypothetically, Hometown's income statement winds up looking like that in Figure A4.1.

From year to year, profits will be determined by how much electricity Hometown delivers to consumers, and costs will fluctuate as well. If revenue turns out to be higher than expenses for several years in a row (and higher than any corresponding increase in costs), regulators can step in and order a rate reduction. Conversely, if revenue comes in lower than anticipated, or costs rise unexpectedly, Hometown can beg the regulators for a rate increase.

Shareholders' Equity	100,000
Multiplied by: Allowed Return on Equity (%)	12
Allowed Profits	**12,000**
Income Taxes (40%)	8,000
Allowed Pretax Profits	**20,000**
Interest Expense (7% on $100 million of debt)	7,000
General Taxes	5,000
Depreciation and Amortization	15,000
Operating and Maintenance Costs	51,000
Fuel Costs and Purchased Power	32,000
Allowed Revenues	**130,000**

Figure A4.1   Hometown Electric's Upside-Down Income Statement (Dollars in Thousands)

Once these regulatory rate cases—which generally take place every few years or so—begin, regulators and utility executives will naturally be on opposite sides of the table. The utility wants to earn higher profits; the regulator is charged with protecting consumers by holding profits down. Everything is on the table: the utility might complain that rising operating costs are hurting profits, while regulators say management isn't operating the business efficiently enough. Management might argue that shareholders deserve a 13 percent return instead of 12 percent; regulators counter by saying 10 percent is more than sufficient. Even the value of the utility's operating assets (a somewhat arbitrary figure known as the *rate base*) can be at issue: Hometown Electric might have spent $10 million to build a new high-voltage transmission line, but if regulators can prove the line could have been built for just $8 million, then $8 million might be the figure used when it comes to setting rates.

Friendly, cooperative regulators know that customers have a vested interest in the utility's profitability. If shareholders can't earn an adequate return, they won't want to provide the capital the utility needs to maintain and expand the existing electric grid over time. Regulators of a more contentious mind-set might acknowledge this in theory, when in fact they aren't inclined to listen to any of the utility's complaints about rising costs or inadequate revenue. In the long run, both shareholders and rate payers may suffer—the former from a lack of decent profits, the latter from less-reliable service.

The regulated utility industry's overall record is one of respectable mediocrity. This mediocrity can make for a worthwhile investment, assuming one sets realistic expectations and pays a reasonable price. About all I ask of a utility is to pay a good, secure dividend and to raise that dividend at least as fast as inflation.

These goals are harder to achieve than you might think. Drawing from historical results, the average regulated utility pays out 60 to 80 percent of its annual earnings through dividends and earns a return on equity of 10 to 12 percent. Taking the midpoint of both figures (a 70 percent payout ratio and an 11 percent ROE) yields a sustainable growth rate of 3.3 percent, not much higher than inflation. If the utility wants or needs to grow faster to accommodate the needs of the regional economy or take advantage of unusual investment opportunities, it will almost certainly have to raise more equity capital by selling additional shares. And as I illustrated with Great Plains Energy (GXP) in Chapter 7, these new shares dilute the value of additional growth for existing shareholders.

Even this modest pace of dividend growth is something of a rarity among the industry's more conservative participants. Many utilities fall short of earning their allowed ROEs, since regulatory rate-setting practices often use yesterday's cost levels to estimate tomorrow's profitability. And growth can easily be as much of a burden as a blessing: A fully integrated regulated utility might need to spend $200 million on assets and raise $100 million in equity capital to score a $10 million gain in annual earnings. After the money has been spent, regulators might look at that $200 million investment, deem it worth only $150 million because of inefficiencies or mistakes of one kind or another, and allow only a $5 million increase for shareholder profits.

Evaluating Utilities

The three primary issues for a utility are fairly simple.

1. What services does it provide—electricity, gas, water, or some combination of the three?
2. What is the mix of regulated versus nonregulated assets?
3. What other kinds of businesses does the utility own?

Type of Service

The prospects of electric utilities tend to be less predictable than those of gas or water utilities, for three reasons: Costs are often more variable than revenue; large chunks of the industry are now deregulated; and when the utility has to add generating capacity; these are large expenditures that the regulators may argue with later. A number of utilities have been forced to cut or eliminate dividends after poorly designed or ineptly managed construction projects—a few have even filed for bankruptcy—and the damage these errors can do to a utility's balance sheet can take decades to recover.

From the standpoint of one interested primarily in stability, natural gas utilities are more likely to earn their allowed ROEs without the drama of the electrics. Unlike their electric cousins, these services don't lend themselves easily to the unpredictable forces of deregulation. Both weather and the cost of natural gas can have massive impacts on revenue, but the way rates are structured—passing along most of the raw cost of gas directly to consumers' monthly bills—results in less volatility for earnings. However, allowed ROEs in this corner of the industry tend to be lower than those of their electrical kin (perhaps 10 percent on average, compared with 11 percent or so for electrics). Their internal growth prospects aren't any better than the electrics', though the fact that the industry is much more fragmented than electricity has provided opportunities for firms like Atmos Energy (ATO) and AGL Resources (ATG) to grow faster through acquisitions.

Unlike electricity and natural gas utilities, most American water utilities are owned by municipalities. The publicly traded water providers are such a small part of the overall industry sector that they barely merit mention, except for the fact that their total return prospects are tiny. Aqua America (WTR) recently traded at a yield close to 2 percent with a dividend growth potential of maybe 3 percent. Much ink has been spilled over the dreadful state of America's freshwater infrastructure, and I suppose a steady acquirer like Aqua America will find opportunities to expand the rate base of its many subsidiaries. But allowed ROEs for water are even lower than for natural gas, making heavy investment a low-growth prospect for shareholders.

Regulated versus Nonregulated

American government at all levels has been gradually relaxing regulatory oversight for nearly 30 years, and the utilities industry is no exception. Local power distribution systems are and probably always will be monopolies, but the electricity itself couldn't be more of a commodity; the 120 volts waiting in the wall socket is 120 volts regardless of how it is generated or where it is made. Coal-generated electrons makes just as good toast as nuclear- or wind-powered electricity.

In the 1990s, many states separated the business of generating electricity from the trade of delivering it. This often split utility companies in two, even if both entities remained under the same corporate roof. The transmission and distribution companies stayed within the tried-and-true allowed ROE framework, while generating stations were taken out of the rate base and forced to compete for customers the same way any other commodity business does: on price. The underlying goal, I suppose, was to encourage existing power plants to become more efficient while enticing new independent power producers to enter the market.

Deregulation didn't turn out to be the panacea that its authors had intended. While the collapse of Enron and the bankruptcy of California's largest utility (Pacific Gas and Electric, PCG) made for widely read headlines, the real failure of deregulation thus far is in the failure of low-cost competition to materialize. The new competitive landscape so frightened traditional utilities that they cut back on investment—the opposite of what deregulation's proponents intended.

Furthermore, the industry's old cost regime has flipped. A decade ago, natural gas–fired plants provided the cheapest means of generating electricity, while nuclear plants were presumed to be the most expensive. Coal, the dominant source of America's electric power, was somewhere in the middle. Now that order has flipped. The nukes have been revealed to be (as they always were) very low-marginal-cost producers, while the cost of natural gas has soared. This is an unpleasant but probably manageable problem for generating assets that are still in regulated rate bases. Regulators might want to squeeze a utility with lots of regulated gas-fired plants on other costs, but consumers still need the power however the utility is able to generate it. For deregulated operations, this has meant both boom (nuke-heavy Exelon, EXC, has made a fortune with its deregulated assets) and bust (Calpine, an independent owner of gas-fired plants, went bankrupt). But even the deregulated owners of nukes shouldn't sleep too easily; that which can be deregulated can certainly be reregulated at lower returns.

Nonutility Businesses

Many utility executives, no doubt frustrated by the industry's lack of growth and glamour, have diversified into other types of business activities. Sometimes these are related to the utility industry. Missouri's Laclede Group (LG), for example, owns a firm called SM&P Utility Resources, which specializes in identifying and marking wires and pipes buried underground. Others are ridiculously far afield. Please tell me how Hawaiian Electric Industries (HE) benefits from owning the state's third-largest bank! Not only does this company's utility business earn poor profits, but the bank isn't earning a decent profit either.

On rare occasions, you might find a utility whose managers have demonstrated a talent for allocating capital in other industries. My hometown utility, Duluth, Minnesota–based Allete (ALE, formerly known as Minnesota Power), has generated solid long-term shareholder returns with investments ranging from auto auctions to real estate. In the aggregate, however, I tend to be skeptical that a utility's management team can deploy capital effectively even in the core operations, let alone elsewhere.

From a dividend investor's standpoint, there's no real need to take chances on utilities with large deregulated or nonutility operations, at least unless those businesses could clearly stand as attractive investments in their own right. I also want to have some sense that regulatory relationships are amicable. Conditions can change quickly, so a state-by-state analysis could be out of date even a year from now. Still, I can generalize:

- *Northeast:* Friendly for transmission and distribution, tough on generators.
- *Southeast:* Perennially friendly.
- *Illinois:* Second only to California in any case study in dysfunctional deregulation (though my own power bill may influence my opinion a bit).
- *Other Midwest:* Tough but usually fair.
- *Northwest:* A bit tougher, but still usually fair.

- ► *California:* Very friendly, at least for now.
- ► *Other Southwest:* Do they even care about shareholders?
- ► *Texas:* Do they even care about rate payers? (TXU, the state's largest utility, is almost insanely profitable as I write this.)

Whatever the region, the long-term state of regulatory relations is bound to show up in earnings and returns on equity. As with any other dividend-paying stock, the guidelines of yield and growth provide us with a basis for analysis.

Utility Dividend: Is It Safe?

Relative to other bastions of dividend income, such as banks, I look at utilities as notable mostly for how often they disappoint loyal, conservative shareholders with dividend cuts. Not every quarter or every year, mind you, but look far enough back in a utility's dividend record, and you're probably as likely as not to find a cutback. Even utilities regarded as industry standard-bearers, from Ohio's American Electric Power (AEP) to Consolidated Edison (ED), have had to trim or eliminate shareholder payouts. Even though these firms are supposedly guaranteed a fair return on their capital investments, bad regulatory relations, bad capital investments, and excessive debt are among the many factors that can prompt a cutback or even elimination of the dividend.

If the situation gets bad enough, as happened with the old Public Service of New Hampshire (now part of Northeast Utilities, NU) in the 1980s, a utility can go bankrupt and bring its conservative shareholders tremendous losses. As of this writing, a handful of traditional utilities aren't paying dividends at all, a group that includes Sierra Pacific Resources (SRP) and Allegheny Energy (AYE).

Even rapid growth can result in dividend cuts. Wisconsin Energy (WEC) slashed its dividend nearly 50 percent in 2000, even though earnings were only in a temporary slump. Management cited a need for heavy capital spending, which was ridiculous. If Wisconsin needs to build new power plants and transmission towers, why can't the company issue new shares? Why should humble income-oriented shareholders suffer?

When looking at a utility, the best starting points are the payout ratio and the balance sheet.

Payout ratio. It's rare to find a utility whose free cash flow exceeds earnings for any length of time, so earnings are the best proxy for dividend-paying ability. A high payout ratio by general standards is okay, but a utility paying out more than 80 percent of average annual earnings is probably asking for trouble. As a side note, a utility stock's price may not always reflect the probability of a cutback. Utility stocks with high payout ratios are also the ones with high yields, but those high yields bring in dividend-seeking investors who might be missing the deteriorating fundamentals.

Balance sheet. Even though the utilities business is presumed to be stable, it's a bad idea for a utility to burden itself with debt more than 55 to 60 percent of total capital. Bondholders recognize that they are competing with shareholder dividends for the utility's cash flow, and too much debt combined with a high dividend payout can result in poor credit ratings and higher interest rates on new loans and bonds. That, in turn, may prompt dividend cuts.

Let's consider Washington's Puget Energy (PSD). It has a terrific CEO in Steve Reynolds, and it operates in a reasonably healthy region of the country, albeit one with some tough regulators. Long before Reynolds took over, this was a picture-perfect case of a utility in trouble; its payout ratio in 2001 was a distinctly unsafe 161 percent. How safe does Puget Energy's dividend look today?

▶ With a $1.00 dividend rate and expected 2007 earnings of $1.60 a share, its payout ratio is 63 percent.
▶ At the end of 2006, Puget Energy had $3.1 billion of debt and $5.2 billion of total capital (debt plus equity of $2.1 billion) for a debt/capital ratio of 59 percent.

Puget Energy's debt/capital ratio is a bit on the high side, but the payout ratio is on the low side. Thus far, I think I can deem this utility's dividend safe.

Then again, this is true only because Puget slashed its quarterly dividend rate from $0.46 to $0.25 a share in 2002. A drought in the Northwest literally dried up the company's cheapest source of electricity (from hydroelectric dams). That might have been a solvable problem if Puget's management and state regulators had a trusting, accommodative relationship, but at the time nothing could have been further from the case. And when regulators and utility executives can't get along, it's the regulators that usually prevail in court.

In most industries, a dividend history that includes cutbacks—especially recent ones—might alone be enough to scare me off. (See Figure A4.2.) But utility dividend cuts are downright commonplace relative to banks or energy master limited partnerships; the list of utility dividends that have *never* been cut or omitted is a pretty short one. Among utilities, at least, a cut in the distant past (more than five years ago) shouldn't rule out a stock whose present dividend rate appears stable.

Payout and debt ratios alone probably won't complete the picture. Among other factors you may want to consider:

▶ *Stability of earnings.* Fluctuations in weather and operating costs (or results from deregulated or nonutility businesses) can prevent a utility from earning the allowed ROE over its equity base. As long as weather alone might be to blame, that's not too much of a problem. While I recognize the

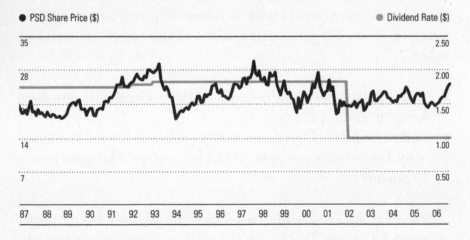

Figure A4.2   Puget Energy (PSD): Share Price and Dividend History

limitations involved in drawing strong conclusions from past performance, I don't like to see back-to-back years in which a utility fell short of covering its dividend. When earnings dip below the dividend rate, borrowing is usually required to make up the shortfall, and the additional debt and interest burden only makes it that much tougher to restore adequate dividend protection.

▶ *Geography.* A utility's fate is in large part a function of the territory it serves. This directly affects dividend growth prospects, but it has an effect on dividend safety as well. All else being equal, a utility in a poor-performing region of the economy, say Michigan or Ohio, is probably not as attractive an investment as one serving healthier and sunnier climes.

▶ *Regulatory relationships.* The health of a utility's relationship with regulators invariably shows up in the ROE. If it's less than 10 to 11 percent for an electric utility these days or 9 percent for a natural gas utility, chances are the company and regulators are at odds over material issues—costs have risen or demand has fallen, and relations between the utility and rate makers aren't healthy enough to restore profitability to reasonable levels. Yet overachievers can be at risk, too; a fully regulated utility earning a 13 to 15 percent ROE is in a tenuous position at best. I came close to recommending Energy East (EAS) in 2005, but the fact that the firm's largest subsidiary, New York State Electric & Gas (NYSEG), was earning close to 15 percent scared me off. (NYSEG was later handed a big rate cut that at least threatens dividend growth.) Thus the prospective or current utility shareholder should pay close attention to any upcoming or pending rate cases—and don't listen only to what the company has to say. Read the local papers if you can get them and, if a rate case is necessary to ensure dividend stability, get hold of the rate case documents themselves.

▶ *Capital expenditures.* When a utility enters a period of very high capital spending, risks to earnings and dividends increase. If the utility makes a bad investment—spending too much on a poorly planned generating station is the most obvious case—regulators may not allow the full value of the investment into the rate base. Never forget that shareholders, not rate payers, will be on the hook for bad investments. At the very least, plans for massive capital expenditures can bring dividend growth to a halt.

Judging Puget Energy on these metrics, I'd term the situation adequate. The company just got rid of its nonutility construction business, a definite plus. New management since 2002 has greatly improved the utility's relationship with regulators, leading to a rate structure and profit stream that is less susceptible to fluctuations in purchased power costs. Regulators have not lost their interest in rate payers, however, and they took advantage of falling costs to stick Puget Energy with a rate cut in early 2007—not a terrible one, but on the basis of current earnings estimates, it looks as if Puget Energy will earn an ROE of only 9 percent in 2007.

Meanwhile, the regional economy remains healthy and growing, if not much faster than the national average. Capital-spending plans appear reasonable for the region's growth potential. In part, Puget Energy hopes to reduce its dependence on purchased power (like many utilities, it doesn't generate all of its own electricity) by building or acquiring additional generating assets. As long as management continues to cooperate closely with regulators, these expenditures don't look large enough to threaten a $1.00 a share dividend rate.

Utility Dividend: Will It Grow?

If I haven't already scared you away from utility stocks and you're satisfied that a utility's dividend is reasonably secure, the next step is to establish a reasonable forecast for dividend growth.

▶ *Allowed and realized ROEs.* This is the single most important factor for regulated utility assets—more important even than the demand growth in the territory it serves. If the utility can't find a way to earn at least 10 percent on incremental investments of shareholders' equity, whatever growth is available will be of little real value to investors.

▶ *Regional demographics.* Assuming regulators allow and management achieves a decent ROE, utilities serving territories with healthy economies and rising populations have the opportunity to invest in their core businesses at a gain for shareholders. The two usually go hand in hand; when a utility is obliged to make large investments to support regional growth, regulators often allow healthy ROEs to ensure the company's access to equity and debt capital on favorable terms. This is not always the case—Arizona and Nevada utilities have had more than their fair share of troubles, but Florida, Texas, and even California have become good states for utilities to invest in.

▶ *Deferred investment.* If a utility is coming off a long stretch of slow asset growth despite generally favorable economic trends in its neighborhood, it might be poised for above-average core growth. For example, many utilities with coal-fired power stations are looking at heavy investments in emission-scrubbing technologies to reduce pollution. If these power stations are in regulated rate bases, pollution-control investments will probably go into the rate base and result in higher earnings. (Nothing is ever guaranteed where regulators are concerned, though.) In other cases, a utility might find itself looking at large outlays for increased generating capacity or transmission system upgrades. Forecasts for capital spending are usually available in utilities' annual reports. If net capital spending (that is, after depreciation) over the next five years points to asset growth greater than local demographic growth, I might use the former in my estimate of core growth.

▶ *Credit rating.* You might figure this belongs under the "Is It Safe?" heading, and a low credit rating might very well point to an insecure dividend. As it pertains to growth, however, a utility with a junk credit rating (BB or lower) faces a significantly higher cost of borrowing than its investment-grade peers. That constitutes a significant competitive disadvantage when it comes to funding growth opportunities.

▶ *Deregulated generation.* If an electric utility happens to own some handsomely profitable nuclear plants, good for it. What I'm interested in is the growth rate from here. I'd be much more wary of heavy planned spending on deregulated generation assets, even nuclear. It's been a long time since the United States launched a new nuke, and I have little doubt that getting one built and approved by regulators will prove tougher than today's nuclear bulls figure. I wouldn't raise my estimate of core growth rates on the basis of blue-sky potential in deregulated generation assets.

▶ *Nonutility businesses.* I'm skeptical of utilities owning and managing nonutility businesses. Though almost always presented as offering superior growth characteristics, these operations usually wind up being a drag on profitability and a poor use of shareholders' capital.

As a rule, I estimate core growth rates as population growth plus 2 percent, and then make company-specific adjustments from there as capital-spending plans might dictate. For stagnant economies (northeastern and some mid-western states), population growth might be nil. For a utility in the Sunbelt like Southern (SO), I might reach as high as 5 percent for core growth, but probably no more than that.

As for ROE, only with great reservation would I assume incremental returns on equity greater than 12 percent. If regulators aren't present to cap returns, competition in deregulated energy markets surely will do so in the long run.

Let's go back to Puget Energy. For ROE, I'll assume that future investments can earn 10 percent—a bit better than Puget Energy is currently making, but not unreasonable, given the current regulatory climate and the fact that the company ought to earn a return on investments that benefit rate payers. As for core growth, I'll use 4 percent—a bit higher than the 2 to 3 percent the regional economy could support, but lower than management's near-term capital-spending plans imply.

It looks as though Puget Energy can afford to fund nearly all of the expenditures necessary to grow at 4 percent annually through retained earnings; its funding gap is negative by just $0.04 a share. (See Figure A4.3.)

Dividend Rate ($)	1.00		Funding Gap ($)	(0.04)
divided by: Share Price ($)	24.00		divided by: Share Price ($)	24.00
Current Yield (%)	**4.2**		**Share Change (%)**	**−0.2**
Core Growth Estimate (%)	**4.0**		Core Growth (%)	4.0
divided by: Return on Equity (%)	10		plus: Share Change (%)	−0.2
multiplied by: Earnings Per Share ($)	1.60		**Total Dividend Growth (%)**	**3.8**
Cost of Growth	**0.64**		plus: Dividend Yield (%)	4.2
			Projected Total Return (%)	**8.0**
Earnings Per Share ($)	1.60			
minus: Dividend	(1.00)			
minus: Cost of Growth ($)	(0.64)			
Funding Gap ($)	**(0.04)**			

Figure A4.3   Puget Energy: Dividend Drill Return Model

The Dividend Drill Return Model's projection for dividend growth is 3.8 percent annually—not much faster than inflation, but it isn't as if low utility growth rates are unusual.

Utility Dividend: What's the Return?

With these estimates, Puget Energy looks like an 8 percent total return prospect. That matches the 8 percent I expect from stocks in general over the long run, but leaves me with no margin of safety. The guidelines I provided in Chapter 8 would require a minimum total return of 9 percent from a stock like Puget with a 4 percent yield.

I may be too conservative, but after running some alternative scenarios, I'm not inclined to think so. With such modest returns on equity and growth prospects, changes in my estimate that would be very large for a real-world regulated utility don't change Puget Energy's potential return much. I'd have to make quite aggressive projections—6 percent core growth and a 12 percent ROE—for Puget Energy's total return prospect to cross my 9 percent hurdle. (See Figure A4.4.)

With dividend growth prospects that aren't likely to be much better than my estimate of 3.8 percent, I'd have to be able to buy this stock with a 5.2 percent yield to clear my return hurdle. With a $1.00 dividend rate, I'd have to find this stock trading around $19. In a case where regulatory relationships can be touchy, a margin of safety is well worth requiring.

Looking at historical total returns from utilities, you might wonder why my description of the industry is so guarded. Even mediocre utilities with little or no dividend growth like Ameren (AEE) have managed to put up double-digit total returns over the past five or ten years. If I thought the stocks could work the same magic over the next decade, I certainly would find some well-run utilities and buy their stocks.

	2% Core Growth	4% Core Growth	6% Core Growth
8% Return on Equity	7.0%	7.3%	7.7%
10% Return on Equity	7.3%	**8.0%**	8.7%
12% Return on Equity	7.6%	8.4%	9.3%

Figure A4.4   Puget Energy: DDRM Scenario Analysis

The trouble is, utilities are at the end of a very long tailwind: falling long-term interest rates. In the early 1980s, utility dividend yields often topped 10 percent; by the early 1990s, yields were down to 7 percent; in 2002, blue-chip utilities could still be had at around 5 percent. Today, the industry's average dividend yield is in the neighborhood of 3 percent. Investors are willing to pay three times as much today as they were 25 years ago for the same dollar's worth of dividends. Expanding valuations have made historical total returns look attractive, but only at the cost of future potential. If future dividend growth potential has improved materially from the 2 to 4 percent historical average, I can't see it.

Even if I could buy Puget Energy shares at $19 and get a 5 percent current yield, I'm not sure I would. The company hasn't raised its dividend since the cut in early 2002. Recall the three basic types of dividend growth I mentioned in Chapter 7: trend, incentive, and hope. There being no trend to rely on, and no clear incentive for management to raise the dividend, the chance of a dividend increase clearly falls into the hope category. I have little doubt that Puget Energy will raise its dividend eventually—its payout ratio is already on the low end of industry norms—but I have no reason to believe this will occur anytime soon. If I want to earn a total return in excess of the stock's 4.2 percent current yield, I have to count on the stock price rising even as the dividend remains flat.

The Bottom Line

Perhaps I've been a bit harsh on utilities. From my stance in mid-2007, I've been exactly wrong on the sector's prospects for several years. I haven't recommended a single utility stock to *Morningstar DividendInvestor* subscribers even as they've collectively generated the best return of any industry over the past one-, three-, and even five-year stretches. I'm an ironclad contrarian by nature; rising prices make stocks less attractive to me, not more. Yet two pieces of the recent boom in utility shares have decent underpinnings:

1. America's energy infrastructure is getting older and creakier, even as the need for reliable sources of power, heat, and clean water grows. The 2003 blackout from Michigan to New England put these needs in high relief.

A number of utilities have announced large capital-expenditure plans that, executed wisely, will enhance their earning power down the road.

2. I underestimated the profit potential of several large utilities' deregulated nuclear and coal assets—firms including the utility where I live, Exelon, and Texas's inelegant but cash-rich TXU. In a power market where the marginal price is set by sky-high natural gas prices, I wish I'd recognized the potential earlier.

However, no one makes a good return from stocks by investing with only the rearview mirror in sight. Investing is a matter of dealing with business prospects as they are, not as recent price action might suggest them to be. In mid-2007, my Dividend Drill analyses across the utilities sector suggested only 6 to 7 percent total returns on average, with only half of that figure looking to come from current yield. In addition to the aforementioned favorable fundamentals, low interest rates and sheer market momentum have driven stock prices to unrewarding levels. At current prices, income investors simply don't need utilities stocks.

I'm reminded of how baseball entrepreneur Bill Veeck responded to a reporter's question just after selling the Chicago White Sox. Was it the high price of free agent players (this was in 1981, mind you) that drove a man of Veeck's modest means out of the business? He said, "It isn't the high price of stars that is expensive, it's the high price of mediocrity."

Even so, I'm sure many investors will continue to crave the steady returns that a well-run, well-positioned utility may offer. In Figure A4.5, I list some of the industry's better businesses, even if they're not necessarily priced for great total returns from where I write today.

Company/Ticker	
AGL Resources ATG	PG & E PCG
Alliant Energy LNT	Piedmont Natural Gas PNY
FPL Group FPL	SCANA SCG
National Fuel Gas NFG	Southern SO
NSTAR NST	Xcel Energy XEL

Note: No utilities were DividendInvestor recommendations as of mid-2007.

Figure A4.5   *Morningstar DividendInvestor's* Favorite Utilities

Appendix 5

Real Estate Investment Trusts

IF THERE'S ONE worthwhile investment we could all agree on, it ought to be real estate. Here's one topic on which Donald Trump and *Gone with the Wind*'s Gerald O'Hara would certainly be in accord. Space in which to exist and live one's life is as essential as air, water, and food, or at least cable TV. Armies fight and die over land. What else would one expect from a scarce asset? Even Will Rogers had a real estate investment strategy to offer: "Buy land. They ain't making any more of the stuff."

True enough. But Will missed two other advantages of real estate. Build or buy a building for investment purposes and the government will allow you to slowly depreciate the cost over time, reducing your taxable income even though the value of that building is probably rising over time. And because real estate is excellent collateral (it usually takes an environmental disaster, natural or man-made, to render it worthless), one can easily borrow against it. This one-two punch of tax benefits and leverage has made many a real estate investor wealthy.

The trouble with land, and real estate generally, is that it is not terribly liquid. Each piece of land and the building that may be on it is unique. Buying and selling land, as any homeowner will tell you, is a lengthy, aggravating, and costly process—certainly more time-consuming than getting into or out of a stock or bond. Though anyone can invest in real estate directly, these facts naturally give an edge to investors with big bucks.

In one of a relatively few nods to investors of ordinary means, the federal government has created a structure to give real estate investments the liquidity benefits of stocks and bonds while preserving their favorable tax and leverage attributes. By passing taxable income down to shareholders through dividends, a firm can avoid paying corporate income taxes itself. The resulting real estate investment trust (REIT) is thus a good place to hunt for dividend income.

Three Kinds of REITs

Not all real estate investments qualify for REIT treatment. To qualify for tax-free treatment at the corporate level a REIT must abide by certain rules. The most important of these are:

► A minimum of 75 percent of the REIT's total assets must be in qualifying real estate investments, principally land, buildings, or loans backed by real estate.

► At least 90 percent of the REIT's taxable income must be paid out through dividends each year.

The way the first rule is drawn allows a REIT to be not just a landlord, but a financier as well. In looking at REITs, it is critical to distinguish among the three basic shapes these businesses can take.

Property REITs

These are the old-fashioned landlords, putting their real estate assets on a paying basis by leasing them out for regular rent payments. The profitability of a property REIT is a function of two factors:

1. *Economic moat.* Unlike banks, not all REITs have sustainable competitive advantages. An apartment building in Manhattan, for example,

bears very different economics than an apartment complex in suburban Dallas. In the congested New York City area, people are willing to pay top dollar to live close to where they work and play. The extreme scarcity of land and enormous cost of construction prevent the supply of residential, office, and retail space from expanding quickly. This in turn gives the Manhattan landlord the ability to raise rents over time—a key driver of future profitability.

In contrast, all you have to do is fly into Dallas–Fort Worth to notice how abundant undeveloped land still is there. Land and construction costs are comparatively cheap. If rents start to rise, developers can throw up new apartment complexes and office parks practically overnight. As the Dallas–Fort Worth area becomes more developed, competition should lessen, but for now, the ever-present threat of additional supply conspires to keep rents low and increases minimal.

A large REIT may also benefit from economies of scale and switching costs, albeit on a low level. Moving a retail store in an effort to keep rent low not only costs money, but regular customers might be inconvenienced by the move at first. Highly profitable retailers are generally averse to trading a proven location for an unproven one.

2. *Capital allocation.* Management's skill at investing shareholders' capital can have just as much influence on future returns as the basic economics of the assets. Does management consistently generate good returns from its asset base, or are individual acquisitions and construction projects hit-or-miss? Are tenants lined up before a building is built, or does the REIT call in the construction crews long before signing leases? There's nothing wrong with new construction; indeed, the returns on equity are often higher than those obtainable through the purchase of already-occupied properties. Then again, this is obviously a riskier strategy than buying proven earners.

Since the rental income from real estate can generate bondlike cash flows, the returns on investment tend to be tied to interest rates, inflation, and the like. If a REIT lays out $20 million for an office building that generates $1.5 million in annual rent, it will earn a 7.5 percent initial return—a figure known as the *capitalization rate*. Cap rates are tantamount to dividend yields, but they don't necessarily capture the property's total return potential: If the

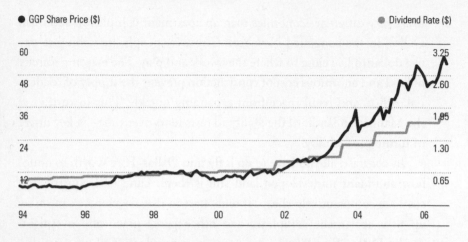

Figure A5.1   General Growth Properties: Share Price and Dividend History

asset is in a good area, well maintained, and properly managed, the landlord may be able to raise rents at the rate of inflation (2 to 3 percent annually) or higher.

When you combine good assets with a great management team, a REIT can generate impressive total returns for shareholders. Of these, mall operator General Growth Properties GGP is certainly one of the best—a fact reflected in the rapid growth of its dividend and market price. (See Figure A5.1.)

Mortgage REITs

Instead of buying real estate and collecting rent, these creations of Wall Street build up portfolios of loans backed by real estate, funded mostly with borrowed money. In a sense, a mortgage REIT functions like a bank, lending money at higher rates than it costs to borrow. For example, a mortgage REIT might be able to buy residential mortgage-backed securities that yield 6 percent while its own borrowing cost is 5 percent. This one-percentage-point spread might not sound like much, but if $20 in assets is backed with just $1 of equity (financial leverage of 20 to 1), this spread can turn into a 20 percent return on equity.

These firms tend to court much, much higher risks than banks do, ranging from interest rate risk (Annaly Capital Management, NLY, depicted in

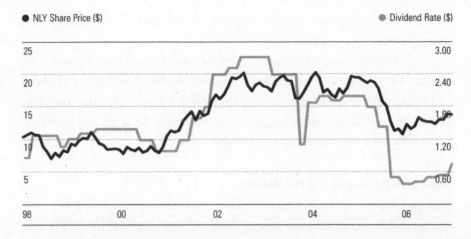

● NLY Share Price ($)   ● Dividend Rate ($)

Figure A5.2   Annaly Capital Management (NLY): Share Price and Dividend History

Figure A5.2) to credit risk (Newcastle Investment, NCT) to funding risk—the ability of the mortgage REIT's lenders to ask for their money back at a moment's notice. As far as I can tell, it's impossible for a business like this to create an economic moat, while their histories of highly variable dividends (and, at times, financial distress) make them poor choices for long-term income investors.

Hybrid REITs

These few firms are neither pure-play landlords nor mortgage investors, but are simply financial services businesses structured as REITs to trim their income tax bills. These firms typically exploit a structure known as a *taxable REIT subsidiary* (TRS). As long as a REIT doesn't invest more than 25 percent of its assets in a TRS, the parent entity can retain its tax-free status while conducting nonconforming business activities inside a tax-paying TRS.

CapitalSource (CSE), a specialty commercial lender, is one such hybrid REIT. Even though it looks like a mortgage REIT at first glance—it even owns some residential mortgage-backed securities to help it comply with the tax rules—I found its management team doing a good job of making high-yield loans at fat margins. It also relies much less on borrowed money to fund its asset base than do its peers. These and other factors prompted me to deem its hefty dividend payment safe in early 2007, while acknowledging that any lending business like this requires careful research and close monitoring thereafter.

Property REITs are a much, much better area to focus your research and capital. While it's possible (if unlikely) that any particular mortgage or hybrid REIT might offer worthwhile dividend potential, I'll grant that the complexities of a CapitalSource or a straightforward mortgage REIT should probably put it into most investors' "too tough" files.

Funds from Operations and FFO Returns

Back in Chapters 6 and 7, I mentioned that accounting earnings didn't provide a terribly accurate picture of true dividend-paying power for REITs and energy MLPs. To take a closer look the alternative financial data for REITs, let's consider the 2006 results of Developers Diversified Realty (DDR), a highly profitable and very well-run operator of shopping centers.

In 2006, DDR earned a profit for common shareholders of $198 million, or $1.82 a share. Meanwhile, dividends totaled $2.36 a share. At first glance, this looks to be an unsafe (if not insane) payout ratio of 130 percent. Dividend investors beware, right?

In economic terms, these reported earnings results bear only a distant relationship to the cash flow DDR hauled in. That's why REIT managers, analysts, and investors have developed an alternative earnings metric statistic for REITs called *funds from operations* (FFO).

According to the National Association of Real Estate Investment Trusts (NAREIT), which publishes standards for calculating this metric, the objective of FFO is to show a REIT's recurring cash-generating power. That explains why one-time gains and losses are excluded while depreciation and amortization—noncash expenses—are added back to net income. Additional items may be added or subtracted to represent the underlying contributions of partnerships and joint ventures, both of which are common in the REIT industry. Virtually every REIT reports FFO along with earnings in its quarterly financial releases, and analyst consensus earnings estimates are generally provided in terms of FFO per share rather than earnings per share.

To illustrate how this calculation works with real numbers, Figure A5.3 shows a summary of DDR's FFO in 2006.

Net Income after Preferred Dividends	198.1
Depreciation and Amortization	185.4
Joint-Venture Adjustments	16.3
Gains on Real Estate Sold	−22.0
Funds from Operations	**377.8**
Average Diluted Shares Outstanding	110.8
FFO Per Share ($)	**3.41**
Dividends Paid	2.36
FFO Payout Ratio (%)	**69**

Figure A5.3   Developers Diversified Realty: Funds from Operations (Dollars in Millions)

True to NAREIT's guidelines, we see that DDR has added back its depreciation and amortization charges and made the necessary adjustments for other items that distort the firm's earning power. Almost all REITs calculate and report FFO in their press releases, so it's not necessary for prospective investors to calculate FFO themselves. Either way, the bottom line has become much more favorable; viewed from the standpoint of FFO, DDR's payout ratio in 2006 was not 130 percent, but a much safer 69 percent.

Taxable versus FFO Payout

To qualify for tax-exempt status, REITs are obliged to pay out 90 percent of their taxable profits. However, taxable profits are typically much lower than FFO, and there are no tax rules stating that a REIT must pay out any particular proportion of its FFO, so FFO payout ratios are usually below 90 percent.

Now let's see how profitable DDR is by looking at return on equity. Calculating ROE is also affected by FFO; after all, the value of DDR's real estate assets probably isn't declining. If we use book equity—which is reduced by the sum of accumulated depreciation charges—to calculate ROE, we'll come up with a very high but irrelevant statistic. If we're going to add depreciation charges back to earnings to consider FFO, it follows that we should also add accumulated depreciation to shareholders' equity to get a true view of ROE. (See Figure A5.4.)

Average Common Shareholders' Equity	1,828,2
Average Accumulated Depreciation	777.0
Adjusted Shareholders' Equity	**2,605.3**
Funds from Operations in 2006	377.8
FFO Return on Equity (%)	**14.5**

Figure A5.4   Developers Diversified Realty: 2006 Return on Equity Based on FFO (Dollars in Millions)

DDR's ROE of 14.5 percent is quite a bit higher than industry averages around 9 percent-11 percent, a tribute to moat-wise capital allocation by management. (See Figure A5.4.) The firm has sought out properties in dense metropolitan areas that face little or no competition from new construction. Clearly it's done a good job of keeping tenants happy and extracting higher rents. (See Figure A5.5.)

Evaluating REITs

Even among property REITs, asset quality and management strategies vary widely. To consider but a few distinguishing characteristics:

▶ *Type of property.* Since every type of real-world economic activity requires real estate, most kinds of real estate will see at least some link to the health of the regional and national economies. Yet some types of property, such

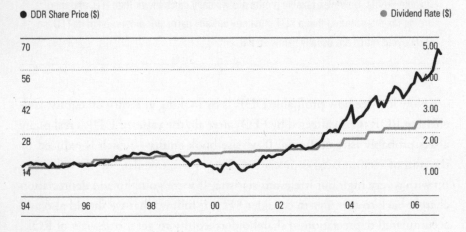

Figure A5.5   Developers Diversified Realty (DDR): Share Price and Dividend History

as retail and residential, tend to be more recession-resistant than others (like office and industrial). Health-care REITs might seem to offer recession-proof economics, but those that are heavily invested in skilled-nursing facilities and hospitals can be influenced by arcane factors such as Medicare reimbursement rules.

▶ *Geography.* Regional economic health drives the demand for real estate and the terms on which it is leased. Areas with perennially sunny economic conditions and rising populations (the Sunbelt, the mid-Atlantic states) lend themselves to safer dividends than midwestern areas that are in relative decline.

▶ *Occupancy trends.* No REIT that I am aware of is 100 percent leased out; there's always a vacant building somewhere. To the extent a REIT can cover its dividend comfortably at current occupancy rates, this figure need not matter much, but a negative trend in occupancy can point to a squeeze in future dividend coverage.

▶ *Tenant concentration.* Some REITs, such as gas station owner Getty Realty (GTY) and hospital owner Universal Health Realty (UHT), obtain the bulk of their rental income from a single tenant. These firms' fates are tied directly to the fates of their tenants; Universal nearly went bankrupt when its onetime parent and largest tenant got into financial trouble. If you buy into a REIT with more than 10 percent of its rental income coming from a single source, you should definitely evaluate the financial health of that tenant. Industry and regional concentration can hurt too, even if no single occupant accounts for a material share of rental income. As a rule, a broadly diversified tenant base makes for a safer dividend.

▶ *Credit rating.* In addition to what a bad credit rating says about a REIT's financial health and dividend safety, it can be a competitive handicap as well. If it costs me 9 percent to borrow and you can get loans at 7 percent, you can easily outbid me for acquisition opportunities. I'd just as soon avoid REITs with subpar credit ratings (lower than Standard & Poor's BB grade).

▶ *Lease duration.* The longer a REIT locks up its tenants, the more predictable its income should be. A handful of REITs write what are known as triple-net leases—bound for 15- or 20-year stretches, tenants pay slightly smaller rents to the REIT while taking responsibility for property taxes, insurance, and maintenance costs themselves. Over these long leases, rent periodically rises at rates and times spelled out in the lease. Now contrast these leases with apartment landlords writing one-year leases. In a regional economic slip-up, these regions are much more prone to experience increased vacancies and downward pressure on rents. The shorter the lease, the less predictable the rental income.

▶ *Fee-based income.* With institutional investors taking an increased interest in real estate, and REIT shares somewhat scarce relative to the size of massive pension funds, several REITs such as AMB Property (AMB) have opened up what are essentially asset-management businesses on the side. In exchange for acquiring and maintaining the property owned by a partnering investor, the REIT skims off healthy management fees. This source of growth can provide a nice source of revenue that doesn't require much capital investment. Moreover, by giving such a REIT an extra incentive to look at more deals, a search for fee income might reveal more and better investment opportunities for the REIT's own balance sheet.

Unlike banks—where even mediocrity is often rewarded with relatively high returns on equity—the past performance and future prospects of individual REITs varies widely. The good REITs almost always make clear who they are through their dividend streams. Dividends that are well supported by FFO and sound balance sheets won't be cut. Management teams that invest shareholders' capital wisely tend to raise their dividends at good rates as well. Unattractive assets, bad balance sheets, and subpar investors reveal themselves with high payout ratios (90 percent-plus), a lack of dividend growth that at least matches inflation, and—in some cases—a dividend record that includes payout cuts.

DDR appears to stack up on the qualitative counts, so let's see what the Dividend Drill has to say.

REIT Dividend: Is It Safe?

Dividend cuts are not unheard of in the REIT industry. Every so often, a REIT will let its payout ratio drift too high on the basis of an overly optimistic outlook, or a downturn in a regional economy or problems at an especially large tenant will hammer cash flow.

Young REITs are more disposed to run into trouble than well-established ones; when going public for the first time, a REIT may set a dividend rate that is too high in an attempt to get a lofty valuation for itself. If the proceeds from the initial public offering aren't invested at the cap rates assumed when setting the dividend, income investors will suffer. But even large, blue-chip REITs aren't exempt from trouble; Equity Office Properties—at the time the nation's largest REIT by market value—was forced to cut its dividend in December 2005 amid declining rents.

When I sit down to evaluate the safety of a REIT's dividend, my top three considerations are as follows:

1. *Sources of income.* You might be surprised to see this listed before even the payout ratio, but it's critical to know how the REIT is earning what it claims for FFO. Some REITs, such as First Industrial Realty Trust FR, stretch the definition of FFO to include gains on property sales. First Industrial has tried to position itself more like an asset manager, turning over large chunks of its asset base on a regular basis. But unpredictable gains on sale simply aren't unreliable as a source of cash for paying dividends, so I'd just as soon rely on ongoing rent income alone for my income.

2. *Payout ratio.* As with any business, a lower payout ratio usually implies greater safety for the dividend, though low payout ratios also correlate to lower yields. On the basis of FFO, I would avoid a REIT whose payout ratio exceeds 85 percent. REIT cash flows are usually stable, but the combination of operating leverage and financial leverage can magnify the bottom-line impact of small fluctuations in occupancy and pricing.

3. *Economic moat.* I'd just as soon avoid exurban apartment complexes and small-city offices. An ill-timed economic downturn can easily hammer occupancy and lease pricing, possibly even forcing a dividend cut.

Probably 90 percent of the time, these three factors will tell you everything you need to know about the safety of a REIT's dividend. (In 80 percent of cases, the payout ratio alone might suffice.) Yet there's one more factor I like to consider, even for REITs whose dividends pass these tests: *debt*. REITs almost always take advantage of cheap debt and preferred stock issues to leverage up returns for common shareholders. However, too much debt—especially combined with pressures on rental income and a high payout ratio—can easily spell a dividend cut.

Turning back to DDR, I see that the firm's reported FFO excludes gains on sale, as it should. In early 2007, the firm raised its dividend rate a nifty 12 percent, to $2.64 a share annually, but FFO is rising too: At midyear, Wall Street was expecting $3.80 per share for 2007. The payout ratio for 2007 looks to be the same as last year's 69 percent. Past ROEs and the nature of DDR's assets—shopping centers in attractive areas—provide ample evidence of an economic moat.

The debt question will take a bit more calculating. Figure A5.6 shows three ways to evaluate a REIT's balance sheet.

The first of these statistics comes straight off the balance sheet: Fixed obligations (debt and preferred stock) make up 72 percent of total capital. On an FFO basis—adding accumulated depreciation back to assets and equity—the debt/capital ratio falls to 64 percent, but even that still looks a bit high in absolute terms.

In DDR's case, it's highly likely that the FFO basis for debt/capital in the second column continues to understate the true value of DDR's assets and equity. Even though we're adding depreciation back to equity when calculating

	Book Basis	FFO Basis	Market Value
Net Real Estate Assets	6,580.9	6,580.9	9,900.5
Add Back: Accumulated Depreciation	—	861.3	861.3
Other Assets	598.9	598.9	598.9
Total Assets	**7,179.8**	**8,041.0**	**11,360.6**
Total Debt	4,248.8	4,248.8	4,248.8
Other Liabilities	312.8	312.8	312.8
Preferred Stock	705.0	705.0	705.0
Shareholders' Equity	**1,913.1**	**2,774.4**	**6,094.0**
Total Debt (and Preferred Stock)	4,953.8	4,953.8	4,953.8
Total Capital (Debt, Preferred, and Equity)	6,866.9	7,728.2	11,047.8
Debt/Capital	**72%**	**64%**	**45%**

Figure A5.6   Developers Diversified Realty: Three Views of Its 2006 Balance Sheet (Dollars in Millions)

this statistic, these historical cost figures might still fall short of the firm's true financial condition. Not only is the value of DDR's property not declining—an adjustment we've already accounted for—it's almost certainly going up. Market value, not historical cost, is the basis on which real estate assets are financed. (If you don't believe me, just ask anyone who bought a house a decade ago and after a refinancing or two, now owes more on his mortgage than what he originally paid for it.)

That's why the industry tends to view debt/capital ratios in terms of the market value of equity (share price multiplied by shares outstanding) instead of book value. In mid-2007, a stock price of $55 for DDR's 110.8 million shares implied an equity value of almost $6.1 billion—triple the book figure and double my FFO basis approach. Measured by market value, DDR's debt is only 45 percent of total capital, a relatively strong figure.

Reluctant as I am to give that fickle Mr. Market credit for valuing the assets of a business properly, analysts and investors have to make do with the best figures available. If a REIT's debt/capital ratio is more than 60 to 65 percent on a market value basis or more than 80 percent on an FFO basis, I would suggest avoiding it.

Still another way to look at a REIT's financial strength is to consider its fixed-charge coverage ratio—a metric similar to the interest coverage ratio I described in Chapter 6. Fixed charges, in this case, represent the interest owed to DDR's banks and bondholders as well as the fixed dividends payable on its preferred stock. (See Figure A5.7.) Compared with balance sheet figures, the market value of a REIT's assets should be directly reflected in its rental income (and, by extension, in its FFO).

Funds from Operations	377.8
Add Back: Interest Expense	221.5
Add Back: Preferred Dividends	55.2
Cash Available for Fixed Charges	**654.5**
Total Interest Expense and Preferred Dividends	276.7
Ratio of Available Cash to Fixed Charges	**2.37**

Figure A5.7   Developers Diversified Reality: Fixed Charge Coverage Ratio in 2006 (Dollars in Millions)

From the data in Figure A5.7, we see that the total amount of cash DDR generated in 2006 exceeds its fixed obligations by a substantial amount—nearly 2.4 times. All else being equal, higher coverage ratios imply a stronger balance sheet. A REIT fixed-charge coverage ratio of 2:1 or better is generally quite healthy; the lower this ratio is, the greater the impact any drop in rental income will have on FFO.

If you choose to tread among highly leveraged REITs, the question of when a company's bonds and loans come due could be very important. If all of a REIT's borrowings come due at the same time—and that time just happens to coincide with indigestion in the credit markets—the REIT could be forced to refinance its debt at higher interest rates. The additional interest expense alone could force a dividend cut; if the firm can't refinance at all, then it's off to bankruptcy court.

REIT Dividend: Will It Grow?

One beautiful attribute of REITs—especially compared with utilities and even banks—is how easy expansion can be. Where investment opportunities are limited in these other industries by regional economics, competitive circumstances, and even regulatory pressures, there are tens of trillions of dollars' worth of real estate out there. Only a tiny proportion of this value is held by REITs, where it can benefit from REITs' tax advantages. There's plenty of growth potential out there.

Furthermore, some (but not all) REITs can expand their earnings over time without additional capital by simply raising rents—not by much, but possibly at or about the rate of inflation. This adds what I call a *free growth* term to the Dividend Drill Return Model.

It's hard to understate the benefit of this free growth term—where you can find it and when it is reliable. If inflation turns out to be higher than 2 to 3 percent in the future, then a well-positioned REIT should be able to pass this inflation along to tenants. This in turn will permit faster dividend increases, helping preserve the real purchasing power of the shareholder's dividend stream.

However, I wouldn't want to buy a REIT whose management was investing willy-nilly in whatever deal happens to cross its desk. Because a REIT can't hope to finance massive quantities of growth with retained earnings—those high payout ratios force them to go begging to the debt and equity markets for most of their expansion capital—the capital markets can act as a check on otherwise bad investment practices. This isn't a perfect block; by the time a bad REIT's investment strategy is well known, a lot of shareholder value might already have been destroyed.

Let's move on to prepare estimates for our DDRM.

Free Growth

The best starting point for this term is zero: that's right, no free growth at all. A REIT without an economic moat—one with lackluster, me-too properties or a poor geographic footprint—will have much more trouble raising rents than a peer with better underlying economics. Better to assume nothing and be surprised on the upside. In some cases—say, the end of a boom in office buildings has left the region with low occupancy rates—this term might well be negative. (You probably won't want to invest in a REIT whose income is set to decline.)

Then again, you might find that a REIT's lease agreements contain rent increases that are contractually known in advance. This is customary for triple-net lease specialists and their 15- and 20-year contracts; Realty Income's (O) lease portfolio carries an average rent increase rate pace of 2 percent.

Somewhere in between—and this is where DDR lies—a REIT with attractive assets and a consistent record of raising rents might deserve a free growth term as well. I wouldn't use a figure higher than the likely rate of inflation—certainly no more than 3 percent—so I'll use 2 percent for DDR.

Core Growth

The actual future of a REIT can be tough to project. A given REIT might plod along for years, content with the assets it already has, and then decide to double itself overnight with a massive acquisition.

This is why I often resort to using the REIT's sustainable growth ratio—one of the rare cases where this single statistic comes in handy. A REIT with a 70 percent payout ratio—meaning it's retaining 30 percent of its FFO—that can reinvest this cash at a 10 percent return will have a sustainable growth rate of 3 percent. For REITs whose record suggests only a passing interest in expansion, this isn't a bad figure to use.

But where management's strategy is clearly and competently articulated, and past rates of asset growth are reasonably consistent, I might be willing to venture beyond this figure. DDR, for example, tripled its asset base between 2001 and 2006—an average growth rate of 25 percent. But as DDR grows larger, it will have a very tough time keeping up this pace, and it certainly isn't the kind of figure I'd want to use in making forward-looking estimates. In no case would I push this figure beyond 10 percent, and I'd curb my enthusiasm further for large REITs (those with assets already greater than $5 billion). Considering DDR's recent past and likely future, I'll estimate core growth at 7 percent. The company may well trounce this conservative estimate, and if the capital is invested wisely, it should result in faster dividend growth than I'd originally expected. But why push it?

Return on Equity

Certainly DDR has been a star performer, what with its 14.5 percent ROE in 2006. However, past returns can easily overstate future potential.

▶ Over time, rent increases will increase the numerator (FFO) in return on equity, but the original cost of the property stays the same. When DDR buys or builds a new shopping center, it won't have the benefit of past rent increases in its returns.

▶ Because of their bondlike cash flows, the cap rates on real estate tend to correlate to interest rates. DDR might (and probably does) own a lot of property purchased when interest rates and cap rates were higher. In mid-2007, with Treasury bonds paying 5 percent instead of 6 or 7 percent, cap rates on new investments will be lower—and so will returns on equity.

For this reason, I don't rely solely on past or even current ROEs as a basis for future projections. Given where interest rates are in mid-2007, I doubt DDR (or any other well-run REIT) would make investments that carried ROEs of less than 9 percent, but DDR's 14.5 percent is almost certainly too high. Figuring that DDR's ROE potential lies somewhere in between, I estimate a 12 percent ROE going forward.

Finally, we've got all of our DDRM estimates. as shown in Figure A5.8.

Dividend Rate ($)	2.64	Funding Gap ($)	(1.06)
Divided by: Share Price ($)	55.00	Divided by: Share Price ($)	55.00
Current Yield (%)	**4.8**	**Share Change (%)**	**−1.9**
Core Growth Estimate (%)	**7.0**	**Free Growth Estimate (%)**	2.0
Divided by: Return on Equity (%)	12.0	Plus: Core Growth (%)	7.0
Multiplied by: Earnings per Share ($)	3.80	Plus: Share Change (%)	−1.9
Cost of Growth ($)	**2.22**	**Total Dividend Growth (%)**	**7.1**
Earnings per Share ($)	3.80	Plus: Dividend Yield (%)	4.8
Minus: Dividend	(2.64)	**Projected Total Return (%)**	**11.9**
Minus: Cost of Growth ($)	(2.22)		
Funding Gap ($)	**(1.06)**		

Figure A5.8   Developers Diversified Reality: Dividend Drill Return Model

REIT Dividend: What's the Return?

DDR's projected total return of almost 12 percent easily clears my 9 percent hurdle rate for stocks with similar yields. This gives me a nice margin of safety in addition to the one my hurdle rate requires.

Better yet, my scenario analysis shows DDR beating my return hurdle rate comfortably, even with very conservative projections. (See Figure A5.9.)

Like utilities, that other redoubt of income seekers, REIT shares have posted awfully attractive total returns in the past five and ten years. Much of this return has been delivered through rising valuations (read: falling dividend yields) rather than dividend growth. Looking backward, REITs' average dividend growth has run at 4 to 5 percent annually, and even that has no doubt benefited from the prolonged decline in long-term interest rates. I wouldn't take any REIT's historical total returns as a proxy for what to expect.

	5% Core Growth	**7% Core Growth**	9% Core Growth
10% Return on Equity	10.1%	10.5%	11.0%
12% Return on Equity	11.0%	**11.9%**	12.7%
14% Return on Equity	11.6%	12.7%	13.8%

Figure A5.9   Developers Diversified Reality: DDRM Scenario Analysis

For a high-yielding REIT (6 percent or more these days) with a safe dividend, I suppose I'd be willing to settle for a total return prospect of 10 percent. Personally, I have a hard time taking REIT stocks with sub-5 percent yields seriously, so I'd demand an especially hefty rate of dividend growth (high single digits at least) and a total return prospect of 11 to 13 percent from a REIT yielding 4 or 5 percent.

The Bottom Line

A well-chosen REIT can serve the income investor very well over time. Even though market prices have appreciated substantially since 1999, I remind myself that REITs started that boom deeply undervalued. In the past, when even blue-chip REITs yielded 8 or 10 percent, I think investors tended to undervalue (or ignore) just how fast a REIT's dividend can grow over time. Those yields may be relics of the past, but from where I write today, I'd take a well-run REIT over a utilities stock any day. See Figure A5.10 for Morningstar's favorite REITs.

Company/Ticker	
AMB Properties AMB	Kite Realty Group KRG
Biomed Realty Trust BMR	Maguire Properties MPG
Developers Diversified Realty DDR	**Realty Income O**
Eastgroup Properties EGP	Regency Centers REG
First Potomac Realty Trust FPO	Simon Property Group SPG
General Growth Properties GGP	**Ventas VTR**
Health Care REIT HCN	Vornado Realty Trust VNO
Kimco Realty KIM	

Note: Names in bold are DividendInvestor recommendations as of mid-2007.

Figure A5.10   *Morningstar DividendInvestor's* Favorite REITs

Appendix 6

Energy Partnerships

FOR THE PAST couple of years, few economic issues have had the same relentless drumbeat as the price of a gallon of gas. Will oil go to $100 a barrel, or even $200, as some so-called experts have claimed? As profitable an investment opportunity as such a future might offer, I can claim no special insight into the right price for oil and natural gas. Except for the energy industry's goliaths like Chevron (CVX) and British Petroleum (BP), few of energy producers pay meaningful dividends anyway.

While I may be lukewarm toward the companies that pump oil and gas out of the ground, you may count me as a huge fan of the small subset of firms specializing in moving this energy from the wellhead to where it needs to go. Just as the easiest profits in the California gold rush went not to the prospectors but to the folks who sold the picks and shovels, the best investments in the energy industry—at least from an income perspective—are found among the enterprises that aren't drilling wells, but rather transporting oil, natural gas, and other products from the wellhead to the end users.

The icing on the cake is this: Because of some favorable provisions in the federal tax code, many of these businesses are structured in a way that leads to hefty cash payouts for investors. Not terribly dissimilar to utilities on the surface, these steady Eddies offer economic characteristics that beat utilities not on just one count or two, but in three entirely positive ways: (1) more predictable cash flows, (2) higher returns on equity, and (3) *much* higher dividend yields.

Pipeline Basics

I love pipelines. Not the kind that surfers seek; even my loving wife laughs at my lack of hand-eye-foot coordination. (The physical activity that comes most naturally to me seems to be typing.) No, I'm talking about steel and concrete pipes buried underground that carry crude oil, refined petroleum products, and natural gas across long distances.

The economic power of a pipeline was evident in the early competitors' attempts to destroy them. The first oil pipelines were built in the 1860s in what was then the center of the global petroleum industry: Pennsylvania and Ohio. At the time, barrel makers, team drivers, barge operators, and railroads were charging stiff prices to carry oil one barrel at a time. A pipeline is essentially a barrel with no bottom—using pumps where necessary, or sometimes just gravity, oil fed into one end could be transported for miles without the expense and grief of filling individual containers. Early attempts to establish pipelines met with predictably fierce resistance, whether through acts of legislatures or acts of sabotage. In the end, though, economics overwhelmingly beat politics and vandalism, and pipelines now carry the vast majority of the nation's liquid and vapor forms of energy. Even today, trucks and railcars can't compete when a pipeline is in place. This fact in itself would endow pipeline assets with narrow economic moats; the only true competitor a pipeline can have is another one—owned by someone else—that runs right alongside.

If that doesn't sound attractive enough, a pipeline only rarely faces direct competition from other pipelines. Just as municipalities grant franchise rights to just one distributor of electricity or natural gas in a particular area, pipeline rights-of-way are very difficult to obtain when another carrier is already in service. Just because someone might see the high returns being earned by an existing pipeline doesn't mean that he will be allowed to lay a competing line. And even if it is allowed, a pair of parallel pipelines would merely split the existing business, greatly diminishing the actual return a new pipeline could expect to earn. What might seem like a narrow economic moat to begin with thus stretches to become a very wide one; *monopoly* would be a fair description.

As yet another benefit, the typical pipeline business provides cash flows that are very stable from year to year. Few pipeline operators attempt to profit on price changes in the oil and gas they carry. Instead, fees are collected based on the volume transported or, better yet, negotiated in advance with customers in exchange for guaranteed carrying capacity. Energy prices can fluctuate wildly, but the annual demand for energy moves in a very narrow band, from perhaps 0 percent growth in a bad year to 2 or 3 percent in a flat-out boom.

While pipelines can be enormously expensive up front, they're not terribly capital-intensive to maintain. Once a pipeline is in the ground, it just sits there, spitting out oil, gas, or refined products for eager customers and cash flow for its owner. Annual spending for upkeep is usually a small fraction of operating cash flow; the rest can be paid out to the pipeline's owners.

Elsewhere in Energy Transportation

For my money, pipelines are the most attractive assets in the energy field, but they're not the only attractive ones. Terminal and storage facilities, if not quite monopolies, can also generate predictable stable cash flows and solid returns.

Another interesting energy business is propane distribution. Propane, which is both a byproduct of natural gas processing and a stand-alone product that can be extracted in the oil refining process, is used by homes and businesses in much the same way that natural gas is; the difference is that it is delivered to end users by truck rather than through pipes. Now that most of the nation's homes are within reach of a natural gas utility, propane demand grows at a snail's pace. It's still a good business, though; like most natural gas utilities, propane distributors charge a fixed markup on each gallon sold, whether the market price of propane is high or low. Revenue may fluctuate wildly as a result of price swings, but gross profits do not. Weather, which determines consumption to a large extent, is a more important short-term variable.

Propane distribution would not have much of an economic moat except for one factor: The distributors, not the customers, own the storage tanks on the customer's site. I mentioned this quirk in Chapter 3 in my discussion of customer switching costs as an attractive type of economic moat. By owning the tank, a distributor prevents any other propane seller from filling it. That in turn leads to handsome returns on equity for the distributor. (Propane distributors' returns aren't subject to regulatory limits like utilities, by the way.) AmeriGas Partners (APU) and Suburban Propane Partners (SPH) are my industry favorites.

Very recently, some oil and gas producers have started to toy with the idea of slipping their mature wells into the master limited partnership structure for the tax benefits. But the cash flows from these partnerships are likely to vary in step with volatile energy prices, and when the wells run dry, so will the cash flow. These are not firms I'm at all interested in owning.

Energy Partnerships

Until the 1990s, the majority of pipeline assets were in the hands of big oil and gas producers, with a handful of independent owners participating as traditional tax-paying corporations. Then a trend took hold that enhanced the value of these assets and provided investors with the opportunity to earn large, stable streams of cash. By placing pipeline assets inside a corporate structure called a master limited partnership (MLP), owners could avoid paying income taxes at the corporate level. Taxable profits would be allocated to investors who in turn would owe tax, but in the process the original earnings would be taxed just once, not twice. (See Appendix 2 for more information on the basic characteristics of partnerships.)

Not just any business lends itself to the MLP format. Tax rules limit the types of trade that can be conducted in an MLP to a handful of activities concentrated in natural resources and real estate. Furthermore, the legal documents that establish and govern the MLP typically require the firm to distribute all or almost all of its cash flow to investors. From an income safety standpoint, this high-payout arrangement lends itself well only to businesses with stable cash flows.

The basic structure of an MLP differs from an ordinary corporation in one key way. There are not one but two classes of equity investors in an

MLP Taxation

There is a chance—albeit an extremely thin one, in my opinion—that the favorable tax treatment of MLPs could one day change for the worse. Everyone agrees the corporate tax code is a mess, even if every individual provision came about for some vested interest at one time or another. But the large-scale tax breaks given to both MLPs and real estate investment trusts (REITs) are meant to encourage investments in these fields. With much of the nation's energy infrastructure in genuine need of capital-intensive upgrades—and the energy industry more than willing to wield its legendary Washington clout—this isn't a risk that keeps me awake at night.

MLP: limited partners and a general partner. The vast majority of the capital comes from those holding limited partnership, or LP, units. The general partner may only own 1 or 2 percent of the MLP's equity. Despite these small stakes, however, general partners hold almost complete control of the MLP's business—whom to hire, what to build or buy, how to finance capital investments, and how much cash to distribute. Furthermore, almost every MLP's partnership agreement entitles the general partner to additional incentive distributions that often enable it to claim a large share of overall cash flow with only minimal investment.

At first glance, this might not sound like a good deal for LP unit holders. Were such an incentive arrangement forced down unwilling investors' throats, it would represent a true travesty of corporate governance. Except for certain extreme circumstances spelled out in the partnership agreement, they can't fire the general partner's management, even if its operating and capital-allocation decisions are questionable. However, the structure of most MLPs provides LP unitholders with a number of critical advantages:

▶ The partnership's formation documents almost always require the MLP to pay out all of its cash flow, so a mere reluctance on the part of the management to pay cash distributions is not the challenge it so often is among traditional dividend-paying corporations.

▶ Management is also prevented from investing in whatever projects happen to suit the fad or fancy of the moment. In the absence of retained cash flow, an MLP has to go hat in hand to Wall Street to fund its growth, not unlike a REIT. Investors thus have a check against bad capital-allocation practices, and dubious deals are less likely to be funded.

▶ A general partner's incentive payments are linked directly to the quarterly cash distributions paid to limited unit holders. Depending on the structure, a 5 percent increase in per-unit payments on LP units can translate to a 10 or 20 percent gain in cash flow to the general partner. But these incentive arrangements also work in reverse: Any potential decrease in per-unit distributions will lead to a much larger cutback in payments to the general partner, providing plenty of incentive for the general partner to run the business in a stable and prudent fashion.

Publicly Traded General Partners

Until recently, almost all general partner interests were either buried inside much larger public companies or held by private interests. In the past few years, however, the owners of general partner stakes have started to take their interests public. To cite one example, the owners of the general partner interests in Magellan Midstream Partners (MMP)—a terrific business in its own right—took their interests public in 2006 as a company known as Magellan Midstream Holdings (MGG).

Magellan Midstream Holdings is also organized as an MLP and, like all MLPs, it has a general partner, but that general partner is not entitled to any incentive payments. All MGG does is collect its incentive payments from MMP and dish them out to MGG's LP unitholders. This leveraged claim on growth is highly compelling; if MMP raises its per-unit distribution 5 percent, MGG might be able to raise its payout to unitholders by 15 percent. In exchange for triple the rate of growth, MGG's yield is only two to three percentage points less than the slower-growing LP units of MMP. MGG's growth rate will eventually converge toward that of MMP, but as of this writing, that day is in the distant future.

There aren't many publicly traded general partners to pick from, and not all of these entities are pure plays on general partner incentive payments: some own LP units as well, or engage in other businesses. But from where I sit today, the yield and growth prospects of these somewhat complicated enterprises looks awfully attractive. At the end of this chapter, I include some of these firms on my list of favorite MLPs.

General partners still have a superior (if riskier) claim on the growth of the MLPs they manage, but that doesn't mean that LP unitholders are suffering as a result. Perhaps the best way to describe life as an LP unitholder is this: The general partner occupies both the cockpit and the first-class cabin. LP unitholders are in business class. But for the general partner to get paid, it has to be willing to take the LP unitholders where they want to go.

MLP Math

As with REITs, differences between the financial reports using generally accepted accounting principles (GAAP) and the underlying economics require MLP investors to sharpen their pencils. Net income and earnings per unit are even less reliable indicators of cash-distributing ability than the same statistics are for a REIT.

Using results from 2006, let's look at Buckeye Partners (BPL), which carries imported refined petroleum products from New York City and Philadelphia to the U.S. Midwest. This is one of my favorite MLPs, and I eagerly recommended it to *Morningstar DividendInvestor* subscribers in January 2007.

If all you look at is earnings per unit—$2.64 for 2006—Buckeye's payout ratio of 115 percent could leave you sputtering. As with REITs, however, net income and earnings per unit are incomplete indicators of cash-distributing ability.

While there is no industry-standard statistic like a REIT's funds from operations for the energy MLP industry, most MLPs calculate their own proxies for cash earnings, called *distributable cash flow* (DCF). Like FFO, distributable cash flow starts with net income and then adds back noncash expenses (principally depreciation and amortization) and any unusual gains or losses. (See Figure A6.1.) The DCF calculation also deducts a portion of capital spending designated as maintenance expenditures—the cash costs of upkeep that merely maintains, rather than expands, the earning power of the partnership's physical assets.

All of the information I needed for Figure A6.1 was available in the company's fourth-quarter press release, with one exception: maintenance capital spending. Buckeye mentioned the number in its quarterly conference call with analysts (anyone can listen in) and listed it in the text of its annual report.

Operating Income	177.1
Less: Interest Expense and Other	−48.6
Less: General Partner Allocations	−25.1
Net Income for Limited Partners	**103.4**
Add Back: Depreciation and Amortization	44.0
Less: Maintenance Capital Spending	−29.8
Distributable Cash Flow	**117.6**
Average LP Units Outstanding (excluding GP Units)	39.2
DCF per LP Unit ($)	**3.00**
Distributions Paid in 2006 per LP Unit	$3.03
Payout Ratio (%)	**101**

Figure A6.1   Buckeye Partners: Distributable Cash Flow in 2006 (Dollars in Millions)

More recently, Buckeye changed the accounting treatment of GP distributions, though not the level of distributions themselves, so at the end of 2007, I may have to hunt for that number as well.

After making these adjustments, Buckeye's payout ratio is still 101 percent. How could I have recommended this MLP for safe income? Have I abandoned my devotion to income safety? Hardly. I'll have more to say on this later.

Getting back to MLP math, we find that DCF, as an alternative metric for earnings, also requires us to look at ROE in a slightly different fashion. By adding accumulated depreciation back to equity, we can match our cash-based earnings and capital statistics on an apples-to-apples basis. (See Figure A6.2.)

Average Partners' Equity	784.2
Average Accumulated Depreciation	134.4
Adjusted Equity	**918.6**
Distributable Cash Flow after GP Incentives	117.6
DCF Return on Equity (%)	**12.8**

Figure A6.2   Buckeye Partners: Cash Return on Equity in 2006 (Dollars in Millions)

Evaluating Energy MLPs

A return on equity in the 12 to 13 percent range (which is fairly typical for the industry) might not sound much better than what utilities can earn. Yet past performance provides evidence to the contrary, as Buckeye Partners' long-term record makes clear. (See Figure A6.3.)

As with utilities, regulators sometimes step in to limit the monopolistic power of pipeline owners. The way this is done, however, differs according to the type of commodity being carried and where the carrying takes place. In every case, the regulatory burden is less than that faced by the typical utility.

▶ *Interstate natural-gas pipelines*, hauling gas from producing areas such as Texas and western Canada to major consuming regions, are regulated with rate bases and allowed ROEs. These lines have some flexibility to negotiate with customers (a much more concentrated and powerful set of vested interests than a widely dispersed group of utility rate payers) and might be able to surpass regulatory limits on ROE. But if depreciation charges routinely exceed capital spending, the rate base will decline—and a declining rate base can spell future reductions in rates, revenue, and earnings.

▶ *Interstate liquid pipelines*, which may deliver crude oil to refineries or carry refined products away to end markets, set prices *initially* with a rate base

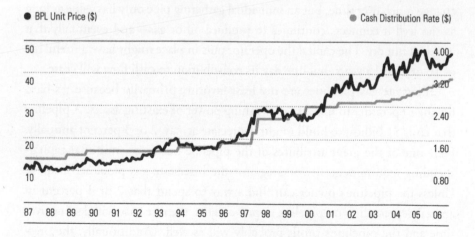

Figure A6.3   Buckeye Partners (BPL): Unit Price and Cash Distribution History

and an allowed return. After that, however, the pipeline operator can raise rates at a pace linked to the producer price index (a proxy for industrial inflation) more or less regardless of the original rate base math.

▶ *Intrastate pipelines*, which connect wellheads to interstate networks, may not be regulated at all, at least with regards to price and profitability. Instead, transport fees are set by agreements between producers and the pipeline.

As far as I'm concerned, interstate liquid pipelines are the cream of the industry's crop. An interstate liquid pipeline, properly maintained, can last for a very, very long time. The Big Inch and Little Big Inch pipelines owned by TEPPCO Partners (TPP) were built during World War II but remain big earners today. Pure-play liquid haulers like TEPPCO or Buckeye Partners are tantamount to inflation-protected bonds with a 6 or 7 percent yield. (Real-world Treasury Inflation-Protected Securities, or TIPS, might yield only 2 percent.) As with a well-positioned REIT, this free-growth potential can help preserve the purchasing power of the investor's income stream in a period of rising inflation. It's hard to find such favorable economics in any industry, let alone one that delivers such handsome income to investors.

The intrastate gathering business can be a good one, too, but there is a catch. The general areas where oil, gas, and refined products originate don't change much over time, but an individual gathering pipe only has value as long as the well it connects continues to produce oil or gas—and eventually that well will run dry. The capital the operator puts in place might have a useful life of 10 or even 15 years, but one day its contribution to cash flow will cease.

Interstate gas pipelines are my least favorite, primarily because it's hard for their operators to increase the earning power of existing assets. A pipeline that costs $1 billion to build might depreciate at, say, 2 or 3 percent annually. Here one of the great attributes of the pipeline business—minimal capital-spending requirements—works against the interstate gas pipeline business. Unless the pipeline's owner can find a way to spend that 2 or 3 percent in annual depreciation on pipeline improvements, the rate base will decline over time and the pipeline's profit probably will as well. (Additionally, the presence of a regulator means the pipeline has someone it can complain to should volume drop and the pipe no longer earns its allowed ROE.)

Energy Producers as MLPs

In the past year or so, a handful of energy exploration and production firms have floated the idea of putting their mature oil and gas producing assets into MLPs, where they, too, can bypass federal income tax bills. BreitBurn Energy Partners (BBEP) and Linn Energy (LINE) have already done so. Like pipeline MLPs, these firms plan to distribute virtually all of their cash flow to investors. Unlike pipelines, cash flows will be highly variable, rising and falling with changes in energy prices. As their wells become less productive over time, volume will fall as well.

Unlike the newly public general partner interests, this new crop of energy MLPs holds no appeal for me at all. If I'm going to invest in an exploration and production concern, it's going to be one of the supermajors like Chevron or BP, whose long-term earning and dividend-paying power doesn't depend on the sustainability of today's high energy prices.

In addition to the relative quality and attractiveness of an MLP's assets, here are some additional factors I consider:

▶ *Cash flow stability.* Because payout ratios are so high, this is the most important aspect of distribution safety. Buckeye's cash flows are super-stable. There's virtually no chance that results will drop 10 or 20 percent in a bad year and then stay there, a situation that would clearly leave the distribution at risk. For the propane distributors, by contrast, whose results can vary widely from year to year because of weather, I would be dubious of a payout ratio north of 85 percent. (This is one of several factors that has kept me out of Ferrellgas Partners FGP, the industry's second-largest player, even though Ferrellgas usually trades at the propane field's highest yield.) I'd also be wary of those few MLPs, such as Plains All American Pipeline PAA, that derive a good chunk of cash flow from energy trading activities. A serious loss in Plains' trading book could restrict the cash available for unitholder distributions.

▶ *Diversification.* As with a portfolio, there's no particular benefit for an MLP to own a lot of lousy assets; better to own a relative handful of good ones. Buckeye's asset base is fairly concentrated, and so is that of Magellan

Midstream Partners, a similar firm whose pipelines run south to north up the middle of the country.

But an MLP that relies heavily on a single asset could pose a problem, especially if it's not a terribly attractive asset to begin with. I once recommended TC Pipelines (TCLP) partly on the back of the partnership's simplicity: It owned minority stakes in just two interstate natural gas pipelines, one (the Northern Border Pipeline) which provided some 90 percent of annual cash flow. Over time, however, I grew concerned. What if shippers and regulators attacked the pipeline's high ROE? In the end, that's exactly what happened. The Northern Border Pipeline went to federal regulators asking for a rate increase but was handed a steep reduction instead. For this and several other reasons (including a disappointing and unexpected lack of distribution growth), I sold.

(Later on, TC Pipelines went on an acquisition spree that added some much-needed diversification. It then started increasing the distribution and the market price shot up. Still, I have no regrets; nothing about TC suggested that such a dramatic strategic shift was in the works, and I had to go with the best information I had at the time.)

▶ *Availability of new projects.* Kinder Morgan Energy Partners (KMP), one of the first mass acquirers of pipeline and storage assets, has recently reacted to lofty asking prices for existing assets by pursuing new construction projects instead. The biggest of these will be the $4 billion Rockies Express natural gas pipeline; when completed, it will deliver Wyoming and Colorado gas to destinations as far away as Ohio and eventually Pennsylvania. Kinder Morgan and other industry players often tout the shifting footprint of America's energy sources as offering tremendous potential for new pipeline construction. With natural gas output shifting from Canada and the Gulf of Mexico to the Texas Barnett Shale, the Rocky Mountains, and ocean-side liquefied natural gas terminals, there should indeed be plenty of opportunity to go around—but not all MLPs in the industry will participate.

▶ *Regulatory threats.* Even though the pipeline business is less regulated than the utility business, interstate natural gas pipes can still experience rollbacks in rates and revenue. Even refined product pipes aren't completely immune, as a long-running dispute in California over a Kinder Morgan

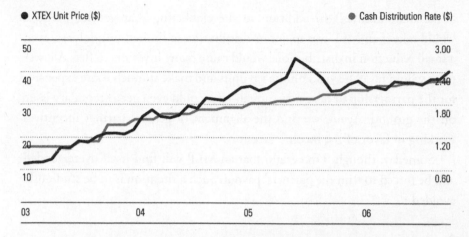

● XTEX Unit Price ($)   ● Cash Distribution Rate ($)

Figure A6.4   Crosstex Energy LP (XTEX): Unit Price and Cash Distribution History

pipe bears witness. Whatever regulatory issues an MLP faces should be listed in the firm's filings with the Securities and Exchange Commission, including the 10-K.

▶ *Interest rates and credit ratings.* As with any capital-intensive enterprise, access to affordable credit can be a key advantage, and the lack thereof a distinct disadvantage. Large quantities of short-term debt—where rising interest expense could threaten DCF—are generally worrisome as well.

Most MLPs have yields and past growth rates that provide an easy basis for future expectations. An investor might do well—emphasis on *might*—simply investing on this basis. The past performance of a Buckeye, or even a younger critter like Crosstex Energy (XTEX), can certainly tempt the investor to skip his homework. (See Figure A6.4.)

Nevertheless, the past—even in the case of MLPs—is not a sufficient basis for making an investment. As with any other business, we look to income safety, growth, and prospective return to evaluate an MLP.

MLP Distribution: Is It Safe?

For a sector with so many high payout ratios, it's astounding that distribution cuts have been so rare. Among the 34 MLPs that Morningstar covered at mid-2007, none—not one!—has ever been forced to cut its cash distributions.

(Take that, utilities!) In addition to the clobbering that general partners would take if an MLP was to cut its distribution to limited unitholders, even a small reduction in distributions would cause many investors to flee. A lower price would raise the yield on the LP units and make it much more expensive for the partnership to raise new capital—if it could even get a secondary issue off the ground. Again, we find the alignment of general partner incentives working in favor of the income investors.

Someday, though, I'm certain that an MLP will find itself overextended and be forced to trim the partners' payout. Such a situation is to be studiously avoided.

Payout Ratios

Earlier, I calculated Buckeye Partners' payout ratio for 2006 at 101 percent. This isn't all that unusual; looking across the MLP sector, payout ratios are often close to 100 percent. That being the case, tiny fluctuations from year to year can nudge the payout ratio over or under 100 percent by a hair. For Buckeye's part, $2 million to $3 million worth of maintenance capital spending that management later characterized as nonrecurring would have made the difference between a 101 percent payout and a superficially superior but economically indistinguishable 99 percent.

Still, I don't want to buy or own an MLP that can't fully cover its distribution with DCF for any length of time. I view the payout ratio of an MLP in the context of additional factors.

▶ *Access to credit.* In the event that distributable cash flow temporarily falls short of actual distributions, does the MLP have access to short-term borrowing? Flipping through Buckeye's 10-K filing on the Internet (okay, I didn't flip—I searched for the word *liquidity* to save time), I notice that the partnership has a $400 million credit line, only $145 million of which was drawn at year-end. Buckeye can tap this credit line for another $255 million—two years' worth of cash distributions—if needed to cover a temporary dip.

▶ *Debt.* Most MLPs stick to a 50/50 debt/equity capital structure. If borrowings were much higher than that, and the MLP didn't have plans to issue new equity soon, I might become nervous. Financial leverage exacerbates the bottom-line impact of changes in revenue and cash flow, and high-payout MLPs by definition have little room for error.

▶ *Predictable growth.* Looking ahead, I have every confidence that Buckeye's earnings will rise enough to bring the payout ratio back below 100 percent. The inflation indexing of its transport fees would pretty much take care of that. Analysts were projecting earnings per unit of $2.97 for 2007; by adding another $0.36 per unit to account for the gap between depreciation and maintenance spending (derived from 2006 results), distributable cash flow of $3.33 provides a 96 percent payout ratio based on the mid-2007 annualized distribution rate of $3.20.

In the end, an appropriate payout ratio will be a reflection of the reliability of the MLP's cash flows. For Buckeye, I'm not troubled by a payout ratio close to 100 percent. But even among MLPs, few have cash flows as stable as Buckeye's, and where there is more variability, the investor should require a lower payout ratio.

Perhaps the best indicator of distribution safety is a slow but steady march skyward in quarterly distributions. As with any other corporation, management isn't going to want to raise distributions to a level that can't be sustained. Buckeye Partners has made a practice of nudging its payout a bit higher every quarter. I suspect that long before some unforeseen unfortunate event comes along to force a distribution cut, regular increases will have come to a halt.

This isn't to say that a temporary halt is necessarily a warning sign; TEPPCO Partners had also been raising distributions every quarter until heavy capital-expansion plans held payouts flat for six quarters beginning in October 2005. TEPPCO, like any pipeline operator, is obliged to lay out cash for new projects today—and make interest payments on borrowings and cash distributions on newly issued units—even though the cash flow from these projects might not come until a year or two down the road. As TEPPCO's projects started paying off, distribution growth resumed in April 2007.

MLP Distribution: Will It Grow?

The key variables for an MLP's distribution growth potential—core growth, return on equity, and even a free growth term in some cases—are very similar to those for REITs.

▶ *Free growth.* This really only applies to refined product haulers like Buckeye Partners; it's an ability to increase prices for no other reason than inflation. Raising prices doesn't require any additional capital, so Buckeye gets a free growth term that most MLPs don't. At the other end of the spectrum—an aging network of gas or crude-oil gathering pipes, for example—I might estimate a negative 1 or 2 percent for this term.

▶ *Acquisition terms.* Most MLPs have come to where they are today by acquiring pipelines and other energy assets from their original builders. Enron's pre-collapse strategy and its subsequent bankruptcy put a lot of attractive assets on the market at dirt-cheap prices. Kinder Morgan bought quite a few of these assets; even Warren Buffett's Berkshire Hathaway bought some. But nothing attracts competition like success; assets that once would have changed hands for six times annual cash flow now sell for multiples of eight or even ten. All else being equal, a lofty price tag reduces the buyer's ROE potential.

Turning again to Buckeye, let's look at what might make good inputs for the Dividend Drill.

▶ *Free growth: 3 percent.* According to Buckeye Partners' SEC filings, the latest federal regulatory pronouncements for refined product pipelines allow rate increases equal to the annual rise in the Producer Price Index (PPI) plus 1.3 percent. I generally figure inflation to run around 3 percent, so I could stick 4.3 percent in for this term, but not all of Buckeye's income comes from PPI-governed pipelines (roughly 20 percent of cash flow comes from terminals and other operations). Free growth is a term best held to a conservative level, so 3 percent is as high as I'll go.

▶ *Core growth: 5 percent.* Buckeye has been improving its existing pipes and making small acquisitions here and there; from an adjusted asset base of $2 billion, a core growth rate of 5 percent implies adding $100 million of new income-generating assets annually. That's probably a conservative figure; if Buckeye makes a couple of large acquisitions in the next few years, core growth could be considerably higher. I'm also aware that majority control of Buckeye's general partner (Buckeye GP Holdings BGH) recently changed hands; surely the new buyers will be looking to

Dividend Rate ($)	3.20	Funding Gap ($)	(1.26)
Divided by: Share Price ($)	51.00	Divided by: Share Price ($)	51.00
Current Yield (%)	**6.3**	**Share Change (%)**	**−2.5**
Core Growth Estimate (%)	**5.0**	**Free Growth Estimate (%)**	3.0
Divided by: Return on Equity (%)	12.0	Plus: Core Growth (%)	5.0
Multiplied by: Earnings per Share ($)	3.33	Plus: Share Change (%)	−2.5
Cost of Growth ($)	**1.39**	**Total Dividend Growth (%)**	**5.5**
Earnings per Share ($)	3.33	Plus: Dividend Yield (%)	6.3
Minus: Dividend	(3.20)	**Projected Total Return (%)**	**11.8**
Minus: Cost of Growth ($)	(1.39)		
Funding Gap ($)	**(1.26)**		

Figure A6.5   Buckeye Partners: Dividend Drill Return Model

expand the MLP more rapidly to make their investment pay off. For now, I'll keep my analytical antennae reeled in.

► *Incremental return on equity: 12 percent.* Earlier I calculated Buckeye's 2006 ROE on a DCF basis and found a return of 12.8 percent. Is 12.8 percent a reasonable proxy for returns on new capital investments going forward? As Buckeye's quarterly distribution continues to rise, the GP incentive will claim a growing proportion of overall cash flow. Also, acquisitions aren't readily available on the favorable terms offered a few years back. Both of these factors will hinder future ROEs, so I tone my estimate down to 12 percent. (See Figure A6.5.)

If you find an MLP whose ROE looks unrealistically high or low, you might want to use a figure like 10 percent or 12 percent. That is quite a bit less than the hurdle rate for most MLPs' investment projects—they usually won't want to build or buy assets unless they can turn at least a mid-double-digit return—but the presence of those general partner incentives reduces the return that is available to LP unit holders. (See Figure A6.5.)

MLP Distribution: What's the Return?

For a 6 percent-ish yield like Buckeye, my basic hurdle rate (see Chapter 8) is 9 percent. With 5.5 percent annual distribution growth, Buckeye stands to beat that by a nice margin. Better yet, this estimate is in the ballpark

	2% Core Growth	5% Core Growth	8% Core Growth
10% Return on Equity	10.2%	11.3%	12.3%
12% Return on Equity	10.4%	**11.8%**	13.2%
14% Return on Equity	10.6%	12.2%	13.8%

Figure A6.6   Buckeye Partners: DDRM Scenario Analysis

of Buckeye's recent pace of quarterly distribution increases, something that raises my confidence in my forecast, if not the individual DDRM estimates as well. Even at a very conservative 2 percent core growth rate and 10 percent ROE, Buckeye should still provide returns of at least 10 percent. (See Figure A6.6.)

Even though most MLPs have yields in that sweet spot of 4 to 7 percent, in practice I tend to look for total returns a point or two higher than my basic hurdle. The high payout ratios make an extra margin of safety well worth obtaining, even if it takes the form of additional dividend growth potential rather than a lower payout ratio. Also, I've observed that over the past couple of years, a number of MLPs have offered prospective returns of 11 percent and higher; with a number to pick from, there's certainly no reason to settle for the first one you research just because it clears the hurdle.

The Bottom Line

Notice the difference between the total returns offered by utilities (6 to 9 percent) and MLPs. If the markets are efficient and prospective total returns fairly reflect risk, why on earth should Buckeye provide *double* the current yield of the average utility *and* faster growth prospects? Well, the markets are not always efficient, and MLPs have two characteristics that distort supply and demand relative to their utilities kin.

Demand

As I described in Appendix 2, the tax treatment of MLPs can make them cumbersome and complicated to own. In addition to the paperwork, MLP distributions are taxed at higher ordinary income tax rates, rather than the maximum 15 percent hit on qualified corporate dividends. (Just as a reminder, again from Appendix 2, returns of capital can allow MLP unitholders to defer much or most of their income tax liability until units are eventually sold.)

Moreover, MLPs are especially difficult to own in tax-deferred accounts where many of the nation's individual investor dollars lie, and institutional buyers are all but prohibited from holding. Since only a relatively small portion of America's investment dollars are available to buy MLP units, these factors combine to limit demand.

By contrast, utilities are easy to own and benefit from the allure (as much marketing as real) of qualified dividend tax treatment. Not only that, but their past performance—attributable mostly to low long-term interest rates and sheer momentum—has made utilities a must-own industry among Wall Street's performance-chasing herd.

Supply

Because MLPs have to issue new LP units to fund their asset growth, existing partnerships are continually providing additional supply to the marketplace. Worse yet, new MLPs are being formed all the time to take advantage of favorable tax treatment. Why any tax-paying corporation would hold these assets directly, when they could keep control and capture much of the upside by simply keeping a general partner stake, is beyond me. Of course, only a limited amount of dollars are available to take on this supply.

Utilities are traditionally regular issuers of new stock as well, but the past few years have provided relatively few secondary issues. Amid such heavy demand, particularly from underweighted institutional investors seeking to beat the indexes, utilities shares have become downright scarce.

Economics 101 teaches that price is a function of supply and demand. Relative to utilities, the demand for MLP units is lower and the supply higher. All else being equal, these circumstances alone keep MLP valuations below those of their utilities peers.

In the end, I think MLPs demonstrate one of the key principles of investing, one I've said before and will say one more time: All else being equal, lower prices equal higher total returns. For those willing to take on the paperwork, many (if not most) MLPs offer an attractive risk/reward trade-off. (See Figures A6.7 and 6.8.)

Company/Ticker	
AmeriGas Partners APU	Magellan Midstream Partners MMP
Boardwalk Pipeline Partners BWP	Nustar Energy NS
Buckeye Partners BPL	**Suburban Propane Partners SPH**
Crosstex Energy LP XTEX	Sunoco Logistics SXL
Kinder Morgan Energy Partners KMP	**TEPPCO Partners TPP**

Note: Names in bold are DividendInvestor recommendations as of mid-2007.

Figure A6.7   *Morningstar DividendInvestor's* Favorite Energy MLPs

Company/Ticker
Atlas Pipeline Holdings AHD
Buckeye GP Holdings BGH
Crosstex Energy Inc. XTXI
Energy Transfer Equity ETE
Enterprise GP Holdings EPE
Magellan Midstream Holdings MGG
Nustar GP Holdings NSH

Note: Names in bold are DividendInvestor recommendations as of mid-2007. Crosstex Energy Inc. is a corporation; all others are MLPs.

Figure A6.8   Publicly Traded Firms Holding General Partner Interests

Appendix 7

Other Dividend Opportunities

I OBSERVED NEAR the beginning of this book that dividend income is not equally distributed among all stocks and sectors. The best plays for income and income growth are concentrated in just a few industries, which Appendixes 3 through 6 broke out in some detail.

At the same time, there are thousands of other dividend-paying stocks outside these four core groups. In general, other sectors of the market tend not to offer terribly attractive yields (3 percent and below is the rule), and dividend growth—while sometimes rapid enough to compensate for modest current income—can be inconsistent. Still, an investor who sticks to bank and utilities stocks stands to miss some real gems.

One case in point is Paychex (PAYX), which provides payroll processing and other human resources services to small businesses. I dare say that very few investors would have deemed this stock worth owning on the basis of its dividend yield. This has always been a growth story, its shares in and out of

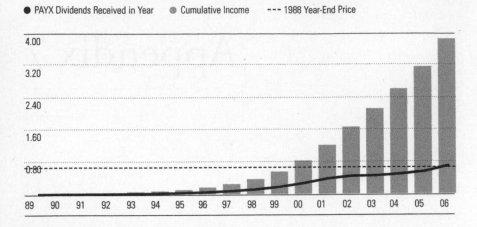

Figure A7.1   Paychex (PAYX): Cumulative Dividend Income

fashion as Mr. Market's mood dictates. Investors don't expect fast-growing companies to pay dividends, and in almost all cases the companies are only too happy to oblige, retaining even earnings that don't need to be reinvested in the business.

Yet Paychex started sharing its earnings with shareholders, even as a very small and young company back in 1988. The dividend yield wasn't much to write home about; it rarely touched even 1 percent until 2001. (See Figure A7.1.) But man, did that dividend ever grow!

At the end of 1988, a share of Paychex sold for just $0.68 (adjusted for many subsequent splits) while paying dividends at a rate just under half a cent a share annually. The yield: just 0.64 percent. From this almost absurdly low starting point, Paychex's dividend grew so quickly that by early 2000, the cumulative dividends paid on that 1988 share were equal to the share's original cost. And by the end of 2006, Paychex's annual dividend rate of $0.84 a share exceeded the stock's price 18 years earlier.

Admittedly, examples of this kind of growth are extremely rare. I sure can't think of another company whose dividend growth averaged 34 percent annually for nearly two decades. But what I can say is this: Paychex management sent a signal very early on that (1) earnings were durable, (2) long-term earning power was rising rapidly, and (3) the company would share this growth directly with shareholders. If you can find a company sending similar signals through its dividend—even if the yield is modest and the growth substantially less—you may still have an excellent long-term investment on your hands.

At the other end of the spectrum we find the rural telephone utilities—Citizens Communications (CZN), Iowa Telecommmunications Services (IWA), Windstream (WIN), and the like. By virtue of their yields, and the longer-term records of a company like AT&T (T) or Verizon (VZ), you might wonder why I haven't spent more time discussing their prospects. That's because these firms, too, are sending signals with their dividends: unexciting ones for the big players, possibly scary ones for the small fry. It's hard for me to get excited about an industry like wire-line communications whose long-term growth prospects are probably zero—and that only under the best of circumstances.

Going through the prospects of every industry with notable ranks of dividend payers could easily fill a book on its own. In most of these cases—consumer products, for example, or Big Pharma—the past dividend record and a forward-looking Dividend Drill analysis should give you a pretty good idea of the company's long-term total return prospects. For industries in a state of significant change—media, telecom, and so on—you'll probably want to develop additional industry knowledge in order to make good Dividend Drill Return Model forecasts.

If you're looking for a place to start, I'm happy to oblige. I've already listed my favorite bank, utility, real estate investment trust, and energy master limited partnership businesses, even if these lists cannot be considered any kind of buy list. Figure A7.2, culled from Morningstar's coverage database, represents an additional group of companies whose prospects I find favorable.

Company/Ticker	Sector
3M Company MMM	Industrial
Abbott Laboratories ABT	Healthcare
Altria Group MO	Consumer Goods
Automatic Data Processing ADP	Business Services
Avery Dennison AVY	Industrial
Avon Products AVP	Consumer Goods
Bemis BMS	Consumer Goods
Carnival CCL	Consumer Goods
Carolina Group CG	Consumer Goods
Chevron CVX	Energy
Clorox CLX	Consumer Goods
Coca-Cola KO	Consumer Goods
Colgate-Palmolive CL	Consumer Goods
Compass Minerals International CMP	Industrial
ConocoPhillips COP	Energy
Eli Lilly & Company LLY	Healthcare
Emerson Electric EMR	Industrial
Federated Investors B FII	Financial
General Electric GE	Industrial
General Mills GIS	Consumer Goods
Gentex GNTX	Industrial
Genuine Parts GPC	Consumer Services
Graco GGG	Industrial
Hershey Company HSY	Consumer Goods
Illinois Tool Works ITW	Industrial
Johnson & Johnson JNJ	Healthcare
Johnson Controls JCI	Industrial
Kellogg K	Consumer Goods
Kimberly-Clark KMB	Consumer Goods
Linear Technology LLTC	Hardware
McCormick & Company MKC	Consumer Goods
McDonald's MCD	Consumer Services
Old Republic International ORI	Financial
PACCAR PCAR	Industrial
Paychex PAYX	Business Services
PepsiCo PEP	Consumer Goods
Procter & Gamble PG	Consumer Goods
Reynolds American RAI	Consumer Goods
Sigma-Aldrich SIAL	Industrial
Sysco SYY	Consumer Services
United Parcel Service B UPS	Business Services
United Technologies UTX	Industrial
Waste Management WMI	Business Services
Whole Foods Market WFMI	Consumer Services
Wm. Wrigley Jr. WWY	Consumer Goods

Figure A7.2   *Morningstar DividendInvestor's* Other Favorite Dividend Payers

Index

A

Accumulated other comprehensive income (accounting data), 51
Accumulated savings, usage, 1
Acquisitions, 65. *See also* Corporate acquisition
  cash returns, 67
  core growth estimation factor, 273
  example. *See* Banks
  impact, 209
Active investment, passive investment (contrast), 202
Adequate returns, requirement, 153–157
ADRs. *See* American depositary receipts
ADSs. *See* American depositary shares
Aeropostale, ROE (impact), 60
After-tax return, 187
  search, 215
Alaska Communications, dividends (initiation), 217
Allegheny Energy, dividends (nonpayment), 284
Allete, long-term shareholder returns, 283
Allied Capital, BDC example, 244–245
Allowed ROE, 288
Altria Group, separation/sale, 233–234

Ameren
  share payment, 72
  total returns, 291
American Capital Strategies, BDC example, 244–245
American depositary receipts (ADRs), 235
  annualized dividend rate, calculation (complexity), 236
  declaration, 254
  dividend income, 256
  research, impact, 236
American depositary shares (ADSs), 235
American Eagle Outfitters, ROE (impact), 60
American Electric Power (AEP), shareholder payouts (reduction), 284
AmeriGas Partners
  cash distributions, issuance, 143
  historical distribution yield/growth, 163f
  industry favorite, 316
  recommendation, 121
  service, 58–59
  stake, 197
Annaly Capital Management, share price/dividend history, 299f
Annaly Mortgage Management, dividend reduction. *See* Mortgage REIT Annaly Mortgage Management

Annual dividends, 230
  growth, implications, 40
Annualized dividend income, subtraction, 197
Annualized dividend rate, 226, 229–230
Annualized portfolio income, 196
Aqua America, yield, 281
Asset-allocation decisions, 2
Asset quality, example, 271f
Asset turnover, 53–54
Associated Banc-Corp
  dividend, increase, 142–143
  record, 14

B
Bad loans
  impact. See Earnings
  recovery, example, 263f
Balances
  growth, withdrawals (usage), 62f
  usage projections, 4f
Balance sheet. See Utilities
  example, 258f, 269f
Bank of America, share price/dividend
      history, 14f
Bankruptcy, filing, 262
Banks
  acquisitions, example, 270–271
  analysis, 257
  basics, 258–261
  dividends
    dispersion, 14
    growth, 272–274
    return, 275
    safety, 268–272
  economic moats, usage, 265–266
  evaluation, 265–268
  expansion, difficulty, 267
  failure, ability, 266
  internal expansion, 274
  Morningstar DividendInvestor selection, 276f
  payout, problems, 272
  profitability, impact, 265
  relationship. See Interest rates
BDCs. See Business development
      corporations
Bear market scenario, 8–9
Bemis Company
  book ROE, tangible ROE (contrast), 136
  DDRM, 136–137
    example, 137f
    scenario analysis, 141f
    total return projections, 157

dividend
  increase, 128
  record, 127f
dividend yield/growth history, 127f
economic moat, 125–126
ROE, 135
Beneficiaries, 246
Berkshire Hathaway, dividend payment
      (absence), 11–12
Biovail Corporation International, 194–195
Bonds
  portfolio, demonstration, 10, 11f
  problems, 9
Book equity, tangible equity (contrast), 270f
Book value, 50
Bristol-Myers, intangible assets, 57
British Petroleum, impact, 16
Brokerage accounts, investment, 214–215
Buckeye GP Holdings, income growth
      (increase), 194–195
Buckeye Partners
  cash ROE, 320f
  core growth, 328–329
  DCF, 320f
  DDRM, 329f
    scenario analysis, 330f
  dividend drill, inputs, 328–329
  estimated tax liability, 251f
  free growth, 328
  gain, comparison, 252f
  incremental ROE, 329
  payout ratio, 319
  pure-play liquid hauler, 322
  taxable cost basis, 251f
  total return, 252f
  unit price/cash distribution history, 321f
Buffett, Warren, 11, 57
  businesses, trading, 12
Business. See Nonutility businesses
  growth, impact, 210
  value. See Intrinsic business value
Business development corporations (BDCs),
      244–245
Buybacks, impact, 132
Buyout, prospect, 31

C
Campbell Soup, dividends (reduction), 80
Capital
  allocation. See Real estate investment trusts
  consumers, DDRM (relationship), 138–140
  expenditures, utilities factor, 287

formation, encouragement, 206
intensiveness, reduction, 96
loss, 29
profits, relationship, 50–51
returns, 243
    impact. *See* Dividends
    problems, 248
    process, 247–249
Capital appreciation, 13. *See also* Long-term
    capital appreciation
    increase, 44–45
Capital gain, 27–28
    calculation. *See* Economic capital gain
    federal tax rates, 206f
    income, receiving, 243
    percentage, 43
    pursuit, 179
    tax codes, favoritism, 206
    unpredictability, 153
Capital-spending plans, 288
Carnival Corporation, dividend
    payments, stability, 83
    record, 83f
Cash
    compounding flow, 178
    dividends payments, 209
    flows, 3
    impact, 25
    payment. *See* Future cash payment
Cash DDR, generation, 308
Cash dividends (special dividends), 34
    payment, 13
Cash flow
    importance, 104
    stability, MLP factor, 323
C corporations, 243
Certificate holders, 246
Charge-off, 262–263
    history, example, 271f
    ratio, 264–265
    reporting, 271
Charles Schwab, revenues/profits, 173–174
Checking deposits, interest payment, 266
Chevron, impact, 16
Cisco Systems, dividends (nonpayment), 32
Citizens Communications
    acquisition, 231
    dividends
        initiation, 217
        opportunity, 335
Coca-Cola
    corporate communications office, usage, 227

dividends, payment, 226
press release, 227
profit, 228
recommendation, 198–199
trade level, 229
Common stock, math (application), 33–34
Commonwealth Telephone, shares
    (buyback), 231–232
Compass Minerals International
    annual operating profit, 113f, 114f
    annual revenue, 113f
    balance sheet, 113f
    dividend payment, 82
    durability examination, 116–117
    earnings/dividends, 114f
    financial leverage, 113
    interest coverage, 114f
    operating leverage, 113
    payout ratio, 117
    revenue fluctuations, 113
    salt miner, 106
    short-term borrowings, access, 117
Competition, impact, 56–57
ConAgra Foods
    dividend
        increase, 118
        maintenance, 118–119
    yield problems, 103
Consolidated Edison
    dividend payments, 40
    dividend record, 40f, 149
    operation, 39
    shareholder payouts, reduction, 284
    stock, prospective return, 175
Consumer staples, dividends (dispersion), 14
Contractual guarantees, 32
Core growth, 136–138
    consideration, 134–135
    estimation, factors, 273
    evaluation, 309–310
    input, 140
        usage, 158
    type, 135
Core growth rate
    DDRM input, 129
    equation, 131
    population growth, impact, 290
Corporate acquisition, 65
Corporate actions, analysis, 208
Corporate assets, 50
Corporate conflicts, solutions, 216–218
Corporate profits, position, 97

Corporate self-discipline, 73
Corporate stocks, migration, 212–213
Corporations
  behavior, 208
  cash, obtaining, 30
  dividends, generation, 49
  incentives, providing, 207
  net worth, 207–208
  self-liquidation, decision, 30
Cost basis, consideration, 248
Credit access. See Master limited
      partnerships
Credit rating, 289
  impact, 303
  MLP factor, 325
Credit spreads, 259
Crosstex Energy LP, unit price/cash
      distribution history, 325f
Cullen/Frost, growth (acceleration), 134
Current dividend rate, DDRM input, 129
Current income
  equation, 35
  providing, 156
Current stock price, DDRM input, 129
Current-year EPS, forecast, 107
Current yield
  appeal, 70–71
  level, reduction, 80
Customer switching costs, economic moat
      source, 266–267

D
Danaher, dividend payments, 80–81
Davis, Christopher, 265
DCF. See Distributable cash flow
DDRM. See Dividend Drill Return Model
Deals, yield (usage), 179
Debt/capital ratios
  evaluation, 111f
  industry perspective, 307
Debt obligations, excess, 120
Deferred investments, impact, 289
Defined-benefit pensions
  disadvantages, 2
  replacement, 2–3
Defined contribution, 2–3
Dell, Inc., dividends (nonpayment), 32
Deluxe Corporation, dividend cuts, 200
Depreciation, recapture, 250
Deregulated generation. See Utilities
Developers Diversified Realty (DDR)
  balance sheet, 306f

DDRM, 311f
  scenario analysis, 311f
  FFO, 301f
  fixed charge coverage ratio, 307f
  profitability, 300
  ROE, 310
    FFO basis, 302f
  share price/dividend history, 302f
Diageo, domestic shareholder payments, 254
Discount brokerage firms, success, 213
Disinflation, impact, 92
Distributable cash flow (DCF), 319–320
Diversification, 193–195
  stability, MLP factor, 323–324
Dividend builder portfolio, 178f
  cash flow forecast, 179f
Dividend Composite Index, 74
Dividend Drill Return Model (DDRM),
      129
  application, 133–137
  example, 274f
  function, 130–133
  inputs, 129, 145
  premises/limitations, 140–142
  relationship. See Capital
  return projections, 162
  scenario analysis, 275f
  usage. See Stocks
  value, usage, 152–153
Dividend growth, 37–41, 198–199.
      See also Maximum dividend growth;
      Real estate investment trusts
  absence. See Past dividends
  case study, 145–147
  determination. See Utilities
  equation, 37
  free growth, addition, 141
  history, 91–92
  implication. See Annual dividends
  inflation, contrast, 94f
  level, 164
  projection, 98–99
  prospects, change, 163
  rate. See Future dividends
    providing, 156–157
Dividend Harvest Portfolio, 192f
DividendInvestor. See Morningstar
      DividendInvestor
Dividend-paying corporations, 317
Dividend-paying stocks
  comparison, 73–76
  ownership, 216

Dividend payment. *See* Final dividends;
    Interim dividends
  analysis, 225
  calendar, 229
  capacity, 104–106
  expectations, 211–212
  pattern, 80–81
  process, 225–228
  receiving. *See* Stockholders
  willingness, 118–119
Dividend rates, 36, 138. *See also* Annualized
    dividend rate
  equation, 37, 43, 132
  increase, demand, 218
  information, usage, 234
  input, usage, 158
  instability, 72
Dividend reinvestment plans (DRIPs),
    20, 202
  advantage. *See* Wealth accumulation
  illustration, 35f
  sponsors, 239
  usage, 238–240
Dividends, 25. *See also* Annual dividends;
    Past dividends; Present dividends;
    Projected dividends; Special dividends;
    Sticky dividends; Variable dividends
  advantage, 175–177
  analysis. *See* Foreign dividends
  announcements, attention, 69–70
  automatic reinvestment, 3
  cuts
    investigation, 80
    warning signs, 120
  date. *See* Ex-dividend date
  demand, increase, 217
  dispersion. *See* Banks
  drill, introduction, 84–85
  examination, 69
  federal tax rates, 206f
  future, 205
  generation. *See* Corporations
  global search, 235–238
  history, example, 268f
  ignoring, 45–46
  impact. *See* Shareholders; Stocks
  income, 3, 13. *See also* Ordinary dividend
    income; Qualified dividend income
    federal rate, extension, 214
    impact, 206
  increase
    demand, 213

    pattern, 81
  monthly payments, 230
  opportunities, 333–335
  pace, comparison. *See* Inflation
  payout ratios, 95–96
  perspectives, shareholders/management
    (contrast), 207–212
  players, *Morningstar DividendInvestor*
    ranking, 336f
  policies, setting, 12
  portfolio
    example, 197f, 198f
    management, 183
  problems, 212–213
  purchase
    absolute justification, 201
    relative justification, 201
  quarterly payments, 230
  records, 80–84, 126–129
    examination, 128
  reinvestment, 19–20
    contrast, 202
    usefulness, 71–72
  relationship. *See* Profits
  returns, 41–47
    ranking, process, 192–193
  rules/plays, 221–223
  safety. *See* Banks; Real estate investment
    trusts
    determination. *See* Utilities
  semiannual payments, 230
  shareholder interest, evidence, 72–73
  shift, returns of capital (impact), 249
  source, 49
  stickiness, 118
  stream, 216
    flatness, 35
    increase, 34
  taxes. *See* Foreign dividends
    relationship, 241
    unfairness, 206–207
  types, 229–234
  usage, 13–17
  uses, 70–72
  virtues, 72–73
  warning signs, 120
  yield, 275
Dividend safety
  absence, 163
  case study, 121–123
  evaluation, 103
  focus, 200

Dividend yield, 13, 37–41. *See also* Standard & Poor's 500
  dividend growth, addition, 140
  equation, 42
  history, 90–91
  information, usage, 234–235
Dollar-cost averaging, 6–7
  reversal, 6–8
Domestic royalty trusts, comparison. *See* Master limited partnerships
DRIPs. *See* Dividend reinvestment plans
Durability. *See* Earnings
  checkpoints, 115–117

E
Earnings
  accounting figures, 105
  assets, 268
  bad loans, impact (example), 264
  durability, 115–117
  estimates, 212
  examination, 104
  example, 258f
  growth, cost, 53f
  impact. *See* Trailing earnings
  payout, absence, 61
  power. *See* Long-term sustainable earning power
  releases, interest, 70
  reports, attention, 69–70
  short-run changes, factors, 112–113
  sources, unsustainability, 120
  stability, 109–115. *See also* Utilities
Earnings per share (EPS), 45, 136
  consideration, 133–134
  DDRM input, 129
  equation, 132
  estimates, 106
  forecast. *See* Current-year EPS
  historical data, usage, 104
  input, 140
    usage, 158
Eastman Chemical, share price/dividend history, 151f
Eastman Kodak
  initiative investments, 210
  share price/dividend history, 211f
eBay, usage, 59
Economic capital gain, calculation, 248–249
Economic moats, 57–59
  absence, 191
  evaluation, 59–60

examination, 115
  sources, 265–267
Economies of scale, 58
  economic moat source, 267
Efficiency ratio, 260–261
  safety, 272
Electricity, generation/delivery (separation), 282
Emerging markets, dividend practices (fluctuation), 236
Energy
  dividends, dispersion, 16
  partnerships, 313, 316–319
  producers, MLP equivalence, 323
  transportation, 315–316
Energy East, recommendation, 287
Energy MLPs, 185–186
  evaluation, 321–325
  math, usage, 106–107
  Morningstar DividendInvestor ranking, 332f
Enron, bankruptcy, 150
EPS. *See* Earnings per share
Equity/assets ratio, 258–259
  determination, 269
  percentage, 270
ETFs. *See* Exchange-traded funds
Exchange-traded funds (ETFs), 22
  choices, 23
  usage, 213–214
Ex-dividend date (ex-date), 226
  market opening, 228
Executive payouts, attention, 209
ExxonMobil
  economies of scale, 58
  impact, 16

F
Federal Deposit Insurance Corporation (FDIC), depositor guarantees, 265–266
Fee-based income, impact, 304
Fees, impact, 23
Final dividends, payment, 235–236
Financial choices, 2
Financial future, impact, 6
Financial leverage, 53, 113
  explanation, 110–112
  illustration, 110f
  impact, 55
  variability driver, 109–110
Financial strength, 185
  evidence, 73

First Horizon National, share price/dividend
    history, 146f
First Potomac Realty Trust
    capital gain, comparison, 249f
    dividend income, collection, 249
    taxable income, 247f
    tax summary, 248f
    total return, 249f
    yields, 191
Fixed income
    demonstration, 11f
    investments
        problems, 9
        usage, 8–11
Fixed interest rate, 32
Fixed monthly payments, 11
Ford Motor Company, economies of scale,
    58
Forecasts, usage, 105–106
Foreign dividends
    analysis, 237
    taxes, 254–255
Forward-looking analysis, usage, 97–98
Forward-looking fundamental research, 267
Forward payout ratio, 107
    information, 108
401(k) account
    savings, usage, 3–4
    usage, 2–3
401(k) plans, advantages, 3
France Telecom, euros payment, 236
Franchise rights, existence, 278
Free growth
    addition, 308
    input, 141
    level, 309
Free market capitalist economies, competi-
    tion (characteristic), 56
Funding
    economic moat source, 266
    gap, 132
Funds from operations (FFO)
    payout, contrast. See Taxable payout
    returns, 300–302
Future cash payment, 29
Future dividends, growth rate, 88

G
Gannett, dividend (increase), 217
GateHouse Media, yield offering, 217
General Electric (GE)
    dividend yield, 161–162

historical dividend yield/growth, 162f
    market value, 74
    pricing, 16–17
    quarterly results, 171
    share price/dividend history, 17f
    stock price, 171–172
General Growth Properties (GGP), share
    price/dividend history, 298f
General Mills
    annual dividend income, share price, 42–43
    dividend return scenarios, 45f
    dividend yield/growth history, 46f
    income generation, 41–42
    problems, 43–44
    purchase, 31
    realized return scenarios, 44f
    relationship, 44–45
    return prospects, 44f
    share price/dividend history, 46f
    year-end market prices, hypothesis, 45
General Motors (GM), shares (ownership),
    206
General partners. See Publicly traded general
    partners
    incentive statements, 318
Genuine Parts GPC
    fixed costs/revenue, 112
    share price/dividend history, 176f
Geography
    core growth estimation factor, 273
    impact, 303
    utilities factor, 287
Goal seek function, 160–161
Goodwill, listing, 58
Google
    dividend, nonpayment, 176
    shares, value, 175–176
Gordon Growth Model, 36–37
    usage, 42–43, 160
Government action, perspective, 208
Graco, dividends
    increase, 38
    payment, 34
    record, 39f
Graco, expansion ability, 39
Graham, Benjamin, 5, 152, 173
Great Plains Energy, DDRM, 138
    example, 139f
    total return projections, 157
Growth
    impact, 93. See also Business
    predictability. See Master limited partnerships

Growth (*continued*)
  problems, ROE (impact), 59–60
  prospects, shrinkage, 47
  relationship. *See* Reinvested income
  retail prices, 65
  trade-up, 201
  variable, 61
Growth-oriented MLP, 253
Growth rate
  equation, 35
  examples. *See* Sustainable growth
  search, 191

H
Heinz, dividends (reduction), 80
Hershey Company
  DDRM, 133f
    total return projections, 157
  growth per share, cost, 132
  ROE, 130
  share, expectations, 131–132
High-dividend-growth stocks, selection
    (ability), 218–219
Higher-yielding stocks, volatility, 211
High-yield equity mutual funds, preference,
    216
High-yield foreign banks, 193
High-yield MLPs
  exclusion, 190
  inclusion, 188
High-yield stocks
  accumulation, 21
  selection, ability, 218–219
Holdings
  dividends, risk, 199
  monitoring, 198–199
Honor system, 32–34
Hope, impact, 144
Hurdle price, determination, 160
Hurdle rate, 155
  equation, 156f
  usage, 157
Hybrid REITs, 299–300

I
Imputation system, 215
Incentive, impact, 143–144
Income. *See* Partnership
  decrease, 9
  derivation, 1
  equation, 33
  growth. *See* Portfolios

  providing, dependability, 8
  statement, example, 261f. *See also* Upside-
    down income statement
  taxes, 260
  types, 242–243
  usage, 101
Independence
  approach, 172–175
  impact, 169
  usage, 177–179
Index comparisons, 74f
Individual retirement accounts (IRAs). *See*
    Roth IRA
  funds contribution, 214
Individual stocks, purchase, 22–23
Inflation
  contrast. *See* Dividend growth
  dividends, pace (comparison), 94–95
  impact, 4, 93–95
  nominal return, representation, 10
  rate, increase, 14
Inflation-adjusted dividend rate. *See*
    Standard & Poor's 500
Intangible assets, 57–58
  listing, 58
Interest coverage ratios, evaluation, 110f
Interest income, withdrawal, 9
Interest-paying liabilities, 259
Interest rate risk, 298–299
Interest rates
  banks, relationship, 259
  MLP factor, 325
Interim dividends, payment, 235–236
Internal Revenue Code, Subchapter C, 243
Internal Revenue Service (IRS), impact, 207
Internet data, impact, 234–235
Interstate gas pipelines, 322
Interstate liquid pipelines, 321–322
Interstate natural gas pipelines, 321
Interstate pipelines, 322
Intrinsic business value, 209
Investment
  account, value, 89
  goals, 2
  importance, 173
  income, tax rates
    deferring, 255
    increase, 215
  plan
    compound value, 89f
    purchasing power, 89f
  strategy, example, 6–8
  vehicles, usage, 213–214

Investors
  expectations, 229
  shares, purchase/sale, 31
IOU
  creation, 26–27
  marketplace, 29
  total return, 27–30
  values, 30–32
Iowa Telecommunications Services, dividend
    opportunity, 335
IRAs. *See* Individual retirement accounts

J
Johnson Controls
  capital allocation, 78
  dividend
    increase, 79
    payment, 78
  Lear, investment comparison, 77f
  outcome, 77–78
  share price/dividend history, 79f
Johnson Controls, Hoover Universal
    acquisition, 76
Johnson & Johnson
  cumulative total returns, 71f
  dividend record, 83f
  growth, percentage, 134
  share price/dividend history, 70f
  success, 72

K
Keogh plans, usage, 187
Kimberly-Clark
  dividends, 37
    record, 38f
  fundamentals, 37
  risk, absence, 38
Kinder Morgan Energy Partners
  cash distributions, payment,
    107, 253
  earnings per unit, 253–254
  projects, availability, 324
Kraft, price increases, 134

L
Laclede Group, SM&P Utility Resources
    ownership, 283
Lear
  dividend
    nonpayment, 78
    payment, 79

investment comparison. *See* Johnson
    Controls
  LBO/debt, 76
  outcome, 77–78
Lease duration, 303–304
Legal ownership, timing, 228
Legal problems, impact, 120
Lewis, Tom, 18
Limited liability corporations, 247
Liquidations, profit, 31
Liquidity, 173
  durability checkpoint, 116
Lloyds TSB Group
  dividend maintenance, 237
  domestic shareholder payments, 254
  stock recommendation, 272
Loan losses
  accounting, 261–265
  allowance, 262
    size, 264
  provisions, 260
Loan/loss ratio, 269
Loans
  problems, example, 263f
  recovery. *See* Bad loans
Long-term capital appreciation,
    197–198
Long-term demand, durability checkpoint,
    116
Long-term ROEs, 56–57
Long-term sustainable earning
    power, 192
Long-term Treasuries, 9
Long-term wealth accumulation, 187
Low-return dividend stream, 179
Lump-sum payment, usage,
    174–175

M
Madison Gas and Electric (MGE) Energy,
    dividends
  growth, absence, 111
  increase, 81
  record, 82f
Magellan Midstream Partners, public
    trading, 318
Management
  guidance, impact, 105
  independence, stock price
    (impact), 209
  perspective, contrast. *See* Dividends
Marginal tax rate, 206

Margin of safety
  equation, 156f
  principle, 152–153
Market
  averages, yield, 17
  beating, 180
  movement, 154
  return, 153
    equation, 156f
Marsh & McLennan, dividend (reduction),
  128–129
Master limited partnerships (MLPs), 16. *See
  also* Energy MLPs; Growth-oriented
  MLP
  acquisition terms, 328
  assets, 323–325
  cash distributions, 251
  credit access, 326
  debt, 326–327
  demand, 330–331
  distribution
    growth, 327–329
    return, determination, 329–331
    safety, 325–327
  domestic royalty trusts, comparison, 246
  factors, 323–325
  format, 316
  free growth, 328
  growth, predictability, 327
  inclusion. *See* High-yield MLPs
  income tax payment, avoidance, 316
  investments, tax math, 250–253
  math, 319–320
    usage. *See* Energy
  ownership
    division, 245–246
    problems, 245–246
  payout ratios, 326–327
  selection, 185
  structure, 316–317
  supply, 331
  taxable cost basis, 251
  taxable income, 246
    characterization, 250
  taxable losses, 253–254
  taxable results, 250
  taxation, 317
  variables, 327–329
Maximum dividend growth, 191
McCormick & Company, share price/
  dividend history, 15f
Means, motive (contrast), 142–144

Merck, intangible assets, 57
Microsoft
  business investments, 210
  special dividend, payment, 234
  switching costs, 59
Moats. *See* Economic moats
Money, command (decision), 5
Monopoly power, abuses, 278
Morningstar coverage, dividend-paying
  stocks (yield sorting), 185f
Morningstar Dividend Composite, 74
Morningstar Dividend Index, S&P 500
  (comparison), 75f
Morningstar DividendInvestor, 22, 117
  case study, 145–147, 165–166
  dividend stock, presentation, 190
  launch, 184
  model portfolio, 177, 197, 199
    usage, 202
  selection. *See* Banks
Mortgage REIT Annaly Mortgage Management, dividend (reduction), 151
Mortgage REITs, 298–299
Mr. Market
  cues, 177
  introduction, 5–6
  investment career, 12
MuniMae, publicly traded business (LLC
  organization), 247
Mutual funds, usage, 213–214

N
National Association of Real Estate Invest-
  ment Trusts (NAREIT), 300
National City
  growth, 134
  recommendation, 201
  share price/dividend history, 165f
  yield
    increase, 201
    trading, 191
Natural gas utilities, ROE earnings, 281
Need matching, usage, 23
Net interest income, 258
Net interest margin, 259–260
Net loan portfolio, reduction, 263
Net margin, 54
Net revenue. *See* Total revenue
Net worth, 50
New Century Financial
  dividend instability, 102–103

share price/dividend history, 102f
yield problems, 101–102
New York State Electric & Gas, earnings,
287
New York Stock Exchange (NYSE), shares
(trading), 174
Nominal income, real income (contrast), 11f
Noninterest expense, 260
Noninterest income, 260
Nonperforming assets, 264
impact, 271
Nonregulated assets, regulated assets
(contrast), 279, 281–283
Nonutility businesses, 283–284
impact, 289
Northern Border Pipeline, rate increase, 324
Novartis, ADR, 254–255

O
Occupancy trends, 303
Omissions, 32
Operating leverage, 113
variability driver, 109
Opportunity
costs, attention, 174–175
set, building, 189–193
Ordinary dividend income, 242
Ownership, questions, 21–22

P
PACCAR, special dividend (payment), 232
Partnership. See Energy
formation document, 317
income, 242
Passive investment, contrast. See Active
investment
Past dividends, 87
growth, absence, 191
Past-due loans, 264
Paychex
cumulative dividend income, 334f
dividend opportunity, 333–334
Pay less principle, 152
Payout
absence. See Earnings
margin safety, 108
reduction, 63
Payout ratio, 61, 131. See also Forward
payout ratio
calculation, 107–109
consideration. See Stocks

constancy, absence, 142
example, 63f
excess, 190
implication, 108
increase, 199
optimum, 64
quality, 61
usage. See Utilities
Peer pressure, impact, 120
Pension obligations, excess, 120
Perpetuity, 30
value, approximation, 34
Per-share rates, 229
Pfizer, intangible assets, 57
Piedmont Natural Gas
DDRM, 159f
dividends
increase, 84
record, 159
reinvestment, hypothesis, 239f
share price/dividend history, 15f
shares, purchase (hypothesis), 238
stock, recommendation, 158
Pilcs, usage, 3–4
Pipelines. See Interstate gas pipelines; Interstate liquid pipelines; Interstate natural
gas pipelines; Interstate pipelines
basics, 314–315
competition, absence, 314–315
economic power, 314
Pollution control investments, 289
Portfolios. See Dividend portfolio
construction, 184
crafting, 195–196
income growth, 196–197
progress, tracking, 196–198
stocks, nonlimitation, 82
usage, 2–3
value, 183
yield, 196
PPI. See Producer Price Index
Preferred stocks, 35–36
Present dividends, 87
Present value, 29
equation, 33, 35, 160
math, application, 32
Press releases, usage, 104
Price, market establishment, 31
Price/earnings ratio, 45
Producer Price Index (PPI), 328
Profitability, 96–98
ceiling, 15–16

Profitability (*continued*)
    evaluation, 51–53
    profit margins, comparison, 52f
    return on equity, comparison, 52f
    viewpoint, 53–55
Profits, 96–98
    determination, 278–279
    dividends, relationship, 60–64
    inequality, 52–53
    relationship. *See* Capital; Virtues
Profit-sharing plans, usage, 187
Progress, tracking. *See* Portfolios
Projected dividends, 87
Projects (availability), stability (MLP factor), 324
Propane distribution, energy analysis, 315–316
Property-owning REITs, 141
Property REITs, 296–298
Property type, impact, 302–303
Prospective return, 36
    equation, 37
Prospects, release, 190–191
Publicly traded firms, general partner interests, 332f
Publicly traded general partners, 318–319
Publicly traded stocks, prices (quoting), 5
Public Service Enterprise Group (PSEG), dividend increase (frequency), 72
Puget Energy
    DDRM, 290f
        scenario analysis, 291f
    · debt/capital ratio, 285–286
    dividend growth, 291
    metrics, judgment, 287–288
    ROE, 290
    share price/dividend history, 286f
    shares, value, 292
    total return prospect, 291
Purchases, justifications. *See* Dividends
Pure-play liquid haulers. *See* Buckeye Partners; TEPPCO Partners

Q
Qualified dividend income, 242

R
Rate base, 279
Real estate, collateral, 295
Real estate investment trusts (REITs). *See* Hybrid REITs; Mortgage REITs;

Property-owning REITs; Property REITs
    balance sheet, evaluation, 306
    capital allocation, 297
    cash-generating power, 300
    corporations, equivalence, 244
    dividends
        capital returns, inclusion, 244
        dispersion, 15–16
        growth, 308–312
        payment, legal obligations, 212
        return, 311–312
        safety, 304–308
    economic moat, 296–297
        consideration, 305
    evaluation, 302–304
    exclusion, 190
    FFO, 300–302, 319
    financial strength, 307–308
    income source, consideration, 305
    math, usage, 106–107
    Morningstar DividendInvestor ranking, 312f
    payout ratio, consideration, 305
    purchase, 308–309
    selection, 185
    structure, 16
    subsidiary. *See* Taxable REIT subsidiary
    sustainable growth ratio, 309
    types, 296–300
    usage, 295
    valuation, increase, 216–217
Real income, contrast. *See* Nominal income
Reality Income, share price/dividend history, 166f
Realized returns, 41–47
Realized ROE, 288
Real-money model portfolio, 184
Real return, 10
Realty Income
    cumulative dividend projections, 22f
    dividend reinvestment, hypothesis, 20f
    share price/dividend history, 18f
    stock price, fluctuation, 19
Recessions, impact, 92
Record date, impact, 227–228
Regional demographics, 288–289
Regulated assets, contrast. *See* Nonregulated assets
Regulation, economic moat source, 265–266
Regulators, impact, 279–280

Regulatory relationships, utilities factor, 287
Regulatory threats, stability (MLP factor), 324–325
Reinvested income, growth (relationship), 61–62
Reinvestment. See Dividends
  income, usage, 11
REITs. See Real estate investment trusts
Required dividend growth, equation, 42
Required return, equation, 33, 35, 42
Residential mortgage-backed securities (RMBSs), 299–300
Retained earnings, path, 96
Retention ratio, 131
Retirement planning, focus (change), 3
Return on equity (ROE). See Allowed ROE; Long-term ROEs; Realized ROE
  average, 137
  calculation, 301
  choice, 274
  comparison. See Profitability
  consideration, 135
  DDRM input, 129
  description, 60
  equation, 54, 131
  examples, 63f
  impact. See Growth
  implication, 267
  increase, 63
  input, 141
    usage, 158
  measurement, 261
  usage, 52
Return on sales, 52
Returns, 25
  defining, 149
  determination, 164
  requirement. See Adequate return
Returns of capital. See Capital
Revenue fluctuations, 113
  variability driver, 109
Revenue sources, core growth estimation factor, 273
Risk
  consideration, 195–196
  dividend approach, 150–152
  standard approach, 150
RMBSs. See Residential mortgage-backed securities
ROE. See Return on equity
Roth IRA

funds contribution, 214
  usage, 187
Roth 401(k) accounts, usage, 187
Royalty trusts, 246

S
Safety. See Dividend safety
  margins. See Margin of safety
  sales, 200
Safeway
  assets, 50–51
  balance sheet (2006), 50f
Sale, timing, 199–202
Same-stock dividend growth, 198f
San Juan Basis Royalty Trust, share price/cash distribution history, 119f
Savings
  account, balance growth, 62f
  balance, increase, 4
  encouragement, 206
  usage. See Accumulated savings; 401(k) account
Schedule K-1, usage, 250, 253
Sears, competitive advantage (decrease), 135
Securities and Exchange Commission (SEC)
  disclosures, 170–171
  filings, 104
  Regulation FD, 171
Security-selection decisions, 2
Senior Housing Properties Trust, yields, 191
SGR. See Sustainable growth rate
Shareholders
  cash, return, 67–68
  deterioration, 200
  dividends, impact, 210–211
  earnings, sharing, 30
  equity, 50
    mechanics, 62
    operation requirement, 258
    percentage, 274
    usage, 51
  improvement, 73
  interest, evidence. See Dividends
  perspective, contrast. See Dividends
  return, mechanics, 62
  wisdom, 212–214
Shares
  buybacks, 65–67. See also Commonwealth Telephone
    usefulness, 209
  changes, 132–133

Shares (*continued*)
  prices
    example, 268f
    input, usage, 158
  rates. *See* Per-share rates
Siegel, Jeremy, 75
Siemens, euros payment, 236
Sierra Pacific Resources, dividends
    (nonpayment), 284
Southwest Gas, dividend increases
    (frequency), 72
Special dividends. *See* Cash dividends
  disadvantages, 229–231
  excess, 243
  governance, 232
  relevance, limitation, 232
  usage, 231–234
Speculation, avoidance, 173
Spin-offs, 34
Spreadsheet, usage, 4
Standard & Poor's 500 (S&P500)
  average, return, 74
  comparison. *See* Morningstar Dividend
    Index
  dividend yield, 13, 95
    illustration, 90f
  inflation-adjusted dividend rate, 94f
  measurement, 180
  payout ratio, 95f
Standard & Poor's 500 (S&P500) Index
  dividend growth, 92f
  dividend rate, 92f
  tracking, 153
  usage, 88
Star Gas Partners, liquidity crisis, 121
Sticky dividends, 72, 104
Stockholders, dividend payments (receiving),
    211
Stock market
  respect, 69
  yield (2007), 88
Stocks
  annualized income, addition, 197
  average price, example, 7
  dividend
    characteristics, 17
    payout ratio, consideration, 113
    representation, 232–233
  example, 18–19
  forecasts, differences, 88–90
  future total return, 88
  long-term returns, 9

pickers, success, 213
price, 136, 138
  adjustment, 211
  equation, 37
  short-run fluctuations, 169–170
promise, 189–190
purchase. *See* Individual stocks
  decision, 199
risk, 7–8
splits, 34
  representation, 232–233
usage, 1
valuation, DDRM (usage), 158–161
value
  dividends, impact, 25–26
  proposition, analysis, 210
volatility. *See* Higher-yielding stocks
yield
  history, 162
  reduction, 151
Strategy, core growth estimation factor, 273
Suburban Propane Partners
  industry favorite, 316
  problems, 121
  share price/dividend history, 122f
Sustainable competitive advantage, 57
  examination, 115
Sustainable earning power. *See* Long-term
    sustainable earning power
Sustainable growth, 64–67
  ratio. *See* Real estate investment trusts
Sustainable growth rate (SGR)
  examples, 63f
  growth estimate, usage, 130
Swap, timing, 199–202
Switching costs, 58–59
Sysco Corporation, 52
  balance sheet, 55
  ROE, earning, 65

T
Takeover, buyout, 31
Tangible equity, contrast. *See* Book equity
Tangible equity/assets ratio, 270
Target yield, 184–186
Taxable accounts, 188
  tax-deferred accounts, contrast, 255–256
Taxable cost basis, 247
Taxable income. *See* Unrelated business
    taxable income
  information, impact, 254
  pretax basis calculation, 253

Taxable loss, allocation, 253
Taxable payout, FFO payout
    (contrast), 301
Taxable REIT subsidiary (TRS), 299
Tax-deferred accounts, 188
    contrast. See Taxable accounts
Taxes
    avoidance, strategy, 219
    bias, reform, 214–216
    code
        adjustments, 241–242
        favoritism. See Capital gain
    increase, responsibility (avoidance), 216
    minimization, strategy, 219
    rates, adjustments, 207
    reduction, 254
    relationship. See Dividends
    status, 187–188
    unfairness. See Dividends
    usage, 188–189
TC Pipelines, cash distributions (raising),
    198–199
Tenant concentration, 303
TEPPCO Partners
    distributions, increase, 327
    pure-play liquid hauler, 322
    unit/cash distribution history, 17f
Third Avenue Funds, 193
3M Company
    profit, 60–61
    ROE, earning, 65
Time horizon, 172–173
Times Company, dividend (increase), 217
TIPS. See Treasury Inflation-Protected
    Securities
Tootsie Roll Industries, stock dividends
    (issuance), 233
Total return
    case study, 165–166
    equation, 28
    trade-offs, 154f
Total revenue (net revenue), 260
Trading costs, minimization, 173–174
Trailing earnings, impact, 105
Treasury Inflation-Protected Securities
    (TIPS), 321
TRS. See Taxable REIT subsidiary
Tuesday Morning
    cash return/dividend policy, 122
    purchase/sale, 144
    share price/dividend history, 123f
TurboTax, usage, 253

U

UAP Holding, trend (building), 143
UGI Corporation, total cash distributions, 143
United Parcel Service (UPS)
    dividend rate, 64
        examination, 115–116
    payout scenarios, 67f
    ROE
        earning, 65
        maintenance, 64
    share, trading level (hypothesis), 66
Unrelated business taxable income, 256
Upside-down income statement, example, 279f
U.S. national income, corporate profit share,
    97f
US Bancorp
    dividends, increase, 84
    yield, trading, 191
Utilities, 277
    assets, mix, 280
    balance sheet, 285
    basics, 277–280
    businesses, ownership, 280
    cost regime, change, 282–283
    debt ratios, 286
    deregulated generation, 289
    dividends
        dispersion, 14
        growth, determination, 288–291
        return, 291–292
        safety, determination, 284–288
    earnings, stability, 286–287
    evaluation, 280–284
    factors, 286–287
    historical total returns, examination, 291
    long-term interest rates, reduction, 292
    Morningstar DividendInvestor
        nonrecommendations, 293f
    payout, 280
        ratio, usage, 285
    problems, 292–293
    selection, 185
    services
        providing, 280
        types, 281
    stocks, nonrecommendation, 292–293
    valuation, increase, 216–217

V

Valley National Bancorp, stock dividends
    (issuance), 233

Value
firm basis, 73
transfer, 208
Value investing, 5
Values, 25
Variability, drivers, 109–110
Variable dividends, 119
Veeck, Bill, 293
Virtues, profits (relationship), 73–76
Volatility, impact, 6
Vornado Realty Trust, share price/dividend
history, 16f

W
Wall Street
consensus, impact, 105
examination, 170–172
Wall Street Journal, television
commercials, 1
Wal-Mart Stores, merchandise purchase/
transport, 58
Wealth accumulation, DRIP
advantage, 240
Wells Fargo Company
share price/dividend history, 146f
switching costs, 59

Westar Energy, 52
ROE, 55
WGL Holdings, dividends (increase), 84
Whitman, Marty, 193
Windstream, dividend opportunity, 335
Wisconsin Energy, dividend (reduction),
139
Withdrawals
decrease, 10
impact, 8
usage projections, 4f

Y
Yield. *See* Portfolios; Target yield
appeal. *See* Current yield
curve, 259
dynamics, 93
history, 161–164
level, change, 163
limit, concept, 186
search, 191
trade-up, 200–201
trouble, 101–102
usage, 188–189. *See also* Deals